W9-AWK-697

THE LOSE WEIGHT NATURALLY COOKBOOK

by Sharon Claessens and
the Rodale Food Center

Editor: Debora Tkac

MJF BOOKS

NEW YORK

Notice: This book is intended as a reference volume only, not as a medical manual. If you suspect that you have a medical problem, we urge you to seek competent medical help. Keep in mind that nutritional needs vary from person to person, depending on age, sex, health status and total diet. The foods discussed and recipes given here are designed to help you make informed decisions about your diet and health. They are not intended as a substitute for any treatment prescribed by your doctor.

mjf

Published by MJF Books
Fine Communications
Two Lincoln Square
60 West 66th Street
New York, NY 10023

Copyright © 1985 by Rodale Press, Inc.

Recipes on the front cover (counterclockwise): Corn Muffins, page 313; Cheese-Stuffed Crepes with Fruit Topping, page 343; Stuffed Flounder Fillets, page 185; Saffron Rice, page 255; Sesame Asparagus, page 73; Mushroom-Spinach Quiche, page 213.

Library of Congress Catalog Card Number 94-75368
ISBN 1-56731-043-5

All rights reserved. No part of this publication may be reproduced or transmitted in any form or by any means, electronic or mechanical, including photocopying, recording, or any information storage and retrieval system, without the prior written permission of the publisher.

Published by arrangement with Rodale Press, Inc.
Manufactured in the United States of America

MJF Books and the MJF colophon are trademarks of Fine Creative Media, Inc.

10 9 8 7 6 5 4 3 2

To my son, Adam, 4, who gave me
the only good reason
I've ever had to gain weight.

Editor: *Debora Tkac*

Rodale Food Center Staff: Recipe Development—*Judith Benn Hurley with the assistance of Nancy J. Zelko, Linda C. Gilbert, Sandy Stiebritz, Susan Burwell, Marie Harrington, Frances J. Fry, Debra Johnston, Pat Singley* Recipe Testing and Nutrient Analysis—*Anita Hirsch, Rhonda Diehl, JoAnn Coponi, Marilen Reed, Pat Singley, Georgine Thear, Fran Wilson, Natalie Updegrove*

Associate Research Chief, Health Books: *Susan Nastasee*

Assistant Research Chief, Health Books: *Holly Clemson*

Research Associates: *Carol Pribulka, Anne Oplinger, Jan Eickmeier, Martin Wood*

Copy Coordinator: *Joann Williams*

Copy Editors: *Claire Kowalchik, Susan Zarrow*

Office Personnel: *Susan Lagler, Roberta Mulliner*

Book Design: *Anita Patterson*

Book Layout: *Darlene Schneck*

Art Direction: *Karen A. Schell*

Project Photographers: *Carl Doney, Sally Shenk Ullman, Mitchell T. Mandel, Alison Miksch, Christie C. Tito, Angelo M. Caggiano*

Food Stylists: *Kay Seng Lichthardt, Laura Hendry Reifsnyder, Barbara Fritz*

Contents

THE LOSE WEIGHT NATURALLY COOKBOOK

How to
Lose Weight Naturally

I hate dieting.

All of the diets I've been on over the years have had just one thing in common: soon after I went off the diets, I gained back the weight—and then some. I could almost guarantee an additional five to ten pounds on my frame every time.

It became so defeating that I finally convinced myself I wasn't meant to be thin and gave up on dieting. And *that's* when I began to lose weight.

Now, before this statement makes any sense to you, you have to understand what dieting was like for me. Chances are, it's a story similar to one of your own.

My weight problems began in college. There, an unlimited supply of rich desserts, meats, and delicious gravies was coupled with hours of studying, doing nothing more strenuous than turning the pages of a book. This combination left me sitting on some hefty assets by sophomore year. Understandably, my self-esteem took a nosedive. Soon, my best "friends" were the sticky buns, sausage sandwiches, and cranberry crunch turned out by the college kitchen staff. I began looking forward to meals the way some people look forward to a long vacation. I loved eating. It was becoming my favorite college pastime.

Late in the school year—around bathing suit season to be exact—reality hit. What I could slip into the year before, I could slip into no longer. I suddenly didn't like the new "me." So, for the lack of anything in the closet, I decided to put on a new resolve: *it's time to lose weight!*

I'd never had to diet before in my life, so I had no idea what I was in for. Ten pounds is all I need to lose, I thought. No sweat. So I literally starved myself, eating the traditional foods so familiar to dieters—cottage cheese, carrot sticks, grapefruit—anything uninteresting and as little of it as possible. Sure enough, the weight just melted off, and in two weeks time I was happily back at the weight I wanted to be—and back in my old eating habits. In another two weeks I was back at my old weight, too. It was the beginning of a syndrome I now refer to as the "Yo-Yo Method of Girth Control."

I used to believe that if the pounds didn't drop off at the rate of five to ten a week, my "diet" wasn't working. I'd practically starve myself, and before long I was feeling so weak, so deprived, and so unhealthy that when I just couldn't stand it any longer I had every excuse I needed to gorge myself on whatever was handy. In just a few short days, I'd manage to make up for the weeks of denial. I soon weighed more than ever. The clothes wouldn't fit again; the guilt would set in. Another diet of lifeless food. The yo-yo syndrome was in full swing—spinning on ball bearings.

My bet is that just about everybody with a weight problem has gone through the same thing: all-out eating, a surge of guilt, remorse, resolution, dieting, then starving again. Some survive on grapefruit and cottage cheese; some choose fad diets that emphasize only a few foods; and still others cut back to a calorie count that couldn't keep a chihuahua happy. Oh, the pounds may come off, but as surely as the sun rises in the morning, they come on again soon after the diet is over.

Why? Because dieting, especially crash dieting or fad dieting, just doesn't work. After all, the reason there are so *many* diets is because there isn't *any* diet that really works. Statistics show that 80 percent of all people who embark on a diet eventually regain all their lost pounds. And that's not very encouraging news.

So, you can understand why after years of yo-yo dieting I gave up dieting altogether. I decided no more ups and downs for me. If my weight was meant to be up—then so be it. But I did decide if I was going to be heavier, I wanted to be healthier—so I decided my eating habits needed a change. I wanted to *feel* better, have more energy. I wanted good health. And I knew I could get it with good food.

I ignored calories but made a conscious effort to eat more wholesome and nutritious foods. It required nothing drastic, just a few basic changes in my diet. I soon found a surge in energy. The hunger pangs were gone. I was happier because I was eating good food. In fact, I was becoming healthier than I had ever been in my life. Then came the bonus: I was losing weight and keeping it off—without ever worrying about calories.

I was doing nothing more than choosing my foods more carefully. The way I look at it now, the foods I eat have to earn their "keep." I have eliminated a lot of things I used to eat, simply because they don't do anything *for* me.

This is an important attitude shift and one you must adopt, if you, too, want to lose weight naturally. I don't feel I'm denying myself special treats and goodies. If certain foods aren't nutritious, if they can take something *away* from me—such as a good self-image—instead of giving something *to* me—such as a healthier body—then they have to go. And because I really care about how I look and feel, letting go of them has gotten progressively easier.

Reduce Your Intake of Fat

4

When I gave up yo-yo dieting, I began to see the connection between healthful eating and losing weight—permanently. The foods I began choosing—mostly whole grains, beans, fruits, and vegetables—offered the vitamins and minerals I needed to boost my energy levels. They also gave me fiber, which left me feeling satisfied. But the added bonus is that these wholesome foods are also low in fat. And fat is *the* foremost thing you must cut down if you want to lose weight and keep it off.

Fat contains more calories, ounce for ounce, than either carbohydrates or protein. In fact, fat has over twice as many calories as an equal amount of sugar: a tablespoon of fat has 120 calories, versus 50 for sugar!

Here again, we can see the connection between eating to lose weight and eating for good health. While high fat intake can lead to obesity, it also can be the prelude to serious heart and circulatory disorders. A diet high in saturated animal fats and cholesterol, many heart researchers believe, encourages deposits of fatty material on the lining of arteries, creating a condition known as atherosclerosis. Fat consumption is also linked to cancer, and the National Cancer Institute has recommended that Americans eat less fat. And, as if that isn't enough, high fat consumption can elevate blood pressure. So, no matter how you look at it, you'll be doing your health—and your figure—a favor by cutting down on fat.

I'm not saying cut out fat, because your body needs some fat to help regulate the appetite, utilize certain vitamins, and maintain healthy skin. But the typical American diet is nearly 50 percent F-A-T—far too high. For good health, and weight control, about half that is the maximum amount of fat your diet should contain.

One way to cut back on fat is to eat less meat. Instead substitute meat meals with poultry or fish. Get accustomed to eating more vegetarian meals. There's a nice big chapter in this book featuring interesting and tasty vegetarian meals (like pizza) that will help you adjust happily to eating less meat.

The box on the following pages shows you ways you can naturally cut back on fat in your diet. Get familiar with them and practice them in your eating and cooking habits every day. They're the first step in losing weight naturally.

Kill a Craving with Fruit 5

As any dieter knows, one thing that makes you so miserable on a diet (in addition to the boring food) is that constant feeling of being hungry. You can really grow to hate your own appetite on a weight-reducing program. It's bound to lead to nothing but trouble (like chocolate cake and giant hamburgers). All the willpower, resolve, and determination in the world can go right out the window (the drive-through window) when a heavy attack of hunger pangs hits. But wholesome foods will help you regulate that appetite.

When you rely on wholesome foods with their full complement of vitamins, minerals, and fiber, your appetite will begin to regulate itself. Instead of an appetite out of control, you'll have an appetite in control. You'll feel hungry only when your body *needs* food. So instead of denying the hunger pangs, you will be able to satisfy them—but with the right foods.

Not all calories are created equal. Refined sugar (or table sugar), for example, upsets the appetite, making it nearly impossible to understand if your body has a real, or artificially induced, craving for more food. But fruit, on the other hand, which contains *natural* sugar known as fructose, actually helps control the appetite.

(continued on page 8)

Ways to Lower Your Fat Intake

Reducing your consumption of fats alone can translate into a tremendous caloric saving. An ounce of fat provides more than twice the calories of an ounce of protein or carbohydrates. Even if you do not follow a strict weight loss plan, it's certainly a good health practice to lower your daily consumption of this calorie-dense food. At first it may require some conscious planning, so the following hints will help you develop some good habits. Eventually you'll discover that good taste in food actually does come from many nonfat sources.

- Use no-stick pans or a no-stick vegetable spray for frying eggs, pancakes, and similar foods.
- Sauté meat, poultry, and fish in a little seasoned stock or liquid instead of in oil or butter.
- If you must use oil to sauté, figure not more than ½ to 1 teaspoon of oil per serving.
- Degrease soups, stocks, and stews before eating. Simply refrigerate them, then skim off all the congealed fat that forms on the top.
- Cook roasts, chops, steaks, meatballs, hamburgers, and other meat patties on a raised broiler pan in the oven so the excess fat will drip away into the lower pan.
- Steam-cook fat-absorbing vegetables such as eggplant. You can also lightly baste eggplant slices with a little oil and broil or bake.
- Instead of frying corn tortillas for Mexican dishes, steam-bake them in the oven. Wrap the tortillas securely in foil and bake just until hot and pliable, about 10 minutes at 375°.
- Poaching is an ideal tasty cooking method for most firm-fleshed fish and boned chicken pieces, and it's quick. Season the poaching liquid with vegetables and herbs.
- Cut away the visible fat from all meat, roasts, steaks, and chops.
- Remove the skin and visible fat from chicken and other poultry.
- Make a quick low-fat meal in a Chinese wok with a no-stick surface. Stir-fry (quick cooking over medium-high heat with constant stirring) vegetables, cubes of meat, poultry, or fish without oil. If liquid seems necessary add a few tablespoons of water or stock.
- Save the meat renderings in the bottom of the broiler pan to make a natural gravy without added fat or starch. To quickly degrease the meat juice, place it in a heat-proof measuring cup. Then submerge the cup in ice water three quarters of the way up. The fat will rise to the top and begin to thicken so you can skim it off easily. Reheat the meat juice and season it with bouillon or herbs and spices to taste.

• When baking or preparing dishes with milk, yogurt, or cheese, always use the nonfat, low-fat, or skimmed dairy products (e.g., low-fat yogurt and cottage cheese, nonfat milk, part-skim mozzarella or Swiss cheese).

• Substitute 1 percent low-fat or dry curd cottage cheese for ricotta cheese in baked or unbaked recipes—you can cut up to half the calories. If a smoother texture is desired, cream the cottage cheese in a blender or food processor first.

• To cut even more dairy calories, you can substitute mashed tofu (a low-fat, high-protein, cholesterol-free soyfood) for ricotta and cottage cheese in recipes. The tofu is milder in flavor than the dairy cheeses, so you may want to add a little more seasoning to the recipe. Taste and see.

• Neufchâtel, a soft dairy cheese used in place of cream cheese, can cut your recipe's calorie count up to 25 percent.

• If adding cheese to a recipe for flavor, calculate not more than 1 tablespoon of shredded hard cheese per serving.

• Always choose tuna (and other canned fish) packed in water rather than oil.

• You can make a baked potato flavorful with a few drops of tamari, soy sauce, or Worcestershire or an herb and spice blend instead of calorie-laden butter or sour cream. See *Baked Potatoes* in "Vegetarian Main Dishes" for many tasty ways to build a low-fat meal around this nutritious vegetable.

• If using traditional oil and vinegar salad dressings, allow about a one-to-one ratio of vinegar to oil (most such dressings typically call for twice as much oil as vinegar). Better yet, try one of the original low-fat dressings in "Dressings, Spreads, and Sauces."

• Avoid the sour cream and fat-rich dairy dips—the calories add up quickly with these. Stick to light nibble food such as vegetables or fruits. Low-calorie dips to complement vegetables and fruits can be found in "Hors d'oeuvres and Appetizers."

• When ordering broiled fish or meats in restaurants, request that no butter or oil be added during their cooking. You can always season the fish or meat to your own taste.

• Given a choice when dining out, choose a baked potato over french fries. It's not the potato but how it's cooked that's fattening.

• If appropriate, bring your own oil-free dressing, spread, or sauce in a small container to the restaurant with you to use on your salad, vegetable, or baked potato or even your fish or meat.

• Even with visible fat removed, meat and poultry will still contribute some fat to your diet. If you are a regular meat eater, consider replacing meat

7

(continued)

Ways to Lower Your Fat Intake—*continued*

several times a week with a healthful vegetarian meal based on satisfying grains or pasta and legumes. See "Vegetarian Main Dishes" for several tasty meal ideas.
- Crackers are often considered a diet food, but don't be fooled. Some crackers contain large amounts of shortening. When buying crackers or similar products, always check the ingredients list on the package. Avoid the product if oil or fat appears among the first three ingredients.
- Think "more flavor, less fat" when making sauces. Use aromatic foods such as tomatoes (fresh or pureed), onions, garlic, mushrooms, peppers, leeks, fresh parsley, basil, and thyme to add flavor to sauces instead of butter, cream, or cheese. Small amounts of such flavor concentrates are all you need.
- Some pureed vegetables (and fruits) can actually be the thickening base of a sauce—tomatoes, carrots, mushrooms, spinach, broccoli, onions, leeks, and watercress, for example, are excellent flavoring and good body for a sauce. Then, if you like, all you have to do is add a little cheese or low-fat milk (figure 1 tablespoon of either per serving) to enrich the sauce.
- If a soup recipe calls for sautéeing vegetables in butter or oil, you can do one of two things. Either steam-sauté the vegetables in a little of the soup liquid in the covered pot or simply omit this step and allow the vegetables to cook along with everything else in the soup. You can always add herbs or other fat-free seasonings for flavor, if necessary, as the soup cooks.
- Oriental sesame oil and extra virgin olive oil or walnut oil are excellent choices in cases where a little oil is absolutely indispensable as a seasoning agent. These oils have highly concentrated flavors, so you need only a few drops of any one to add taste to any dish—soups, salads, vegetables, sauces.
- A hot-air popcorn popper is a handy appliance to have around to make batches of a warm, wholesome oil-free snack if you are prone to such cravings.

8

Yale University researchers found that consuming certain types of sugar affects hunger and the quantity of food eaten the rest of the day. Participants in their study were given a daily dose of either fructose (fruit sugar), glucose (table sugar and the type of sugar most easily absorbed into the bloodstream), or plain water.

Those who took the glucose mixture ate an average of nearly 500 calories per day more than those who took the fructose mixture. And those who drank only plain water ate an average of 225 calories more than the fructose group. They also experienced more feelings of hunger than any of the other participants.

You can control your appetite in the same way. Satisfy your own cravings for sweetness with fruits and natural foods. Eat cereals without sugar (there are plenty in this book to choose from). Forego the pastries and candy. When the stomach starts to grumble, reach for an apple or a peach or anything else that's fresh and in season. Not only will you feel better and less hungry, but you'll also consume fewer calories—another step in losing weight naturally.

More Food for Fewer Calories

As I said, when I gave up dieting, I made some basic changes in my eating habits. I began eating certain foods more frequently and in greater quantity. I cut back on others (like meat), and some I eliminated altogether (like sugar).

First, let's talk about eating *more*. Yes, you read it right. This is a weight loss plan that encourages you to eat more.

Let me explain. Do you ever sit down to a lunch of a sandwich, with perhaps a thin piece of cheese and a modest slice of turkey or some roast beef between two skinny slices of white bread? Doesn't take up much room on the plate, does it? Neither does it take much time to eat.

Now change that white bread to whole wheat. The texture alone tells you there's more to chew. Place two thick slices of tomato in between (you can still keep the cheese and turkey, if you like), add a pile of alfalfa sprouts or grated zucchini and a few nice leaves of spinach. Surround the sandwiches with crunchy carrot sticks, radishes, and celery.

Now you have a sandwich you can really wrap your mouth around. It will last longer, taste better, and make you feel a whole lot more satisfied—and the additional calories are negligible. What you're adding to the sandwich is something it surely lacked before—fiber. And fiber is at the top of the list of the things you should be getting more of in your diet.

What is it about fiber that makes it such a magic diet food? For one thing, it takes longer to chew foods that are fiber-full. This gives your appetite the chance to be satisfied *before* you've overeaten. (Remember, it takes 20 minutes for the brain to signal the stomach that it's had enough.) And fiber is satisfying—its bulk helps give a feeling of satiety after eating.

And if that's not enough, fiber works to help keep your entire digestive tract healthy because it speeds the transit time of foods. That means wastes aren't sitting around irritating delicate linings. Fiber itself is not digested, which means it adds no calories of its own.

There's even evidence that shows that foods rich in fiber can reduce the number of calories absorbed as they pass through the digestive tract. And studies have shown that those who eat high-fiber diets eat fewer calories a day than those whose diets are low in fiber. What more incentive do you need to put more fiber into your life? But you won't find fiber in meats and cheese, and there's very little in white flour bread. Fiber comes from plant food and grains.

Now, let's take a look at those foods you should eat more often to lose weight naturally.

Whole grains. Whole grains are foremost on the fiber list because they have their bran layer intact. And what's bran? Valuable fiber. In addition, whole grains contain the germ, or heart of the seed, which holds many of the important vitamins and minerals vital to your good health. Remember, you're not solely interested in weight loss, but increased health and vitality as well.

How do you spot whole grains? First, they're usually darker than refined grain products. But be careful, especially when you choose bread, that the deep hearty-looking appearance doesn't come from caramel coloring. That's why it's important to read labels. Choose bread made with "stone-ground whole wheat flour" or "whole wheat flour." If the label just says "wheat flour," it's not whole wheat, but a bleached flour that doesn't even claim to be "enriched." Better yet, make your own whole grain bread. There's an entire chapter in this book on whole grain breads just perfect for the weight conscious.

Choose stone-ground, whole grain cornmeal for baking. Rye, oat, and buckwheat flours are good choices, too. All whole grain flours should be refrigerated.

Choose brown rice over its pale, less nutritious counterpart, white rice. Brown rice has a rich, nutty flavor that adds a tasty note to casseroles, soups, and side dishes. And, again, brown rice contains its valuable germ.

Select whole wheat pastas or get valuable exercise by kneading up a batch of your own—homemade. Whole wheat noodles are hearty and satisfying and can be the basis of a filling, nutrition-rich meal. Yes, you can have pasta and lose weight, too!

If you are just moving into whole wheat pastas, you might want to start by mixing half whole wheat and half regular pasta until you become accustomed to the heartier taste. (My husband soon asked me to eliminate the white pasta I had begun using for his benefit, since he far preferred the whole wheat.)

Bulgur, another grain with much of its bran layer intact, is tasty and versatile. It is the main ingredient in the popular Middle Eastern salad known as tabbouleh. It also makes a nice pilaf and breakfast cereal. Because bulgur is precooked before it is cracked, it cooks quickly, and when soaked in water for tabbouleh, needs no cooking at all. This is a grain worth getting accustomed to.

Corn tortillas and taco shells are made from simple ingredients: whole grain cornmeal, water, and lime juice. They are protein-rich when served with beans, in traditional Mexican style. Recipes in this book make good use of corn tortillas.

Legumes.   Dried beans, peas, and lentils all make up the fiber-rich food group known as legumes. High in protein, high in fiber, and low in fat, legumes offer an unbeatable combination for dieters. While somewhat higher in calories than ordinary vegetables, legumes are a prize example of the axiom "A little goes a long way." Why? Because they contain a lot of fiber.

Get familiar with them all. Lentils and yellow or green split peas are the easiest to work with because they can be cooked without presoaking. For other dried beans, you'll have to rinse and pick over them, then soak over-night in enough water to cover. Next day, drain, then cover generously with water, bring to a boil, lower the heat, cover, and simmer until tender. This will vary from about 1½ hours for lima, kidney, and small white beans to about 3 hours for chick-peas, adzuki, and soybeans.

By combining beans or lentils and whole grains, you will be able to create robust, filling meals while holding calories well within reason. The psychological satisfaction that comes from sitting down to a hearty meal is as important as the nourishment so abundant in these vegetarian combinations.

11

Fresh fruits and vegetables. You'll never go wrong eating too much of these low-calorie, high-health foods. Vegetables provide a wide range of vitamins and minerals. They can be served raw as an appetizer with a low-calorie dip, thinly sliced for salads, or lightly steamed as side dishes. The simpler, the better is a good rule of thumb to go by for cooking vegetables. Slightly steamed with a touch of herbs is best.

Fresh fruits can be a valuable part of your weight loss efforts, especially when you eat them instead of a rich dessert. Try some of the more exotic fruits—papaya, mango, or kiwi fruit—when you feel you need an extra treat. You'll still be satisfied by an intriguing flavor, without having to resort to high-calorie fare.

Whole grains, legumes, fresh vegetables, and fruits—these are the fiber-filled foods you'll want to add to your menu. Make sure you get your fair share every day.

Flavor without Fat

There are plenty of helpful cooking techniques and tips you should get familiar with in your quest for lower fat and more healthful cooking. At the top of my list is the use of herbs.

Herbs. Herbs are important for flavor when you don't want to rely on butter and other fats. Sprinkle them over vegetables. You'll discover you don't need butter. Use them generously in meat, fish, and poultry dishes. Lemons squeezed over fish, chicken, or vegetables also can provide flavor satisfaction without a lot of added calories.

Yogurt. Yogurt, the overly sweetened, fruity version eaten straight from the container, can add to your weight problems. But used as a condiment, low-fat plain yogurt can help in cutting down on fat. Use it in place of sour cream, or if you really need that sour cream flavor, mix two parts yogurt to one part sour cream. The mixture cannot be stirred into very hot dishes, however, or it will curdle. Try it as a baked potato topping. Yogurt can also be mixed half and half with mayonnaise to make a tangy dressing. Substitute this mix for plain mayonnaise in salads and on sandwiches. You'll be adding valuable calcium and cutting down on fat. You'll find low-fat yogurt used quite extensively in the book but only in small amounts. It makes a wonderful garnish.

Flavored vinegars. You'll want to make the acquaintance of the delicious flavored vinegars on the market: tarragon, thyme, blueberry, malt vinegars, and others. They add great flavor to salads. They contain zero fat, close to nothing in calories, and superb flavor for salad dressings. Experiment to your heart's content to find the flavors you like best, or create your own. You can be a gourmet in this area without one shred of guilt.

Sprouts. Sprouts are high in nutrients—all the potential vitamins and minerals needed to nourish a growing plant are released when seeds germinate. So it only makes sense that you want to make them part of your new eating habits. Sprouts make a healthful, low-calorie addition to salads, sandwiches, casseroles, soups, breads, or snacks. And you can pile them high to give you the visual effect of a bountiful meal.

Thirst quenchers. When you're in the mood for a beverage, we have several important suggestions. The first one is water. When you're thirsty, it's simply the best, noncaloric thirst quencher you'll find. Sometimes a feeling of hunger can often be a craving for water. (After all, many foods contain a lot of it.) Water can serve as an appetite suppressant.

Next, try some herbal teas. They come in such a wide range of flavors that you are sure to find one or two that are bound to become favorites. You might try mixing herbal teas with fruit juices or combining fruit juices with sparkling mineral water. They're low calorie and refreshing.

Fresh fruit and skim milk can also be combined for delicious, potassium-rich drinks. Use a touch of vanilla extract, which increases perceived sweetness. Vanilla is also useful in flavoring yogurt and desserts. You'll find more low-calorie and nutritious drinks in the beverage chapter.

13

Foods to Cut Back

Sugar and other sweeteners. Sugar epitomizes the idea of "empty calories." As I've already pointed out, it can trigger the appetite. Weight loss specialists say it can even trigger binge eating in many people. That alone is enough reason to want to avoid it. You'll also want to go easy on natural sweeteners—honey and molasses. Although they are used in this book, they're used only in small amounts. While they do contain trace nutrients, it's not enough to justify overindulging. Go easy on *all* sweeteners.

Chocolate. Chocolate is naturally bitter, so it requires a lot of sugar and other sweeteners before it assumes a pleasing taste. The devilish combination of fat and sugar, which spells doom to losing weight, is reason enough to forego chocolate.

Salt. Because of its connection with high blood pressure and the fact that it causes water retention, salt is another thing you'll want to cut back. Start by avoiding salt at the store. With the exception of bread, you'll find none in these recipes. You'll also want to eliminate, or at least cut down on, highly salted foods such as pickles, olives, and anchovies. Weight watchers just don't need to wrestle with water retention.

White flour. White flour and the baked goods made with it are best left to minimal use. Better yet, avoid white flour altogether. (You won't find much of it in this book.)

White flour has had nearly all of its natural fiber removed, and even when the label says "enriched," only a few of the vitamins and minerals that have been stripped from the whole grain are replaced. To maximize your health with the food you put into your body, whole wheat is the way to go.

Caffeine. Caffeine is found in many soft drinks, including diet soft drinks, as well as coffee and black tea. Since caffeine tends to disrupt sleep, add to a sense of jittery nerves, and artificially stimulate the system, it adds nothing to your quest for a healthier lifestyle. And when you're not feeling well, it's hard to stick to a weight-loss program.

Alcohol. You should also cut back on alcohol if you want to lose weight. Alcohol contributes little to your health for its sizable contribution of calories. It can also stimulate the appetite. Just one scotch and soda has close to 100 calories. For two drinks you could be eating a gigantic health salad, a hearty bowl of soup, or even a piece of the pizza featured in this book. Serious weight watchers should save their calories for nourishing food.

Fried foods. Since we already know that an important part of weight loss means controlling the amount of fat in meals, let's eliminate all fried foods: french fries, chips, and anything deep fat-fried.

14

Gravies.   You can pass on the gravy, too. You'll find enough low-calorie sauces in this book for your meats, poultry, and other foods that you'll never even miss it. Gravy only means two things: calories and fat.

Processed meats.   Items such as bologna, salami, pepperoni, ham, and other luncheon meats are not only high in fat but high in salt, as well. Eliminate them. Instead fill your sandwiches with poultry, fish, or lots of vegetables. The sandwich chapter provides excellent low-calorie, high-nutrient sandwiches.

Coconut and coconut oil.   Both of these are highly saturated. When scientists want to study the effects of bad circulation, they often rely on coconut fats to clog up the systems of the experimental animals. Reason enough to steer clear.

It is important to read the fine print on labels when shopping for oils. Many times "pure vegetable oil" may mean a mixture containing coconut oil or palm oil (which is also highly saturated).

Stick to sunflower, corn, or safflower oils, with the occasional use of virgin olive oil.

15

The Three-Star Calorie Counter

When I think back to the diets I tried in the past, I remember becoming obsessed with calories. I measured and weighed my foods, I added and added—and soon the calories themselves became more important than the quality of the food I was eating and how it made me feel. At times it was also discouraging to know how little I was eating and how little I was losing. There's nothing productive about calorie counting. That's why you'll find none of it in this book.

Instead, I've devised three calorie categories: three stars (Weight Loss), which represents the dishes considered very low in calories; two stars (Maintenance), which represents dishes slightly higher in calories; and one star (Treat Yourself Thin), which represents dishes moderate in calories that should only be eaten occasionally. (The following chart gives you the calorie ranges for various types of dishes: fish, poultry, main vegetarian, etc.)

(continued on page 18)

Charting Your Way

Below you will find the calorie ranges per serving for the Lose Weight Naturally recipes. Approximately 50 percent of them fall under Weight Loss (designated by three stars) because they represent recipes with the lowest calories; 30 percent under Maintenance (two stars), which are slightly higher in calories; and 20 percent under Treat Yourself Thin (one star), which are the recipes highest in calories.

By dividing your eating in a similar ratio—that is, eating on the low side about five or six days a week, the maintenance range about once or twice a week, and treating yourself thin occasionally—you should have no trouble losing weight naturally and permanently.

When you reach your ideal weight, you can enjoy more Maintenance and Treat Yourself Thin recipes, interspersing them with low-calorie recipes on an as needed (or as desired) basis.

	Weight Loss	Maintenance	Treat Yourself Thin
Appetizers	80 and under	81-115	116-135
Beverages	50 and under	51-75	76-90
Breads, Rolls, Crepes, etc.	80 and under	81-90	91-115
Breakfasts: Cereals (including milk), Pancakes and Waffles (including topping)	150 and under	151-220	221-275
Desserts	75 and under	76-150	151-240
Dips (per tablespoon)	15 and under	16-20	21-25
Dressings (per tablespoon)	10 and under	11-20	21-35
Egg Dishes	200 and under	201-255	—

	Weight Loss	Maintenance	Treat Yourself Thin
Fish	200 and under	201-275	276-350
Hors d'oeuvres (per piece)	10 and under	11-25	26-45
Meat	250 and under	251-325	326-375
Muffins	100 and under	101-125	126-160
Pasta	250 and under	251-300	301-350
Poultry and Game	250 and under	251-300	301-375
Rice and Other Grains	130 and under	131-175	176-225
Salads, side dish	75 and under	76-135	136-160
Salads, main dish	225 and under	226-250	251-300
Sandwiches	175 and under	176-250	251-300
Sauces and Toppings (per tablespoon)	15 and under	16-25	26-45
Side Dishes	50 and under	51-75	76-135
Soups, light	100 and under	101-150	151-185
Soups, hearty	225 and under	226-275	276-350
Spreads, including Purees and Pâtés (per tablespoon)	20 and under	21-30	31-40
Vegetarian Main Dishes	250 and under	251-300	301-350

In this way, though you won't be totally ignoring calories, they won't become the be-all and end-all. You can begin to move more confidently through your menu planning, learning to trust your appetite and make healthful food choices that can stay with you for life.

With the Lose Weight Naturally plan, you'll still be able to regulate how quickly you lose weight. All you need to do is follow the stars. If you stick to the three-star recipes, you will be able to trim pounds slowly and surely.

If you begin adding more Maintenance or Treat Yourself Thin dishes and find yourself staying at a plateau, you can decide to go back to the Weight Loss dishes or simply enjoy being where you are for a while, before trimming pounds again.

By tackling your girth problem as a slow-but-sure process and not a do-or-die proposition, you will give yourself an important psychological advantage. You're no longer "on" or "off" a diet, no longer seeing yourself as "good" or "bad," but rather giving yourself the chance to be an individual moving toward your highest potential. As long as you stick with the recipes or foods suggested in this book, you know you'll be eating the foods right for your diet.

Now that you have a basic guideline of what to expect in this book, it's time to explore. Since sudden changes can often make us uneasy, I would recommend moving into this new way of eating slowly. Don't expect to change your eating habits overnight.

Page through this book. Find recipes made with food you know you like. Choose dishes that sound exciting, exotic, or maybe, if you're in a hurry, just plain easy to prepare.

Gradually you will build up a repertoire of dishes that appeal to you. And, since the range of choices is so wide, you will be able to find things the whole family can enjoy. Your loved ones may not have excess weight to lose, but everyone benefits from a healthy diet.

I think you are going to find the recipes in this book an enjoyable part of losing weight, so enjoyable that you will happily incorporate them into your lifelong eating plan. My wish is for your good health and the long-lasting satisfaction I know you will have in your new trim and healthy body.

18

Hors d'oeuvres and Appetizers

Appetizers can be a powerful ally to prevent overeating when you're trying to lose weight. Having something in your stomach before you sit down to a large meal can take the edge off your appetite, leaving you in better control when a full meal is put in front of you.

This is especially important when you are dining out, entertaining, or being entertained. At times like these, we tend to lose track of what we are eating, so it is best to reduce our appetites by eating low-calorie, nutritious "nibble food" rather than by munching on the traditional cheese and crackers, chips and dip, or deep-fried hors d'oeuvres that often are offered before a meal.

The selection of recipes I have given here will help to keep your appetite in check on these special occasions, while keeping a hold on calories.

This chapter is divided into two sections: hors d'oeuvres and appetizers. The hors d'oeuvres include dips, spreads, and an assortment of "finger food" you'll want to serve at a cocktail party or an informal gathering before going to the dinner table. Some of the hors d'oeuvres, such as *Madras Cauliflower, Zucchini and Carrot Pickles,* and *Cilantro Tomatoes* are nice low-calorie fare you might even want to keep on hand in the refrigerator as snack food.

Calorie ratings for the hors d'oeuvres were given per tablespoon for dips and spreads and per piece for the finger foods, such as meatballs, chicken wings, etc. Remember, the idea is to eat a little, not a lot.

The appetizers—foods you can serve as a first course before dinner—are rated according to servings. Because they're only an appetizer, you can expect the servings to be small—just enough to take the edge off your appetite but still leave room for what is to follow. To serve as a main course, just double the serving size. Star ratings will be the same.

In fact, on hot summer days you may choose to skip dinner altogether and just serve a varied and tasty selection of cold hors d'oeuvres and appetizers. I've found that being able to enjoy a variety of tastes is a nice change of pace when you're dieting. But if you're going to do this, stick with the 3-star dishes only. It's the one sure way to keep your calories in check.

Hors d'oeuvres

Crudités ★ ★ ★

Crudités—from the French word *cru*, meaning raw—are nothing more than an assortment of fresh, raw vegetables served buffet-style with one or a variety of dips. They've become *de rigueur* for cocktail parties and buffet tables—a great blessing for weight watchers!

The success of a crudité display depends a lot on its attractiveness. Select an array of colorful vegetables and take the time to cut them in a variety of different shapes and sizes. Containers of dips, too, should be innovatively displayed. Use only the dips suggested in the following pages. They're all low in calories and were created to complement raw vegetables.

There's no need to worry about serving size here. Crudités (but not the dip) can almost be considered calorie free!

—————————— CONTAINERS FOR DIPS ——————————

globe artichoke, hollow out the center

small pumpkin, remove center

croustade (rye bread), cut off top and scoop out center

acorn squash, remove center

savoy or purple cabbage, core, remove outer leaves and pull away center

—————————— FOR THE VEGETABLES ——————————

carrot sticks, cut with a crinkle cutter or slice in quarters lengthwise

celery sticks, cut stalks to three inches, cut tiny slits halfway down each piece and drop in ice water for hour to make fans

radishes, cut into roses and drop in ice water before serving

broccoli florets

cauliflower florets

cherry tomatoes

rutabaga, cut into sticks or half moons

sugar snap peas

whole white mushrooms

zucchini, cut into sticks and rounds or slice in quarters lengthwise

cucumbers, cut into sticks and rounds (for rounds, peel cucumber if waxed; run tines of a fork down all sides, then slice) or slice in quarters lengthwise

scallions

Jerusalem Artichokes

fennel bulbs cut into sticks

Chinese cabbage, ribs only

celeriac, slice into thin rounds

brussels sprouts

icicle radishes, cut into rounds or cut into sticks with a crinkle cutter

daikon radishes, cut into strips

green beans

gold, green, and red peppers, cut into strips

jicima, cut into half moons and sticks

Recipes for italicized ingredients can be found by checking the index.

Creamy Horseradish Dip ★ ★ ★

Makes 2 cups

¾ cup low-fat cottage cheese
¾ cup low-fat yogurt
½ cup crumbled feta cheese
1 tablespoon prepared
     horseradish
2 tablespoons chopped
     scallions
1 tablespoon minced fresh
     parsley
½ teaspoon basil
½ teaspoon oregano
1 clove garlic, minced

Place the cottage cheese, yogurt, feta cheese, horse-radish, scallions, parsley, basil, oregano, and garlic in a food processor or blender. Process on low to medium speed until smooth, scraping down the sides of the container as necessary. Place in a serving container and refrigerate until ready to serve.

Dutch Tarragon Dip ★ ★ ★

This dip is exceptionally good when made with fresh tarragon.

Makes approximately ¾ cup

6 tablespoons low-fat yogurt
1 tablespoon *Lighten-Up
     Mayonnaise*
1 tablespoon minced sweet
     red peppers
1 tablespoon minced green
     peppers
1 tablespoon minced celery
2 teaspoons minced shallots
2 teaspoons minced fresh
     tarragon or ½ teaspoon
     dried tarragon
   tarragon sprigs (garnish)

In a small bowl, combine the yogurt, mayonnaise, red peppers, green peppers, celery, shallots, and tarragon. Place in a serving container, garnish with tarragon, and chill before serving, if desired.

Chick-Pea Puree ★ ★

A traditional Middle Eastern dip also known as hummus.

Makes about 3 cups

2   tablespoons chopped fresh
       parsley
⅓   cup tahini (sesame butter)
⅓   cup lemon juice
¼   cup water
2   tablespoons olive oil
2   cloves garlic
2   cups cooked chick-peas

Place all of the ingredients in a food processor or blender. Process on medium speed until smooth, stopping the blender and scraping down the sides as necessary. Store tightly covered in the refrigerator until ready to serve.

★ ★ ★ *VARIATION:* Chick-Pea Puree *makes a nice sandwich spread.*

Creamy Red Onion Dip ★ ★ ★

Dip or dressing? Try it on salads, too, and see how you like it best.

Makes ¾ cup

½   cup low-fat cottage cheese
¼   cup chopped red onions
1   tablespoon skim milk
       dash of ground cumin
       dill sprig (garnish)

Place the cottage cheese, onions, milk, and cumin in a food processor or blender. Process on low to medium speed until very smooth. Place in a small bowl, garnish with dill, and chill before serving, if desired.

★ ★ *VARIATION: Use as is for a salad dressing or add 1 teaspoon olive oil before blending.*

Apple Delhi Dip ★ ★ ★

This is a dip for fresh fruit slices.

Makes ¾ cup

½   cup low-fat cottage cheese
¼   cup apple juice
½   teaspoon curry powder
       (preferably Madras)
       dash of cinnamon
       dash of nutmeg
       mint sprig (garnish)

Place the cottage cheese, apple juice, curry, cinnamon, and nutmeg in a blender. Process on low to medium speed until very smooth. Place in a small bowl, chill, and garnish with mint before serving, if desired.

Golden Guacamole ★ ★ ★

Makes 2½ cups

1   cup low-fat cottage cheese
¼   cup chopped fresh parsley
½   small onion, chopped
1   tablespoon minced
        hot chili peppers
1   tablespoon lime juice
1   tablespoon chopped fresh
        coriander
½   clove garlic
1   avocado, quartered
1   tomato, seeded and
        chopped

Place the cottage cheese, parsley, onions, chili peppers, lime juice, coriander, and garlic in a food processor or blender. Process on medium speed until smooth, scraping down the sides of the container as necessary. Add the avocado and continue processing on medium speed until all of the ingredients are combined. Place in a serving container and top with the tomatoes. Serve immediately.

24

Madras Cauliflower ★ ★ ★

A dip for steamed cauliflower.

Makes 1 cup dip

1   large head cauliflower
¾   cup low-fat yogurt
¼   cup *Lighten-Up Mayonnaise*
1   teaspoon curry powder
        (preferably Madras)
1   clove garlic
    parsley sprigs (garnish)
    cherry tomatoes (garnish)

Break the cauliflower into florets and steam just until crisp-tender, about 2 to 3 minutes. Rinse under cold water until thoroughly cooled.

In a small bowl, combine the yogurt with the mayonnaise and curry. Add the garlic by pushing it through a garlic press into the bowl. Stir to combine.

Place the bowl of dip in the center of a serving plate and arrange the cauliflower around it. Garnish the plate with parsley and cherry tomatoes, if desired.

★ ★ ★ *VARIATIONS: Serve the cauliflower raw instead of steamed or substitute raw broccoli florets for all or part of the cauliflower. Or, serve very lightly blanched asparagus spears along with the cauliflower.*

Pâté de Poisson ★ ★ ★

Use leftover flounder or other white fish to make this quick pâté.

Makes 1¼ cups

6 tablespoons low-fat cottage
    cheese
1 tablespoon Dijon mustard
1 teaspoon dill
1 teaspoon parsley
1 teaspoon chives
1 cup cubed cooked fish
    dill sprig (garnish)

In a blender or food processor, puree the cottage cheese, mustard, dill, parsley, and chives. Add fish and puree on medium to high speed until combined. Scoop into a pretty bowl or crock, garnish with dill sprig, if desired, and chill, covered, for at least 2 hours. Serve with whole grain crackers.

Mushroom-Almond Puree ★ ★

Makes about 2 cups

¾ cup blanched, slivered
    almonds
1 small onion, minced
½ tablespoon olive oil
1 pound mushrooms, minced
2 teaspoons tamari or soy
    sauce
1 teaspoon minced fresh
    tarragon or ½ teaspoon
    dried tarragon
1 clove garlic
1 egg
    cherry tomatoes, seeded
        and cut into thin strips
        (garnish)
    scallion tops cut into thin
        strips (garnish)

25

Place the almonds in a medium-size iron skillet. Set over low to medium heat and cook, stirring frequently, until the almonds are golden brown.

Place the almonds in a blender or food processor and process with short bursts on high speed until the nuts are ground.

Place the onions in a medium-size skillet with the oil and set over medium heat. Cook, stirring frequently, until the onions are translucent. Add the mushrooms, tamari, and tarragon. When the mushrooms have released most of their liquid and most of the liquid has evaporated, add the garlic by pushing it through a garlic press into the skillet. Cook, stirring, until all of the liquid has evaporated from the pan, about 1 to 2 minutes.

Stir the mushroom mixture into the ground almonds in the blender, then stir in the egg. Blend, scraping down the sides as necessary, on low to medium speed until all of the ingredients are combined but the mixture is still a little coarse.

Pack the spread into a small crock and chill. Decorate the top with a design of cherry tomato and scallion strips, if desired.

Mushrooms Oreganata ★ ★ ★

As an hors d'oeuvre, marinated mushrooms are always a welcome item. Choose small mushrooms with tight caps.

Makes 1½ cups

¼	cup water
2	tablespoons olive oil
3	tablespoons lemon juice
2	tablespoons white wine vinegar
½	teaspoon marjoram
¼	teaspoon oregano
¼	teaspoon thyme
1	clove garlic
1	bay leaf
1	pound mushrooms

Place the water, oil, lemon juice, vinegar, marjoram, oregano, thyme, garlic, and bay leaf in a medium-size saucepan. Bring to a boil over medium heat. Add the mushrooms and return to a boil. Reduce heat and simmer for 10 minutes. Remove from heat. Remove the garlic clove and bay leaf. Cool, then chill before serving, if desired.

26

Pâté de Poulet ★ ★ ★

Serve on whole grain bread sliced into "fingers."

Makes about 3 cups

½	pound chicken livers
⅓	cup *Chicken Stock*
1½	teaspoons butter
½	cup minced onions
2	shallots, minced
2	hard-cooked eggs, quartered
1	head Boston lettuce minced fresh parsley (garnish)

Place the chicken livers in a small saucepan with the stock. Bring to a boil, then reduce heat and simmer just until the insides of the livers are pink, about 8 minutes.

While the livers cook, melt the butter in a small skillet. Add the onions and shallots and cook just until the onions are translucent.

Drain the livers and place them in a blender or food processor with the cooked onions and shallots and the eggs. Process on medium speed until blended, adding some of the stock if needed to make a smooth mixture.

Line a serving plate or bowl with lettuce leaves. Mound the pâté on top. Garnish with parsley, if desired.

Herb Cheese Spread ★ ★ ★

Who needs expensive, imported herb cheeses? Not you! As an hors d'oeuvre, serve in a small bowl flanked by thinly sliced black bread and red radishes.

Makes 1¼ cups

1 cup low-fat cottage cheese
1 tablespoon low-fat yogurt
1 small onion, minced
1 small clove garlic, minced
1 teaspoon minced fresh coriander (optional)
¼ teaspoon thyme
¼ teaspoon oregano
  minced fresh parsley (garnish)

Place the cottage cheese in a medium-size mixing bowl. Mash with the back of a wooden spoon until fairly smooth. Stir in the yogurt, onions, garlic, coriander, thyme, and oregano. Chill until ready to serve, then garnish with parsley, if desired.

NOTE: Do not keep spread more than a day or two before serving.

★ ★ ★ VARIATION: Herb Cheese Spread *can also be used to stuff celery. Garnish stuffed celery with thinly sliced radishes and minced parsley, if desired.*

27

Zucchini and Carrot Pickles ★ ★ ★

Pickled vegetables make a tangy hors d'oeuvre or relish.

Makes 2 cups

1 tablespoon tamari or soy sauce
3 tablespoons rice vinegar
1 teaspoon mustard seeds
1 dried red chili pepper
1 ¼-inch slice ginger
1 clove garlic
2–3 small zucchini, cut into 2 × ½-inch sticks (1 cup)
2–3 medium-size carrots, cut into 2 × ½-inch sticks (1 cup)

Combine tamari, vinegar, mustard seeds, chili pepper, ginger, and garlic in a small bowl. Place zucchini and carrots in a shallow dish or bowl and pour marinade over them. Cover and chill at least overnight, stirring occasionally.

Acapulco Chili Dip ★ ★ ★

Makes 1½ cups

1 cup cooked red kidney beans
½ cup low-fat yogurt
½ small onion, coarsely chopped
1 clove garlic, minced
1 tablespoon chili powder
1 teaspoon ground cumin chopped scallions (garnish)

Place the beans and yogurt in a food processor or blender and process. Add onions and garlic and blend. Add the chili powder and cumin, and process on medium speed until smooth. Pour into a small bowl. Garnish with scallions and chill before serving, if desired.

Sicilian Spread ★ ★

Serve with apple and pear wedges dipped in lemon juice to prevent darkening.

Makes 1 cup

½ cup finely crumbled Gorgonzola cheese
½ cup low-fat cottage cheese
2 tablespoons low-fat yogurt watercress sprigs (garnish)

In a small bowl, mix the Gorgonzola and cottage cheese together with a wooden spoon. Add the yogurt and stir until smooth. Mound the spread in a small serving bowl. Garnish with watercress, if desired.

Mousseline de Saumon ★ ★ ★

Makes 8 servings

1¾ cups flaked, cooked, red salmon
3 tablespoons *Lighten-Up Mayonnaise*
1 stalk celery, minced
2 shallots, minced
2 tablespoons minced fresh coriander or fresh parsley

In a medium-size bowl, combine the salmon and mayonnaise and mix until smooth. Stir in the celery, shallots, and coriander. Cover and chill before serving.

★ ★ ★ *VARIATION: Spread ¼ cup on whole grain bread, toasted if desired, top with vegetable garnish of your choice, and serve as an open-faced sandwich.*

Cilantro
Tomatoes ★ ★ ★

Makes an attractive hors d'oeuvre served on a bed of fresh spinach leaves.

Makes about 24 hors d'oeuvres

2   cups cherry tomatoes
⅔   cup low-fat cottage cheese
1   small scallion, minced
1   tablespoon minced fresh
     parsley
½   clove garlic
½   teaspoon basil
¼   teaspoon marjoram
     dash of curry powder
     spinach leaves (garnish)
     parsley sprigs (garnish)

Cut the top third of the cherry tomatoes almost through, to form a lid. Carefully scoop out the seeds with a melon ball cutter and discard. Let the hollowed-out cherry tomatoes drain upside down on a kitchen towel while preparing the filling.

In a small bowl, mix together the cottage cheese, scallions, and parsley. Add the garlic by pushing it through a garlic press into the bowl. Add the basil, marjoram, and curry and stir well.

Use a small spoon to fill the cherry tomatoes with the cheese mixture. Use enough of the cheese so that the lids are held partly open and the stuffing is visible. Chill before serving, if desired.

Arrange the spinach leaves on a serving platter. Arrange the stuffed cherry tomatoes on top. Garnish with parsley sprigs, if desired, and serve.

29

Baliñas ★ ★

A Portuguese dish—white fish rolled into little balls.

Makes 12 hors d'oeuvres

⅓   cup chopped, cooked
     white fish
¼   cup shredded Muenster
     cheese
1   shallot, minced
½   teaspoon marjoram
½   teaspoon thyme
2   teaspoons toasted wheat
     germ
1   teaspoon minced fresh
     parsley
2   radishes, thinly sliced
12   watercress leaves

Mash the fish and cheese together in a blender on medium speed or in a food processor. Place in a small bowl with the shallots, marjoram, and thyme and mix well. Form 12 balls and roll each in wheat germ and parsley to cover. Spear each ball with a toothpick and add a radish slice and watercress leaf.

Ukrop ★ ★ ★
Russian dilled egg spread.

Makes 8 servings

4   hard-cooked eggs, chopped
2   tablespoons low-fat yogurt
1   tablespoon *Lighten-Up Mayonnaise*
¼   cup minced sweet red peppers
1   tablespoon minced fresh dill or ½ tablespoon dried dill
¼   teaspoon ground coriander fresh dill (garnish)

Combine the eggs with the yogurt, mayonnaise, red peppers, dill, and coriander in a medium-size bowl. Place the mixture in a serving bowl, garnish with dill, if desired, and surround the bowl with crackers.

30

Russian Minted Meatballs ★

Makes approximately 48 hors d'oeuvres

1½   pounds very lean ground round
2   eggs, beaten
¾   cup whole wheat bread crumbs
2   medium-size onions, minced
¼   cup minced fresh parsley
1   tablespoon minced fresh mint
¼   teaspoon cinnamon
¼   teaspoon ground allspice
2   tablespoons *Basic Brown Stock*
1   bunch parsley (garnish)

Combine the meat, eggs, bread crumbs, onions, parsley, mint, cinnamon, and allspice in a large bowl. Cover and refrigerate several hours or overnight.

Form the meat mixture into bite-size meatballs (about ½ ounce of meat per meatball). Sauté half the meatballs in half the stock until browned. Keep warm. Repeat with the remaining meatballs. Serve with toothpicks, garnishing the serving plate generously with parsley, if desired.

Chinese Chicken Wings ★

Serve with plenty of napkins!

Makes 28 hors d'oeuvres

14	chicken wings (about 2 pounds)
⅓	cup tamari or soy sauce
⅓	cup pineapple juice
2	tablespoons water
1	tablespoon sunflower oil
1	tablespoon honey
1	teaspoon grated fresh ginger
1	teaspoon minced garlic

Cut the chicken wings apart at the joints and discard the wing tips. Combine the tamari, pineapple juice, water, oil, honey, ginger, and garlic in a small bowl. Place the chicken wing parts in a 9 × 13-inch baking dish and pour marinade over them. Cover and refrigerate overnight.

Line a baking sheet with aluminum foil. Remove the chicken wing parts from the marinade and arrange on the foil. Pour ½ cup of the marinade over the wings. Bake at 350° for 30 to 40 minutes.

NOTE: The baked wings can be frozen, then reheated before serving.

31

Chinese Chicken Livers ★

Makes approximately 18 hors d'oeuvres

1	pound chicken livers
1	cup water
½	cup chopped scallions
¼	cup tamari or soy sauce
2	tablespoons sherry wine vinegar
1½	teaspoons minced fresh ginger
1	teaspoon honey
¼	teaspoon aniseed
1	large daikon radish, shredded
¼	cup rice vinegar

Place the livers and water in a medium-size saucepan and bring to a boil. Turn off heat and drain the cooking liquid from the livers, reserving ½ cup of the liquid.

Combine the reserved liquid with the scallions, tamari, vinegar, ginger, honey, and aniseed. Pour the mixture over the chicken livers in the saucepan.

Return the livers to a boil, reduce heat, cover, and simmer for 15 minutes. Cool, then remove the livers from the stock and cut into bite-size pieces. Return the livers to the stock and chill.

Toss the radishes with the rice vinegar. To serve, drain the livers well and pat them dry. Place in a wide strip down the middle of a serving platter and arrange the radishes on each side. Serve with toothpicks.

Appetizers

Ali Baba's Eggplant ★ ★ ★

If you like Middle Eastern foods, you'll like this oilless version of Baba Ghannouj.

Makes 8 servings

1	medium-size eggplant
⅓	cup minced fresh parsley
¼	cup lemon juice
¼	cup tahini (sesame butter)
2	cloves garlic
	parsley sprigs (garnish)
	paprika (garnish)

Place the eggplant, unpeeled, on an ovenproof glass pie plate coated with no-stick spray. Bake at 500° for 45 minutes or until the skin is charred and the eggplant is soft.

Scoop the eggplant out of the skin and place the pulp in a blender. Add the parsley, lemon juice, and tahini. Add the garlic by pushing it through a garlic press into the blender. Process on low speed until smooth, scraping down the sides of the container as necessary. Place the eggplant puree in a tightly covered container and chill for 2 to 3 hours before serving.

To serve, place the dip on eight small serving plates. Garnish with parsley sprigs, dust with a little paprika, and serve with a variety of raw vegetables.

Rashid's Artichokes ★ ★ ★

Makes 4 servings

4	large artichokes
¼	cup low-fat yogurt
2	tablespoons *Lighten-Up Mayonnaise*
1	tablespoon sour cream (optional)
½	teaspoon curry powder (preferably Madras)
½	clove garlic

Cut off the stems of the artichokes close to the base. Using kitchen shears, snip off the tips of the leaves about ½ inch from the ends.

Bring a large pot of water to a boil. Add the artichokes and cover. Cook the artichokes at a low boil for 30 minutes or until tender. Drain and cool.

Combine the yogurt, mayonnaise, sour cream (if used), and curry in a small bowl. Add the garlic by pushing it through a garlic press into the bowl. Divide the dip among four small bowls.

Serve the artichokes on plates large enough to accommodate the leaves. Place a small bowl of dip by each plate.

Terrine of Turkey ★ ★

Serve chilled and sliced. This easy-to-make, elegant appetizer is really just a glorified version of meatloaf.

Makes 16 servings

 2 pounds ground turkey
    meat
 1 medium-size onion,
    minced
⅓ cup minced fresh parsley
 2 cloves garlic, minced
½ cup whole wheat bread
    crumbs
½ cup water
¼ cup tomato paste
 2 tablespoons Dijon
    mustard
 1 tablespoon tamari or soy
    sauce
 1 teaspoon thyme
 2 eggs, beaten
    red leaf or Boston lettuce
    leaves (garnish)
16 scallions (garnish)
    cherry tomatoes (garnish)

Place the turkey in a large bowl. Add the onions, parsley, garlic, bread crumbs, water, tomato paste, mustard, tamari, and thyme. Mix the ingredients together, then add the eggs and mix again until well combined. Press the turkey mixture into a 9 × 5-inch loaf pan.

Cover the terrine with foil. Bake at 325° for 1¼ hours. Remove from oven, let cool for an hour. Place another 9 × 5-inch loaf pan on top of the terrine and fill with dried beans or other heavy material, such as a can of food, or cover with foil and top with something heavy. Refrigerate for 2 to 3 days.

To serve, place lettuce leaves on small plates. Cut terrine into 16 slices and lay on top of lettuce. Garnish each plate with a scallion and cherry tomatoes, if desired.

NOTE: To make an attractive garnish with scallions, cut them to a length of 4 inches. Make thin, lengthwise cuts at each end, then place in ice water until the ends curl.

33

Summer Fruits ★ ★

Mango highlights this seasonal fruit salad.

Makes 4 servings

 1 mango, diced
 1 cup seedless green grapes
 1 cup cherries, pitted
 1 cup sliced nectarines
    mint sprigs (garnish)

Gently mix together the mango, grapes, cherries, and nectarines. Spoon into decorative glass dishes and garnish with mint sprigs, if desired. Chill before serving.

Pickled Cauliflower ★ ★ ★

Makes 8 servings

1   head cauliflower
1   small red onion, cut into thin slices
½   cup olive oil
⅓   cup tarragon vinegar
2   teaspoons minced fresh dill or 1 teaspoon dried dill
½   teaspoon honey
½   teaspoon Dijon mustard
¼   teaspoon dry mustard
    minced fresh parsley (garnish)

Separate the cauliflower into florets, cutting the larger florets in half or quarters. Steam the cauliflower until crisp-tender, about 10 minutes.

While the cauliflower steams, separate the onion slices into rings and arrange these on the bottom of a large serving bowl.

Combine the oil, vinegar, dill, honey, Dijon mustard, and dry mustard in a small jar or bowl and shake or stir until well combined.

Place the steamed cauliflower in the serving bowl on top of the onion rings. Slowly pour the dill dressing over the hot cauliflower until all of the cauliflower is lightly coated with dressing.

Without stirring, allow the cauliflower to cool, then refrigerate 6 to 8 hours or overnight. Before serving, toss the onions and cauliflower in the dressing, then drain well. Arrange on serving dishes and garnish with minced parsley, if desired.

34

Mandarin-Stuffed Mushrooms ★ ★ ★

Makes 4 servings

8   very large mushrooms
1   tablespoon bulgur
1   tablespoon safflower oil
2   teaspoons tamari or soy sauce
1   clove garlic
½   teaspoon grated fresh ginger
¼   cup crumbled tofu
2   tablespoons minced fresh Italian parsley
    parsley sprigs (garnish)

Carefully remove the stems from the mushrooms. Soak the bulgur in the oil and tamari. Push the garlic through a garlic press into the bulgur mixture and add the ginger. When the bulgur has soaked about 10 minutes, stir in the tofu and parsley.

Place the stuffing in the mushroom caps and arrange them in a shallow 8 × 8-inch baking dish. Add enough water just to cover the bottom of the baking dish. Cover loosely with aluminum foil. Bake at 350° for 20 minutes. Serve hot.

Tomato Granita ★ ★ ★

Put a freeze on the wilt of hot weather with an unusual sherbet-like appetizer. Use garden tomatoes for best flavor. Prepare the tomatoes the day before you plan to serve this dish.

Makes 6 servings

10 large tomatoes
¾ cup *Chicken Stock*
½ cup chopped red onions
    mint sprigs (garnish)

Cut 4 tomatoes in quarters. Remove any tough fibers from the stem area. Squeeze out the seeds. Place the tomatoes on a baking sheet and freeze.

Cut the top quarter off the remaining 6 tomatoes and carefully scoop out the seeds and pulp and reserve for another use. Cover and refrigerate the shells (do not freeze).

Just before serving, place the frozen tomato quarters in a blender with the stock and onions. Process on low speed until smooth, scraping down the sides of the container if necessary. (Do this quickly, as the blended mixture must not have a chance to defrost.)

Quickly spoon the blended tomato mixture into the tomato shells and serve in sherbet glasses. Garnish with mint sprigs, if desired, and serve at once.

NOTE: You can omit the tomato shells and serve the granita garnished with mint directly in a sherbet glass.

35

Dilled Shrimp ★ ★ ★

Prepare the day before and marinate in the refrigerator until the flavors are well blended.

Makes 6 servings

¾ pound medium-size shrimp, peeled and deveined
2 lemon slices
1 bay leaf
¾ cup water
¼ cup tarragon vinegar
¼ cup minced fresh dill or 2 tablespoons dried dill
2 scallions, chopped
1 small stalk celery, minced
1 head Boston lettuce

Place the shrimp in a medium-size saucepan with the lemon slices, bay leaf, and just enough water to cover. Bring to a boil, then reduce heat and simmer until the shrimp are opaque and cooked through, about 2 minutes. Drain the shrimp and place them in a medium-size bowl with the ¾ cup of water, the vinegar, dill, scallions, and celery. Marinate for at least 24 hours.

Drain the marinated shrimp. Place lettuce leaves on a serving plate and arrange the shrimp on top.

Shrimp Zucchini Boats ★ ★

Makes 4 servings

1½ cups water
1 lemon slice
1 bay leaf
¼ pound medium-size shrimp, peeled and deveined
¼ cup small whole wheat pasta shells
4 small zucchini (about 6 inches long each)
½ cup very small broccoli florets
1 small carrot, cut diagonally into thin slices
32 snow peas
2 tablespoons low-fat yogurt
2 teaspoons *Lighten-Up Mayonnaise*
2 teaspoons minced sweet red peppers
2 teaspoons minced green peppers
2 teaspoons minced celery
1 teaspoon minced shallots
1 teaspoon minced fresh tarragon or ¼ teaspoon dried tarragon
½ clove garlic
tarragon sprigs (garnish)

36

In a small saucepan, bring the water, lemon, and bay leaf to a boil, then reduce heat, add shrimp, and simmer just until the shrimp are opaque, about 3 to 5 minutes. Drain and set aside to cool.

Cook the pasta shells in boiling water just until al dente, 6 to 12 minutes, then drain and rinse under cold water until cool. Set aside in a medium-size bowl.

Cut the zucchini in half lengthwise and steam for about 3 to 4 minutes or until crisp-tender. Rinse under cold water until cool.

Hollow out the zucchini halves, leaving enough of the shell intact to hold their shape well.

Steam the broccoli, carrots, and snow peas for about 2 to 3 minutes or until crisp-tender. Rinse under cold water until cooled. Add the broccoli to the pasta in the medium-size bowl. Set aside the carrots and snow peas.

In a small bowl, combine the yogurt, mayonnaise, red peppers, green peppers, celery, shallots, and tarragon. Add the garlic by pushing it through a garlic press into the bowl. Stir to combine.

Chop the shrimp and add to the pasta and broccoli in the medium-size bowl. Add the dressing mixture and toss until combined.

Stuff the shrimp and pasta mixture into the zucchini halves. Arrange the carrot slices on top of the zucchini boats. Place each zucchini half on a small plate and arrange a fan of snow peas along one side. Garnish with tarragon sprigs, if desired.

Nachos ★

Authentic nachos are generally a high-calorie snack served with refried beans. We've replaced the beans with herbs and low-calorie vegetables. The tortillas are oven crisped for additional calorie savings.

Makes 12 servings

1	medium-size zucchini, shredded
1	medium-size carrot, shredded
1	medium-size onion, minced
½	teaspoon ground cumin
½	teaspoon ground coriander
½	teaspoon garlic powder
2	cups shredded part-skim mozzarella cheese
12	*Corn Tortillas*
1	tablespoon corn oil
1	small anaheim (mild green chili) pepper, seeded and very thinly sliced (optional)

Drain the zucchini in a colander for 10 to 15 minutes. Squeeze out additional moisture. Mix the zucchini, carrots, onions, cumin, coriander, garlic powder, and mozzarella in a medium-size bowl.

Cut the tortillas into quarters. Brush one side of the tortilla chips lightly with oil. Place the tortillas on two cookie sheets. Bake one sheet at a time at 450° for 8 to 12 minutes or until crisp and browned. (Watch carefully because they can overcook quickly.)

Remove from oven and spread half the vegetable-cheese combination over the baked tortilla chips. Broil for 2 to 3 minutes or until the cheese is melted and bubbly. Garnish with pepper rings, if desired. Repeat with second sheet of tortillas.

37

Soups

Here's news that should put a smile on every dieter's face. Those who add soup to their daily diet are more successful at losing weight than those who don't.

In a study at the University of Pennsylvania, researchers monitored weight loss in two groups of dieters—those who ate soup and those who didn't. After ten weeks, those who ate soup every day lost an average of 20 percent of their extra weight, while those who didn't eat soup lost only 15 percent. The researchers discovered that the soup eaters, no matter how diverse their other eating habits, consumed fewer calories in a day's time than those who didn't eat soup. And this by no means was an isolated case.

At the University of Nebraska Medical Center and the Swanson Center for Nutrition, researchers analyzed the diets of approximately 28,000 individuals. They were not put on a specific diet; they were told only to write down whatever they ate each day. At the end of the experiment, the researchers tallied the calories. They, too, found that those who ate soup on a routine basis consumed fewer calories than those who didn't.

Weight loss experts say that the fact that soup eaters eat less isn't all that surprising. No matter how thick and filling, soup is still made up largely of water, so it's generally not calorically dense. Also, soup often contains lots of vegetables, which also helps keep calories low. Perhaps even more important, soup is served hot, so we tend to eat it *slower* than we do other foods. And therein lies a tactic that weight loss experts have been encouraging dieters to practice for years. By eating slowly, it's easier to stretch a meal out to 20 minutes—the amount of time it takes the brain to signal the stomach that enough has been eaten.

In this chapter, you won't find any recipes with heavy cream, whole milk, or a lot of butter and oil—needless high-calorie items that often "sneak" into the soup pot. Thickening is done by pureeing vegetables in a blender or food processor. Higher calorie items, such as beans and rice, are always coupled with lower calorie vegetables, giving you loads of taste without loads of calories. And the creamy soups are "creamed" with skim milk *only.*

The first section of this chapter is devoted to stocks. Stock is something I think every weight watcher should always have on hand. While you can eat these stocks as you would soup, their real purpose in this book is twofold: they are used as a base for soup and serve as a low-calorie substitute for butter and oil in sautéing meat and vegetables. The recipes in this book rely heavily on the stocks you'll find on the next few pages. Every time you substitute a tablespoon of stock for butter or oil, you're saving yourself about 100 calories (even more for some oils). That's a pretty significant savings—both in calories and unwanted fat.

And, yes, I do think it's worth your while to make your own stock. Even though *all* stocks are generally low in calories, most commercial brands tend to be a bit on the fatty side and are also high in salt. And you don't need that extra salt. Not only can it launch a case of high blood pressure, but it can also saddle your cells with extra water—and water retention causes temporary weight gain, which can be discouraging.

When you make your own stock, you also avoid excess fat. The fat in the finished stock will rise to the top if you refrigerate the stock overnight. Then all you need do is lift off the layer of fat and throw it away. (This should be a practice when making *all* your soups and stews.)

Just remember, stock made without salt spoils more quickly than salted ones. So, if you're not going to use the stock within two days, it's best to divide it in batches and freeze it. One nice idea is to freeze stock in ice cube trays. The little blocks are handy when you need stock for sautéing.

We've provided enough stocks on the following pages to suit all your cooking needs. While most of the recipes in this book call for a specific stock, feel free to use whatever you want or have on hand. The poultry and vegetable stocks, in particular, are basically interchangeable.

The other sections of this chapter are devoted to light soups—those intended to be served as an appetizer—and hearty soups—those designed to serve as the main dish. (You'll also notice that calorie ranges differ for the two. A three-star hearty soup can have twice the calories of a three-star light soup.)

I've found that serving a light soup as an appetizer is a nice way to take the edge off your appetite. Putting something in your stomach helps you face the main part of the meal—the part with the largest concentration of calories—with much more restraint.

You would be doing your waistline justice to take advantage of the nice range of oriental soups featured in the light soups section. Such dishes as *Seven Happiness Soup, Chinese Cucumber Soup,* and *Japanese Sea Vegetable Soup* are about as low in calories as soup can get. You should find their unique tastes pleasantly satisfying.

You needn't limit yourself to eating light soups only as an appetizer. Coupled with a tasty one- or two-star salad, any one of these light soups makes a nice lunch or even dinner that can only help your weight loss efforts.

As for the hearty soups, you'll want to limit these (except for the specified few) to main course fare. The hearty soups have a lot more calories than the light soups because they contain a lot more bulk, so there's plenty there to fill you up. Feature them for lunch or dinner, especially during the winter when something warm is always so appealing. A three-star hearty soup, a nice green salad, and a slice of whole grain bread can make a diet meal downright delightful.

Stocks

Chicken Stock ★ ★ ★
A basic stock, easy to make and keep on hand.

Makes 1 quart

2 pounds chicken pieces or bones (or 2 chicken carcasses)
6 cups water (or water to cover, if using carcasses)
1 large onion, quartered
1 large carrot, thickly sliced
2 stalks celery, halved
1 bay leaf
2 sprigs fresh parsley
1 teaspoon cider vinegar or herbed vinegar
1 clove garlic, halved (optional)

Place all of the ingredients in a large stockpot. Bring to a boil and skim off any foam that rises to the surface. Reduce heat, cover, and simmer gently for 1½ to 2 hours. Strain and refrigerate overnight. Remove fat from surface, refrigerate or freeze.

41

Basic Oriental Stock ★ ★ ★
Use in *Egg Drop and Sprout Soup* or substitute for *White Poultry Stock* or *Chicken Stock* in clear soups.

Makes 7 cups

2 pounds chicken bones
8 cups water
2 ¼-inch slices ginger
1 cup shredded Chinese cabbage
2 cloves garlic

Place chicken bones, water, ginger, and cabbage in a large stockpot. Add the garlic by pushing it through a garlic press into the stockpot. Bring to a boil and skim off any foam that rises to the surface. Reduce heat, cover, and simmer gently for 2 hours. Strain and refrigerate overnight. Remove fat from surface and refrigerate or freeze.

White Poultry Stock ★ ★ ★

Make use of your holiday turkey carcass and substitute it for chicken in this stock.

Makes 5 cups

2   pounds chicken pieces or bones (or 2 chicken carcasses)
6   cups water (or water to cover, if using carcasses)
1   cup thickly sliced carrots
1   cup thickly sliced leeks
1   cup thickly sliced celery
½   cup sliced turnips
½   cup shredded spinach
1   clove garlic
1   bay leaf
½   teaspoon turmeric

Combine all ingredients in a large stockpot. Bring to a boil and skim off any foam that rises to the top. Reduce heat, cover, and simmer for 3 hours. Strain and refrigerate overnight. Remove fat from the surface, refrigerate or freeze.

42

Basic Brown Stock ★ ★ ★

Makes 4 cups

3   pounds beef shin or neck bones cut into manageable pieces
5   cups water
⅓   cup chopped celery
⅓   cup chopped carrots
⅓   cup chopped leeks or onions
4   sprigs parsley
3   peppercorns
1   bay leaf

Place all the ingredients in a large stockpot and bring to a boil. Reduce heat to a simmer and skim off any foam that rises to the top. Partially cover and continue to cook over very low heat for 2½ hours. Strain and refrigerate overnight. Remove fat from the surface and refrigerate or freeze.

NOTE: For a browner stock, heat bones at 400° for about 30 minutes or until browned. Then use in recipe as you would fresh bones.

Sausalito Fish Stock ★ ★ ★

Use as a base for chowders, fish soups, and stews.

Makes 3½ cups

3   cups water
1   cup rice vinegar
2   pounds fish heads, bones, and shells
¼   cup lightly packed fresh parsley
1   bay leaf
¼   cup fresh thyme or 1 tablespoon dried thyme, secured in cheesecloth
½   cup sliced onions
2   cloves garlic
5   peppercorns

Combine all ingredients in a large stockpot. Bring to a boil and skim off any foam that rises to the surface. Reduce heat, cover, and simmer gently for 1½ hours. Strain, cool, cover, and refrigerate or freeze.

43

Vegetable Stock ★ ★ ★

Choose your own vegetables, even leftovers, if desired. Just make sure to use twice as much liquid as vegetables.

Makes 4 cups

5   cups water
½   cup chopped spinach
½   cup chopped tomatoes
½   cup sliced turnips
½   cup sliced onions
½   cup coarsely chopped celery
1   bay leaf
1   clove garlic

Combine all ingredients in a large stockpot and bring to a boil. Remove any foam that might come to the top. Reduce heat, cover, and simmer slowly for 1½ hours. Strain, cool, cover, and refrigerate or freeze.

Vegetarian Stock ★ ★ ★

I rarely peel potatoes, but when I do, I save the peels for this delicious stock. Keep vegetable trimmings in a plastic bag in the freezer until you have enough for stock.

Makes about 2 quarts

10–12	cups potato peels
12	cups water
14	cloves garlic, sliced
2	medium-size onions, chopped
1	stalk celery, sliced
3	sprigs parsley
1	bay leaf

Place all of the ingredients in a large stockpot. Bring to a boil. Remove any foam that may come to the top. Reduce heat, cover, and simmer for 1½ to 2 hours. Strain the stock, cool, cover, and refrigerate or freeze.

44

Light Soups

Curried Potato Soup ★ ★

Makes 4 servings

1	medium-size onion, minced
1	tablespoon safflower oil
2½	cups *Chicken Stock*
2	large potatoes, diced
1	large tomato, peeled, seeded, and chopped
¼	teaspoon curry powder
¼	teaspoon paprika
2	tablespoons minced fresh parsley
	minced fresh parsley (garnish)

Place the onions and the oil in a medium-size saucepan and cook over medium heat, stirring frequently. When the onions are softened and just beginning to turn golden, add the stock, potatoes, tomatoes, curry, paprika, and parsley. Bring to a boil over medium heat, then reduce heat, cover, and simmer slowly for 30 minutes.

Remove about 1½ cups of the potatoes with a slotted spoon and place in a warmed serving bowl. Place the remaining soup in a blender and process on low speed until smooth. Add the blended soup to the potatoes in the serving bowl and stir. Garnish with parsley, if desired, and serve.

Old-Fashioned Chicken and Rice Soup ★ ★ ★

Like Grandma used to make.

Makes 8 servings

1	large Spanish onion, chopped
4	cups *White Poultry Stock*
4	cups sliced carrots
5	tomatoes, chopped
10	cloves garlic, thinly sliced
1	bay leaf
1	sprig tarragon or ¼ teaspoon dried tarragon
¼	teaspoon thyme
	dash of powdered saffron
1	cup cooked brown rice
4	teaspoons tamari or soy sauce
2	tablespoons minced fresh parsley

Place the onions with 2 tablespoons of the stock in a large saucepan. Cook over medium heat until the onions are translucent.

Add the rest of the stock, carrots, tomatoes, garlic, bay leaf, tarragon, thyme, and saffron. Bring to a boil, then reduce heat and simmer, covered, for 1 hour. Add rice. Remove from heat. Stir in the tamari and parsley and serve.

45

Avocado Soup ★ ★ ★

Good hot or cold.

Makes 4 servings

1½	cups *Chicken Stock*
1	teaspoon grated onions
1	cup cubed avocado
¼	teaspoon finely grated lemon rind
¾	cup low-fat yogurt
	parsley sprigs (garnish)

In a medium-size saucepan, bring the stock to a boil. Add the onions, reduce heat, and simmer 2 to 3 minutes.

Place the avocado in a blender. Add the stock and blend on low speed until smooth.

Add the lemon rind and ½ cup of the yogurt, then blend until combined. Pour into individual bowls and serve at once, garnished with dollops of the remaining yogurt and the parsley sprigs, if desired.

NOTE: To serve the soup cold, pour into individual bowls and chill 2 to 4 hours. Serve garnished with dollops of yogurt and a dusting of nutmeg, if desired. Omit parsley.

Vegetable Mélange ★ ★ ★

Makes 8 servings

1	medium-size red onion, chopped
4	medium-size carrots, sliced
1	stalk celery, sliced
½	cup corn
¼	cup barley
5	cloves garlic, minced
2	tablespoons minced fresh parsley
5	cups water
3	medium-size tomatoes
½	teaspoon marjoram
1	cup peas
1	cup packed spinach leaves, chopped
½	cup tomato paste
1	tablespoon tamari or soy sauce

Place the onions, carrots, celery, corn, barley, garlic, parsley, and 3 cups of the water in a large saucepan.

Place the remaining 2 cups of water, the tomatoes, and marjoram in a blender and process on low to medium speed until smooth. Add to the saucepan. Bring to a boil, then turn down heat, cover, and simmer for 1¼ hours.

Add the peas, spinach, tomato paste, and tamari, cover, and simmer for 10 minutes more.

NOTE: If you are using very mature garden peas, add them 10 to 15 minutes sooner.

Russian Tomato Borsht ★ ★ ★

Makes 4 servings

1¼	cups *White Poultry Stock*
1	cup chopped onions
2	cups tomato juice
1	cup shredded savoy cabbage
½	cup shredded carrots
½	cup shredded spinach
¼	teaspoon tamari or soy sauce
	yogurt (garnish)

In a large saucepan, heat 2 tablespoons of stock and sauté the onions for 5 minutes. Add the tomato juice and the rest of the stock and bring to a boil. Then turn down heat and simmer for 30 minutes. Add cabbage, carrots, spinach, and tamari and cook 15 minutes more. Serve hot with yogurt garnish, if desired.

46

Italian Escarole Soup ★ ★

Prepared this way, you'll have extra chicken for sandwiches or salad.

Makes 10 servings

2   whole chicken breasts, halved and skinned
12   cups water
2   large carrots
2   small onions
2   stalks celery
2   cups sliced carrots
1   cup sliced parsnips
1   cup chopped leeks
3   cups chopped escarole

Place the chicken in a large stockpot with the water, whole carrots, onions, and celery. Bring to a boil, skim off any foam, then reduce heat, cover, and simmer for 45 minutes. Remove the chicken and set it aside. Continue to simmer the stock for 30 minutes, then remove and discard the carrots, onions, and celery.

When the chicken is cool, remove the meat from two of the pieces and cut it into bite-size chunks. Reserve the remaining two pieces of chicken for another use.

Add the sliced carrots, parsnips, and leeks to the chicken stock. Bring to a boil, then reduce heat and simmer until the vegetables are tender, about 30 minutes. Add the escarole to the soup and cook an additional 10 minutes. Add the chicken meat and heat through before serving.

47

Gazpacho ★ ★ ★

Keep the ingredients in the refrigerator so the soup will be cold when you make it.

Makes 4 servings

6   large tomatoes, seeded, peeled if desired, and coarsely chopped
4   scallions or 1 small onion, chopped
½   sweet red pepper, chopped
1   tablespoon olive oil
2   tablespoons tarragon vinegar
½   teaspoon oregano
    dash of cayenne pepper
½   cucumber, finely chopped
    parsley sprigs (garnish)

Place the tomatoes in a blender with the scallions, peppers, oil, vinegar, oregano, and cayenne. Process on low to medium speed until the ingredients are finely chopped and well combined.

Divide the soup among four serving bowls. Sprinkle each with cucumbers. Garnish with parsley sprigs, if desired. Keep chilled until ready to serve.

Dilled Split Pea Soup
as an appetizer ★
as a main dish ★ ★ ★

Makes 8 servings

2   cups dried split peas
8   cups water
2   tablespoons *Chicken Stock*
1   small onion, minced
1   medium-size carrot, diced
2   stalks celery, chopped
2   tablespoons minced
    fresh dill
1   tablespoon tamari or soy
    sauce
¼   cup low-fat yogurt
    (garnish)
8   sprigs dill (garnish)

Bring the split peas and water to a boil in a large saucepan. Reduce heat, partially cover, and simmer for 30 minutes.

While the peas cook, place the stock in a large skillet and set over low to medium heat. Add the onions, carrots, celery, and dill. Cook slowly, stirring occasionally, until the vegetables are golden brown. Add more stock if necessary to prevent scorching.

Drain the split peas but save the cooking liquid. Stir the split peas into the vegetables in the skillet so that they can absorb the flavor. Cook for about 3 to 4 minutes over low heat. Return to soup pot.

Add the split pea cooking liquid and the tamari. Continue to cook the soup for an additional 30 minutes. Puree the soup in batches in a blender on low speed. Reheat, if necessary, before serving.

To serve, place the soup in individual bowls. Place a dollop of yogurt and a dill sprig in the center of each bowl, if desired.

Puree of Cauliflower Soup ★ ★ ★

In winter, the French in the northern province of Upper Saone enjoy this savory potage.

Makes 4 servings

2   cups cauliflower florets
½   cup chopped potatoes
4   cups *White Poultry Stock*
½   cup chopped leeks
1   bay leaf
¼   teaspoon ground caraway
    seeds
2   tablespoons chopped chives
    (garnish)

Steam the cauliflower and potatoes for 20 minutes. Combine with stock, leeks, bay leaf, and caraway seeds in a large saucepan and simmer for 20 minutes. Remove bay leaf. Puree in blender or food processor a cup at a time. Return to the pot and heat through. Pour into serving bowls and garnish with chives, if desired.

48

Creamy Cauliflower Soup ★ ★ ★

Makes 6 servings

1   large onion, chopped
4   cups *Chicken Stock*
2   medium-size carrots, thinly sliced
1   head cauliflower, separated into florets
½   cup packed watercress, coarsely chopped
1   cup skim milk
½   teaspoon ground coriander
    dash of nutmeg
    dash of cayenne pepper

Place the onions and 1 tablespoon of stock in a large stockpot or flameproof casserole. Cook over medium heat, stirring occasionally until the onions are translucent. Stir in the carrots and cauliflower and cook over medium heat for about 3 to 4 minutes. Add the remaining stock and watercress. Cover and simmer for 30 minutes or until the vegetables are quite tender.

With a slotted spoon, remove about three-fourths of the cauliflower from the soup and place in a blender with the skim milk. Process on low to medium speed until smooth. Return the blended cauliflower to the soup, add the nutmeg and cayenne, heat through, and serve.

Sunchoke Soup ★ ★ ★

Makes 6 servings

1½   cups finely diced Jerusalem artichokes
1½   cups finely diced carrots
1   sweet red pepper, minced
1   medium-size onion, minced
½   cup finely chopped leeks
1½   cups *Chicken Stock*
1½   cups skim milk
2   cloves garlic
½   teaspoon grated fresh ginger
¼   teaspoon ground coriander
    fresh dill (garnish)

Place all of the ingredients except dill in a large saucepan. Bring to a boil, then reduce heat and simmer, partially covered, for 30 minutes or until the vegetables are tender.

Place about a third of the soup in a blender and process on low to medium speed until smooth. Transfer the blended soup to a warmed serving bowl. Blend another third of the soup and add to the serving bowl. Stir in the remaining soup without blending. Garnish with fresh dill, if desired, and serve.

Celeris à la Crème ★ ★ ★

A classic cream of celery soup from France's Loire Valley.

Makes 2 to 4 servings

2	cups chopped celery
1/3	cup minced sweet red peppers
3	scallions, minced
2	tablespoons *Chicken Stock*
1	tablespoon whole wheat flour
1	teaspoon tamari or soy sauce
1¾	cups skim milk
	dash of nutmeg
	dash of ground coriander
	sweet red pepper rings (garnish)
	parsley sprigs (garnish)

Steam the celery for 10 minutes. Set aside.

Cook the peppers and scallions in the stock in a large saucepan over low heat, stirring often, for 5 minutes. Stir in the flour and remove from heat.

Place the tamari and ¾ cup of the milk in a blender with the celery and process on low to medium speed until smooth.

Add the blended mixture along with the remaining milk, the nutmeg, and coriander to the saucepan. Set over low heat and simmer about 5 minutes before serving. Garnish with pepper rings and parsley, if desired.

Spinach Gazpacho ★ ★ ★

A slight variation from the tomato variety. Adjust the seasoning to your taste *after* chilling soup.

Makes 4 servings

2½	cups chopped spinach
3	cups *White Poultry Stock*
1	clove garlic, minced
2	tablespoons lemon juice
1	cup peeled, seeded, and coarsely chopped cucumbers
½	cup chopped tomatoes
½	cup chopped red onions
½	teaspoon thyme

Simmer the spinach in the stock for 5 minutes. Add garlic and lemon juice and refrigerate until cool. Puree the spinach in a food processor or blender on medium to high speed. Add cucumbers, tomatoes, onions, and thyme. Refrigerate overnight. Stir before serving. Serve in chilled bowls.

50

Broccoli and Cheddar à la Crème ★ ★

Makes 6 servings

1	tablespoon *Chicken Stock*
10	scallions, chopped
3	tablespoons chopped fresh parsley
4	teaspoons whole wheat flour
1	clove garlic
4	cups skim milk
1	large bunch broccoli
¼	cup shredded sharp Cheddar cheese
	paprika (garnish)

Pour stock in a large saucepan, then add the scallions. Cook over low heat, stirring frequently until the scallions are limp. Stir in the parsley, and when it is wilted, add the flour. Stir until the flour coats the scallions, then add the garlic by pushing it through a garlic press into the saucepan. Add the milk a little at a time, stirring to break up any lumps of flour. Turn heat to medium.

Cut the florets from the broccoli, making them about 1½ inches long. Peel any tough outer skin from the stems of the florets. Cut the florets in thin, lengthwise strips. Add the broccoli florets to the saucepan, and when the milk comes to a boil, reduce heat, partially cover, and simmer for 20 minutes. Remove from the heat. Add the cheese and stir until the cheese melts.

51

Broccoli Bud Soup
as an appetizer ★ ★
as a main dish ★ ★ ★

Makes 4 servings

1	small carrot, sliced
1	stalk celery, sliced
1	small onion, chopped
1	clove garlic, minced
½	teaspoon marjoram
¼	teaspoon basil
½	cup *Chicken Stock* or *Vegetable Stock*
2	cups skim milk
2	cups coarsely chopped broccoli
½	cup cooked macaroni
	dash of nutmeg
	low-fat yogurt (garnish)

Place the carrots, celery, onions, garlic, marjoram, basil, and stock in a medium-size saucepan. Bring to a boil, then reduce heat, cover, and simmer for 10 minutes.

Add the milk and broccoli. Return to a boil, reduce heat, then simmer for an additional 5 to 7 minutes or until the broccoli is tender. Add the macaroni and nutmeg and heat through.

Remove some broccoli buds from the soup and place in a serving bowl. Place the remaining soup in a blender and process on low speed, until the soup is smooth, holding down the lid so no hot liquid spills out.

Pour the soup into the serving dish. Place the yogurt in a separate dish on the table so that each diner can garnish his or her soup, if desired.

Cream of Broccoli, Leek, and Fennel Soup ★ ★

Makes 6 servings

1	large stalk broccoli
1	tablespoon butter
2	cups chopped leeks
1	cup minced fennel bulb
1	tablespoon water
1½–2	cups *Chicken Stock*
1½	cups low-fat milk
¼	teaspoon ground coriander
	dash of nutmeg
	lemon slices (garnish)
	fennel sprigs (garnish)

Peel the broccoli stem. Cut the stem into thick slices. Separate the broccoli tops into small florets. (There should be about 3 cups of broccoli altogether.)

Melt the butter in a large saucepan. Add the broccoli, leeks, fennel, and water. Slowly steam-sauté the vegetables over low heat, stirring until they begin to soften, about 20 minutes.

Add 1½ cups of the stock, the milk, coriander, and nutmeg. Bring just to a boil, cover, and simmer over low heat for about 15 minutes or until the vegetables are quite tender.

Process the soup in a blender on low speed or in a food processor until smooth. Add more stock, if desired, to thin the soup slightly.

Heat through, if necessary, before placing in a warmed soup tureen. Float lemon slices topped with fennel sprigs on the soup, if desired. Serve immediately.

52

Zucchini Zuppa ★ ★ ★

Makes 4 servings

2¼	cups *Chicken Stock*
3	small zucchini, cubed
1	small green pepper, diced
6	scallions, cut diagonally into thin slices
1	cup skim milk
	dash of cayenne pepper
	dill sprigs (garnish)

Heat 2 tablespoons of the stock in a medium-size skillet over low to medium heat. Add the zucchini, green peppers, and scallions. Cover and cook for about 10 minutes, stirring occasionally. Add more stock, if necessary, to prevent scorching.

Place half the vegetables with the rest of the stock in a blender. Process on low speed until smooth. Return this mixture to the skillet. Bring to a boil, then simmer for 5 minutes. Remove from heat. Stir in the milk and cayenne. Chill and serve garnished with dill, if desired.

Herbed Zucchini Soup ★ ★ ★

Makes 4 servings

2   scallions, chopped
2   tablespoons *Chicken Stock*
2   cups shredded zucchini
3   cups skim milk
2   tablespoons minced fresh parsley
1   teaspoon minced fresh thyme or ½ teaspoon dried thyme
¼   teaspoon ground coriander
¼   cup low-fat yogurt (garnish)
4   tarragon sprigs (garnish)

In a large saucepan, cook the scallions in the stock until limp, stirring constantly. Add the zucchini and cook until tender, about 7 to 10 minutes. Add the milk, parsley, thyme, and coriander. Bring to a boil, then turn heat to low and simmer for 20 minutes.

Place three-fourths of the soup in a blender and process on low to medium speed until smooth. Stir back into the soup in the pan. To serve, place the soup in individual bowls. Garnish each bowl of soup with a tablespoon of yogurt and a tarragon sprig, if desired.

French-Style Onion Soup ★ ★

Makes 6 servings

4   large onions
2   teaspoons olive oil
1   tablespoon whole wheat flour
1   clove garlic
5   cups *Chicken Stock*
1   tablespoon tamari or soy sauce
½   cup shredded Gruyère or Swiss cheese

Cut the onions in half lengthwise, then slice crosswise into thin half-circles. Heat the oil over low heat in a very large skillet or large flameproof casserole. Add the onions, cover, and cook slowly, stirring occasionally. Add a few drops of water if necessary to prevent the onions from scorching.

When the onions are tender and begin to turn golden brown, sprinkle the flour on them. Add the garlic by pushing it through a garlic press into the pan. Stir until the onions are coated with flour. Cook, stirring, 2 to 3 minutes.

Add the stock and tamari, cover, and cook over low heat for about 15 minutes.

To serve, divide the soup among four ovenproof serving bowls. Sprinkle each with the cheese and bake at 400° or place under a broiler until the cheese is melted and golden brown. Serve hot.

Onion Soup Gratinée
as an appetizer ★
as main dish ★ ★ ★
Looks and tastes wonderful!

Makes 4 servings

2	large onions, thinly sliced
1	tablespoon olive oil
1	clove garlic
4	cups *Chicken Stock*
1	tablespoon tamari or soy sauce
½	teaspoon blackstrap molasses
1	bay leaf
4	slices stale or toasted whole wheat bread
4	thin slices part-skim mozzarella cheese

Cook the onions in a large saucepan over low heat in the oil, stirring often. When the onions are translucent, push the garlic through a garlic press into the pan.

Immediately pour in the stock, then add the tamari, molasses, and bay leaf. Cover, bring to a boil, then reduce heat and simmer for about 40 minutes.

Remove bay leaf. Place the soup in individual ovenproof serving dishes or in a 1½-quart ovenproof casserole. Top with the bread and place a slice of cheese on each piece of bread.

Place under a broiler until the cheese is melted and begins to brown slightly. Serve hot.

54

Fennel Vichyssoise ★ ★ ★
This is my variation of vichyssoise. The fennel adds a delicate flavor of anise. This is one of the few occasions when I suggest peeling potatoes; it maintains the delicate color of the soup.

Makes 8 servings

4¼	cups *Chicken Stock*
3	large leeks, white part only, chopped
1	large onion, chopped
1	large fennel bulb, chopped
4	large potatoes, peeled and cubed
1	tablespoon tamari or soy sauce
1	cup skim milk
	chopped watercress or Italian parsley (garnish)

Put 2 tablespoons of stock in a large, heavy-bottom pot. Add the leeks, onions, and fennel and cook over low heat for 3 to 4 minutes, stirring often, until the vegetables are wilted. Do not let the vegetables brown. Add more stock, if necessary.

Add the potatoes, the rest of the stock, and tamari. Bring to a boil, then reduce the heat, cover, and simmer for about 20 minutes or until all of the vegetables are quite tender. Remove from the heat and stir in the milk.

Puree the soup in small batches in a blender and place in a tureen or individual bowls. Garnish with the watercress or parsley, if desired.

Corn and Carrot Bisque ★ ★

Makes 4 servings

4 cups *White Poultry Stock*
2 tablespoons Italian dried mushrooms, rinsed and broken into oat-size pieces
½ cup sliced yellow onions
1 cup shredded carrots
1 cup corn, processed in a blender for 5 to 10 seconds
1 egg, beaten
4 sprigs parsley (garnish)

In a large saucepan, simmer the stock, mushrooms, onions, and carrots for 20 minutes. Add corn and simmer 10 minutes more. Slowly bring to a boil and stir in the egg. Remove from heat and serve immediately, garnished with parsley, if desired.

55

Gingered Carrot Bisque ★ ★

Makes 4 servings

5 small carrots, diced
2 tablespoons *Chicken Stock*
1 cup diced Jerusalem artichokes
1 tablespoon minced fresh ginger
2 cloves garlic, halved
2 cups skim milk
2 teaspoons whole wheat flour minced fresh parsley (garnish)

Place the carrots and stock in a large skillet. Set over low heat, cover, and cook, stirring occasionally, for 15 minutes or until the carrots are crisp-tender.

While the carrots cook, place the Jerusalem artichokes, ginger, garlic, and milk in a medium-size saucepan. Bring to a boil, then reduce heat, cover, and simmer for 15 minutes.

Sprinkle the flour over the carrots in the skillet and stir until the carrots are coated. Add the Jerusalem artichokes and milk mixture to the carrots and stir. Simmer for 15 to 20 minutes.

Place the soup in a blender. Process on low, then medium speed until smooth, stopping and scraping down the sides as necessary. Put the soup through a strainer and press out liquid with the back of a wooden spoon to thin the soup. Return to the skillet or a saucepan and heat through. Garnish with parsley, if desired.

Spiced Cream of Carrot Soup ★ ★ ★

This is so low in calories that you can have 2 servings and still be within the weight loss calorie range!

Makes 6 servings

2	cups sliced carrots
2½	cups *Chicken Stock*
1	bay leaf
½	teaspoon grated orange rind
	dash of cinnamon
	dash of ground cumin
	dash of chili powder
½	cup orange juice
2	tablespoons low-fat yogurt
	carrot curls (garnish)
	dill sprigs (garnish)

Place the carrots, stock, bay leaf, orange rind, cinnamon, cumin, and chili powder in a large saucepan. Bring to a boil, then reduce heat, cover, and simmer until the carrots are soft, about 15 to 20 minutes.

Place the cooked carrot mixture in a blender. Add the orange juice and yogurt. Process on low speed until smooth. Place in a soup tureen or individual bowls and garnish with carrots and dill, if desired. Serve immediately or chill.

56

Corn and Carrot Soup ★ ★ ★

Because sea vegetables are so nutritious and low in calories, it's worth getting acquainted with them. The sea vegetable in this recipe yields a delicate stock in which the other ingredients simmer.

Makes 8 servings

6	cups water
1	5-inch piece of kombu
1	medium-size onion, chopped
1	stalk celery, chopped
⅓	cup dried navy beans or dried baby lima beans
2	cups corn
1	cup diagonally sliced carrots
¼	cup millet
4	teaspoons tamari or soy sauce

Place the water in a large saucepan. Add the kombu and bring to a boil. Reduce heat, cover, and simmer for 5 to 8 minutes. Remove the kombu.

Add the onions, celery, beans, and corn to the stock. Bring to a boil, reduce heat, and cover. Simmer for 1¼ hours, stirring occasionally.

Add the carrots and millet. Simmer, covered, an additional 30 to 45 minutes, stirring occasionally. Remove from the heat. Stir in the tamari and serve hot.

NOTE: Kombu is available in oriental groceries or natural food stores.

Seven Happiness
Soup ★ ★ ★

A light vegetable soup from Canton.

Makes 4 servings

4 cups *Basic Oriental Stock*
½ cup shredded Chinese
cabbage
⅓ cup coarsely chopped tofu
⅓ cup thinly sliced
mushrooms
⅓ cup snow peas, ends and
strings removed
⅓ cup slivered bamboo
shoots
⅓ cup thinly sliced water
chestnuts
⅓ cup sliced carrots (use a
crinkle cutter to slice
decoratively)

Combine all ingredients in a large saucepan and
simmer gently for 20 minutes. Serve hot.

57

Egg Drop and Sprout
Soup ★ ★ ★

Makes 2 servings

2 cups *Basic Oriental Stock*
1 egg
1 tablespoon water
¼ cup bean sprouts
1 tablespoon minced fresh
scallions

Bring the stock to a boil in a medium-size saucepan. While the stock heats, beat the egg with the water
in a small bowl. When the stock boils, begin stirring it
and slowly pour in the egg, while stirring. When all
of the egg is added, quickly stir in the sprouts and
scallions, remove from heat, and serve.

Chinese Cucumber Soup ★ ★ ★

Makes 4 servings

4   cups *Basic Oriental Stock*
2   cups diced, peeled
     cucumbers
3   shiitake mushrooms,
     rinsed and slivered
½   cup shredded bamboo
     shoots
½   cup shredded spinach
½   cup chopped raw shrimp
1   clove garlic
1   ¼-inch slice ginger
1   teaspoon tamari or soy
     sauce

In a large saucepan, combine all ingredients. Simmer gently for 20 minutes. Remove garlic and ginger. Serve hot.

58

Misoshiru ★ ★ ★

This Japanese clear soup with red soybean paste is somewhat sweeter than other Japanese soups. Although traditionally served toward the end of a formal meal, Misoshiru is by no means a dessert soup and is delightful as the focal point of a luncheon or as a light evening meal.

Makes 4 servings

4   cups *Basic Oriental Stock*
⅓   cup red miso (red soybean
     paste)
½   cup diced tofu
¼   cup thinly sliced scallions
     (garnish)
¼   cup thinly shredded
     spinach (garnish)

Simmer the stock in a medium-size saucepan. Put a strainer over the saucepan and, with a wooden spoon, rub the miso through the strainer. Simmer until heated through, about 10 minutes. Add tofu. Pour into individual bowls and garnish with scallions and spinach, if desired.

Japanese Sea Vegetable Soup ★ ★ ★

A tasty introduction to nori, a Japanese sea vegetable.

Makes 4 servings

4 cups *Basic Oriental Stock*
1 clove garlic
2 shiitake mushrooms, rinsed and slivered
½ cup shredded nori
¼ cup diced water chestnuts
¼ cup chopped scallions (garnish)

In a large saucepan, combine the stock, garlic, mushrooms, nori, and water chestnuts. Simmer for 20 minutes. Remove garlic. Serve hot, garnished with scallions, if desired.

NOTE: Nori is available in oriental groceries or natural food stores.

White Waterfall Soup ★ ★ ★

The name comes from the shirataki noodles that alternately float and fall through the soup.

Makes 4 servings

4 cups *Basic Oriental Stock*
2 shiitake mushrooms, rinsed and slivered
1 cup shirataki (yam threads), rinsed and cut into 2-inch pieces
3 scallions including green tops, cut in half lengthwise, then at 2-inch intervals
2 teaspoons tamari or soy sauce

Combine the stock and shiitake mushrooms in a medium-size saucepan and bring to a boil. Reduce heat and simmer for 10 minutes. Add shirataki, scallions, and tamari and serve immediately.

NOTE: Shirataki is available, canned, in oriental food stores.

Hearty Soups

Cuban Black Bean Soup ★ ★

Popular in Latin America, this soup is a storehouse of nutrients and as satisfying a soup as you'll find. Ginger is a nontraditional addition.

Makes 8 servings

1   pound dried black beans
6   cups water
2   medium-size onions, chopped
2   tablespoons minced fresh ginger
4   cloves garlic, minced
3   stalks celery, thinly sliced
2   hot peppers, seeded and minced
¼   cup minced fresh parsley
1   teaspoon thyme
1   bay leaf
5   cups water
2   cups *Chicken Stock*
4   teaspoons tamari or soy sauce
   low-fat yogurt (garnish)

Soak the black beans overnight in the 6 cups of water.

Drain the beans. Place in a very large ovenproof casserole or small roasting pan. Add the onions, ginger, garlic, celery, peppers, parsley, thyme, and bay leaf. Add enough water to cover the ingredients (about 5 cups), then stir in the stock and tamari.

Bake at 375° for 2 hours or until the beans are tender. Remove the bay leaf. Serve hot with a spoonful of yogurt in the center of each serving, if desired.

Beacon Hill Fish Chowder ★ ★

Makes 4 servings

2   cups skim milk
1   large tomato, seeded
3   medium-size potatoes, cubed

Place 1 cup of the milk in a blender with the tomato and process on low speed until smooth. Place the blended mixture, the remaining milk, the potatoes, and onions in a large saucepan. Bring to a boil, reduce

1 large Spanish onion, chopped
1 pound haddock fillets, cut into bite-size pieces
1 cup corn
   dash of thyme
   dash of marjoram
   dash of paprika (garnish)
   minced fresh parsley (garnish)

heat, and simmer for 15 minutes.

Stir in the haddock, corn, thyme, and marjoram. Return to a boil, then reduce heat and simmer for 5 minutes or until the fish is cooked through. Serve hot, garnished with paprika and parsley, if desired.

Italian Wedding Soup ★ ★ ★

Makes 8 servings

8-10 cups of *Vegetable Stock*
 ½ pound lean ground beef
 1 tablespoon minced fresh parsley
 1 tablespoon minced onions
 ¼ teaspoon minced garlic
 ¼ cup whole wheat bread crumbs
 5 tablespoons skim milk
 1 pound escarole, washed
 2 medium-size carrots, coarsely chopped
 1 stalk celery, coarsely chopped
 2 eggs, beaten with 2 tablespoons cold water
 1 tablespoon chopped parsley
 1 hard-cooked egg, sliced (garnish)

In a 6-quart saucepan, bring the stock to a slow boil. Simmer, covered, while preparing the meatballs.

In a medium-size bowl, combine the ground beef, the parsley, onions, garlic, bread crumbs, and milk. Mix well. Using your hands, roll into 1-inch balls. Place on a broiler pan and bake at 375° for about 25 minutes or until browned. Remove from pan and set aside.

Steam escarole for about 5 minutes or until tender. Coarsely chop.

Add carrots and celery to the stock. Simmer 20 minutes or until vegetables are tender.

Add meatballs and escarole to the stock. Heat through. Add eggs, stirring until eggs are set, about 20 seconds. Turn off heat.

Serve with parsley sprinkled on top and garnish with egg slices, if desired.

61

Country Chicken and Barley Soup ★ ★

Makes 4 servings

4	chicken thighs, skinned
½	cup barley
5½	cups *Chicken Stock*
1	stalk celery, chopped
3	small carrots, sliced
1	large tomato, peeled and chopped
2	cloves garlic, minced
1	tablespoon tamari or soy sauce
½	teaspoon basil
	dash of oregano
	dash of thyme
	dash of cayenne pepper
2	tablespoons minced fresh parsley

Place all of the ingredients except the parsley in a large saucepan. Bring to a boil, cover, and reduce heat.

Simmer the soup for 1¼ hours, stirring occasionally.

Remove the chicken thighs from the soup. When they have cooled slightly, remove the meat, cut into bite-size pieces, and return the meat to the soup.

Simmer for an additional 15 minutes, stir in the parsley, and serve.

Curried Chicken-Rice Soup ★ ★

Makes 10 servings

2	whole chicken breasts, halved, skinned, boned, and cut into bite-size pieces
1½	tablespoons butter, melted
2	large onions, chopped
2	stalks celery, chopped
3	leeks, chopped
7	cups *Chicken Stock*

In a large heavy-bottom saucepan, sauté the chicken in ½ tablespoon of melted butter. Remove the chicken and set aside.

Add the remaining butter to the saucepan. Cook the onions, celery, and leeks over low to medium heat until they are soft and lightly browned.

Stir 3 cups of the stock, apples, and curry into the vegetables. Combine the vegetable and apple mixture and remaining stock. Process a few cups at a time in a blender on low speed until smooth. Place in a 3-quart

2 tart apples, chopped
3 tablespoons curry powder
  (preferably Madras)
3 cups cooked brown rice
2 tablespoons tamari or soy
  sauce
1 tablespoon lemon juice
2 teaspoons blackstrap
  molasses
1 clove garlic

container and allow flavors to blend for 2 to 4 hours or overnight.

Return the blended mixture to the saucepan and bring to a boil. Stir in the cooked chicken pieces, rice, tamari, lemon juice, and molasses. Push the garlic through a garlic press into the soup. Return to a boil, reduce heat, cover, and simmer for about 15 minutes. Serve hot.

Chicken Gumbo ★ ★ ★

Makes 6 servings

5 cups water
½ pound collard or mustard
  greens
1 pound spinach, shredded
6 sprigs parsley
1 bay leaf
1 pound chicken breast meat,
  cut into 1-inch pieces
½ pound okra, cut into 1-inch
  pieces
½ cup minced onions
½ cup minced celery
¼ cup minced scallions
¼ cup whole wheat flour
¾ cup coarsely chopped
  Italian plum tomatoes
2 cloves garlic, minced
½ teaspoon thyme
¼ teaspoon cayenne pepper
¼ teaspoon ground allspice
½ teaspoon tamari or soy
  sauce

In a medium-size saucepan, bring water to a boil. Drop in the greens, spinach, and parsley tied together with the bay leaf. Reduce heat to low and cook, partially covered, for 1 hour or until greens are tender. Discard bay leaf and parsley and strain the greens through a sieve over a bowl, pressing down firmly on the greens. Reserve the strained cooking liquid. Puree the greens in a food processor or blender on medium to high speed.

In a medium-size skillet coated with no-stick spray, sauté the chicken until browned, adding some of the cooking liquid if necessary to prevent scorching. Remove chicken and sauté okra in a little more cooking liquid until "roping" has stopped (white threads disappear). Remove the okra, add more cooking liquid, and sauté the onions, celery, and scallions until wilted.

In a medium-size saucepan, make a paste with the flour and ½ cup of the cooking liquid, heating slowly and stirring. Whisk vigorously to make the mixture free of lumps. Add remaining cooking liquid, stirring until combined. Whisk, if necessary. Add reserved greens, chicken, okra, onions, celery, scallions, tomatoes, garlic, thyme, cayenne, allspice, and tamari. Bring to a boil, reduce heat to low, and simmer, partially covered, for 30 minutes or until vegetables are almost tender.

63

Lancaster Bean and Vegetable Soup ★

Makes 6 servings

- 1 medium-size onion, chopped
- 1 tablespoon safflower oil
- 2 tablespoons whole wheat flour
- 4 cups *Vegetable Stock* or *Chicken Stock*
- 2 medium-size carrots, sliced
- ¼ teaspoon marjoram
- 3 cups halved brussels sprouts
- 2 cups cooked dried baby lima beans
- 2 tablespoons minced fresh parsley

Place the onions and oil in a large heavy-bottom saucepan and cook the onions until lightly browned, stirring often. Stir in the flour. Add the stock, carrots, and marjoram. Bring to a boil, then reduce heat and simmer for 10 minutes.

Add the brussels sprouts. Return to a boil, then simmer for another 10 minutes. Add the beans and parsley. Stir and cook until heated through before serving. (Do not overcook; the brussels sprouts should remain crisp-tender.)

★ *VARIATION: For a vegetarian main meal, serve over 3 cups of cooked brown rice.*

64

German Cheese Soup ★ ★ ★

Bread, cheese, and milk—a fondue-like course with no "dipping." Delicious and hearty in cool weather.

Makes 4 servings

- 2¾ cups skim milk
- 1¾ cups fresh whole wheat bread crumbs
- 2 teaspoons Dijon mustard
- 1 cup shredded Muenster cheese
  nutmeg (garnish)
  paprika (garnish)
  minced fresh parsley (garnish)

Place 1½ cups of the milk in a blender with the bread crumbs and mustard and process on low speed until smooth. Place the mixture in a medium-size saucepan with the remaining milk and the cheese. Cook over low heat, stirring constantly, until the cheese melts and the soup is heated through. Do not boil.

Pour the soup into individual bowls. Sprinkle with nutmeg and paprika and place a pinch of parsley in the center of each serving, if desired.

Caspian Sea Split Pea
as a main dish ★ ★ ★
as an appetizer ★ ★

Makes 6 servings

6   cups water
2   large tomatoes
1   cup shredded cabbage
½   cup dried split peas
½   cup barley
2   large carrots, sliced
      diagonally
3   tablespoons minced fresh
      parsley
1   tablespoon tamari or soy
      sauce
2   cloves garlic

Place 2 cups of the water in a blender with the tomatoes. Process on low speed until smooth. Place the tomato mixture, cabbage, split peas, and barley in a large saucepan. Bring to a boil over medium-high heat. While the mixture is heating, add the carrots, parsley, and tamari. Add the garlic by pushing it through a garlic press into the saucepan.

When the soup boils, stir, cover, and reduce heat to simmer. Cook for about 1¼ hours or until the barley is tender.

Harvest Pea Soup
with Fennel ★ ★ ★

Makes 10 servings

8   cups water
1½   cups dried split peas
4   cups chopped fennel bulb
1   cup chopped celery
2   tablespoons minced
       shallots
2   tablespoons *Chicken Stock*
1   tablespoon minced fresh
       basil or ½ teaspoon
       dried basil
4   medium-size potatoes,
       diced
2   cups peas
2   tablespoons minced fresh
       parsley
     fennel sprigs (garnish)

Place the water, split peas, fennel, and celery in a large saucepan. Bring to a boil, reduce heat, cover, and simmer for 45 minutes.

While the soup simmers, sauté the shallots in the stock in a small skillet until they are translucent. If using dried basil, stir into the shallots, then remove from heat. Stir the shallots into the soup as it simmers.

After it has simmered for 1 hour, puree the soup in batches in a blender. Return the blended soup to the pot.

Add the potatoes and simmer for 15 minutes. Then add the peas and basil (if using fresh) and simmer until the peas are tender. Stir in the parsley and remove from the heat. Garnish with fennel sprigs, if desired.

65

Creamy Corn Chowder
as a main dish ★ ★ ★
as an appetizer ★ ★

Served with a three-star green salad, you'll still have a meal well under 300 calories.

Makes 4 servings

2   tablespoons *Chicken Stock*
1   small sweet red pepper, finely diced
3   scallions, minced
1   shallot, minced
1   tablespoon whole wheat flour
2   cups corn
1¾ cups skim milk
     dash of nutmeg
1   teaspoon tamari or soy sauce
     sweet red pepper rings (garnish)
     minced fresh parsley (garnish)

Place the stock in a large saucepan over medium heat. Add the peppers, scallions, and shallots. Cook, stirring frequently, until the peppers are crisp-tender, about 3 minutes. Add a bit of water, if necessary, to prevent scorching. Stir in the flour and cook 1 to 2 minutes more, stirring constantly, then remove from heat.

Place 1 cup of the corn in a blender or food processor with 1 cup of the milk. Process on low speed until smooth, stopping and scraping down the sides if necessary. Add the blended mixture, the remaining corn and milk, the nutmeg, and tamari to the peppers in the large saucepan. Set over medium heat and bring just to the boiling point, stirring frequently.

Reduce heat and simmer for about 5 minutes. Place in a warmed soup tureen or individual bowls. Garnish with red pepper rings and parsley, if desired.

Lentil Stew ★ ★ ★

Makes 6 servings

8   cups *Vegetable Stock*
1   cup dried lentils
1   large sweet red pepper, cut into narrow, 1-inch-long strips
6   scallions, sliced
3   medium-size carrots, sliced
1   small zucchini, sliced
1   tablespoon tamari or soy sauce
¼   teaspoon oregano
¼   teaspoon rosemary

Place the stock and lentils in a stockpot over medium-high heat and bring to a boil.

Add the peppers, scallions, carrots, zucchini, tamari, oregano, and rosemary. Bring to a boil. Cover, reduce heat, and simmer for about 45 minutes. Serve hot.

Lentil and Corn Soup ★ ★ ★

Makes 8 servings

1   medium-size onion,
       chopped
2   medium-size carrots,
       sliced
1½ tablespoons safflower oil
7   cups water
¾   cup dried lentils
2   medium-size tomatoes,
       peeled and chopped
1   cup corn
1   small sweet potato, diced
4   teaspoons tamari or soy
       sauce
1   cup cooked brown rice
2   tablespoons chopped fresh
       parsley

Place the onions and carrots in a large, heavy-bottom saucepan with the oil. Cover and cook over low heat, stirring occasionally, until the onions are translucent.

Add the water, lentils, tomatoes, corn, and sweet potatoes. Bring to a boil, then reduce heat, cover, and simmer for 25 minutes. Add the tamari, rice, and parsley and heat through before serving.

67

Curried Lentil Soup
as a main dish ★ ★ ★
as an appetizer ★

Makes 4 servings

½   cup diced carrots
½   cup diced onions
½   cup chopped celery
1   16-ounce can chopped
       tomatoes with juice
¾   cup dried lentils
4   cups water
2   teaspoons curry powder
       (preferably Madras)
2   tablespoons low-fat yogurt
       (garnish)

Puree the carrots, onions, and celery in a food processor or blender on medium to high speed. Place in a large stockpot with the tomatoes and juice, the lentils, water, and curry. Bring to a boil, then reduce heat and simmer for 3 hours. Serve with yogurt as a garnish, if desired.

Salads

Salads and diets are synonymous. That's because salad fixings are about as low in calories as you can get. Unfortunately, many do-it-yourself salad makers are short on imagination and long on dressing when it comes to doing what's best for the waistline. As a result, it doesn't take too many days before the I-can't-stand-the-thought-of-one-more-salad type of thinking starts intruding on all of your good intentions.

All the rabbit food in the world—no matter how modest the calories—isn't going to do you much good if you heap it with lots of oil-based dressings (which are what you usually find in the bottle or served in restaurants). Every tablespoon of ordinary salad dressing contains anywhere from 75 to 100 calories—mostly fat calories, I might add. Yet, plain ordinary greens, even accompanied by some onions and a radish or two, can be pretty tired-looking and tasteless without it. No wonder salads are the downfall of many diets.

But you'll find none of that in this chapter. There's no reason in the world why a salad has to be boring, for just about *anything* that's good for you can taste great in a salad. To prove it, I'm offering some 50 different salad recipes in this chapter—and not one has a piece of iceberg lettuce in it.

Greens should only be thought of as a *base* on which to hold your salad. Rice, beans, nature's entire array of fresh vegetables, nuts, and the whole gamut of fresh fruit can be turned into an appetizing salad to accompany any meal. And there's an entire section on main dish salads to show you that potatoes, grains, apples, fish, poultry, and even beef can be added to your salad-eating pleasure.

I like the idea of making a meal out of a salad. Since it's the only thing you're going to eat at the meal (except maybe for a light soup), there's little need to worry about the calories. So don't be timid about piling it high with extra vegetables or fruits.

But *do* worry about the calories in the dressing. Use only the dressings suggested in this book. Some of the dressings are directly incorporated into the recipes. Others call for a specific dressing from the "Dressings, Spreads, and Sauces" chapter. *All* the dressings in this book contain only a modest amount of calories—some contain hardly any at all.

Make sure you eat a salad a day—twice a day is even better. Salad greens are important to your health, providing large amounts of vitamin A and other essential nutrients. They take long to eat, making the meal last longer and helping you to fill up easier. Choose the freshest ingredients you can find, both for their crunch and to enjoy them when they're at their nutritional best.

Side Dish Salads

Red Lettuce Bowl ★ ★ ★

Makes 6 servings

2 cups halved green beans
2 cups broccoli florets
½ head red leaf lettuce or 1 head raddiccio lettuce
6 mushrooms, sliced
½ sweet red pepper, diced
2 tablespoons minced fresh parsley
1 slice red onion, separated into rings
½ cup *Russian Dressing*

Place the green beans in a steaming basket over boiling water. Steam for 5 minutes, then add the broccoli and steam an additional 3 to 4 minutes or until the broccoli is crisp-tender. Remove from steamer and rinse under cold water until cool.

While the vegetables steam, tear the lettuce leaves in half crosswise. Arrange the top halves around the outside of a plate or shallow serving bowl. Place the bottom halves in the middle.

Place the mushrooms on the lettuce in the center. Layer the beans and broccoli on top of the mushrooms. Sprinkle the peppers and parsley over the salad and arrange the onion rings on top. Serve the dressing in a small dish on the side.

Garden Salad ★ ★ ★

Here's a basic, but very tasty, fiber-filled salad that you'll want to accompany a main meal. Make the salad and dressing in big batches, so you'll always have it on hand.

Makes 6 servings

½   head Boston lettuce
6   large leaves romaine
      lettuce
½   cup shredded red cabbage
½   sweet red pepper, cut
      lengthwise into thin
      strips
1   small zucchini, sliced
1   small carrot, sliced
2   tablespoons coarsely
      chopped fresh dill
4   tablespoons lemon juice
4   tablespoons rice vinegar
½   teaspoon basil
½   teaspoon thyme
¼   teaspoon dry mustard

Tear the Boston and romaine lettuces into large bite-size pieces. Place in a large salad bowl. Add the cabbage, peppers, zucchini, carrots, and dill.

In a small jar, combine the lemon juice, vinegar, basil, thyme, and mustard. Shake well and pour over vegetables. Toss well.

70

Salade aux Epinards ★ ★ ★

This salad of shredded spinach with sweet peppers and mushrooms is so low in calories you can help yourself to seconds—and even thirds—without a twinge of guilt.

Makes 4 servings

2   cups shredded spinach
1   cup mushroom caps,
      blanched for 30 seconds
1   cup thinly sliced sweet
      red peppers
¼   cup cider vinegar
1   teaspoon Dijon mustard
1   teaspoon tarragon

Toss the spinach, mushroom caps, and peppers in a large salad bowl. In a small jar, combine the vinegar, mustard, and tarragon. Shake well and pour over vegetables. Toss well and chill. Toss again before serving.

Red Spinach Salad ★ ★

Makes 4 servings

4 cups firmly packed spinach
2 medium-size tart red
     apples, chopped
½ small red onion, sliced
2 teaspoons chopped fresh
     tarragon
1 tablespoon chopped
     walnuts
¼ cup *Lemon Yogurt Dressing*

Tear the spinach into bite-size pieces and place in a serving bowl with apples. Toss to combine. Separate the onion slices into rings and arrange on top of the salad. Sprinkle with the tarragon and walnuts. Drizzle the dressing over the salad or serve the dressing separately.

Celebration Salad ★ ★ ★

Company coming? This is a bonanza of a green salad.

Makes 8 servings

2 cups packed spinach leaves
1 bunch watercress
¼ cup chopped scallions
¼ cup minced fresh dill
½ pound mushrooms, sliced
1 hard-cooked egg
½ cup *Green Onion Dressing*

Tear the spinach into large bite-size pieces and place in a large salad bowl. Remove the stems from the watercress. Add the watercress and scallions to the bowl along with the dill and mushrooms and toss.

Press the hard-cooked egg through a sieve into the center of the salad or mince the egg and place it in the center.

At the table, pour some of the dressing over the salad and toss. Pass the remaining dressing, if desired.

71

Escarole, Apple, and Mushroom Salad ★

Makes 4 servings

2 cups packed escarole
1 large tart apple, sliced
1 cup sliced mushrooms
¼ cup sunflower oil
1 tablespoon lemon juice
1 tablespoon low-fat yogurt
1½ teaspoons Dijon mustard
     dash of marjoram

Tear the escarole into bite-size pieces. Place in a salad bowl with the apples and mushrooms.

In a small bowl, combine the oil, lemon juice, yogurt, mustard, and marjoram. Beat together well. Pour the dressing over the salad, toss, and serve.

Green Bean Salad with Sunflower Seeds ★ ★ ★

Makes 6 servings

1   pound green beans
1   tablespoon olive oil
2   tablespoons sunflower seeds
1   large clove garlic
4   teaspoons tarragon vinegar
    spinach leaves, shredded
       (optional)
    chopped scallions (garnish)

Steam the beans until just crisp-tender, about 3 or 4 minutes.

While the beans steam, place the oil in a small skillet with the sunflower seeds and cook, stirring, over medium heat until the sunflower seeds are golden brown. Do not overcook. Remove from heat.

Push the garlic through a garlic press into the skillet. Stir well. When the sunflower seeds have cooled slightly, stir in the vinegar.

In a large bowl, toss the beans with the sunflower seed mixture. Cool, then chill. To serve, arrange the beans over spinach and garnish with scallions, if desired.

72

Fuji Salad ★ ★ ★

Named for the sacred Japanese mountain on which a fountain of youth is said to be hidden.

Makes 4 servings

2   cups sliced (2 × ½-inch)
       daikon radishes
1   cup sliced carrots
½   cup diced sweet red
       peppers
1   cup sugar snap peas, ends
       and strings removed
¼   cup rice vinegar
1   tablespoon tamari or soy
       sauce
½   teaspoon crushed ginger
1   clove garlic

Steam the radishes and carrots for 5 minutes, then cool. In a large bowl, toss them with the peppers and peas.

In a small jar, combine the vinegar, tamari, and ginger. Add garlic by pushing it through a garlic press into the jar. Shake well and pour over vegetables. Toss and serve.

Sesame Asparagus ★ ★

A wonderful way to savor this special spring vegetable. Use only rice vinegar, which is milder in flavor than most vinegars.

Makes 4 servings

1   pound asparagus
¼   cup rice vinegar
1   tablespoon oriental sesame oil
2   teaspoons honey
1   teaspoon tamari or soy sauce
1   tablespoon sesame seeds
    lemon slices (garnish)

Use a vegetable peeler to remove the thin layer of skin from the bottom of the asparagus spears nearly to the green tips. Steam the asparagus just until crisp-tender, 2 to 3 minutes. Rinse under cold water to stop the cooking.

Combine the vinegar, oil, honey, and tamari. Arrange the asparagus in one layer in a shallow dish. Pour the marinade over the asparagus. Chill, covered, for 3 to 5 hours or overnight.

Before serving, place the sesame seeds in a small, dry, iron skillet and toast them lightly over medium heat until light golden brown. Sprinkle over the asparagus and garnish with lemon slices, if desired.

73

Bermuda Beet Salad ★ ★ ★

Apples and onions give crunch and flavor to this beet salad.

Makes 6 servings

1   medium-size Bermuda onion, sliced
2   medium-size tart red apples, thinly sliced
¼   cup lemon juice
¼   cup cider vinegar
½   teaspoon caraway seeds
1   teaspoon tamari or soy sauce
5   beets, cooked, peeled, and thinly sliced

Separate the onion slices into rings and place in a 1- to 1½-quart glass or enamel serving dish. Arrange the apple slices over the onion rings. Mix together the lemon juice, vinegar, caraway seeds, and tamari in a small bowl or jar. Pour over the apples and onions.

Toss the beets with the apple and onion mixture. Marinate in the refrigerator for about 4 hours and toss before serving.

Jack Sprat's Beets with Watercress ★ ★ ★

A typically English salad, this is another low-calorie dish you can keep on eating.

Makes 4 servings

½	pound young beets
2	cups trimmed watercress
⅓	cup white wine vinegar
1	teaspoon prepared horseradish
1	teaspoon Dijon mustard
4	leaves romaine lettuce

In a medium-size saucepan, boil the beets for 20 to 30 minutes until tender. Peel and slice into matchstick-size pieces. Let cool, then toss with watercress.

In a small bowl, combine vinegar, horseradish, and mustard and toss with beets and watercress. Chill at least 1 hour. Toss briefly, divide in fourths, and serve on romaine lettuce.

Greek Green Beans ★ ★ ★

74

Makes 4 servings

¾	pound green beans
1	tablespoon Greek oregano
⅓	cup red wine vinegar
1	teaspoon Dijon mustard
1	clove garlic

Steam the beans until just crisp-tender, about 3 or 4 minutes. In a small bowl or jar, combine oregano, vinegar, and mustard. Add garlic by pushing it through a garlic press into the bowl. Toss dressing with beans. Chill. Toss again and serve.

Green Bean Salad with Walnut Dressing ★ ★

Elegant picnic fare.

Makes 4 servings

¾	pound green beans
½	cup walnuts
3	tablespoons rice vinegar
1	tablespoon packed fresh dill
¼	teaspoon Dijon mustard
1	tablespoon minced sweet red peppers

Steam the beans until just crisp-tender, about 3 to 4 minutes. Cool.

Place the walnuts, vinegar, dill, and mustard in a blender. Process on low to medium speed until smooth, stopping frequently to scrape down the sides of the blender.

Toss the beans with the walnut mixture and the minced peppers.

Saratoga Salad ★ ★ ★
Beautiful and delicious.

Makes 4 servings

¾ pound green beans
¼ cup *Tomato Vinaigrette*
1 sweet red pepper, cut into
      8 rings
4 dill sprigs (garnish)

Steam the beans until crisp-tender, about 3 to 4 minutes. Rinse under cold water until cool.

Divide the beans among four serving plates and arrange them together in bunches. Spoon a band of dressing across the middle of the beans. Arrange 2 pepper rings on each serving and top each with a dill sprig. Chill before serving, if desired.

Summer Tomato Salad ★ ★

Makes 4 servings

4 large tomatoes
2 ounces part-skim mozzarella
      cheese, cut into 4 slices
4 sprigs marjoram, dill, or
      basil
2 cups shredded spinach
1 tablespoon olive oil

Cut a thick slice from the center of each tomato. Reserve the remaining tomato for another use. Use a cookie cutter or a knife to cut a design in the cheese slices, making them smaller than the circumference of the tomato slices.

Place a piece of cheese on each of the tomato slices. Top each with a sprig of marjoram.

Arrange the tomato slices on a bed of spinach on a serving dish or four individual salad plates. Spoon a little of the olive oil over each serving.

★ ★ ★ *VARIATION: When tomatoes are deep red and lusciously fresh, omit the oil. It's only a waste of calories.*

75

Harvest Moon Salad ★ ★ ★

Makes 4 servings

4 large tomatoes, thinly
      sliced
1 medium-size red onion,
      thinly sliced
¼ cup minced watercress
1 clove garlic, minced
¼ cup *Tomato Vinaigrette*

Place the tomato slices in a serving dish. Layer the onion slices over the tomato slices and sprinkle with the watercress.

Mix the garlic with the dressing. Pour over the salad. Refrigerate, covered, for about 2 to 4 hours or overnight. Toss before serving.

Herbed Tomato Fontina ★ ★ ★

Makes 6 servings

4   scallions, cut into thin, 2-inch-long strips
1½ ounces fontina cheese, cut into thin, 2-inch-long strips
5   tomatoes, cut into wedges
¼   cup red wine vinegar
½   teaspoon Dijon mustard
1   teaspoon basil
½   teaspoon parsley

In a serving bowl, gently combine scallions, cheese, and tomatoes. Place vinegar, mustard, basil, and parsley in a small jar and shake well. Pour over the salad and toss. Chill and toss again before serving.

76

Celeriac Remoulade ★

This Bavarian dish is usually made with a large quantity of oil. By decreasing the amount of oil and replacing it with yogurt, calories are reduced.

Makes 8 servings

2   pounds celeriac, shredded or julienned
1   egg
1   tablespoon lemon juice
1   tablespoon Dijon mustard
⅓   cup corn oil
½   cup low-fat yogurt
1   tablespoon chopped scallions
    dash of white pepper

Place the celeriac in a large mixing bowl. Place the egg, lemon juice, and mustard in a food processor or blender. Process briefly. Slowly add the oil, beginning with a few drops and increasing the flow as the mixture thickens.

Transfer the thickened dressing to a bowl and fold in the yogurt, scallions, and pepper.

Pour the dressing over the celeriac and mix. Refrigerate for at least 2 hours before serving to allow the flavors to blend.

Greek Cabbage Salad ★ ★

One of my favorites!

Makes 4 servings

4 cups chopped cabbage
½ cup crumbled feta cheese
1 tablespoon minced fresh dill
2 tablespoons olive oil
3 tablespoons lemon juice
1 tablespoon grated
      Parmesan cheese
¼ teaspoon dry mustard
¼ teaspoon oregano

Place the cabbage, feta, and dill in a large bowl.

Put the oil, lemon juice, Parmesan, mustard, and oregano in a small bowl or jar and stir or shake until combined. Pour the dressing over the salad and toss until well mixed.

Minted New Potato Salad ★ ★

Makes 8 servings

5 cups quartered new
      potatoes
¼ cup minced fresh mint
2 tablespoons minced red
      onions
2 tablespoons minced sweet
      red peppers
2 tablespoons low-fat yogurt
2 tablespoons lemon juice
½ tablespoon minced fresh
      basil or ¼ teaspoon dried
      basil
½ teaspoon honey
¼ teaspoon dry mustard
      mint sprigs (garnish)
      sweet red pepper or red
      onion rings (garnish)

Place the potatoes in a large pot of water and bring to a boil. Reduce heat and cook until tender, about 10 minutes.

While the potatoes cook, combine the mint, onions, and peppers in a large serving bowl. Place the yogurt, lemon juice, basil, honey, and mustard in a small jar or bowl and shake or stir until blended.

When the potatoes are tender, drain and place in the serving bowl with the mint mixture. Pour on the dressing and toss lightly until combined. Serve hot or cool slightly and chill. Garnish with mint and pepper or onion rings, if desired.

NOTE: You can substitute ½ teaspoon dried spearmint and 2 tablespoons of minced fresh parsley for the fresh mint.

Old Mill Corn Salad ★

This easy-to-assemble salad keeps well.

Makes 4 servings

2	cups cooked brown rice
1	cup cooked corn
⅓	cup minced celery
1	shallot, minced
¼	cup *Tomato Vinaigrette*
	romaine lettuce leaves
	sweet red pepper rings
	(garnish)

Combine the rice, corn, celery, and shallots in a medium-size mixing bowl. Drizzle with the dressing and toss. Serve on lettuce and garnish with red pepper rings, if desired.

North Indian Coleslaw ★ ★ ★

Makes 8 servings

4	cups shredded cabbage
1	sweet red pepper, chopped
1	stalk celery, thinly sliced
1	tablespoon minced fresh parsley
¾	cup *North Indian Dressing*

Combine the cabbage, peppers, celery, and parsley in a large bowl. Pour the dressing over the salad and toss well. Cover tightly and chill, if desired.

NOTE: This will keep nicely for a day or two in the refrigerator.

Pear Salad Noel ★ ★ ★

The combination of red and green vegetables makes this a holiday-perfect salad selection.

Makes 4 servings

12	large leaves spinach
2	pears, thinly sliced
2	scallions, cut into thin, 2-inch strips
1	radish, minced
¼	cup *Ginger Lime Dressing*

Arrange the spinach on four salad plates. Arrange the pear slices in a circle over the spinach. Place the scallions in the middle of the pears. Sprinkle with the radishes. Drizzle the dressing over the salads and serve at once.

NOTE: If you do not intend to serve the salad immediately, sprinkle the pear slices with lemon juice to prevent darkening, then make the salads, cover, and chill.

Fantasy Fruit Salad ★ ★ ★

Layer this fruit salad in a straight-sided glass bowl so the full effect of color and shape can be appreciated by your guests.

Makes 6 servings

2 large peaches, sliced
1 small banana, sliced diagonally
1 cup watermelon balls
¾ cup seedless green grapes
1 cup blueberries
½ cup cantaloupe or honeydew balls
1 kiwi fruit, peeled and sliced

Layer the peaches in the bottom of a glass serving bowl. Add the bananas to the bowl along with the watermelon balls and grapes. Then layer the blueberries and cantaloupe balls in the bowl. Arrange the kiwi fruit on top. Chill, tightly covered, for 2 hours before serving.

NOTE: Because peaches and bananas tend to darken when standing, add a few drops of lemon juice to these before adding to the bowl if the fruit salad is being prepared well in advance of serving.

Avocado with Orange ★ ★

Pretty—and perfect for entertaining.

Makes 6 servings

2 tablespoons olive oil
1 tablespoon lemon juice
1 tablespoon orange juice
1 teaspoon minced fresh parsley
¼ teaspoon grated orange rind
dash of dry mustard
1 large avocado, peeled
2 navel oranges, sectioned
parsley sprigs (garnish)

Combine the oil, lemon juice, orange juice, parsley, orange rind, and mustard in a small bowl.

Cut the avocado in half lengthwise, then into thin, lengthwise slices. Peel the membranes off the orange sections, if desired.

Arrange the avocado slices and orange sections in a wheel shape on a round serving dish. This can be done by alternating orange sections with avocado slices or by making an inner wheel of orange sections and placing the avocado slices around the outside.

Pour the dressing over the orange and avocado arrangement. Garnish with the parsley sprigs and chill briefly before serving, if desired.

NOTE: This salad must be served promptly, before the avocado slices turn brown.

Swedish Cabbage ★ ★ ★

A fresh perspective on coleslaw.

Makes 4 servings

1 cup low-fat yogurt
2½ cups shredded cabbage
½ cup shredded carrots
½ cup halved seedless red
    grapes
½ cup sliced celery
¼ cup orange juice
1 tablespoon lemon juice
½ teaspoon celery seeds
1 teaspoon parsley

Place the yogurt in a strainer lined with cheese-cloth and allow to drain for 2 hours. In a large bowl, toss together the cabbage, carrots, grapes, and celery.

In a small bowl, mix the yogurt (the amount should be reduced by half), orange juice, lemon juice, celery seeds, and parsley. Toss with cabbage mixture 30 times. Chill for at least one hour. Toss again and serve.

80 Louisiana Lentil Salad ★ ★

Makes 6 servings

2 cups cooked lentils
1 cup cooked corn
2 tablespoons sunflower oil
1 tablespoon tarragon vinegar
1 teaspoon water
1 tablespoon minced
    watercress
1 tablespoon minced fresh
    parsley
½ teaspoon thyme
3 slices red onion, separated
    into rings (garnish)
1 hard-cooked egg, sliced
    (garnish)

Combine the lentils and corn in a serving bowl.

In a small bowl, mix together the oil, vinegar, water, watercress, parsley, and thyme. Pour over the lentils and corn and toss lightly until combined. Top the salad with the onion rings and egg slices, if desired.

Summer Melon Salad with Red Onions ★ ★ ★

Makes 4 servings

½ small cantaloupe or ⅓ honeydew melon
½ cup blueberries
2 tablespoons chopped red onions
8 large leaves spinach
½ cup *Ginger Lime Dressing*
2 scallions, chopped (garnish)

Carve out the melon using a small melon baller. Place in a medium-size bowl and toss with the blueberries and onions.

Arrange the spinach on a serving plate or individual salad plates or bowls. Top with the melon ball mixture. Drizzle with the dressing, then sprinkle with chopped scallions, if desired.

Main Dish Salads

Yamamoto Beef ★ ★
A nice way to use leftover *Buckingham London Broil.*

Makes 4 servings

1 pound cooked lean beef, diagonally cut into ¼-inch-thick slices
1 green pepper, cut into thin strips
½ cup sliced radishes
¼ cup thinly sliced bamboo shoots
3 tablespoons lime juice
1 teaspoon tamari or soy sauce
1 teaspoon honey
2 cloves garlic, minced
4 leaves lettuce

In a large bowl, combine the beef, peppers, radishes, and bamboo shoots.

In a small bowl, whisk together the lime juice, tamari, honey, and garlic. Pour over the meat mixture and toss until all pieces are coated.

Arrange lettuce on a platter and mound meat mixture over it. Chill and serve.

Breast of Duck with Raspberry Mayonnaise ★ ★ ★

Makes 4 servings

1   pound lean duck breast meat, skinned and cut into 2 × ½-inch pieces
¾   cup chopped watercress
½   cup quartered water chestnuts
¼   cup *Lighten-Up Mayonnaise*
1   tablespoon raspberry vinegar or ½ teaspoon raspberry jelly combined with 1 tablespoon rice vinegar
4   leaves curly red leaf lettuce
1   tablespoon chopped fresh parsley (garnish)

In a large bowl, gently combine the duck, watercress, and water chestnuts.

In a small bowl, combine the mayonnaise and vinegar. Pour over the duck mixture and toss until all pieces are coated.

Arrange lettuce on a serving dish, curly side towards the edge, and gently mound duck mixture in the middle. Garnish with parsley, if desired, chill, and serve.

82

Mariner's Salad ★ ★ ★

Makes 4 servings

1   pound cooked white fish (such as cod or haddock), cut into 1½-inch chunks
¾   cup shredded spinach
¼   cup julienned carrots
¼   cup minced scallions
⅓   cup low-fat yogurt
1   tablespoon lemon juice
1   tablespoon chopped fresh parsley
1   clove garlic
1   lemon, sliced (garnish)

In a large bowl, gently combine the fish, spinach, carrots, and scallions.

In a small bowl, combine the yogurt, lemon juice, and parsley, and add the garlic by pushing it through a garlic press into the bowl. Pour the dressing over the salad and toss gently until all the pieces are covered. Mound on a serving dish and arrange lemon slices around the edges, if desired. Chill and serve.

Scallop and
New Potato Salad ★ ★ ★

A wonderful main dish salad that's packable for picnics.

Makes 4 servings

1	lemon slice
1	whole clove
1	bay leaf
1	cup water
½	pound sea scallops
3	cups halved new potatoes
¾	cup coarsely chopped broccoli florets
¼	cup minced sweet red peppers
¼	cup minced red onions
1½	tablespoons sunflower oil
1½	tablespoons lemon juice
1	tablespoon minced fresh mint or 1½ teaspoons dried mint
1	tablespoon minced fresh dill or 1½ teaspoons dried dill
½	tablespoon minced fresh parsley
½	teaspoon honey
¼	teaspoon dry mustard
	thinly sliced radishes (garnish)
	mint, watercress, or parsley sprigs (garnish)

Place the lemon slice, clove, bay leaf, and water in a medium-size skillet. Bring to a boil, add the scallops, and poach just until the scallops are cooked through, about 4 to 5 minutes. Drain the cooked scallops, let cool, and cut into ¼-inch slices.

Place the potatoes in a large saucepan with enough water to cover. Bring to a boil, reduce heat, cover, and cook just until the potatoes are tender, about 10 to 15 minutes.

While the potatoes cook, steam the broccoli just until crisp-tender, about 3 to 4 minutes. Rinse under cold water to stop the cooking.

To make the dressing, combine the peppers, onions, oil, lemon juice, mint, dill, parsley, honey, and mustard in a small bowl. Stir until well combined.

To assemble the salad, place the hot potatoes and broccoli in a large mixing bowl and toss with the dressing. When the mixture has cooled slightly, toss with the cooked scallops and chill immediately.

To serve, toss again and place the salad on a flat serving plate. Garnish with radishes and arrange a generous amount of mint around the perimeter of the serving plate, if desired.

83

Dilled Salmon and Spiral Salad ★ ★

Makes 6 servings

3 cups whole wheat sesame
    pasta spirals
1 pound asparagus
¾ pound salmon fillets
2 cups cherry tomatoes
1 tablespoon minced fresh dill
¼ cup *Dilled Cucumber Sauce*
    dill sprigs (garnish)

Place a large pot of water over high heat and bring to a boil. Add the pasta and cook until al dente, about 8 to 10 minutes. Drain and rinse under cold water until cool.

While the pasta cooks, trim the tough ends from the asparagus and peel the stems halfway up the stalk. Cut diagonally into 2-inch pieces. Steam the asparagus until crisp-tender, 3 to 4 minutes. Rinse under cold water until cool.

In a medium-size saucepan with about ½ inch of simmering water, poach the salmon fillets until firm throughout, about 8 minutes. Flake or cut into bite-size pieces.

Place the pasta, asparagus, salmon, tomatoes, dill, and sauce in a medium-size serving bowl. Toss and garnish with dill, if desired.

84

Neptune Salad Primavera ★

Makes 4 servings

2 cups whole wheat sesame
    pasta spirals
¾ pound white fish fillets
    (such as haddock, cod,
    flounder)
2 cups broccoli florets
1 sweet red pepper, cut into
    strips
4 scallions, cut into 2-inch
    strips

Bring a large saucepan of water to a boil, add the pasta, and cook until al dente, about 8 to 10 minutes. Rinse under cold water until cool. Set aside.

In a large skillet, bring about ½ inch of water to a boil, reduce heat, add the fish fillets, cover, and poach just until opaque, about 8 to 10 minutes. Remove the fish carefully and set aside to cool.

Steam the broccoli just until slightly tender, about 3 minutes. Rinse under cold water until cool.

Place the pasta, broccoli, red peppers, scallions, and cherry tomatoes in a medium-size serving bowl.

2 cups cherry tomatoes
2 tablespoons olive oil
1 tablespoon Dijon mustard
2 tablespoons tarragon
   vinegar
2 teaspoons minced fresh
   parsley
1 teaspoon lemon juice
½ teaspoon marjoram
¼ teaspoon dry mustard
   dash of thyme

In a small bowl, combine the oil, Dijon mustard, vinegar, parsley, lemon juice, marjoram, mustard, and thyme. Pour over the salad and toss well.

Cut the fish into bite-size pieces, add to the salad, and toss gently until combined. Serve at once or chill, tightly covered.

Minnesota Chicken Salad ★ ★ ★

Makes 6 servings

1 whole chicken breast,
   boned and skinned
1 egg white
1 tablespoon cornstarch
1 tablespoon *Chicken Stock*
2 cups cooked brown rice
¾ cup cooked wild rice
3 tablespoons chopped
   walnuts
1 cup chopped celery
1 cup halved green grapes
2 tablespoons minced fresh
   parsley
¼ cup *Lemon Yogurt Dressing*
   butterhead lettuce leaves
   grated lemon rind (garnish)

Cut the chicken into bite-size pieces. Place in a small mixing bowl with the egg white and stir to coat. Stir in the cornstarch. Allow to sit 5 to 10 minutes.

Heat the stock in a medium-size skillet over medium heat, then add the chicken and cook, stirring occasionally, until the chicken is opaque throughout and lightly browned. Arrange the chicken in a single layer on a plate. Let cool for 5 minutes, then cover and refrigerate. Chill for at least ½ hour.

In a serving bowl, combine the brown rice, wild rice, walnuts, celery, grapes, and parsley. Add the chicken and the dressing. Serve on a bed of lettuce and garnish with lemon rind, if desired.

Dilled Chicken Salad ★ ★

Leftover chicken goes a long way in this dish.

Makes 3 servings

1   cup whole wheat elbow
     macaroni
1   cup shredded spinach
1   cup diced, cooked chicken
2   tablespoons minced sweet
     red peppers
¼   cup *Spring Garden Dill
     Dressing*
     orange slices (garnish)
     dill sprigs (garnish)

Cook the macaroni in boiling water until al dente, about 7 to 8 minutes. Drain immediately and rinse under cold water until cool.

In a medium-size mixing bowl, toss the macaroni, spinach, chicken, and peppers together.

Pour the dressing over the salad and toss. Garnish with orange slices and dill, and chill before serving, if desired.

86

Kiwi-Lime Chicken Salad ★

Makes 4 servings

1½   cups diced, cooked
      chicken
2   cups cooked brown rice
2   tablespoons sunflower oil
1½   tablespoons lime juice
1   teaspoon lemon juice
½   teaspoon honey
¼   teaspoon dry mustard
      dash of turmeric
1   kiwi fruit, peeled and
      sliced
      spinach leaves
      mint sprigs (garnish)

Place the chicken and rice in a large bowl.

Combine the oil, lime and lemon juices, honey, mustard, and turmeric in a small bowl or jar with lid. Stir or shake until well combined.

Pour the dressing over the chicken and rice and toss to combine. Add the sliced kiwi fruit and toss again, gently. Chill, if desired, before serving.

To serve, place on top of spinach in a serving bowl or on individual plates. Garnish with mint, if desired.

Red Potato and Broccoli Salad ★ ★ ★

Makes 4 servings

4 small new potatoes, quartered
2 cups broccoli florets
3 radishes, thinly sliced
¼ cup *Tomato Vinaigrette*
    minced fresh parsley (garnish)

Place the potatoes in a large saucepan. Add enough water to cover. Bring to a boil, then reduce heat, cover, and simmer until the potatoes are tender, about 10 to 15 minutes. Drain and let cool slightly.

Steam the broccoli until crisp-tender, about 3 to 4 minutes. Rinse under cold water until cool. Place in a large serving bowl with the potatoes.

To serve at room temperature, add the radishes and just enough dressing to moisten the salad. Toss and garnish with the minced parsley, if desired.

To serve chilled, add enough of the dressing to moisten the potatoes and broccoli and toss. Chill. Add the radishes just before serving, toss, and garnish with parsley, if desired.

87

Wenatchee Rice Salad ★ ★ ★

Wenatchee, Washington, is the apple capital of the world, but use tart apples from anywhere in this zesty apple and rice salad.

Makes 4 servings

2 cups cooked brown rice
1½ cups thinly sliced tart apples
½ cup chopped celery
¼ cup sunflower seeds
½ cup shredded spinach
2 tablespoons apple juice
2 tablespoons lemon juice
½ teaspoon grated fresh ginger
½ teaspoon parsley
4 leaves romaine lettuce

Place rice, apples, celery, sunflower seeds, and spinach in a large bowl and toss.

In a small jar, combine apple juice, lemon juice, ginger, and parsley and shake. Pour over rice mixture and toss. Arrange lettuce on a platter and scoop one-fourth of the salad on each leaf.

Rice and Chick-Pea Salad ★ ★

Makes 6 servings

1   cup brown rice
1   small red onion, chopped
1   tablespoon tamari or soy
      sauce
1   tablespoon paprika
2   cups water
6   medium-size carrots, sliced
      diagonally
1   clove garlic
1   cup broccoli florets
1   medium-size sweet red
      pepper, diced
2   cups cooked chick-peas
¼   cup sunflower oil
2   tablespoons tarragon
      vinegar
½   teaspoon Dijon mustard
¼   teaspoon dry mustard
      dash of turmeric
½   teaspoon tarragon
      sweet red pepper rings
      (garnish)

Place the rice, onions, tamari, paprika, and water in a medium-size saucepan and bring to a boil over medium heat. Boil for 1 to 2 minutes, then cover and reduce heat to as low as possible. Cook for 45 minutes, without lifting the lid or stirring.

When the rice has cooked about 20 minutes, place the carrots and the garlic in another medium-size saucepan with a small amount of water. Cook over low to medium heat until the carrots are crisp-tender, about 10 minutes. Remove from heat, drain off the liquid, and remove the garlic.

Steam the broccoli and red pepper just until crisp-tender, about 3 to 4 minutes. Place in the saucepan with the carrots, cover, and keep warm.

Steam the chick-peas for about 1 minute, then cover and turn off the heat. Keep covered so the chick-peas are heated through.

In a small bowl, stir together the oil, vinegar, Dijon mustard, dry mustard, turmeric, and tarragon.

In a large mixing bowl, combine the rice, carrots, broccoli, red peppers, chick-peas, and dressing. Toss until mixed.

Serve the salad on a large, warmed platter and garnish with red pepper rings, if desired.

Tasty nibbles need not be off the diet when the buffet contains such appetizing hors d'oeuvres as *Dilled Shrimp*, *Baliñas*, and *Cilantro Tomatoes*.

Egg Drop and Sprout Soup and *Yamamoto Beef* are a nice change of taste for a soup and salad meal.

Londonderry Vegetable Salad ★ ★ ★

Makes 4 servings

3 cups halved green beans
3 cups cauliflower florets
3 cups broccoli florets
2 tablespoons sesame seeds
1 tablespoon minced garlic
3 tablespoons sunflower oil
2 tablespoons vinegar
1 tablespoon honey
1 tablespoon tamari or soy sauce

Steam the green beans for 2 minutes, then add the cauliflower and broccoli. Steam for another 4 to 6 minutes or just until the vegetables are crisp-tender. Do not overcook. Rinse the vegetables under cold water until they are cool.

While the vegetables cook, begin making the marinade. Place the sesame seeds in a small skillet over low heat and toast lightly. Add the garlic and oil and cook, stirring, over very low heat for about 2 minutes. Do not allow the garlic to brown at all or the taste will be bitter. Remove from the heat and stir in the vinegar, honey, and tamari.

Place the cooked vegetables in a shallow serving dish. Spoon the marinade over the vegetables. Cover tightly and refrigerate for 4 to 6 hours or overnight.

91

Bulgur with Fennel and Peas ★ ★ ★

Makes 6 servings

½ cup bulgur
½ cup hot water
¼ cup lemon juice
1 cup peas
1 medium-size carrot, shredded
½ medium-size fennel bulb, julienned
¼ cup sunflower seeds
3 tablespoons olive oil
lettuce leaves
parsley sprigs (garnish)

Place the bulgur, water, and lemon juice in a medium-size bowl and let the bulgur soak for about 20 minutes.

While the bulgur soaks, cook the peas in a small amount of water just until crisp-tender, about 3 minutes. Toss the bulgur with the peas, carrots, fennel, sunflower seeds, and oil. Serve on a bed of lettuce and garnish with parsley sprigs, if desired.

Kidney Bean and Apple Salad ★ ★ ★

Makes 8 servings

2   cups cooked kidney beans
1½   cups cooked wheat kernels
½   cup chopped red onions
6   radishes, thinly sliced
⅓   cup chopped walnuts
2   tablespoons minced fresh parsley
1   teaspoon minced fresh dill or tarragon or ½ teaspoon dried dill or tarragon
2   small, tart apples, thinly sliced
½   cup *Ginger Lime Dressing*
     spinach leaves
     red onion rings (garnish)
     dill or tarragon sprigs (garnish)

Place the beans, wheat kernels, onions, radishes, walnuts, parsley, and dill in a large bowl. Toss until combined.

Add the apples and enough dressing to moisten the salad. Toss gently.

To serve, cover a large serving plate or individual plates with spinach leaves. Place the salad on top of the spinach. Garnish with onion rings and dill and chill before serving, if desired.

Tabbouleh Maghreb ★

A refreshing summer salad from Morocco.

Makes 4 servings

1   cup bulgur
1   cup hot water
½   cup lemon juice
½   teaspoon grated lemon rind
3   tablespoons olive oil
1½   cups minced fresh parsley
¾   cup minced scallions
2   cups cherry tomatoes
     lettuce leaves
     parsley sprigs (garnish)

Place the bulgur, water, lemon juice, lemon rind, and oil in a large bowl. Set aside to soak for about 30 minutes or until the liquid is absorbed.

Toss the soaked bulgur with the parsley, scallions, and cherry tomatoes until well mixed. Serve on a bed of lettuce and garnish with parsley sprigs, if desired.

White Bean Tabbouleh ★ ★ ★

Makes 4 servings

½ cup bulgur
½ cup hot water
¼ cup lemon juice
5 scallions, chopped
1½ cups minced fresh parsley
2 tablespoons olive oil
1 cup cooked white beans
1 cup cherry tomatoes (garnish)
  spinach leaves (garnish)

Place the bulgur, water, and lemon juice in a small bowl and set aside for 20 minutes.

Place the soaked bulgur in a medium-size serving bowl. Add the scallions, parsley, and oil and toss together well. Add the beans and gently toss again.

Place the cherry tomatoes on top of the tabbouleh and arrange the spinach around the outside of the bowl. Cover and chill if desired.

NOTE: Tabbouleh will keep for about 1 week in the refrigerator, so you may want to double the recipe and keep some on hand. Stir well before serving.

Treasure Island Salad ★ ★ ★

Pineapple adds a tropical highlight to this traditional salad, which makes a wonderful main-dish lunch.

Makes 4 servings

¼ pineapple, chopped
3 medium-size carrots, shredded
¼ cup raisins
¼ cup sunflower seeds
¼ cup low-fat yogurt
1½ tablespoons lemon juice
½ teaspoon grated orange rind
  orange slices (garnish)
  watercress sprigs (garnish)

Combine the pineapple, carrots, raisins, and sunflower seeds in a large bowl.

Combine the yogurt, lemon juice, and orange rind in a small bowl or jar. Mix or shake until well blended. Pour over the salad. Serve in individual bowls, garnished with orange slices and watercress, if desired.

Bali Fruit Salad ★ ★ ★

Just a hint of the exotic. Serve for breakfast or a luncheon main meal.

Makes 4 servings

1   grapefruit, sectioned
2   bananas, sliced diagonally
1   papaya, cubed
¼   pineapple, cubed
     lime wedges (garnish)

Peel the membrane off the grapefruit sections and remove the seeds. Toss the grapefruit, bananas, papaya, and pineapple together. Garnish with lime wedges and chill before serving, if desired.

Winter Fruit Salad
as a main dish salad ★ ★ ★
as a dessert ★

Look no further for a holiday salad or a dessert for company.

Makes 6 servings

¼   cup chopped dried apricots
¾   cup water
     orange juice
¼   cup raisins
2   medium-size tart red
       apples, sliced
1   pear, sliced
2   oranges, sectioned
½   grapefruit, sectioned
2   kiwi fruits, peeled and
       sliced
2   tablespoons sesame seeds
     dash of cinnamon
     dash of nutmeg
1   cup low-fat yogurt
2   drops vanilla extract

Place the apricots and water in a small bowl and soak overnight. Drain the water into a measuring cup and add enough orange juice to make ¾ cup of liquid.

Place the apricots, juice, and raisins in a small saucepan and bring to a boil. Reduce heat and simmer for 5 minutes. Turn off heat.

Combine the cooked fruit with the apples, pears, oranges, grapefruit, and kiwi fruits in a medium-size serving bowl. Add the sesame seeds, cinnamon, and nutmeg. Toss together gently with the cooking liquid from the apricots. Chill before serving, if desired.

Combine the yogurt with the vanilla extract and serve on the side.

94

Dressings, Spreads, and Sauces

It takes experiencing just one diet to know that little things can mean a lot when it comes to calories. Little things like jam on your breakfast bread, mayonnaise on your sandwich, dressing on your salad, icing on your cake, or butter melted over your baked potato. Just *one* tablespoon of jam is 50 calories—more than half the calories in the bread itself. Mayonnaise and salad dressing can each add as much as an extra 100 calories a tablespoon to an otherwise innocent dish. Icing adds nearly 100 extra calories to a small sliver of white cake—half the calories of the cake itself. And for every tablespoon of butter you eat, you could almost be eating an entire baked potato. No wonder people hate to diet.

Yet eating without such things can make for some pretty dull meals. Imagine eating your morning toast dry, your salad plain with just lemon (that's the way many *other* diet books say you should eat it), or your spaghetti with nothing but parsley on top. I'm sure it doesn't appeal to you any more than it does to me. That's why we decided to take the calories *out* of some of your favorite condiments, so you can keep on eating them—without the guilt.

We experimented and came up with a whole array of dressings, spreads, and sauces that prove it doesn't take a lot of calories to get great flavor. These recipes are so low in calories, you needn't worry about limiting yourself to a smidgen of sauce or a drizzle of dressing. After all, we know how defeating it is to try to stretch one tablespoon of dressing over a gigantic health salad.

All we ask is that you use common sense in dishing out these recipes. The three-star recipes are pretty conservative as far as calories go.

But remember, they're for a tablespoon—not a cup. This is important to keep in mind when you are serving heavier sauces, such as tomato, spaghetti, or marinara. Also, you'll want to use the same judgment when serving the dessert toppings. A low-calorie topping over a low-calorie dessert sounds like heaven. And it can be—as long as you keep to one serving.

One thing you might want to take advantage of are our savory sauces for fish and poultry. Fish or chicken breast simply poached and topped with *Mustard Sauce, Lemon-Thyme Sauce,* or *Sauce Corsica* make elegant low-calories meals.

And forget about butter (it's mostly fat anyway) over your baked potato. At less than 15 calories a tablespoon, *Baked Potato Topping* just can't be matched. As for mayonnaise, make a big batch of *Lighten-Up Mayonnaise* and keep it on hand. You'll never have to eat your sandwiches dry again.

This is the chapter you'll want to turn to every time you make a salad or are looking for a sauce or dessert topping to cap an elegant dinner. I found my favorites, and I know you will too.

96

Dressings

Tomato Vinaigrette ★ ★ ★
Use this no-oil version on greens, cold meats, or fish.

Makes ⅓ cup

½ cup chopped, peeled
     tomatoes
2   tablespoons white wine
     vinegar
½ teaspoon basil
½ teaspoon thyme
½ teaspoon Dijon mustard

Combine all of the ingredients in a blender or food processor. Blend on medium to high speed for about 25 seconds or until combined. Will keep refrigerated, for 2 days. Shake well before using.

Ginger Lime Dressing ★ ★ ★

Makes ¾ cup

½ cup low-fat yogurt
2 tablespoons lime juice
¼ teaspoon crushed fresh
    ginger

Place yogurt in a strainer lined with cheesecloth and let drain for 2 hours. (Amount will be reduced by half.) In a small bowl, combine yogurt with lime juice and ginger. Will keep in the refrigerator for about 1 week. Stir before using.

Lemon Yogurt Dressing ★

Makes 1½ cups

2 tablespoons lemon juice
2 tablespoons white wine
    vinegar
1 teaspoon Dijon mustard
¼ cup olive oil
1 cup low-fat yogurt

Combine the lemon juice, vinegar, and mustard in a food processor or in a blender on low speed. With the motor running, add the oil very slowly. When the oil is incorporated, add the yogurt. Process on low to medium speed until smooth, scraping down the sides of the container as necessary. Will keep for about 1 week in the refrigerator. Stir before serving.

97

North Indian Dressing ★ ★ ★

Serve on cold fish salads, in coleslaw, or on sandwiches.

Makes ¾ cup

¾ cup low-fat yogurt
1 tablespoon tomato paste
½ teaspoon Dijon mustard
½ teaspoon tamari or soy
    sauce
¼ teaspoon lemon juice
    dash of ground coriander
    dash of ground cumin
    dash of ground ginger
    dash of cayenne pepper

Place all of the ingredients in a small bowl and beat together well. Store, tightly covered, in the refrigerator. Will keep for about 1 week.

Rosewood Strawberry Dressing ★ ★ ★

A unique dressing to serve with fruit and vegetable salad combinations.

Makes 1 cup

½   cup low-fat yogurt
⅓   cup chopped red onions
¼   cup sliced strawberries
3   tablespoons lemon juice
2   teaspoons tarragon vinegar
1   teaspoon honey
1   teaspoon paprika
½   teaspoon grated lemon rind
    dash of dry mustard

Place all of the ingredients in a blender. Process on medium speed until smooth. Store tightly covered in the refrigerator. Will keep for 3 to 5 days. Stir before serving.

Creamy Blue Cheese Dressing ★ ★ ★

Rich and creamy, for salad greens or sandwiches.

Makes 1 cup

1   cup low-fat cottage cheese
2   tablespoons crumbled blue
    cheese
2   tablespoons skim milk
1   clove garlic

Place the cottage cheese, blue cheese, and milk in a blender or food processor. Push the garlic through a garlic press into the blender. Process for about 20 seconds. (The blue cheese will still be chunky.) Keeps for 1 week in a tightly covered jar in the refrigerator.

Country Chateau Dressing ★ ★

Makes 1 cup

⅓   cup water
¼   cup white wine vinegar
2   tablespoons olive oil
2   tablespoons tomato paste
1   teaspoon honey
1   clove garlic
    dash of cayenne pepper

Place all of the ingredients in a blender and process on high speed until smooth. Will keep for about 1 week in the refrigerator. Shake well before serving.

Spring Garden
Dill Dressing ★ ★ ★

This creamy and tangy dressing for salad also makes a nice dip for raw vegetables.

Makes 1 cup

½   cup low-fat cottage cheese
½   cup low-fat yogurt
3   tablespoons minced fresh
      dill or 1 tablespoon
      dried dill
1   tablespoon minced fresh
      parsley or 1½ teaspoons
      dried parsley
½   teaspoon Dijon mustard
1   tablespoon lemon juice

Combine all of the ingredients in a food processor or in a blender on medium to high speed for 30 seconds. Chill before serving. Will keep, refrigerated, for 1 week. Stir before serving.

99

Green Onion
Dressing ★

Makes 1 cup

2   scallions, coarsely chopped
½   cup low-fat yogurt
½   cup packed watercress
1   teaspoon minced fresh
      tarragon or ½ teaspoon
      dried tarragon
3   tablespoons olive oil
2   tablespoons tarragon
      vinegar
1   clove garlic

Place all of the ingredients in a blender. Process on low to medium speed until smooth. Store tightly covered in the refrigerator. Will keep for 5 to 7 days. Stir before serving.

Russian Dressing ★ ★

Less than half the calories of high-fat Russian dressings, this is great on greens and cold shellfish.

Makes ¾ cup

½ cup *Lighten-Up Mayonnaise*
2 tablespoons catsup
2 tablespoons minced fresh chives
1 teaspoon prepared horseradish
1 tablespoon minced pickle
1 teaspoon lemon juice
1 teaspoon paprika

Combine all of the ingredients in a food processor or in a blender on low to medium speed for 30 seconds. Will keep, refrigerated, for 1 week.

100

Spreads

Lighten-Up Mayonnaise ★ ★ ★

Mayonnaise can't get much lower in calories than this recipe. Tastes like the real thing, too.

Makes 1½ cups

2 eggs
 dash white pepper
1 tablespoon honey
1 teaspoon mustard
2 teaspoons cornstarch
1 cup skim milk
2 tablespoons lemon juice
1 tablespoon vegetable oil

Blend all ingredients together in a food processor or blender on medium speed. Pour into a saucepan with a no-stick surface. Cook over medium heat, stirring constantly until mixture thickens. *Do not boil.* Refrigerate. Will keep for 1 week.

NOTE: This will thicken to a mayonnaise consistency in the refrigerator.

Golden Nile Spread ★

A nice spread for *Whole Wheat Pitas.*

Makes 4 cups

2½ cups sprouted chick-peas
   (1 cup dry)
3 tablespoons chopped fresh
   parsley
⅔ cup tahini (sesame butter)
⅔ cup water
½ cup lemon juice
½ cup olive oil
2 cloves garlic
   dash of cayenne pepper
   (garnish)

Place the chick-peas in a large saucepan and cover generously with water. Bring to a boil, then reduce heat and simmer until tender, about 1¼ hours.

Place the parsley, tahini, water, lemon juice, and oil in a blender or food processor. Add the garlic by pushing it through a garlic press into the blender. Process on low to medium speed until smooth.

Add the cooked, drained chick-peas about a cup at a time and process until all the chick-peas are added and the mixture is smooth. To serve, spread the hummus on flat plates and garnish each with a dash of cayenne, if desired.

NOTE: To sprout chick-peas, place 1 cup of dried chick-peas in a large bowl and cover generously with water. Let stand 8 hours or overnight until the chick-peas have expanded. Drain well. Rinse with water 3 to 5 times each day, draining well each time, until the chick-peas are sprouted. (Should have 2½ cups sprouted chick-peas.) This will take about 3 days. Sprouting chick-peas considerably reduces their cooking time.

101

Fresh Blueberry Jam ★ ★ ★

There's no need to give up jam when you're watching your weight. This one tastes as great as it looks.

Makes 1½ cups

1 pint blueberries
1 tablespoon maple syrup
2 teaspoons unflavored
   gelatin
¼ cup cold water

Place the berries and syrup in a medium-size saucepan. Stir the gelatin into the water until it dissolves. Add the gelatin mixture to the saucepan. Bring to a boil, then reduce heat and simmer for 6 to 8 minutes. Place in a sterilized jar, cool, then refrigerate.

Horseradish
Cheese Spread ★ ★ ★

Who needs expensive, imported herb cheeses? Serve on bread or crackers like you would soft cheese.

Makes 1¼ cups

1	cup low-fat cottage cheese
1	tablespoon low-fat yogurt
1	tablespoon prepared horseradish
1	small onion, minced
1	small clove garlic, minced
1	teaspoon minced fresh coriander (optional)
¼	teaspoon thyme
¼	teaspoon oregano
	minced fresh parsley (garnish)

Using the back of a spoon, push the cottage cheese through a sieve or strainer into a small bowl. Stir in the yogurt, horseradish, onions, garlic, coriander, thyme, and oregano.

Chill until ready to serve. Garnish with parsley, if desired.

102

Keystone Savory
Cheese ★

This cheese spread is nice on sandwiches. Or use as a bread spread instead of butter. At less than half the calories of butter, it can't be beat. It will keep in the refrigerator for 1 week.

Makes 1¼ cups

1	8-ounce package Neufchâtel cheese
¼	cup low-fat cottage cheese
¼	cup tofu
1	teaspoon chopped chives
¼	cup minced scallions
1	teaspoon minced fresh parsley
½	teaspoon paprika

Combine all of the ingredients in a small bowl and chill.

★ ★ ★ *VARIATION: This can also be turned into a low-calorie dip. Simply add 2 tablespoons of skim milk to the recipe.*

Apricot Spread ★ ★

Use on crepes or spread on homemade whole grain bread or muffins.

Makes ½ cup

¼ cup dried apricot halves
¾ cup apple juice

Place the apricots and apple juice in a small saucepan. Bring to a boil, then reduce heat, cover, and simmer until the apricots are soft and only about ¼ cup of liquid remains. Place the cooked apricots and juice in a blender and process on low speed until smooth. Store tightly covered in the refrigerator.

★ ★ ★ *VARIATION: To make Apricot-Orange Spread, cook the apricots in water instead of apple juice. Add 1 tablespoon orange juice and ¼ teaspoon grated orange rind when blending the apricots.*

Keystone
Breakfast Cheese ★

A sweet variation of *Keystone Savory Cheese.* Great for a breakfast spread on *Keystone Whole Grain Bread.*

103

Makes 2 cups

1 8-ounce package
   Neufchâtel cheese
¼ cup low-fat cottage cheese
¼ cup tofu
1 teaspoon honey
1 tablespoon chopped raisins
1 tablespoon chopped
   sunflower seeds

In a small bowl, combine all of the ingredients and chill.

Sweet Sauces

Creamy Whipped Dessert Topping ★ ★

A creamy topping for your sensible desserts.

Makes 1 cup

1   cup part-skim ricotta
    cheese
1   tablespoon honey
¼   teaspoon vanilla extract

Place all of the ingredients in a blender. Process on low speed until smooth and creamy. Refrigerate unused portion tightly covered.

Light and Creamy Dessert Sauce ★ ★ ★

Perfect over fresh fruit or whenever you want a touch of sweetness without a barrel of calories.

Makes 1 cup

¾   cup low-fat yogurt
½   banana
1   teaspoon honey
    dash of vanilla extract

Place all of the ingredients in a blender. Process on low speed until smooth. Use immediately or banana may darken.

Orange Sauce ★ ★ ★

A nice topping for pancakes or waffles.

Makes about ¾ cup

¾   cup orange juice
1   tablespoon maple syrup
1   teaspoon cornstarch

Place ½ cup of the orange juice in a small saucepan with the maple syrup and set over low heat. Dissolve the cornstarch in the remaining orange juice, then add to the saucepan. Bring to a boil over medium heat, then simmer for 2 to 3 minutes until the sauce begins to thicken. Serve hot or cold.

Orange Crème ★ ★ ★

An alternative to sugar-filled icings. It goes well with *Orange Angel Cake*.

Makes ½ cup

1 cup low-fat yogurt
1 teaspoon orange extract
1 teaspoon grated orange rind
1–2 teaspoons honey

Place the yogurt in a strainer lined with cheesecloth and place over a bowl to catch the liquid. Let the yogurt sit for 2 hours and discard the liquid. In a small mixing bowl, combine the yogurt with the orange extract, orange rind, and honey.

Maple Yogurt Sauce ★ ★ ★

Especially good over apple desserts.

Makes ½ cup

½ cup low-fat yogurt
2 teaspoons maple syrup
dash of vanilla extract

Stir the ingredients together in a small bowl. Chill, tightly covered, before serving.

105

Breakfast Fruit Sauce ★ ★ ★

Serve hot over pancakes or waffles; or at room temperature over filled crepes, cakes, or pies.

Makes 2 cups

1¼ cups apple juice
1 large, tart apple, peeled and sliced
1 tablespoon arrowroot
¼ teaspoon grated lemon rind
1 drop vanilla extract
dash of nutmeg
½ cup blueberries
½ cup sliced strawberries

Place 1 cup of the apple juice and the apples in a medium-size saucepan and bring to a boil.

Reduce heat, cover, and simmer for about 5 minutes or until just crisp-tender.

Stir the arrowroot into the remaining ¼ cup of apple juice. Add it to the pan along with the lemon rind, vanilla, and nutmeg and cook, stirring until the sauce thickens. Remove from heat and stir in the blueberries and strawberries. Serve hot or at room temperature.

Cherry Yogurt Sauce ★ ★ ★

A delicious crepe filling.

Makes about ¾ cup

¼	cup low-fat cottage cheese
¼	cup low-fat yogurt
½	teaspoon honey
¼	teaspoon vanilla extract
½	cup pitted sweet cherries

In a blender, process the cottage cheese, yogurt, honey, and vanilla until smooth. Add the cherries and blend in short pulses until the cherries are finely chopped but not pureed.

Pineapple Yogurt Sauce ★ ★ ★

Wonderful over fresh fruit desserts and fruit kabobs. A creamy luscious blend with its own natural fiber.

Makes 1 cup

1	cup chopped pineapple
¼	cup apple juice
¼	cup low-fat yogurt

Place the pineapple and apple juice in a small saucepan. Bring to a boil, then reduce heat, cover, and simmer for 10 minutes, stirring occasionally. Let cool.

Place the cooled pineapple in a blender with the yogurt. Process on low speed until smooth. Cover and chill, if desired.

Pineapple Sauce ★ ★ ★

A tropical-flavored topping for pancakes and waffles.

Makes 1 cup

2	teaspoons butter
1	cup finely minced pineapple
¼	cup apple or pineapple juice
1	teaspoon honey
	dash of nutmeg

Melt the butter in a medium-size saucepan. Add the remaining ingredients and bring to a boil. Reduce heat and simmer for about 5 minutes, stirring frequently. Serve hot or cold.

Apricot-Pineapple Dessert Topping ★

Tasty on cakes and pies.

Makes about 1 cup

½	cup dried apricot halves
1½	cups water
½	cup honey
2	tablespoons lemon juice
1	teaspoon grated lemon rind
½	cup minced pineapple

Place the apricot halves, water, honey, lemon juice, and lemon rind in a small saucepan. Bring to a boil, reduce heat, cover, and simmer for 20 minutes.

Place the apricot mixture in a blender or food processor fitted with the steel blade. On medium speed with the blender, or with several short bursts in the processor, blend the ingredients until smooth.

Return the apricot mixture to the saucepan. Stir in the pineapple. Place in a serving bowl and chill, if desired. Keep unused portion refrigerated, tightly covered.

Apricot Sauce ★ ★ ★

Serve over crepes, pancakes, and fresh fruit desserts.

Makes 1 cup

4	apricots, pitted
3	tablespoons apple juice
2	tablespoons maple syrup
1	drop almond extract

Place the apricots in a blender or food processor with the apple juice, maple syrup, and almond extract. Process on medium speed until smooth. Store unused portions, tightly covered, in the refrigerator.

Strawberry Sauce ★ ★ ★

A treat during fresh berry season. Try it over *Golden Dream Pie.*

Makes 2 cups

2½	cups sliced strawberries
1	tablespoon maple syrup

Place 1½ cups of the strawberries in a blender with the maple syrup. Process on medium speed until smooth. In a serving bowl, stir the remaining cup of strawberries into the blended mixture and serve.

NOTE: This sauce can be heated and served warm.

Strawberry-Rhubarb Sauce ★ ★ ★

When both strawberries and rhubarb are in season, make enough sauce to freeze. Use young rhubarb shoots, if possible, or peel tough, older stalks before slicing. Use as a crepe stuffing.

Makes 2½ cups

3	cups sliced rhubarb
1	cup sliced strawberries
¼	cup honey
1	tablespoon water

Place all of the ingredients in a medium-size saucepan, cover, and set over low to medium heat. Bring slowly to a boil, stirring occasionally. Reduce heat to lowest setting and slowly simmer the ingredients for about 30 minutes.

Gooseberry Sauce ★ ★

This sauce is especially good over home-canned pears.

Makes about 4 cups

7	cups gooseberries
1	cup apple juice
1½	tablespoons lemon juice
1	cup honey
	dash of cinnamon

Place all of the ingredients in a large saucepan, bring to a boil, reduce heat, and simmer, stirring occasionally, until the mixture is reduced by about half and is thickened. Store, tightly covered, in the refrigerator or freezer.

Savory Sauces

Baked Potato Topping ★ ★ ★

Serve over baked potatoes or stir into mashed potatoes. You may find you like it even better than butter.

Makes ¾ cup

½	cup low-fat cottage cheese
¼	cup low-fat yogurt
1	tablespoon grated Parmesan cheese
¼	teaspoon basil

Place all of the ingredients in a blender. Process on low to medium speed until smooth.

Mixed Wild Mushroom Sauce ★ ★ ★

Pair this sauce with poached white fish. To serve with a stronger-flavored fish, like bluefish, add thyme and a dash of hot pepper sauce. If you are adept at hunting wild mushrooms, use your "finds" to replace the shiitake mushrooms. Begin the sauce before the fish because it requires slow cooking.

Makes 1½ cups

¼ cup packed dried porcini mushrooms
6 dried shiitake mushrooms
2 cups warm water
1 medium-size onion, minced
1 small sweet red pepper, diced
1 teaspoon tamari or soy sauce
½ teaspoon fresh rosemary or ¼ teaspoon dried rosemary, crumbled
2 cloves garlic, minced
2 tablespoons rice vinegar

Soak the porcini and shiitake mushrooms in the water for 30 minutes. Remove mushrooms from the water, reserving the liquid. Chop the porcini into ¼-inch pieces. Remove and discard the stems from the shiitake mushrooms and cut the caps into thick strips.

Strain ½ cup of the soaking water through a paper-towel-lined strainer into a small saucepan, reserving the rest. Bring to a boil and add the onions, peppers, and tamari. Cover, reduce heat, and simmer for 15 minutes. Uncover and cook to evaporate the liquid. Add the rosemary and garlic and cook, stirring occasionally, allowing the onions to brown slightly. Add the vinegar and stir well, scraping the browned bits into the sauce. Puree the onion mixture in a blender or food processor using extra soaking water from the mushrooms if necessary.

Return to saucepan and add the mushrooms. Strain the remaining soaking water into the saucepan. Simmer for 30 to 40 minutes until reduced to almost half, about 1½ cups.

109

Mustard Sauce ★ ★

Serve over fish or poultry.

Makes ⅔ cup

2 egg yolks
½ teaspoon dry mustard
1½ teaspoons honey
¼ cup tarragon vinegar
2 tablespoons skim milk
1 tablespoon Dijon mustard
1 tablespoon lemon juice

Place the egg yolks, dry mustard, and honey in the top of a double boiler over boiling water. Add the vinegar and stir until the mixture has thickened. Add the milk and continue to cook, stirring, for 4 to 5 minutes. Remove from heat and stir in the Dijon mustard and lemon juice. Store in the refrigerator, tightly covered.

Horseradish Sauce ★ ★ ★

Excellent with cold poached fish.

Makes ½ cup

½	cup low-fat cottage cheese, whipped in a blender
2	tablespoons prepared horseradish
1	teaspoon minced fresh parsley

Combine all of the ingredients in a small bowl.

Lemon Thyme Sauce ★ ★ ★

Makes ½ cup

½	cup low-fat cottage cheese, whipped in a blender
1½	teaspoons lemon juice
2	tablespoons skim milk
1	teaspoon minced fresh parsley
1	teaspoon basil
½	teaspoon thyme

Combine all of the ingredients in a small bowl.

★ ★ *VARIATION: Add 2 tablespoons more skim milk and serve as a salad dressing.*

Sauce Corsica ★ ★ ★

The calories in this sauce are almost nonexistent, so feel free to splurge. Summer-ripe tomatoes make it a truly excellent topping for hot poached fish or shrimp.

Makes ¾ cup

¾	cup minced tomatoes
1	tablespoon balsamic vinegar
2	tablespoons minced fresh coriander or 2 tablespoons minced fresh parsley

Combine all of the ingredients in a small bowl. Chill 2 hours before serving.

NOTE: If fresh parsley is used, add a dash of ground coriander.

No-Oil Pesto ★ ★

Serve with pasta, spaghetti squash, or over fish. This is not a cooking sauce and should be used only to top already cooked foods.

Makes ¾ cup

2	tablespoons sunflower seeds
1	clove garlic, minced
1	tablespoon Dijon mustard
½	cup low-fat cottage cheese
1	cup trimmed, fresh basil
¼	cup trimmed, fresh parsley

Place sunflower seeds, garlic, and mustard in a blender or food processor. Puree on medium to high speed until smooth. Add cottage cheese and blend again. Add basil and parsley and blend until smooth, pushing herbs down with a rubber spatula.

NOTE: To use on cooked pasta or spaghetti squash, drain the pasta or squash, saving 2 tablespoons cooking water. Combine the water with ½ cup pesto and toss with pasta. Serve immediately.

Dilled Cucumber Sauce ★ ★ ★

Another sauce very low in calories. Excellent with poached salmon, as a dip for raw vegetables, or as a dressing for salad greens.

111

Makes 1 cup

½	cup peeled, seeded, and minced cucumbers
½	teaspoon cider vinegar
½	cup low-fat yogurt
1	teaspoon Dijon mustard
1	tablespoon chopped chives
1½	teaspoons dill

Combine all of the ingredients in a small bowl.

Hot Taco Sauce ★ ★ ★

Makes 2½ cups

3	tomatoes, minced
1	small onion, minced
2	green chili peppers, seeded and minced
2	teaspoons cider vinegar
1	teaspoon minced fresh coriander (optional)

Combine all of the ingredients in a small bowl. Store, tightly covered, in the refrigerator.

Barbecue Sauce ★ ★

Makes 1¹/₃ cups

¼   cup shiitake or porcini
      mushrooms or other
      dried mushrooms
¾   cup minced onions
1   teaspoon safflower oil
1   cup *Tomato Sauce*
1   tablespoon lemon juice
3   tablespoons Worcestershire
      sauce
3   tablespoons cider vinegar
1   tablespoon frozen apple
      juice concentrate
2   teaspoons dry mustard
1   cup water

Soak the mushrooms in warm water for 20 minutes.

Sauté the onions in the oil for about 5 minutes in a large saucepan. Add the tomato sauce, lemon juice, Worcestershire sauce, vinegar, apple juice, mustard, and water.

Strain the mushrooms and mash them to a paste. Add to the pan and simmer gently for 1 hour.

Marinara Sauce ★ ★ ★

Makes 6 cups

½   cup minced onions
1   tablespoon *Chicken Stock*
2   cloves garlic, minced
¼   cup minced celery
5   cups coarsely chopped
      plum tomatoes, with
      juice
4   cups water
2   tablespoons red wine
      vinegar
2   teaspoons oregano
2   teaspoons thyme
1   bay leaf
2   teaspoons dried parsley

In a medium-size saucepan, sauté the onions in the stock for 5 minutes. Add the garlic, celery, tomatoes, water, and vinegar. Bring to a boil, then simmer gently, uncovered, for 2 hours. Add oregano, thyme, bay leaf, and parsley and simmer 30 minutes longer. Remove bay leaf.

NOTE: This sauce freezes well.

Vegetarian Spaghetti Sauce ★ ★ ★

Nice served over spaghetti squash.

Makes 3 cups

3	large tomatoes, chopped
1	medium-size onion, chopped
1	large sweet red pepper, chopped
2	teaspoons tamari or soy sauce
2	cups cooked kidney beans
1½	teaspoons marjoram
1	teaspoon basil
½	teaspoon oregano

Place the tomatoes, onions, peppers, and tamari in a blender. Process on low, then medium speed until smooth.

Place the sauce in a large skillet. Add the beans, marjoram, basil, and oregano. Bring to a boil, stirring frequently. Reduce heat, cover, and simmer for 30 minutes, stirring occasionally.

113

Tomato Sauce ★ ★ ★

The lack of oil makes this a super-low-calorie treat. Make several batches when tomatoes and peppers are ripe and freeze.

Makes about 4 cups

6	medium-size tomatoes, quartered
2	large sweet red peppers, coarsely chopped
1	medium-size onion, coarsely chopped
½	cup tomato paste
5	cloves garlic
½	teaspoon basil
¼	teaspoon oregano
¼	teaspoon marjoram

Place half of the tomatoes, half of the peppers, half of the onions, half of the tomato paste, the garlic, basil, oregano, and marjoram in a blender. Process on medium speed until smooth, stopping the blender and scraping down the sides as necessary. Pour into a medium-size saucepan.

Process the remaining tomatoes, peppers, onions, and tomato paste in the blender on medium speed until smooth. Add to the saucepan. Over medium heat, bring the tomato sauce to a boil, cover, reduce heat, and simmer for 30 to 40 minutes.

Pasta

What's this? An entire chapter on pasta—in a *diet* book? That's right. Pasta is finally living down its reputation as being a high-calorie food and is taking its rightful place where it belongs—as a health-promoting, energy-promoting, *and* weight loss-promoting food.

There's no underestimating the psychological value of having an attractive, visually satisfying main dish to look forward to when you're watching your weight. And, to me, pasta is right at the top of the list. After all, how can you feel deprived eating spaghetti with cheese sauce?

When I speak of pasta, of course, I'm referring to pasta made from whole grains—a chief source of the fiber, complex carbohydrates, vitamins, and minerals that are all-important to your weight loss efforts. Whole wheat pasta contains the full complement of vitamins and minerals found in a hearty loaf of whole wheat bread. Combined with tasty seasonal vegetables, well-chosen low-fat cheeses and low-calorie sauces, whole grain pasta can be the mainstay of a weight reducing program—not just an occasional splurge that ends in regret.

In this chapter you'll find a wide array of pasta dishes well within the 250 calorie-per-serving Weight Loss range. You'll be able to fill up on lasagna, macaroni, and even manicotti without having to worry about filling out. In fact, there's not one recipe in this chapter higher than 350 calories a serving. What more proof do you need that pasta is not a high-calorie food?

You can buy your whole wheat pasta dried and in the box from the supermarket shelf, but I recommend that you make your own. One good reason is that you'll be able to control calories even more if you make your own. For example, *Basic Whole Wheat Pasta* is nothing more than flour, egg, and water—about as low in calories as pasta can get. (I'll even let you in on a little secret: It's only 110 calories a serving!)

The second reason is that making your own will help you *burn* calories—provided, of course, you work by hand and *not* with an electric pasta machine. Whole wheat flour makes a rather firm dough, which requires a little extra muscle behind it when kneading. Think of your pasta-making time as an exercise routine, working your hands, arms, and upper torso.

The third reason is that you just can't beat the taste of freshly made pasta.

On the following pages you'll find a half-dozen ways to make your own pasta. In addition to *Basic Whole Wheat Pasta*, there's *Whole Wheat Pasta I* and *II*. These are a little more traditional in nature because they incorporate a bit of oil and more eggs, although the recipes themselves vary slightly. These are also low in calories (about 170 calories a serving).

You'll also find a recipe for *Eggless Whole Wheat Pasta* for those who want to limit their intake of cholesterol (like *Basic Whole Wheat Pasta*, it too, is *very* low in calories). There are also recipes for *Tomato Pasta*, a colorful version of *Basic Whole Wheat Pasta* you might want to serve to impress a dinner crowd, and *Buckwheat Pasta*, for just a change of taste.

All the basic pasta recipes make approximately ½ to 1½ pounds of noodles, although the weight will vary depending on conditions, such as air, moisture, temperature, and altitude. It can be used at once, but it will stay fresh wrapped in a slightly damp towel and refrigerated for a day or two. Or you can put it in a plastic bag and freeze it. Noodles can also be draped over a drying rack (improvise if you don't have your own) and stored in a jar or box in the pantry where they will keep indefinitely.

To cook homemade pasta: Cook the pasta in a large pot of boiling water—7 quarts of water per pound of pasta—so the pasta has enough room to "swim" around. Make certain the water is boiling rapidly before adding the pasta. Add in small amounts so as not to disturb the boil. Cook the pasta, uncovered, stirring gently with a wooden spoon to distribute it evenly while it cooks. Should the water cease to boil after you add the pasta, cover the pot, leaving the cover slightly ajar, until the water begins to boil readily again. Uncover immediately.

The amount of time it takes to cook the pasta depends a lot on the size and shape of the pasta. But it is finished when it is firm-tender or al

115

dente—"to the tooth." In our kitchen tests, these fresh pasta recipes were finished in anywhere from 6 to 12 minutes with 7 to 8 minutes as the average. It's best to begin testing after 2 minutes. Fresh pasta will cook more quickly than dried.

Cut your pasta in any length or width you wish. Serve with *Tomato Sauce, Marinara Sauce,* or *No-Oil Pesto* for a three-star entrée. Homemade noodles are also featured in many of the other recipes in this chapter.

A plate of pasta . . . a big green salad . . . a slice of whole grain bread. A winning combination for a three-star meal.

You'll have to admit, being on a diet does have it's rewards!

Whole Wheat Pasta I ★ ★ ★

116

Makes 1 to 1¼ pounds, serving 8 to 10

2 cups whole wheat flour
1 cup gluten flour
4 eggs
1 tablespoon sunflower oil
3-4 tablespoons warm water

Combine the flours and place in a mound on a sturdy work surface. Make a well in the center of the mound large enough to hold the eggs.

Place the eggs in the well and begin beating them with a fork, incorporating the flour gradually. When the egg mixture becomes stiff, add the oil and begin to knead in the flour with your fingers.

Add enough water to make a smooth ball of dough as you knead in the flour. Knead the dough an additional 10 minutes, until it is elastic and shiny. Set the dough under an overturned bowl to rest for 30 minutes.

Divide the dough into 6 sections and roll out each section to a thickness of about ¹⁄₁₆ inch or as thin as possible without tearing the dough.

Dry the rolled dough slightly by letting it rest, uncovered, on the work counter for 10 minutes or so, turning once. Dust with flour and roll up jelly-roll style. Cut noodles to desired width. Unroll noodles and cut to desired length.

Whole Wheat Pasta II ★ ★ ★

Makes approximately 1 pound, serving 8

2	cups whole wheat pastry flour
2	eggs
1½	teaspoons sunflower oil
2–3	tablespoons warm water

Place the flour in a mound on a sturdy work surface. Make a well in the flour large enough to hold the eggs.

Place the eggs in the well and beat with a fork, incorporating the flour gradually. When the egg mixture becomes stiff, add the oil, then work in the remaining flour with your fingers, adding enough water to make a smooth ball of dough. Set the dough aside to rest for 30 minutes under an overturned bowl.

Divide the dough into quarters, and roll out, one quarter at a time, to a thickness of about ¹/₁₆ inch or as thin as possible without tearing the dough.

Dry the dough slightly by letting it rest, uncovered, for 10 minutes, turning it over once. Dust with flour, then roll up jelly-roll style and cut noodles to desired width. Unroll and cut noodles to desired length.

117

Basic Whole Wheat Pasta ★ ★ ★

This oilless version is about as low in calories as you can get. If you're really calorie conscious, you'll want to use this recipe while you're trying to lose weight.

Makes approximately 1 pound, serving 8

2	cups whole wheat flour
1	egg, beaten
¹/₃–½	cup warm water

Place the flour in a medium-size bowl. Add the egg and just enough of the water to make a very firm dough.

Knead the dough on a lightly floured board for about 20 minutes or until it is very smooth and elastic.

Divide the dough into quarters and roll out one quarter of the dough to a thickness of about ¹/₁₆ inch or as thin as possible on the lightly floured board. Keep the remaining dough well wrapped to prevent drying out.

Dust the rolled-out dough lightly with flour, then roll up jelly-roll style and cut noodles to desired width. Unroll and cut to desired length.

Eggless Whole Wheat Pasta ★ ★ ★

Makes approximately 1½ pounds, serving 12

2½	cups whole wheat flour
¼	cup soy flour
1⅓	cups low-fat yogurt

Combine the flours and place in a mound on a sturdy work surface. Form a well in the center of the mound large enough to accommodate the yogurt.

Place the yogurt in the well, and using a fork, beat the yogurt lightly, slowly incorporating the flour.

When the mixture gets too thick to beat with a fork use your hands to knead the remaining flour into the yogurt. Roll the dough into a ball and let it rest under an overturned bowl for 5 minutes.

Knead the dough on a lightly floured surface for about 8 to 10 minutes or until it is smooth. Divide the dough into quarters.

Roll out the dough, one quarter at a time, to a thickness of about ⅛ inch. Keep the remaining dough under an overturned bowl so it does not dry out. Set aside rolled out dough and cover loosely with a kitchen towel. Let the rolled out dough rest for 20 minutes under the towel, turning it over after 10 minutes.

Lightly dust the dough with flour, roll up jelly-roll fashion, and cut the noodles to desired width. Unroll and cut to desired length.

118

Tomato Pasta ★ ★ ★

When cooked, these noodles take on a delicate color that makes any pasta combination special.

Makes approximately 1 pound, serving 8

2	cups whole wheat flour
2	eggs, beaten
¼	cup tomato paste
1	tablespoon warm water

Place the flour in a mound on a sturdy work surface. Beat the eggs and tomato paste together.

Make a well in the center of the flour large enough to accommodate the egg mixture. Beat the egg mixture with a fork, slowly incorporating the flour.

When the mixture gets stiff, use your fingers to knead in the remaining flour. Add the water and continue to knead until the dough is smooth.

Knead for about 10 minutes more or until the dough is shiny. Set under an overturned bowl and let the dough rest for about 30 minutes.

Divide the dough into quarters. Roll out each quarter until it is about ¹/₁₆ inch thick or as thin as you can roll it without breaking the dough.

Let the rolled out dough dry slightly by leaving it on the counter for 10 minutes, turning once. Dust with flour, then roll up, jelly-roll fashion, and cut the noodles to desired width. Unroll the noodles and cut to desired length.

Buckwheat Pasta ★ ★ ★

Makes approximately ½ pound,
serving 4

¾	cup whole wheat flour
¼	cup buckwheat flour
1	egg
1	tablespoon corn oil
1½–2	tablespoons warm water

Combine the flours and place in a mound on a sturdy work surface. Form a well in the center of the flour and place the egg in the well.

Carefully beat the egg with a fork, slowly incorporating the flour. When the egg mixture gets too thick to beat with the fork, pour on the oil and begin to knead the dough. Add enough water to make the dough smooth and shiny as you knead. Continue kneading for about 10 minutes.

Divide the dough into two sections. Let rest 15 minutes under an overturned bowl. Roll out each section to a thickness of ¹/₁₆ inch or as thin as possible without tearing the dough.

Dust lightly with flour, then roll up dough, jelly-roll fashion, and cut noodles to desired width. Unroll and cut noodles to desired length.

Tomato Pasta
with Ricotta
Cream Sauce ★ ★ ★

Makes 8 servings

1   pound *Tomato Pasta*
1   cup peas
½   cup low-fat yogurt, at room
      temperature
½   cup part-skim ricotta
      cheese, at room
      temperature
¼   cup grated Parmesan
      cheese

Cook the pasta in boiling water until al dente (see cooking instructions on page 115).

Meanwhile, steam the peas until crisp-tender, about 10 minutes.

Place the yogurt and ricotta in a blender and process on medium speed until smooth.

Drain the pasta and toss with the peas in a large bowl. Place on a heated serving platter or individual plates and spoon on the ricotta sauce. Sprinkle with Parmesan and serve.

120   Stuffed Jumbo Shells
with Broccoli ★

Makes 6 servings

6   quarts water
12   ounces jumbo whole wheat
      pasta shells
½   bunch broccoli
2   cups low-fat cottage cheese
2   eggs, beaten
½   teaspoon basil
      dash of grated nutmeg
3   cups *Tomato Sauce*

Bring water to a boil in a large pot. Add the shells and cook until al dente, about 10 to 12 minutes. *Do not overcook.* Drain the shells immediately, then rinse under cold water until cool. Separate the shells carefully and set aside.

Peel the tough outer layer from the broccoli stems and steam the broccoli until crisp-tender, about 10 minutes. Cut off the broccoli florets to a length of about two inches. Mince the broccoli stems. Place the minced broccoli stems in a large mixing bowl with the cottage cheese, eggs, basil, and nutmeg. Mix together well.

Stuff the cooked shells with the cheese mixture. Layer a few spoonfuls of tomato sauce in the bottom of two shallow 8 × 8-inch baking dishes. Place the stuffed shells in the baking dishes along with the broccoli florets. Top with the remaining tomato sauce. Bake uncovered at 400° for 20 minutes.

Golden Stuffed Manicotti ★ ★ ★

Makes 4 servings

6   quarts water
8   manicotti tubes
2   cups mashed cooked winter squash
¼   cup grated Parmesan cheese
1   tablespoon minced fresh parsley
½   teaspoon freshly grated nutmeg
1½ cups *Marinara Sauce*

Bring water to a boil in a large pot. Add manicotti and cook the tubes until al dente, about 10 minutes. Drain carefully and set aside to cool.

In a medium-size bowl, mix together the squash, Parmesan, parsley, and nutmeg. Using a spoon or a pastry bag fitted with a large tube, fill each manicotti tube with about 4 tablespoons of squash mixture.

With no-stick spray, coat a 9 × 13-inch baking dish. Arrange manicotti in the dish. Cover with sauce.

Bake at 350° for about 20 minutes, until heated through.

Pasta Primavera with Scallops ★ ★ ★

Makes 6 servings

12 ounces whole wheat spaghetti
½   large onion, chopped
½   cup *Chicken Stock*
½   cup sliced mushrooms
1   medium-size carrot, cut into thin slices
2   cups chopped broccoli
1   teaspoon tamari or soy sauce
    dash of cayenne pepper
¼   pound sea scallops, quartered
    minced fresh parsley (garnish)

Cook the spaghetti until al dente (see cooking instructions on page 115).

Meanwhile, place the onions in a large skillet with ¼ cup of the stock and cook over medium heat until translucent. Add the mushrooms, carrots, broccoli, remaining stock, tamari, and cayenne. Bring to a boil, then reduce heat to low, cover, and simmer just until the broccoli is bright green but still quite hard, about 10 minutes.

Stir the scallops into the vegetables and cook until the scallops are cooked through and opaque and the vegetables are crisp-tender, 1 to 2 minutes.

Drain the spaghetti, place on a serving plate, and spoon the vegetable mixture on top. Garnish with minced parsley, if desired.

★ ★ *VARIATION: Use ½ pound of scallops.*

121

Fettuccine with Tofu and Vegetables ★ ★ ★

A delicious combination.

Makes 8 servings

8	ounces tofu, crumbled
2	tablespoons tamari or soy sauce
1½	cups water
1	tablespoon red wine vinegar
1	teaspoon basil
½	teaspoon oregano
½	teaspoon marjoram
½	teaspoon savory
¼	teaspoon thyme
	dash of cayenne pepper
1	pound whole wheat fettuccine
½	cup *Chicken Stock*
½	large onion, chopped
6	cloves garlic, sliced
1	cup chopped mushrooms
2	cups sliced broccoli florets
½	sweet red pepper, diced
¼	cup minced fresh parsley
2	tablespoons grated Parmesan cheese

122

Place the tofu in a large bowl with the tamari, ½ cup of the water, the vinegar, basil, oregano, marjoram, savory, thyme, and cayenne. Toss to combine. Cover and marinate in the refrigerator for several hours or overnight.

Drain the tofu in a fine sieve and discard the liquid. Press the tofu gently with the back of a wooden spoon and set aside.

Cook the fettuccine until al dente (see cooking instructions on page 115).

While the pasta cooks, place the stock in a large skillet. Add the onions and cook over medium heat until the onions are translucent. Add the garlic and the mushrooms and stir to combine.

Add the tofu and the remaining water. Bring to a boil, then reduce heat, cover, and simmer for about 10 minutes.

Steam the broccoli and peppers until crisp-tender, 5 to 8 minutes.

Stir the parsley and Parmesan into the tofu mixture and simmer another 1 to 2 minutes.

Drain the fettuccine and toss with tofu mixture in a large bowl. Arrange the fettuccine mixture on a serving platter. Spoon the steamed vegetables on top. Serve at once.

Poultry, pasta, and vegetables are combined to make this meal-in-one entrée—
Fettuccine Giordino with Chicken.

One of the secrets to dining on a diet is to put variety into the menu. This Japanese-style meal calls for *Beef Sukiyaki, Sushi Bowl with Tamago,* and *Japanese Sea Vegetable Soup.*

Fettuccine Giordino with Chicken ★

Makes 8 servings

1	pound whole wheat fettuccine
1	cup peas
1	cup cauliflower, cut into florets
1	cup corn
1	cup broccoli, cut into florets
1	cup diced green and red peppers
1	cup green beans or sugar snap peas
2	whole chicken breasts, skinned, boned, and cut into small pieces
¼	cup *Chicken Stock*
3	medium-size tomatoes, chopped
½	cup chopped fresh parsley
½	cup chopped fresh basil
2	teaspoons tamari or soy sauce
½	teaspoon black pepper
1	teaspoon oregano
2-3	cups sliced mushrooms

Cook the fettuccine until al dente (see cooking instructions on page 115).

Meanwhile, steam the peas, cauliflower, corn, broccoli, peppers, and beans until tender, about 10 minutes. Do not overcook.

In a large skillet, sauté the chicken in 2 tablespoons of the stock, until cooked through, about 5 minutes. Add tomatoes, parsley, and basil. Remove from heat when tomatoes are warm and wilted. Add tamari, pepper, and oregano.

In another medium-size skillet, sauté the mushrooms with the rest of the stock.

Combine the steamed vegetables, chicken mixture, and mushrooms in a large bowl.

Drain the fettuccine and place on a large serving platter. Top with vegetable-chicken-mushroom mixture and serve hot.

125

Macaroni with Tomato Sauce ★ ★ ★

Makes 4 servings

4	cups hot macaroni, cooked until al dente (2 cups dry)
1½	cups *Tomato Sauce*
2	tablespoons minced fresh parsley (garnish)

Toss the macaroni with the tomato sauce. Serve garnished with minced parsley, if desired.

Spaghetti with Cheese Sauce ★ ★ ★

Makes 8 servings

1   pound whole wheat spaghetti
½   cup low-fat cottage cheese
¼   cup crumbled feta cheese
½   teaspoon basil
1   egg
1   tablespoon minced fresh parsley (garnish)

Cook the spaghetti until al dente (see cooking instructions on page 115).

Meanwhile, place the cottage cheese, feta, and basil in a blender or food processor. Puree on medium speed until creamy.

Beat the egg in a large serving bowl. When the spaghetti is done, drain quickly, then immediately place in the serving bowl and toss with the egg until coated. Add the cheese sauce and continue tossing until well mixed. Serve garnished with parsley, if desired.

126   Pasta with Broccoli and Chevre ★ ★ ★

Chevre is a mild goat cheese.

Makes 4 servings

8   ounces *Basic Whole Wheat Pasta* (thin strips)
¾   cup *Chicken Stock*
½   bunch broccoli, broken into florets
1   teaspoon minced fresh thyme or ½ teaspoon dried thyme
¼   pound chevre, softened

Cook the pasta until al dente (see cooking instructions on page 115).

While noodles are cooking, put ¼ cup of the stock in a medium-size skillet with the broccoli and sauté for several minutes until crisp-tender. Transfer to a plate and set aside.

Add remaining stock, thyme, and cheese to skillet. Stir with a whisk until creamy.

Return broccoli to pan. Add cooked pasta and toss to combine.

NOTE: If goat cheese is unavailable in your area or is too strong for your taste, you can substitute a creamy garlic and herb cheese such as Boursin.

Mediterranean Mixed Cheese Linguine ★ ★

Makes 4 servings

8 ounces linguine
¾ cup peas
1 egg
¼ cup crumbled feta cheese
2 tablespoons grated
    Parmesan cheese

Cook the linguine until al dente (see cooking instructions on page 115). Cook the peas in a small amount of water just until tender but still bright green, about 10 minutes.

While the pasta is cooking, place the egg in a serving bowl, beat lightly, and add the cheeses. Beat until well blended.

When the pasta is cooked, drain and toss immediately with the peas and cheese sauce. Serve hot.

Vegetarian Lasagna ★ ★ ★

Makes 9 servings

8 ounces whole wheat
    lasagna noodles
4 large tomatoes, peeled if
    desired, and seeded
½ cup tomato paste
2 scallions
1 tablespoon tamari or soy
    sauce
2 cloves garlic
2 teaspoons basil
1 teaspoon oregano
½ teaspoon marjoram
3 cups low-fat cottage cheese
2 eggs, beaten
¼ cup grated Parmesan
    cheese
4 ounces part-skim mozza-
    rella cheese, thinly
    sliced

Bring a large pot of water to a boil and cook the lasagna noodles until al dente, about 10 to 12 minutes. Drain and rinse under cold water. Spread out flat until ready to use.

Meanwhile, place the tomatoes in a blender with the tomato paste, scallions, tamari, garlic, basil, oregano, and marjoram. Process on low to medium speed until smooth.

Combine the cottage cheese with the eggs and Parmesan.

To assemble the casserole, layer about ½ cup of the tomato sauce in the bottom of a 9 × 13-inch baking dish coated with no-stick spray. Place a third of the lasagna noodles across the bottom of the dish, overlapping as necessary. Spread half the cheese mixture over the noodles. Top with another third of the noodles. Then layer the remaining cheese and noodles and pour the rest of the sauce over the noodles. Arrange mozzarella on top.

Bake at 375° for 35 to 45 minutes. Let stand about 10 minutes before serving.

Spinach Lasagna ★ ★

Makes 9 servings

½ pound spinach
12 ounces lasagna noodles
1 cup part-skim ricotta cheese
2 cups low-fat cottage cheese
2 tablespoons grated Parmesan cheese
2 eggs, beaten
dash of grated whole nutmeg
2 tablespoons butter
2 tablespoons whole wheat flour
1 cup skim milk
2 ounces part-skim mozzarella cheese, shredded
1 cup *Tomato Sauce*
flat leaf parsley sprigs (garnish)

Clean the spinach well and discard the stems. Place the spinach in a large saucepan and steam in the water that clings to the leaves, stirring frequently, until the spinach is wilted. Set aside to drain.

Bring a large pot of water to a boil and cook the lasagna noodles until al dente, about 10 to 12 minutes. Drain and rinse under cold water. Spread out flat until ready to use.

While the noodles are cooking, combine the ricotta cheese, cottage cheese, Parmesan, eggs, and nutmeg in a large bowl. Squeeze the liquid from the spinach, then chop and add to the cheese mixture.

Melt the butter in a medium-size skillet and stir in the flour. Stir over low heat a minute or so, then add the milk all at once and stir to eliminate lumps. When the mixture has thickened, stir in the mozzarella. Remove from heat.

To assemble the lasagna, spread a few tablespoons of the tomato sauce over the bottom of a 9 × 13-inch baking dish coated with no-stick spray.

Layer one-fourth of the lasagna noodles on top of the tomato sauce, then half of the spinach-cheese mixture. Layer another fourth of the noodles and the remaining spinach and cheese.

Add another layer of lasagna noodles and spoon the mozzarella cheese sauce over top. Add a final layer of noodles and spoon the remaining tomato sauce over all.

Cover the lasagna loosely with foil and bake at 350° for 30 minutes. Remove from the oven and let stand about 10 minutes before serving. Garnish with parsley, if desired.

Mixed Cheese and
Vegetable Lasagna ★ ★ ★

Makes 9 servings

8	ounces whole wheat lasagna noodles
1	cup part-skim ricotta cheese
1¾	cups low-fat cottage cheese
¼	cup grated Parmesan cheese
¼	cup wheat germ
2	eggs, beaten
1	cup cooked cauliflower or broccoli florets, sliced
2	cups *Tomato Sauce*

Bring a large pot of water to a boil and cook the lasagna noodles until al dente, about 10 to 12 minutes. Drain and rinse under cold water to cool. Spread out flat until ready to use.

In a medium-size bowl, combine the ricotta cheese, cottage cheese, Parmesan, wheat germ, and eggs.

To assemble the lasagna, layer one-third of the noodles on the bottom of a 9 × 13-inch baking dish coated with no-stick spray. Spread with half the cheese mixture. Top with ½ cup of cooked vegetables and ½ cup of tomato sauce.

Top with another third of the noodles. Repeat the layering with remaining cheese mixture, vegetables, and another ½ cup of tomato sauce.

Top with the remaining noodles, then spoon the rest of the tomato sauce over the noodles.

Bake, covered, at 375° for 20 minutes. Uncover and bake an additional 20 minutes. Remove from oven and wait 10 to 15 minutes before serving.

129

Macaroni and
Peas with Feta ★ ★

Makes 4 servings

1	cup peas
1	egg
¾	cup crumbled feta cheese
3	cups hot cooked macaroni (1½ cups dry)

Cook the peas in a little water in a small saucepan for 4 to 5 minutes or until firm-tender. Drain.

In a medium-size serving bowl, beat the egg, then beat in the cheese.

Mix the hot macaroni and peas and immediately toss with the egg and cheese mixture until well coated. Serve hot.

Broccoli Bake with Macaroni ★

Makes 4 servings

2 quarts water
½ pound fresh broccoli
4 cups cooked macaroni
     (2 cups dry)
¾ cup low-fat cottage cheese
2 eggs
¼ teaspoon black pepper
¼ teaspoon paprika
¼ teaspoon dry mustard
1 cup shredded low-fat
     mozzarella cheese

Put the water in a large pot and bring to a boil. Meanwhile, chop the broccoli but separate the stems from the florets. When the water boils, add the broccoli stems and allow them to cook for 3 minutes. Then add the chopped broccoli florets and cook for another 3 minutes. Drain.

Mix the broccoli, macaroni, and cottage cheese together in a large bowl. Set aside. Coat an 11 × 7-inch baking dish with no-stick spray. Spread the macaroni-broccoli-cottage cheese mixture in the dish.

Beat the eggs. Add the pepper, paprika, and mustard to the eggs and pour this mixture over the broccoli. Top with mozzarella. Bake at 350° for 30 minutes or until the top is golden brown.

130

Macaroni-Spinach Tart ★ ★ ★

Makes 6 servings

1 cup chopped onions
¼ cup *Chicken Stock*
¾ cup crumbled feta cheese
3 eggs, beaten
2 tablespoons skim milk
½ teaspoon basil
     dash of nutmeg
1 pound spinach, lightly
     steamed and minced
1 cup macaroni, cooked
     until al dente (½ cup
     dry)
2 tablespoons wheat germ
1 orange, sliced (garnish)
6 parsley sprigs (garnish)

Cook the onions slowly in the stock in a medium-size skillet until they are translucent and tender.

In a large mixing bowl, combine the cheese, eggs, milk, basil, and nutmeg. Stir in the spinach, macaroni, and onions. Transfer the mixture to a 9- or 10-inch pie plate or tart pan. Sprinkle with the wheat germ.

Bake at 350° for 40 minutes. Cut into wedges and serve hot. Garnish with orange slices and parsley, if desired.

Pasta and Cheese with Cauliflower ★ ★ ★

Makes 6 servings

2 cups sliced cauliflower florets, lightly steamed
1½ cups sesame whole wheat pasta spirals, cooked until al dente
¾ cup shredded sharp Cheddar cheese
2 eggs, beaten
¾ cup low-fat cottage cheese
¼ cup skim milk
2 tablespoons wheat germ
1 tablespoon grated Parmesan cheese
dash of paprika

In a 2-quart ovenproof casserole, layer one-third of the cauliflower, one-third of the pasta, and one-third of the Cheddar. Repeat the layering twice.

Place the eggs, cottage cheese, and milk in a blender. Process on low to medium speed until smooth. Pour over the layered pasta mixture, using a spoon to help the sauce reach the bottom of the casserole in several places. Top with the wheat germ, Parmesan, and paprika. Bake at 375° for 35 minutes or until the top is golden brown.

131

Pesto Pasta with Feta ★ ★
A cold pasta plate.

Makes 8 servings

2 cups chopped broccoli florets and stems
½ sweet red pepper, diced
½ cup peas
1 pound sesame whole wheat pasta spirals, cooked until al dente
¼ cup *No-Oil Pesto*
2 tablespoons crumbled feta cheese

Steam the broccoli and red peppers until crisp-tender, about 10 minutes, then rinse under cold water until cool.

Cook the peas in a small amount of boiling water until tender, about 10 minutes, then drain and rinse under cold water until cool.

Combine the pasta, broccoli, peppers, peas, pesto, and feta in a serving bowl. Toss until the pesto sauce is evenly distributed. Cover and chill before serving, if desired, or serve at room temperature.

Meats

If you're a meat lover embarking on a diet for the first time, it's pretty jolting to look at a calorie chart and discover that your all-time favorite meal—a 12-ounce sizzling sirloin steak—weighs in at well over 1,600 calories. It brings the problem immediately into focus. You gasp, "No wonder I have to go on a diet!"

All is not as bad as it first may seem, however. For one thing, if you cut the fat away from that steak, especially if you do it *before* you put it on the grill, you'll be cutting away a sizable portion of those calories—about half. (See, the news is getting better already.) And therein lies the first lesson in cooking. *Always trim away the fat.*

The second may be a little harder to swallow—at least at first. You really don't *need* all that meat. Four ounces per serving is all you really should be eating. Less is even better.

As you've already learned, in order to lose weight naturally, you must *increase* your intake of complex carbohydrates and *decrease* your intake of fat. And since a large portion of the calories in meat comes from fat (for some cuts that's 50 percent or even more), that means you should learn how to get by on less.

Sure, meat can be the focal point of the meal. The idea is to fill out the meat dish with other low-calorie and tasty ingredients. Take shish kabobs, for example. Four ounces of meat can go a long way when it is cubed and put on skewers with low-calorie fresh vegetables and served over rice or chopped fresh spinach. Stir-frying strips of beef Chinese style with lots of tasty vegetables (you get a lot of crunch this way) is another way to stretch out a meat meal. You get enough meat to satisfy your craving and plenty of complex carbohydrates to give you a full and satisfying meal—but without a lot of calories. The vegetables also give you the fiber that meat lacks. *Beef Sukiyaki, Julienne of Beef with Broccoli and Spinach, Hearty Shamrock Stew, Thai Pork with Cellophane Noodles,* and *Ragout of Lamb with Garden Vegetables* are but a few of the excellent recipes in this chapter that prove meat can go a long way.

But you'll find recipes for steaks and chops, too, like *Pennsylvania Pot Roast, Tournedos of Beef Athéné,* and *Grilled Greek Lamb Chops.* The trick to enjoying full meat meals without a lot of calories is to incorporate important fat-cutting tips in the cooking process. For one thing, avoid sautéing your meat in butter or oil. There's enough fat in the meat itself without adding even more at the stove. Instead, we found that meat browns quite nicely in stock. A tablespoon or two is all you need. If, for some reason, you do use oil, use as little as possible—a teaspoon per serving is plenty. And always drain the meat—even ground meat—on paper towels after sautéing, even if you're sautéing in stock. The meat releases a lot of fat in those first few minutes of quick cooking.

When making stews and pot roasts, refrigerate the dish for several hours after cooking it. The refrigeration will coagulate the fat, which will rise to the top. You can easily just lift it off. Then all you need to do is reheat it and serve it. While this may sound like a lot of extra work, it's well worth it as far as your diet is concerned.

Also, restrict yourself to only the leanest cuts of meat. While it may cost a little more, the expense is well worth it in terms of your diet and your health. When buying ground beef pick out your own cut (sirloin is good) and ask the butcher to grind it for you or do it yourself. Round steak and flank steak are among the beef cuts lowest in calories. Both can be tenderized in marinades. But avoid any roasts or steaks that are well marbled or pocked with fatty areas. Also avoid eating meat with ribs—the meat is usually connected to the ribs with a healthy portion of fat. Some of the worst offenders are rib roasts and corned beef.

Although pork has long been maligned as a high-calorie meat, its image is beginning to change. Pork producers are now breeding leaner animals, which are resulting in leaner cuts on your dinner plate. But the caveat here is still the same. *Cut away the fat.* The best cut of meat here in terms of your diet is the pork tenderloin. A lightly cured ham is also lean, but it's also high in salt, a real drawback for the dieter. Forget bacon and sausage. The calories are way too high and so is the fat—some 75 percent of their calories come from fat.

As for lamb, some cuts are better than others, of course, and leg of lamb is at the top of the list. If you want lamb cubes, have it cut from the leg. Rack of lamb, although very expensive, also is a lean and tender meal—as long as you steer clear of the fat!

While you don't have to give up meat, we want to say again that you should make an effort to cut back on it—both for the sake of your diet and your health. In addition to being high in calories, meat is high in saturated fats. If you eat meat every day, start cutting back to every other day, then cut back even more until you're eating meat only once or twice a week. Not only will you *be* healthier, you'll *look* healthier, too.

Beef Sukiyaki ★

134

Called "the friendship dish" in Japan because family and guests participate in the preparation of this cook-at-the-table entree.

Makes 4 servings

2 tablespoons tamari or soy sauce
⅓ cup *Basic Brown Stock*
½ cup mirin (sweet rice vinegar)
1 pound beef sirloin, sliced paper thin
8 small scallions, cut diagonally into 2-inch pieces
½ cup bean sprouts
1 cup loosely packed spinach leaves
1 cup mushroom caps
1 cup cubed tofu

Combine the tamari, brown stock, and mirin to make sukiyaki sauce and pour into a small pitcher or bowl.

Arrange the beef, scallions, sprouts, spinach, mushrooms, tofu, and bamboo shoots attractively on a large platter and set on the table with the sukiyaki sauce.

Place an electric frying pan on the table. Coat with no-stick spray and heat to medium. Add one-fourth of the beef and scallions and pour in one-fourth of the sukiyaki sauce. Cook 2 to 4 minutes, depending on desired doneness. Add one-fourth of the sprouts, spinach, mushrooms, tofu, and bamboo shoots, keeping them separate. Cook another 30 seconds to 2 minutes. Repeat with 3 remaining portions.

Serve and eat while cooking or let the diners help themselves, adding more ingredients to the frying pan

½ cup sliced bamboo shoots
1 cup *Chicken Stock*
¼ cup cooked rice

as the food is eaten. Do not overcook. After all of the ingredients have been eaten, pour in the chicken stock and rice, bring to a boil, and serve as a soup, in small cups.

NOTE: Mirin is available at oriental groceries.

★ *VARIATION: For a more authentic recipe, substitute ½ cup of yam noodles cut into 2-inch lengths for the rice. You can find the noodles in an oriental grocery store.*

Beef Stroganoff ★ ★

Savory—without the calories of sour cream.

Makes 4 servings

1 pound lean beef, cut into ½-inch cubes
2 cups sliced mushrooms
1½ cups sliced onions
½ cup sliced celery
1 tablespoon safflower oil
1 teaspoon onion powder
1 teaspoon savory
¼ teaspoon paprika
½ cup *Basic Brown Stock*
½ cup water
1½ teaspoons sweet rice powder or cornstarch
1 tablespoon *Basic Brown Stock*
½ cup low-fat cottage cheese
½ cup buttermilk
¼ teaspoon lemon juice
1 tablespoon chopped fresh parsley

Place the beef on a rack in a broiler pan filled with water. Bake at 400° until the meat is browned on all sides, about 10 minutes. Drain the meat on paper towels.

In a heavy medium-size saucepan, sauté the mushrooms, onions, and celery in the oil until soft, about 5 minutes. Add the onion powder, savory, paprika, ½ cup of stock, and water. Cover and simmer gently until the vegetables are tender, about 15 to 20 minutes.

Dissolve the rice powder in the tablespoon of stock, add to the saucepan, and cook, stirring, until thickened.

Puree the cottage cheese in a blender on medium to high speed until smooth and creamy. Add the buttermilk and lemon juice and puree.

Add the meat to the vegetable mixture and remove from heat. Slowly stir in the cottage cheese-buttermilk mixture and parsley. Serve immediately.

135

Barbecued Beef Satay ★ ★ ★

Makes 4 servings

1 pound round steak, cut into 1-inch cubes
1 medium-size onion, minced
2 teaspoons grated fresh ginger or ½ teaspoon ground ginger
1 teaspoon caraway seeds
½ teaspoon ground coriander
½ teaspoon turmeric
½ teaspoon cayenne pepper
2 teaspoons tamari or soy sauce
2 tablespoons *Basic Brown Stock*
2 tablespoons lemon juice
1 clove garlic

Place all of the ingredients except the garlic in a medium-size ceramic bowl. Add the garlic by pushing it through a garlic press into the bowl. Mix the ingredients, cover, and let marinate for 2 hours in the refrigerator. Spear the meat onto small skewers, reserving the marinade. Broil 4 inches from the heat for 6 minutes, turning once and brushing with the marinade.

In a small saucepan, bring any reserved marinade to a simmer. Serve the beef with the warm marinade as a dipping sauce.

★ *VARIATION: This will also serve 8 as an appetizer.*

Tournedos of Beef Athéné ★ ★ ★

Tournedos are the center, most tender part of the fillet.

Makes 4 servings

4 tournedos of beef (4 ounces each)
¼ cup *Basic Brown Stock*
¾ cup coarsely chopped tomatoes
¼ cup minced red onions
1 teaspoon basil
½ teaspoon thyme

In a large skillet coated with no-stick spray, brown the tournedos in the stock over medium-high heat for 5 minutes on each side or until cooked to desired degree. Drain on paper towels. Arrange the tournedos on a platter.

In a medium-size bowl, combine the tomatoes, onions, basil, and thyme. Gently drizzle over the tournedos and serve immediately.

Beef Heart Braised in Cider ★ ★

Makes 10 servings

3 pounds beef heart
1½ cups apple cider
1 cup *Chicken Stock*
2 medium-size onions, chopped
1 tablespoon tamari or soy sauce
parsley sprigs (garnish)
cherry tomatoes (garnish)

Trim off visible fat from the beef heart and cut out large veins if this has not already been done by the butcher.

Place the heart with the cider, stock, and onions in a deep, 1½-quart ovenproof casserole. Cover and bake at 325° for 2½ hours.

Remove the heart from the casserole and strain the cooking liquid. Puree the onions in a blender on medium speed with one cup of liquid to make a gravy. Season with the tamari.

Thinly slice the heart and arrange the slices on a serving platter. Spoon the gravy over top. Garnish the platter with parsley and cherry tomatoes, if desired.

Julienne of Beef with Broccoli and Spinach ★ ★ ★

Crisp vegetables and tangy ginger dressing complement this dish, which is served at room temperature.

Makes 4 servings

1 pound flank steak, 1 inch thick
1½ cups ½-inch-wide shreds spinach
1 cup bite-size broccoli florets
2 tablespoons tamari or soy sauce
2 tablespoons *Basic Brown Stock*
¼ cup rice vinegar
½ teaspoon grated fresh ginger
1 clove garlic, minced
1 teaspoon honey

Broil the steak for 6 minutes on each side or until cooked to desired degree. Let cool and slice into ¼-inch-thick strips. Slice each strip lengthwise and place in a large mixing bowl.

Place the spinach in a colander. Bring a 5-quart pot of water to a boil and blanch the broccoli for 30 seconds. Don't overcook. Pour the entire contents of the pot over the spinach. The hot rushing water will blanch, but not cook, the spinach. Drain the spinach and broccoli well and add to the bowl of meat.

Combine the tamari, stock, vinegar, ginger, garlic, and honey in a small bowl, whisking briskly to make a clear, amber dressing. Toss the beef and vegetables with the dressing, arrange on a platter, and serve at room temperature.

137

Buckingham London Broil ★ ★ ★

Quick cooking is essential to keep this lean meat tender.

Makes 4 servings

1   pound flank steak, 1 inch thick
2   tablespoons tamari or soy sauce
1   tablespoon honey
¾   cup red wine vinegar
1   teaspoon minced fresh ginger
1   bay leaf
1   clove garlic

Pierce the steak on both sides with a thin knife or skewer. Place in a 9 × 13-inch glass dish. In a medium-size bowl, combine the tamari, honey, vinegar, ginger, and bay leaf, and add garlic by pushing through a garlic press into the bowl. Pour over the steak and refrigerate, covered, for at least 4 hours, turning meat once or twice. (Marinating longer will impart a more robust flavor to the meat.)

Remove the steak from the marinade and broil for 5 to 7 minutes on each side or until cooked to desired degree. Slice thinly and arrange on a serving platter.

★ ★ ★ *VARIATION: Serve with* Horseradish Sauce.

138

Braised Beef Milanese ★ ★ ★

This meat is refrigerated, then reheated in order to remove all excess fat before eating.

Makes 8 servings

½   teaspoon oregano
¼   teaspoon minced garlic
¼   teaspoon basil
     dash of thyme
1   tablespoon minced fresh parsley
2   pounds bottom round or rump roast, tied
½   cup minced onions
¼   cup minced carrots
¼   cup minced celery

In a small bowl, mix together the oregano, garlic, basil, thyme, and parsley. With a small, sharp knife, make incisions in the beef and insert some of the spice mixture into each incision. Place the meat on a rack in a broiler pan. Broil until browned, about 10 minutes, and remove.

Sauté the onions, carrots, and celery in 1 tablespoon of the stock in a large skillet over medium heat for 5 minutes or until tender. Place the vegetables in a shallow 2-quart baking dish.

Place the beef on top of the vegetables. In a small saucepan, combine the rest of the stock, tomatoes, and

1 cup *Basic Beef Stock*
½ cup coarsely chopped
    tomatoes
1 bay leaf
    black pepper to taste

bay leaf. Bring to a boil, lower heat, and simmer for 5 minutes. Pour over the meat and vegetables. Cover tightly. Braise in the oven at 350° for 2 hours or until the meat is tender.

Remove the bay leaf. Remove the meat from the baking dish and pour the vegetables and liquid into a small saucepan and refrigerate for 2 to 3 hours. Return the meat to the baking dish, cover, and refrigerate. When ready to serve, skim the fat from the top of the saucepan using a slotted spoon. Heat the liquid to boiling, add the pepper, and simmer for 2 to 3 minutes.

Slice the meat thinly. Spoon the sauce over the meat. Cover and bake at 350° for 15 minutes or until heated through.

Pennsylvania Pot Roast ★ ★ ★

This pot roast should be made in advance and reheated before serving.

Makes 4 servings

1 pound round roast
½ cup crushed tomatoes with
    juice
¾ cup water
½ medium-size onion,
    sliced
¼ cup diced carrots
¼ cup diced celery
¼ cup diced turnips
1 small bay leaf
4 black peppercorns
¼ teaspoon thyme
1 tablespoon chopped fresh
    parsley

Place the meat on a rack in a broiler pan. Broil until all sides are browned, about 4 minutes on each side. Drain on paper towels.

Place the meat, tomatoes and juice, water, onions, carrots, celery, turnips, bay leaf, peppercorns, and thyme in a large skillet coated with no-stick spray. Simmer, covered, for 2 to 3 hours until meat is tender, adding water if cooking liquid evaporates. Refrigerate skillet and contents for at least 4 hours or until the fat rises to the surface and can be skimmed off.

When ready to serve, remove the skillet from the refrigerator and lift off the fat. Add the parsley, cover, and cook gently over low heat until heated through. Remove the meat to a hot serving platter. Turn heat to medium and cook the sauce until slightly thickened. Remove the bay leaf. Pour the sauce over the meat and serve.

Beef Stew with
Adzuki Beans ★ ★ ★

Flavorful beans add fiber and low-fat protein to this delicious stew.

Makes 10 servings

1	cup adzuki beans
1	pound lean beef cubes
¼	cup whole wheat flour
3	tablespoons *Basic Brown Stock*
1	small onion, finely chopped
10	cups water
4	medium-size tomatoes, peeled and chopped
6	medium-size carrots, cut in thick slices
2½	cups quartered mushrooms
8	small white onions
2	sweet red peppers, diced
1	cup corn
⅔	cup tomato paste
4	garlic cloves, minced
1	bay leaf
1	teaspoon basil
½	teaspoon thyme
¼	teaspoon oregano
¼	teaspoon rosemary, crumbled
¼	teaspoon marjoram
3	tablespoons tamari or soy sauce
¼	cup minced fresh parsley

140

Soak the beans overnight in water to cover. Drain. Dredge the beef in the flour. Place the stock in a large, heavy-bottom saucepan. Sauté the beef cubes, half at a time, until they are lightly browned. Set aside until all are browned, then return the beef to the saucepan and add the chopped onions.

Cook over medium heat until the onions are translucent. Add the water, beans, tomatoes, carrots, mushrooms, onions, peppers, corn, tomato paste, garlic, bay leaf, basil, thyme, oregano, rosemary, and marjoram.

Stir well, to loosen any bits of flour or meat stuck to the bottom of the pan. Bring the stew to a boil, then reduce heat, partially cover, and slowly simmer until meat is tender, about 2 hours. Refrigerate 2 to 4 hours or overnight. Remove fat from top of stew and reheat, about 15 to 20 minutes.

Stir in the tamari and parsley. Serve hot.

Sautéed Liver
with Vegetables ★ ★

Makes 2 servings

½ pound calf's liver
1 tablespoon whole wheat flour
2 teaspoons corn oil
½ cup chopped leeks
½ cup chopped sweet red peppers
2 tablespoons chopped raisins
3 tablespoons water
1 teaspoon chili seasoning
1 teaspoon cinnamon
1½ teaspoons tamari or soy sauce
½ teaspoon ginger

Trim any membranes away from the liver and cut into thin strips. Pat the liver dry, then dust with the flour.

Place the oil in a medium-size skillet with the leeks and peppers. Cook over medium heat for about 5 minutes, until the vegetables are slightly tender. Add a few drops of water, if necessary, to prevent scorching.

Stir in the raisins, then add the strips of liver, the water, chili seasoning, cinnamon, tamari, and ginger. Stir, then cover and steam until the liver is just slightly pink inside, about 5 minutes. Do not overcook. Serve at once.

141

Braised Liver with
Endive and Bay ★

Makes 4 servings

1 pound calf's liver
1½ cups water
2 bay leaves
¾ cup diced carrots
½ cup sliced celery
¼ cup sliced onions
4 Belgian endives, halved lengthwise

In a medium-size saucepan, combine the liver, water, and 1 of the bay leaves. Cover and braise at a gentle simmer for 20 minutes. Remove from the liquid, place on a serving tray, and keep warm.

Combine the carrots, celery, onions, endives, and remaining bay leaf and steam for 10 minutes. Arrange over the liver and serve.

Hearty Shamrock
Stew ★ ★ ★

Cut calories by preparing this zesty Irish stew ahead of time. Overnight refrigeration solidifies the fat so you can simply lift it off before reheating to serve.

Makes 4 servings

1   pound beef chuck, cut into 1-inch cubes
1   cup *Basic Brown Stock*
1   cup water
1   bay leaf
1   medium-size onion, sliced into rings
½   cup diced turnips
½   cup sliced carrots
½   cup diced potatoes
½   teaspoon black pepper
2   tablespoons whole wheat flour
2   teaspoons marjoram
1   tablespoon tamari or soy sauce

In a large saucepan, combine the beef, stock, water, and bay leaf. Bring to a boil over medium-high heat, reduce heat, cover, and simmer for 20 minutes. Add the onions, turnips, carrots, potatoes, and pepper. Simmer for 45 minutes. Remove from heat and refrigerate for at least 5 hours.

Remove the fat from the top of the stew. Remove ½ cup of the liquid, combine it with the flour, and stir to make a smooth paste. Add to the stew with the marjoram. Heat and stir until the stew thickens and is heated through, about 12 minutes. Stir in the tamari and serve.

Beef and Lentil
Stew ★ ★ ★

You'll enjoy the taste while learning to do a lot with a little bit of meat. Add additional chili powder and cumin or even a finely chopped hot pepper if your taste buds favor Mexican dishes. Freeze some for later.

Makes 8 servings

1   tablespoon corn oil
½   pound lean ground beef
2   medium-size onions, chopped
1   sweet red pepper, chopped

Place the oil in a large, heavy pot. Add the beef and brown over medium heat. Stir in the onions and cook until translucent.

Add the peppers, carrots, mushrooms, and garlic. Turn heat to low and stir occasionally.

Place the tomatoes, 2 cups of the water, and the tomato paste in a blender with the tamari, marjoram,

2 medium-size carrots,
   thinly sliced
2 cups mushrooms, thinly
   sliced
2 cloves garlic, minced
2 medium-size tomatoes,
   halved
3½ cups water
⅔ cup tomato paste
1 tablespoon tamari or soy
   sauce
2 teaspoons marjoram
1 teaspoon basil
1 teaspoon chili powder
1 teaspoon ground cumin
¼ teaspoon oregano
1 cup lentils

basil, chili powder, cumin, and oregano. Process on low to medium speed until smooth.

Add the blended mixture, the remaining water, and the lentils to the beef mixture. Bring to a boil, stir well, reduce heat, and simmer about 40 minutes, until all the vegetables are tender.

★ VARIATION: Serve over cooked noodles or spaghetti, approximately ½ cup per serving.

143

Sweet and Spicy Pork ★ ★ ★

Makes 6 servings

1½ pounds boneless lean
   pork, trimmed of fat
   and cubed
¾ cup apple cider
1 small onion, halved
3 cloves garlic
1 tablespoon honey
1 tablespoon peanut butter
1 tablespoon tamari or soy
   sauce
¼ teaspoon black pepper
¼ teaspoon cinnamon
¼ teaspoon ground allspice
¼ teaspoon ground cloves
¼ teaspoon ginger

Place pork in a large bowl.

In a blender, combine the cider, onion, garlic, honey, peanut butter, tamari, pepper, cinnamon, allspice, cloves, and ginger. Process on medium speed until smooth.

Pour the marinade over the pork cubes and stir so all of the pork is coated with marinade. Refrigerate several hours or overnight.

Place the pork cubes on metal skewers. Set over a hot grill or under a broiler until the pork is well done throughout, about 20 minutes. Remove from the skewers to serve.

Jamaican Pork ★ ★ ★

Stir-frying without oil makes this a low-calorie Caribbean feast.

Makes 4 servings

2 tablespoons tamari or soy sauce
⅓ cup *Basic Brown Stock* or *Vegetable Stock*
1 ¼-inch slice ginger
¼ teaspoon ground allspice
1 bay leaf
1 clove garlic, halved
¾ pound pork shoulder, cut into ¼-inch strips
½ cup sliced mushrooms
⅓ cup sliced celery
½ cup thinly sliced sweet red peppers
1 teaspoon cornstarch
1 teaspoon honey

In a large mixing bowl, combine the tamari, stock, ginger, allspice, bay leaf, and garlic. Add the pork, cover, and marinate in the refrigerator for at least 4 hours, turning several times. Remove the pork from the bowl and reserve the marinade.

Heat a wok or large skillet coated with no-stick spray and stir-fry the pork strips over medium-high heat for 3 to 5 minutes, adding a bit of marinade if necessary to prevent scorching. Remove the pork strips and drain on paper towels. Wipe the wok clean of all fat.

Reheat the wok and sauté the mushrooms, celery, and peppers with 1 tablespoon of the marinade over medium-high heat for 1 minute. Remove the vegetables from the wok.

In a small bowl, combine ¼ cup of the marinade, the cornstarch, and honey. Return wok to medium-high heat and add the sauce, stirring until thickened and shiny. Quickly add the pork and vegetables, tossing to coat with the sauce. Serve immediately.

Diamond Head Pork with Pineapple ★ ★ ★

This Hawaiian feast is served in a pineapple shell.

Makes 4 servings

½ cup pineapple juice
2 tablespoons tamari or soy sauce
3 tablespoons cider vinegar
1 teaspoon minced fresh ginger
2 tablespoons minced onions
1 clove garlic

In a medium-size bowl, combine pineapple juice, tamari, vinegar, ginger, and onions. Add garlic by pushing it through a garlic press into the bowl.

Slice the pork against the grain into paper-thin pieces, add to bowl and let marinate for 4 hours.

Cut pineapple in half lengthwise, leaving green top intact. Reserve one half for another use. With a sharp knife, loosen flesh from the other half, scoop out

144

¾ pound boneless pork
   chops, trimmed of fat
1 ripe pineapple
1 teaspoon cornstarch
1 green pepper, cut into
   thin strips
1 red pepper, cut into thin
   strips

with a spoon, and cut into ½-inch strips. Set the pineapple and shell aside.

Drain marinade from pork, reserving ½ cup. Heat a wok or large no-stick skillet over medium-high heat and add 3 tablespoons of marinade. Stir-fry pork until just brown. Don't overcook. Remove from pan and add the rest of the reserved marinade plus cornstarch and stir constantly, until thick, about 20 seconds. Quickly add green peppers, red peppers, pineapple strips, and pork. Toss and remove from heat. Pile into pineapple shell and serve immediately.

Thai Pork with Cellophane Noodles ★ ★ ★

Tangy and aromatic.

Makes 4 servings

¾ cup cellophane noodles
2 tablespoons fermented
   black beans, rinsed and
   chopped
1 tablespoon mirin (sweet
   rice vinegar)
5 tablespoons *Basic Brown
   Stock*
2 teaspoons cornstarch
1 clove garlic
1 ¼-inch slice ginger
¾ pound lean pork, sliced
   paper thin
1 cup shredded spinach
¼ cup chopped water
   chestnuts
¼ cup slivered red sweet
   peppers

In a medium-size mixing bowl, cover the noodles with hot water and let them soak for 20 minutes, then drain. Cut into 1-inch pieces with scissors.

Combine the beans, mirin, 2 tablespoons of the stock, and cornstarch and set aside.

In a wok or large skillet, cook the garlic and ginger in the remaining stock over medium-high heat for 1 minute. Discard the garlic and ginger and stir-fry the pork and noodles for 3 minutes or until cooked through. Add the spinach, water chestnuts, peppers, and sauce. Toss to heat through and serve immediately.

NOTE: Mirin is available in oriental groceries.

Smothered Pork with Peppers ★ ★ ★

Makes 6 servings

6   pork chops, trimmed of fat
2   tablespoons water
1   tablespoon sunflower oil
2   medium-size onions, thinly
       sliced
1   sweet red pepper, diced
1   green pepper, diced
2   cloves garlic, minced
4   cups sliced mushrooms
2   cups chopped, cooked
       plum tomatoes with juice
1   teaspoon marjoram
½   teaspoon oregano
¼   teaspoon thyme

Place the pork chops in a large skillet with the water and cook over medium heat until the water evaporates and the pork chops begin to brown. Remove the chops to a large, shallow baking dish and arrange in one layer.

Heat the oil in a large skillet and when it is warm, add the onions, the red peppers, and the green peppers. Cook until the onions are translucent, then add the garlic. Stir over medium heat for 2 to 3 minutes. Add the mushrooms and cook until they release their liquid and the liquid has evaporated.

In a blender, combine the tomatoes with the marjoram, oregano, and thyme on medium speed until the mixture is smooth. Combine with the onion mixture in the skillet.

Pour the tomato and onion mixture over the pork chops in the baking dish. Cover with foil and bake at 325° for 1 hour. Remove the foil and bake an additional 15 minutes.

Grilled Greek Lamb Chops ★ ★ ★

Makes 4 servings

4   lamb chops, ¾ inch thick,
       trimmed of fat
2   tablespoons lemon juice
1   tablespoon minced fresh
       mint
1   teaspoon paprika
     dash of ground cinnamon
     dash of ground nutmeg
1   clove garlic, sliced
     mint sprigs (garnish)
     lemon slices (garnish)

Prick the lamb chops with a sharp fork, then place in a shallow bowl.

In a small bowl, combine the lemon juice, mint, paprika, cinnamon, nutmeg, and garlic and pour over chops, turning them once so that all of the surfaces are covered. Refrigerate several hours or overnight.

Drain the chops. Cook on a grill or broil 5 minutes on each side. Do not overcook.

Garnish with mint sprigs and lemon slices, if desired.

★ ★ *VARIATION: Serve 2 lamb chops per person.*

Curried Lamb
Matari ★ ★

Makes 4 servings

1	pound lean lamb, cut into 1-inch cubes
1¼	cups *Basic Brown Stock*
½	cup coarsely chopped onions
½	cup coarsely chopped celery
¾	cup coarsely chopped tart apples
1	tablespoon chopped raisins
1	tablespoon sesame seeds
1-2	tablespoons curry powder

In a medium-size skillet, cook the lamb briskly in 2 tablespoons of the stock for 10 minutes or until browned. Add more stock as needed. Add the onions and celery and continue to cook 1 minute more. Lower heat and add the apples, raisins, sesame seeds, curry, and the rest of the stock and cook 5 minutes longer or until the sauce is thick.

Broiled Noisettes
of Lamb ★ ★ ★
Quick, elegant, and slimming.

Makes 4 servings

1	teaspoon crushed black peppercorns
2	teaspoons ground coriander
2	tablespoons *Basic Beef Stock*
1	clove garlic
4	slices of lamb tenderloin (4 ounces each and 1½-inches thick), trimmed of fat

In a small bowl, combine the pepper, coriander, and stock, and add the garlic by pushing it through a garlic press into the bowl. Rub the lamb with the mixture. Broil for 8 to 10 minutes on each side or until cooked to desired degree.

Mongolian Lamb ★ ★

Makes 4 servings

1	pound lean lamb, trimmed of fat
2	tablespoons mirin (sweet rice vinegar)
1	tablespoon tamari or soy sauce
1	tablespoon red miso (red soybean paste)
1	tablespoon sesame seeds
2	teaspoons safflower oil
1	clove garlic
1	¼-inch slice ginger
¼	cup julienned carrots
1	cup shredded Chinese cabbage
¾	cup shredded spinach

Slice the lamb paper thin across the grain and cut into 1 × ½-inch pieces. In a medium-size mixing bowl, marinate the lamb with 1 tablespoon of the mirin and the tamari for 30 minutes.

In a small bowl, combine the miso, the remaining mirin, and the sesame seeds to make a sauce. Set aside.

Heat the oil in a wok or medium-size skillet over medium-high heat. Add the garlic and ginger and stir-fry for 1 minute, then discard. Drain the lamb and reserve liquid. Add lamb to the wok and stir-fry for 1 to 2 minutes, then remove. Add the carrots and stir-fry for 30 seconds with just enough of the lamb liquid to create steam. Add the lamb and the miso sauce, toss quickly, and serve immediately over a bed of Chinese cabbage and spinach.

NOTE: Mirin is available in oriental groceries.

Ragout of Lamb with Garden Vegetables ★ ★

Makes 6 servings

1½	pounds lamb shank meat, cut into 1-inch cubes
2	cloves garlic, minced
½	teaspoon basil
½	teaspoon rosemary, crumbled
1	bay leaf
¼	teaspoon caraway seeds dash of thyme

In a large no-stick skillet, cook the lamb over medium heat, a few pieces at a time, until well browned. Remove from pan and drain on paper towels. Add the garlic to the skillet and cook for 1 minute. Put the lamb back in the skillet, add the basil, rosemary, bay leaf, caraway seeds, thyme, pepper, and rice flour. Add the stock slowly, stirring constantly. Bring to a boil, cover, and simmer for about 1 hour or until the lamb is tender, stirring occasionally.

Add the onions, carrots, and mushrooms. Bring

dash of black pepper
1   tablespoon sweet rice flour
    or cornstarch
2   cups *Basic Beef Stock* or
    Chicken Stock or water
6   ounces pearl onions
    (¾–1 cup)
4   medium-size carrots, cut
    diagonally into 2-inch
    pieces
1   cup mushroom caps
1   tablespoon chopped
    fresh parsley

to a boil, cover, and simmer for 30 minutes or until the vegetables are tender.

Transfer the ragout to a warm serving dish and sprinkle with the parsley.

Lamb with Tabbouleh ★ ★

Lamb lends its gentle flavor to this tasty Middle Eastern dish.

149

Makes 4 servings

¼   cup bulgur
½   cup boiling water
1   pound lean lamb, cut into
    ½-inch cubes
¼   teaspoon black pepper
½   cup chopped scallions
½   teaspoon oregano
    dash of ground coriander
1   cup coarsely chopped
    tomatoes
½   cucumber, peeled, seeded,
    and cut into 2-inch
    sticks
1½ teaspoons chopped fresh
    parsley
4   leaves lettuce
    chopped fresh mint
    (garnish)

In a small bowl, combine the bulgur and boiling water. Let stand for 1 hour. Drain and press out excess water.

In a no-stick skillet, cook the lamb over medium-high heat for 10 minutes or until browned on all sides. Let cool.

In a large mixing bowl, combine the bulgur, lamb, pepper, scallions, oregano, coriander, tomatoes, cucumbers, and parsley. Toss gently.

Arrange the lettuce on a serving platter. Place a scoop of the lamb mixture on each leaf. Garnish with mint, if desired, and serve at room temperature or slightly chilled.

Tunisian Lamb Kabobs with Yogurt Cucumber Sauce ★ ★

Makes 4 servings

KABOBS
1   clove garlic, chopped
2   tablespoons lemon juice
2   tablespoons *Vegetable Stock*
1   hot dried chili, seeded and minced
¼   cup low-fat yogurt
1   teaspoon ground coriander
¼   teaspoon turmeric
1   pound lean lamb, cut into 1-inch cubes
2   medium-size onions, quartered and separated into layers

SAUCE
1   cup low-fat yogurt
½   cup peeled, seeded, and chopped cucumbers
¼   cup low-fat cottage cheese
½   teaspoon ground coriander
     dash of black pepper
¼   teaspoon dry mustard

To make kabobs: Combine the garlic, lemon juice, stock, chilies, yogurt, coriander, and turmeric. Pour over the lamb and marinate overnight.

Skewer the lamb cubes alternately with the onion pieces.

Broil for 10 to 13 minutes or until cooked to desired degree, turning often.

To make the sauce: Line a strainer with cheesecloth and let the yogurt drain for 2 hours. Combine the yogurt with the cucumbers, cottage cheese, coriander, pepper, and mustard in a blender. Process on medium speed until blended but not smooth. Drizzle over the kabobs. Serve at room temperature.

150

Moussaka ★ ★

Makes 8 servings

1   pound lean ground lamb
1   medium-size eggplant, cubed

Lightly brown the lamb in a medium-size no-stick skillet. Drain and set aside.

Steam the eggplant for 10 minutes. In a medium-size saucepan, boil the potatoes in water to cover until tender, 10 to 15 minutes.

6 small potatoes, peeled and quartered
4 cups cooked plum tomatoes with juice
1 medium-size onion, minced
2 cloves garlic, minced
½ teaspoon oregano
dash of cinnamon
dash of grated whole nutmeg
⅓–½ cup hot skim milk
¼ cup finely crumbled feta cheese

Place the tomatoes in a blender and process on medium speed until finely chopped. Place in a medium-size saucepan with the onions, garlic, oregano, cinnamon, and nutmeg. Bring to a boil, reduce heat, and simmer 10 to 15 minutes, uncovered.

Drain the potatoes. Mash with enough of the hot milk to make a loose mixture.

To assemble the casserole, place half the eggplant in the bottom of a 9 × 13-inch baking dish coated with no-stick spray. Top with half of the meat, then half of the sauce.

Repeat with remaining eggplant, meat, and sauce. Sprinkle with the feta cheese. Spread the mashed potato mixture over the top of the casserole. Bake, uncovered, at 325° for 1 hour. Let stand about 15 minutes before cutting into serving pieces.

Skinny Beef Tacos ★

Makes 4 servings

½ pound lean ground beef
¼ cup water
2 tablespoons *Tomato Sauce*
1 tablespoon whole wheat flour
1 tablespoon chili powder
2 teaspoons ground cumin
¾ cup cooked red kidney beans
8 taco shells
1½ cups shredded lettuce
1 cup chopped tomatoes
½ cup grated sharp Cheddar cheese
¼ cup alfalfa sprouts
1 cup *Hot Taco Sauce*

Place the beef in a large no-stick skillet and brown, adding a few drops of water, if necessary, to prevent sticking. Remove from skillet and drain on a paper towel to remove excess fat. Return to skillet with the remaining water, the tomato sauce, flour, chili powder, and cumin. Stir together over medium heat until well blended with the meat.

Stir in the kidney beans and partially mash them with a fork or the back of a wooden spoon. Stir the meat and bean mixture occasionally while the mixture heats through. Turn off heat and cover skillet. Heat the taco shells in the oven at 350° for about 5 minutes before assembling tacos.

To assemble the tacos, place some of the meat mixture in the bottom of a heated taco shell. Top with some lettuce, tomatoes, cheese, and sprouts. Add taco sauce.

Viennese Stuffed Cabbage ★ ★ ★

Makes 4 servings

1	small head savoy cabbage, cored
3	cups boiling water
½	cup minced onions
¼	teaspoon minced garlic
½	cup cooked rice
1	egg white
½	pound lean ground beef
1	teaspoon tamari or soy sauce
1½	tablespoons paprika
	dash of marjoram
	dash of black pepper
½	cup water
½	cup crushed tomatoes with juice
	low-fat yogurt (garnish)

Remove 8 leaves from the cabbage, wash, and place them in a large bowl. Reserve the remaining cabbage. Pour the boiling water over the cabbage leaves. Let stand until the leaves are slightly soft, about 8 minutes. Remove the leaves from the water with tongs and place them on paper towels to dry.

In a medium-size mixing bowl, combine the onions, garlic, rice, egg white, ground beef, tamari, 1 tablespoon of the paprika, the marjoram, and pepper. Mix well.

Cut out any heavy end core from each cabbage leaf. Place 2 tablespoons of filling on each leaf. Fold the thick end of each leaf over the filling, then fold the sides over and roll each leaf tightly.

Shred 3 cups of reserved cabbage. Spread 1 cup in the bottom of a 1½-quart ovenproof casserole. Place 4 cabbage rolls on top of the shredded cabbage. Top with 1 cup shredded cabbage. Place the remaining rolls on top. Top with the remaining cabbage.

In a small bowl, combine the ½ cup water and the tomatoes with their liquid. Pour the mixture over the cabbage rolls. Bake, covered, at 325° for 1½ hours or until the cabbage is tender. Sprinkle with the remaining ½ tablespoon of paprika. Top with yogurt, if desired. Serve immediately.

152

Spinach-Stuffed Meat Roll ★ ★ ★

This savory meat roll is easy to make and a great dish to serve to company. Leftovers freeze well—just thaw in the refrigerator. Can be served cold like a paté or terrine.

Makes 8 servings

½	pound lean ground beef
½	pound lean ground lamb
2	eggs
⅓	cup bread crumbs

In a food processor, mix together the beef, lamb, 1 egg, the bread crumbs, tomato paste, onions, pepper, coriander, and thyme until thoroughly combined. Set aside.

¼   cup tomato paste
⅓   cup minced onions
¼   teaspoon black pepper
¼   teaspoon ground coriander
½   teaspoon thyme
1   cup low-fat cottage cheese
1   tablespoon grated Romano
         cheese
1   tablespoon grated
         Parmesan cheese
2   tablespoons parsley
1   cup chopped spinach

In a medium-size bowl, mix together the cottage cheese, Romano, Parmesan, parsley, spinach, and the other egg.

On a sheet of aluminum foil about 15 inches long, form the meat mixture into a rectangle about ⅜-inch thick. Spread the spinach mixture over the meat. Keep the mixture ½-inch away from the edges of the meat. Roll the meat up tightly jelly-roll style by gently lifting the foil at the short side of the rectangle.

Seal the ends of the roll. Carefully place the meat roll, seam side down, on a rack in a broiler pan and bake at 350° for 50 to 55 minutes. (If after 20 minutes the top is too brown, cover with foil for the remaining cooking time.) Cool about 5 minutes before slicing. Serve hot or cold.

Lamb Pilaf ★ ★   *153*

Makes 6 servings

¾   pound lean ground lamb
1   large onion, chopped
1   tablespoon sunflower oil
1   tablespoon mustard seeds
2   cloves garlic, minced
1   cup long grain brown rice
1   teaspoon ground coriander
1   cup peeled, seeded, and
         chopped tomatoes
2   small carrots, thinly sliced
2   cups *Chicken Stock*
1   tablespoon tamari or soy
         sauce
     minced fresh dill (garnish)
     cherry tomatoes (garnish)

Place the lamb in a medium-size skillet with a tablespoon or two of water. Cook just until all the pinkness has disappeared. Drain on paper towels and set aside.

Place the onions in a large, heavy-bottom saucepan with the oil and stir over medium heat until the onions are translucent. Add the mustard seeds, garlic, and rice, stirring until the rice turns opaque. Stir in the coriander, tomatoes, carrots, stock, tamari, and lamb.

Bring the ingredients to a boil, then reduce heat to lowest setting, cover the pan tightly, and steam the pilaf for 45 minutes. Remove from heat and let stand 10 minutes. Stir ingredients together and place on a serving platter. Garnish with dill and tomatoes, if desired.

Stuffed Sweet Peppers ★ ★ ★

Makes 4 servings

½ pound lean ground lamb
4 sweet red peppers
½ cup cooked rice
½ cup minced onions
¼ cup minced celery
½ cup finely diced carrots
1½ teaspoons oregano
1 teaspoon thyme
1 teaspoon minced fresh
    parsley
¾ cup water

Brown the lamb in a skillet coated with no-stick spray. Remove the lamb from the pan and drain on paper towels.

Cut tops from the peppers and remove the seeds and spines.

Combine the rice, onions, celery, carrots, oregano, thyme, and parsley with the lamb. Fill the peppers with the mixture and place in a baking dish with the water. Cover and bake at 350° for 40 minutes, then uncover and bake for 15 minutes more so the tops will brown nicely. Serve immediately.

154

Blue Ribbon Meat Loaf ★ ★

Makes 6 servings

2 cups cooked rice
1 large carrot, shredded
1 large onion, finely chopped
2 celery stalks, finely
    chopped
1 pound lean ground beef
2 eggs, beaten
¼ cup skim milk
2 tablespoons tamari or soy
    sauce
½ teaspoon basil
¼ teaspoon thyme
    dash of marjoram
⅔ cup tomato paste
1 tablespoon water

In a large mixing bowl, combine the rice, carrots, onions, celery, beef, eggs, milk, tamari, basil, thyme, and marjoram. Stir in ½ cup of the tomato paste.

Pack the meatloaf in a 2-quart ovenproof casserole. Mix the remaining tomato paste with the water and spread over the loaf. Bake at 350° for about 1 hour.

To serve, cut like a cake.

Poultry and Game

Think of diet food and you think of chicken—pale, insipid, plain-on-the-plate chicken breast. Sure, chicken is a great diet food—because lean, skinless, light meat chicken is low in calories. Ounce for ounce, chicken contains as much protein, but far less fat, than red meats. It is for this reason that poultry and reducing diets go hand in hand. However, the range of poultry dishes that can be enjoyed by a dieter is far greater than ordinary chicken breast. The possibilities that can be spun from chicken and its cousins are almost endless.

In this chapter, I will give you a taste of the culinary creations that can be savored when poultry is handled with imagination and an eye on the calorie counter. When you add turkey, pheasant, Cornish game hens, quail, and even duck to your repertoire you come up with an exciting balance of flavor, nutrition, and eye-pleasing appearance that will bump the blahs right out of the poultry picture.

Let's not forget turkey for your diet list. In fact when it comes to poultry, turkey beats out chicken as a low-calorie food. And don't worry about the size of the bird. If the family is small, just buy the turkey breast (it's the part of the bird that's lowest in calories anyway). Turkey breast is increasingly available and can be stuffed as easily as a large bird. Turkey breast fillet can be substituted for boned chicken breasts in any recipe. Two special offerings, *Turkey Stroganoff* and *Turkey Fillets Provençal,* make delicious use of turkey breast fillets.

Rabbit is becoming more popular and rivals chicken in being high in protein and low in fat. Rabbit can be substituted in most recipes calling for chicken, especially highly flavored dishes, such as curries.

Duck, you say? That's right. You can even fit duck into the Lose Weight Naturally system. For it's not the meat on the duck that gives the poor bird its bad name, it's the skin. So we'll just cook the duck without the skin. And in answer to your next question—no, it will not be dry and tasteless. In fact, you might want to serve *Ragout of Duck* at your next dinner party, proving to your guests that changing eating habits on the favorable side of the calorie scale can be far from boring.

Yes, this is a section that you'll want to turn to when you're having guests and you don't want to let anyone know that you're dieting. *Pecan-Stuffed Quail* makes an impressive main course. Filled with bran-rich brown rice, it is a delicate blend of minced vegetables and just enough pecans to give it that nutty flavor. *Roast Pheasant with Apples* is yet another elegant choice for those times you want to treat yourself thin and others, too.

156

Poached Chicken
Ericana ★ ★ ★

Makes 4 servings

1½	cups water
½	cup lemon juice
1	bay leaf
1	clove garlic, minced
2	whole chicken breasts, halved, boned, and skinned
¾	cup coarsely chopped tomatoes
1	teaspoon chopped chives
1	teaspoon rosemary, crumbled

In a shallow 10-inch pan, combine the water, lemon juice, bay leaf, garlic, and chicken and simmer, covered, over low heat. Allow the liquid to come to a boil, then simmer gently. Total cooking time, from when the chicken is first placed in the pan, should be 25 minutes. Remove chicken and keep warm. Strain poaching liquid.

In a small saucepan, place 2 tablespoons poaching liquid, tomatoes, chives, and rosemary. Bring to a simmer and cook for 5 minutes. Serve over chicken.

157

Elegance on a calorie budget? Why not! *Pecan-Stuffed Quail*, *Broccoli a la Grecque*, and *Tomatoes Oregano* fill the bill quite nicely.

158

On those times when the occasion calls for something special, serve this Treat Yourself Thin meal: *Roast Turkey Breast* with *Barley Stuffing*, *Puree of Sweet Potatoes*, *Brussels Sprouts with Chestnuts and Oranges*, and *Apple Crisp*.

South India Poached Chicken ★ ★ ★

This sauce is good on both hot and cold chicken.

Makes 4 servings

1 cup water
1 cup rice vinegar
2 ¼-inch slices ginger
1 clove garlic, minced
2 whole chicken breasts, halved, boned, and skinned
½ cup low-fat yogurt
1 tablespoon minced orange rind

In a shallow 10-inch pan, combine the water, vinegar, 1 piece of ginger, garlic, and chicken and simmer, covered, over low heat. Allow the liquid to come to a boil then simmer gently. Total cooking time from when chicken is placed in the pan is 25 minutes. Remove chicken and keep warm. Strain poaching liquid.

In a small bowl, combine 2 tablespoons poaching liquid, the yogurt, and orange rind. Mince the remaining ginger and stir into the sauce. Serve over chicken.

Chestnut-Stuffed Chicken Breasts ★ ★

An autumn treat baked in apple cider.

Makes 4 servings

1 cup boiled chestnuts
¼ cup currants
¼ cup minced tart apples pinch of nutmeg
2 whole chicken breasts, halved, boned, and skinned
2 teaspoons butter
1 teaspoon paprika
1 cup apple cider

In a medium-size mixing bowl, combine the chestnuts, currants, apples, and nutmeg.

Flatten each piece of chicken by placing it between 2 sheets of waxed paper and pounding with a mallet or the flat side of a meat cleaver until ¼ inch thick.

Roll one-fourth of the stuffing in each chicken piece.

Place the stuffed chicken, seam side down, in a shallow 8 × 8-inch baking dish. Mix butter and paprika and drizzle over chicken. Add the apple cider to the dish. Cover tightly with foil and bake at 350° for 30 minutes. Remove foil, baste, and bake for another 30 minutes, basting 2 or 3 more times.

Chicken and Apricot Stir-Fry ★ ★ ★

Makes 4 servings

1   clove garlic
2   whole chicken breasts, boned, skinned, and cubed
3   fresh apricots, pitted and sliced
2   tablespoons chopped scallions
3   tablespoons orange juice
1   tablespoon tamari or soy sauce
1   teaspoon cornstarch
¼   teaspoon grated fresh ginger

Coat a wok or 10-inch skillet with no-stick spray and toss the garlic on medium-high heat for 30 seconds. Remove garlic, add chicken, and stir-fry for 5 minutes. Add apricots and scallions and stir-fry for one minute longer. Remove chicken and apricots.

In a small bowl, combine orange juice, tamari, cornstarch, and ginger. Add to wok and cook briskly, stirring, until thick and shiny (no more than 30 seconds). Turn off heat, add chicken and apricots to sauce, and toss. Serve immediately.

Chicken-Stuffed Tofu with Mushroom Sauce ★ ★ ★

This dish has a rich flavor and is naturally low in saturated fats.

Makes 4 servings

TOFU
1   pound tofu
1   scallion, chopped
1   tablespoon tamari or soy sauce
2   tablespoons rice vinegar
¼   cup apple juice
2   cloves garlic

To make the tofu: Cut the tofu into 4 triangles. Scoop out 1 to 2 tablespoons from the center of each triangle.

In a small bowl, combine the scallions, tamari, vinegar, and apple juice. Add the garlic by pushing it through a garlic press into the bowl and combine.

Place the tofu triangles in a single layer in a 1-quart casserole. Pour the marinade over the tofu, cover, and refrigerate for 8 hours or overnight.

STUFFING
¼ pound chicken breast
   meat, minced
1 scallion, minced
1 teaspoon oriental sesame
   oil
1 teaspoon tamari or soy
   sauce
½ teaspoon minced fresh
   ginger
1 teaspoon toasted sesame
   seeds
3 water chestnuts, diced
1 clove garlic, minced

SAUCE
1 teaspoon oriental sesame
   oil
½ cup sliced mushrooms
1 tablespoon cornstarch
2 teaspoons tamari or soy
   sauce
1 cup water
½ teaspoon honey
1 teaspoon currant or
   apricot jelly
1½ teaspoons minced fresh
   ginger
2 tablespoons diced bamboo
   shoots

To make the stuffing: In a small bowl, combine the chicken, scallions, oil, tamari, ginger, sesame seeds, water chestnuts, and garlic. Remove tofu from marinade and gently fill each piece with the chicken mixture.

Place a steaming rack in a large wok or pot and add enough water to come just below the rack. Place the casserole on the rack, cover the wok or pot, and bring the water to a boil. Steam until the chicken is cooked and the tofu is steaming, about 30 minutes.

To make the sauce: While the tofu cooks, heat the oil in a medium-size skillet. Add the mushrooms and sauté until tender, about 5 minutes.

In a small bowl, combine the cornstarch and tamari to form a paste. Slowly whisk in the water and add to the mushrooms. Stirring constantly, add the honey, jelly, ginger, and bamboo shoots. Cook until syrupy, about 4 to 5 minutes. Pour over the stuffed tofu and serve.

161

Chicken Curry Supreme ★ ★

Makes 4 servings

1   large onion, chopped
4   cups *Chicken Stock*
2   whole chicken breasts, halved, boned, and skinned
1½–2   tablespoons curry powder (preferably Madras)
1   tablespoon minced fresh ginger
¼   cup raisins
2   tablespoons ground almonds
1   small banana, diced

Cook the onions in 1 tablespoon of stock in a large skillet or saucepan over low heat. When the onions are quite soft, remove from the pan and set aside.

Cut the chicken into bite-size pieces. Add 1 tablespoon of stock to the pan and turn the heat up to medium high. Sauté the chicken pieces quickly, just until they are cooked through. Remove the chicken from the pan and set aside.

Return the onions to the pan. Stir in the curry and remaining stock. Add the ginger, then, over high heat, rapidly boil down the stock until it is reduced almost by half. This should take about 20 minutes. Stir in the raisins, almonds, and bananas. Simmer together for about 5 minutes. Stir in the chicken and heat through for a minute or so before serving.

NOTE: Because the sauce is reduced, unsalted chicken stock is necessary. If you use canned stock, use half water, half stock.

162

Marinated Grilled Chicken with Tarragon ★ ★ ★

Makes 4 servings

2   whole chicken breasts, halved, boned, and skinned
½   cup tarragon vinegar
1   tablespoon grated onions
1½   teaspoons tarragon
2   teaspoons tamari or soy sauce
1   clove garlic

Flatten each piece of chicken by placing it between 2 sheets of waxed paper and pounding it with a mallet until ¼ to ½ inch thick.

Place the chicken pieces in an 8 × 8-inch baking dish.

In a small bowl, combine the vinegar, onions, tarragon, and tamari. Add the garlic by pushing it through a garlic press into the bowl and stir. Pour the marinade over the chicken, cover, and refrigerate for at least 2 hours, turning the chicken once or twice.

Grill or broil the chicken pieces until cooked through, about 20 to 30 minutes, brushing with additional marinade every 10 minutes as the chicken cooks.

Poached Chicken Dijonnaise ★ ★ ★

A cold dish, perfect for a summer luncheon or light dinner.

Makes 4 servings

2   cups *White Poultry Stock*
3   teaspoons tarragon
5   peppercorns
2   whole chicken breasts, halved, boned, and skinned
½   cup low-fat cottage cheese, whipped
1   teaspoon Dijon mustard

In a shallow 10-inch pan, combine the stock, 2 teaspoons of tarragon, peppercorns, and the chicken and simmer, covered, over low heat. Allow the liquid to come to a boil, then simmer gently. Cooking time from when chicken is first placed in the pan should be 25 minutes. Remove chicken, cool, and refrigerate. Strain poaching liquid.

While chicken cools, whip together 1 tablespoon of the poaching liquid, the cottage cheese, mustard, and remaining tarragon. Serve over cold chicken.

Baked Chicken with Tomato Sauce ★ ★ ★

Fresh tomatoes give a fine flavor to the sauce. This is low enough in calories to serve over spaghetti (½ cup per serving) for a complete Weight Loss dinner.

Makes 4 servings

2   whole chicken breasts, halved and skinned
4   cups chopped tomatoes
1   small onion, coarsely chopped
2   tablespoons tomato paste
½   sweet red pepper, coarsely chopped
1   teaspoon basil
1   teaspoon thyme
½   teaspoon oregano
2   cloves garlic, minced
¼   teaspoon crushed red pepper (optional)

Arrange the chicken in the bottom of a large oven-proof casserole coated with no-stick spray.

Place the tomatoes, onions, red peppers, tomato paste, basil, thyme, oregano, garlic, and crushed red pepper in a blender. Process on medium speed until smooth.

Pour the tomato sauce over the chicken. Cover and bake at 350° for 30 minutes. Remove the cover and continue baking for another 10 minutes.

Chicken Italian Style ★ ★ ★

Makes 4 servings

2 whole chicken breasts, halved, boned, and skinned
1 tablespoon olive oil
½ pound mushrooms, sliced
1 medium-size onion, chopped
2 sweet red peppers, chopped
2 cloves garlic
5 tomatoes, seeded and chopped
⅓ cup packed parsley sprigs
½ teaspoon marjoram
¼ teaspoon thyme
¼ teaspoon oregano

Brown the chicken in the oil in a large skillet, turning to cook both sides. Remove from the pan and set aside.

Place the mushrooms, onions, and peppers in the skillet and cook over low to medium heat for 3 minutes. Add the garlic by pushing it through a garlic press into the skillet and stir.

Add the tomatoes, parsley, marjoram, thyme, and oregano.

Return the chicken to the pan and spoon the vegetables over the chicken as much as possible. Cover and simmer until the chicken is tender, about 25 minutes.

To serve, transfer the chicken to a serving plate and spoon the vegetables on top. Keep warm. If there is a lot of liquid in the pan, quickly boil down over high heat, uncovered, until only ¼ cup or less remains. Spoon this over the chicken and vegetables.

★ ★ *VARIATION: In place of the tomatoes, substitute 1 cup* Chicken Stock *mixed with ⅔ cup tomato paste.*

164

Chicken Sauté with Vegetables ★ ★ ★

Makes 4 servings

2 whole chicken breasts, halved, boned, and skinned
1 egg white
1 tablespoon cornstarch
2 tablespoons *Chicken Stock*
½ cup sliced mushrooms
2 small zucchini, cut into 2-inch strips

Flatten each piece of chicken by placing it between 2 sheets of waxed paper and pounding it with a mallet until about ¼ inch thick. Cut the chicken into bite-size pieces.

Place the chicken in a medium-size mixing bowl. Add the egg white and stir until the chicken is coated. Stir in the cornstarch thoroughly. Let the chicken sit for about 10 minutes, then place in a large heated skillet with the stock. Sauté, stirring occasionally, just until the chicken is opaque throughout.

6 scallions, cut into 2-inch strips
1 large tomato, chopped
2 teaspoons tamari or soy sauce

Remove the chicken from the skillet using a slotted spoon. Add the mushrooms to the pan and stir over low to medium heat until the mushrooms begin to release their liquid. Add the zucchini, scallions, tomatoes, and tamari and cook over medium heat, stirring frequently, until the vegetables are crisp-tender. Stir in the chicken and heat through before serving.

Chicken Baked with Lemon-Sesame Sauce ★ ★ ★

Makes 4 servings

1 lemon
1 tablespoon minced fresh ginger
1 clove garlic, minced
2 tablespoons tahini (sesame butter)
2 tablespoons water
1 teaspoon tamari or soy sauce
½ Spanish onion, sliced and separated into rings
4 small carrots, cut diagonally into thin slices
2 whole chicken breasts, halved, boned, and skinned
2 tablespoons *Chicken Stock* or water
4 scallions, chopped
    minced fresh mint or parsley (garnish)

Carefully remove the rind from the lemon. Reserve the lemon and cut the rind into very thin, 1-inch strips. Place the strips in a small saucepan with about 1 inch of boiling water. Boil for 5 minutes, drain, and rinse the rind under cold water until cool.

Coat a small skillet with no-stick spray. Add the ginger. Cook over medium heat, stirring constantly, until the ginger is slightly golden. Remove from the heat and stir in the garlic.

Juice the lemon. Add the lemon juice, cooked lemon rind, tahini, water, and tamari to the skillet with the ginger. Stir to combine.

Place the onions in the bottom of a shallow 8 × 8-inch baking dish. Arrange the carrots over the onions.

Flatten each chicken piece by placing it between 2 sheets of waxed paper and pounding with a mallet until about ¼ inch thick. Arrange over the carrots in the baking dish. Add the stock. Spread the sauce over the chicken. Sprinkle with the scallions. Cover tightly with foil and bake at 350° for 30 to 40 minutes. Garnish with mint or parsley, if desired. Serve hot.

165

Chicken Enchiladas ★

Makes 4 servings

1   whole chicken breast,
      halved and skinned
1   cup chopped onions
1   egg
1   tablespoon water
1   tablespoon minced fresh
      coriander (optional)
2   cups red chili sauce
8   *Corn Tortillas*
¼   cup shredded Monterey
      Jack cheese
½   cup low-fat yogurt
½   cup chopped scallions

Place the chicken in a small saucepan with enough water to cover. Bring just to a boil, then reduce heat to simmer, partially cover the pan, and poach the chicken until tender, about 25 minutes.

Meanwhile, heat a medium-size skillet over low to medium heat. Add the onions and cook, stirring, until they are translucent. Turn the heat to low and let the onions cook for another 5 minutes or until tender. (Do not brown. Add a few drops of water, if necessary, to prevent scorching.) When the onions are tender, beat the egg with the tablespoon of water and the coriander and add to the skillet. Stir occasionally and remove from heat when the egg is set.

When the chicken is tender, remove from the heat and drain. When cool enough to handle, remove the bones and cube the meat. Combine the chicken with the onion and egg mixture.

To assemble the casserole, place 1 cup of the red chili sauce in a small skillet just large enough to hold a tortilla. Bring the sauce to a boil, then reduce heat, and as the sauce simmers, dip a tortilla into the sauce just long enough to soften the tortilla. Roll one-eighth of the chicken mixture in the tortilla, then place, seam side down, in a 9 × 13-inch baking dish. Repeat with the remaining tortillas and filling, placing the enchiladas side-by-side in the baking dish.

Pour all of the remaining sauce over the enchiladas and sprinkle with the cheese. Cover loosely with foil and bake at 350° for 30 minutes. Remove from the oven and spoon the yogurt down the center of the row of enchiladas. Sprinkle the chopped scallions on top of the yogurt. Serve hot.

Chicken Lasagna ★

You can bake the lasagna one day, refrigerate it overnight, and warm it for dinner the next day. It tastes even better this way because the flavors have time to blend.

Makes 4 servings

1   medium-size onion,
      minced
2   medium-size carrots, finely
      diced
1   green pepper, minced
2   cloves garlic, minced
3   cups tomato puree
½   teaspoon basil
½   teaspoon thyme
1   bay leaf
½   teaspoon black pepper
¼   cup coarsely chopped
      Italian parsley
2   chicken breasts, halved,
      boned, and skinned
1   medium-size eggplant, cut
      lengthwise into ¼-inch
      slices
1   cup low-fat cottage cheese
      dash of black pepper
½   teaspoon oregano
¼   cup shredded part-skim
      mozzarella cheese

Place the onions, carrots, peppers, and garlic in a 2-quart saucepan with ¼ cup of the tomato puree. Steam-sauté the vegetables in the puree over medium-high heat until they are wilted, about 10 minutes. Add the remaining tomato puree, the basil, thyme, bay leaf, pepper, and parsley and simmer for 30 minutes. Remove the bay leaf.

Lay one piece of chicken on a cutting board and, using a thin, sharp knife, cut it in half horizontally, as if you were cutting a sandwich roll, leaving the top and bottom attached to each other by a thin, uncut strip. Repeat with the remaining chicken.

Lay one of the chicken pieces on the board and open it up like a book. Cover with a sheet of waxed paper and pound it with the bottom of a heavy skillet until it is very thin. Repeat with the remaining chicken.

Place the chicken on a lightly oiled baking sheet and broil for 2 minutes on each side. Set aside.

Broil the eggplant until lightly browned, about 2 to 3 minutes on each side. Set aside.

Mix the cottage cheese, dash of pepper, and oregano.

In a 9 × 9-inch baking pan, begin layering the lasagna by lining the bottom with ½ of the eggplant slices. Top with a small amount of the sauce. Layer half of the chicken breasts, more sauce, the cottage cheese mixture, and top with a thin layer of sauce. Layer the remaining eggplant, a little sauce, the remaining chicken, and the remaining sauce. Top with the mozzarella. Cover with aluminum foil and bake at 375° for 25 minutes.

167

Chicken Stew ★ ★ ★

Makes 4 servings

1   whole chicken breast, halved, boned, and skinned
1   tablespoon olive oil
2   medium-size onions, chopped
½   cup sliced mushrooms
6   small carrots, thickly sliced
1   large zucchini, halved and sliced
3   tomatoes, peeled and halved
3   cups *Chicken Stock*
2   tablespoons tamari or soy sauce
    dash of basil
    dash of marjoram
    dash of paprika
    minced fresh parsley (garnish)

Cut the chicken into bite-size pieces. Brown briefly in a large skillet coated with no-stick spray. Remove with a slotted spoon and set aside.

Heat the oil in the skillet over medium heat and add the onions. Cook, stirring, until the onions begin to turn translucent. Add the mushrooms and cook, stirring occasionally, until the mushrooms give up their liquid and the liquid evaporates.

Return the chicken to the pan. Add the carrots, zucchini, tomatoes, stock, tamari, basil, marjoram, and paprika. Bring to a boil, then reduce heat and simmer for 45 minutes. Serve hot, garnished with the minced parsley, if desired.

Chicken and Leek Tart ★

Makes 8 servings

CRUST

4   tablespoons butter
1   cup whole wheat flour
½   cup low-fat cottage cheese

To make the crust: Cut the butter into the flour with a pastry blender. Place the cottage cheese in a blender and process on low speed until smooth, scraping down the sides of the container as necessary.

FILLING

3	tablespoons *Chicken Stock*
3	cups chopped leeks
2	tablespoons whole wheat flour
1¾	cups milk
½	cup peas
1½	cups chopped, cooked chicken
2	eggs, beaten
½	teaspoon marjoram
½	teaspoon basil
	dash of nutmeg
2	tablespoons wheat germ
	dill or tarragon sprigs (garnish)

Using a fork, stir the cottage cheese into the butter-flour mixture just until combined. Press the dough into the bottom and up the sides of a 9-inch pie plate coated with no-stick spray. (The dough can also be chilled, then rolled out to fit the pie plate.)

To make the filling: Heat the stock in a large skillet over medium heat for about 1 minute. Stir in the leeks and cook over low heat, stirring frequently, until tender and translucent. Do not brown.

Stir in the flour until the leeks are coated. Add the milk, stir well, then stir in the peas. Simmer until the sauce thickens.

Remove the skillet from the heat. Stir in the cooked chicken, then rapidly beat in the eggs. Stir in the marjoram, basil, and nutmeg.

Pour the chicken–leek mixture into the crust and sprinkle with the wheat germ. Bake at 350° for about 30 minutes or until the tart is puffed, golden, and cooked through. Let the tart rest for 10 minutes before cutting. Garnish with dill or tarragon, if desired.

169

Chicken Pilaf ★

A delicious dish with an accent of India.

Makes 4 servings

1	tablespoon sunflower oil
1	small onion, minced
1	teaspoon mustard seeds
1	cup brown rice
4	chicken thighs, skinned
2	cups *Chicken Stock*
½	teaspoon ground coriander
	dash of cayenne pepper
2	cloves garlic
1	cup peas

Place the oil and onions in a large, heavy saucepan. Cook over low heat, stirring, until the onions are translucent. Add the mustard seeds and the brown rice. Stir for 4 to 5 minutes.

Add the chicken, stock, coriander, and cayenne. Add the garlic by pushing it through a garlic press into the pan. Bring to a boil, simmer for 5 minutes, then cover tightly and reduce heat to very low. Cook for 40 minutes. Quickly add the peas, cover the pan, and cook for another 5 minutes. Remove from heat and set aside, covered, for 5 minutes before serving.

NOTE: Large peas may take a little longer to cook. They can be boiled separately in a small saucepan and added just before serving. (Don't overcook peas. Remove from boiling water while they're still plump.)

Skillet Chicken Livers with Cherry Tomatoes ★ ★ ★

The cherry tomatoes add color and flavor to this dish.

Makes 4 servings

6	scallions, white part only, chopped
1	tablespoon olive oil
1	pound mushrooms, quartered
¼	teaspoon thyme
	dash of nutmeg
1	pound chicken livers, halved
2	teaspoons tamari or soy sauce
2	cups cherry tomatoes
2	tablespoons minced fresh parsley

Place the scallions in a large skillet with half of the oil. Cook over low heat until the scallions are translucent. Add the remaining oil and the mushrooms. Stir over low to medium heat until the mushrooms begin to give up their liquid. Add the thyme and nutmeg. Cover the pan and turn heat to low. Cook for 5 minutes.

Add the chicken livers and tamari and stir. Cover and cook, stirring occasionally, just until the livers are slightly pink inside, about 5 minutes. Do not overcook.

Place the cherry tomatoes on top of the livers. Cover the pan and cook on low heat just until tomatoes are heated through. Sprinkle with minced fresh parsley and serve right from the skillet.

170

Roast Turkey Breast ★ ★ ★

Makes 10 servings

3½–4	pound turkey breast
1	tablespoon Dijon mustard
½	cup *Chicken Stock*
	Italian Parsley sprigs (garnish)

Preheat oven to 450°. Rinse turkey and pat dry. Rub the skin with the mustard. Place on a rack in a roasting pan and place in the oven. Immediately turn heat down to 325°. After 15 minutes, baste the turkey with the chicken stock. Continue baking, basting occasionally, for another 1 to 1¼ hours or until golden, tender, and cooked through. Remove from oven, cover loosely with foil, and let stand for 10 minutes.

Slice the turkey and arrange on a platter garnished with parsley, if desired. Serve hot. To serve cold, allow the turkey to cool, then chill before slicing.

★ *VARIATION: Stuff with 3 to 4 cups of* Barley Stuffing *and proceed as above.*

Turkey Steaks ★ ★ ★

Makes 4 servings

1   pound boned, skinned
      turkey breast
1   tablespoon butter
2   cups sliced mushrooms
2   tablespoons *Chicken Stock*
1   teaspoon tamari or soy
      sauce
      minced fresh parsley
      (garnish)
      minced chives (garnish)

Cut the turkey breast into four serving pieces. Flatten each piece by placing it between two sheets of waxed paper and pounding with a mallet until about ¼ inch thick.

Melt the butter in a large skillet. Add the turkey and sauté for 5 to 7 minutes on each side. Remove from the pan and keep warm.

Add the mushrooms, stock, and tamari to the skillet. Cook until the mushrooms have released their liquid and most of the liquid in the pan has evaporated.

Spoon the mushrooms over the turkey steaks and garnish with minced parsley and chives, if desired.

Turkey Fillets Provençale ★ ★ ★

171

Makes 6 servings

1½   pounds boneless turkey
        breast fillets
  2   tablespoons whole wheat
        flour
  ¼   teaspoon thyme
  2   tablespoons *Chicken Stock*
  1   medium-size onion,
        chopped
  1   cup sliced mushrooms
  2   large tomatoes, chopped
  ¼   cup minced fresh parsley
  2   teaspoons tamari or soy
        sauce
  1   teaspoon thyme
  1   teaspoon basil
  2   cloves garlic
  2   cups hot cooked rice

Flatten the turkey fillets by placing them between two sheets of waxed paper and pounding with a mallet until about ¼ inch thick. Cut into serving-size pieces, allowing 2 pieces per person. Combine the flour and thyme and dredge the fillets in the mixture.

Heat the stock in a large skillet and add the turkey fillets. Sauté briefly, turning once, then transfer to a 9 × 13-inch baking dish.

Place the onions and mushrooms in the skillet, adding a few drops of stock, as needed, to prevent sticking. Cook over medium heat until the mushrooms begin to give up their liquid.

Add the tomatoes, parsley, tamari, thyme, and basil. Add the garlic by pushing it through a garlic press into the skillet and stir over medium heat until the mixture is heated through and most of the liquid has evaporated.

Spoon the vegetable mixture over the turkey, cover with foil, and bake at 350° for 40 minutes. Serve over rice.

Turkey Stroganoff ★ ★

Makes 6 servings

1½	pounds boneless turkey breast fillets
2	tablespoons whole wheat flour
2	tablespoons *Chicken Stock*
2	tablespoons minced shallots
1	pound mushrooms, sliced
3	tablespoons minced fresh parsley
2	teaspoons basil
1	large tomato, peeled, seeded, and chopped
¾	cup *Chicken Stock*
2	teaspoons tamari or soy sauce
1	clove garlic
¼	cup low-fat yogurt
2	cups hot cooked rice

Flatten the turkey breasts by placing them between two sheets of waxed paper and pounding with a mallet until about ¼ inch thick. Cut the turkey into bite-size pieces. Dredge the turkey in the flour.

Heat the two tablespoons of stock in a large skillet over medium heat. Stir in the shallots. When the shallots are translucent, add the turkey and brown lightly, turning frequently.

Add the mushrooms, parsley, basil, tomatoes, stock, and tamari, then push the garlic through a garlic press into the pan. Bring to a boil, then reduce heat, cover, and simmer for about 40 minutes, stirring occasionally. Remove from heat and gently stir in yogurt.

Place the rice on a serving platter. Spoon the turkey mixture over the rice and serve.

Curried Turkey on Toast ★ ★ ★

Makes 4 servings

2	tablespoons *Chicken Stock*
2	tablespoons whole wheat flour
1	teaspoon curry powder (preferably Madras)
1¼	cups skim milk
1	cup peas
1½	cups diced, cooked turkey
4	slices whole-grain bread, toasted

Place the stock, flour, and curry in a large skillet and cook over low heat, stirring occasionally, for about 2 minutes.

Add the milk and stir until combined. Add the peas and bring to a boil. Reduce heat and simmer about 2 minutes. Stir in the turkey, heat through, and serve over the toast.

★ ★ *VARIATION: Try serving the curried turkey on whole wheat pasta shells or other whole-grain pasta instead of toast.*

172

Turkey Cabbage Rolls ★ ★ ★

Makes 6 servings

1   medium-size head
      cabbage
1   pound ground turkey
1¼ cups cooked rice
½   cup chopped onions
½   cup applesauce
2   eggs, beaten
2   tablespoons chopped dates
1   teaspoon curry powder
      (preferably Madras)
1   cup *Chicken Stock*

Bring a large pot of water to a boil. Add the head of cabbage and boil until the leaves separate easily, about 20 to 30 minutes. Drain.

Separate 12 leaves from the cabbage. Remove the hard center vein, part way up the leaf.

Combine the turkey, rice, onions, applesauce, eggs, dates, and curry. Divide the filling among the 12 cabbage leaves and roll up each leaf from the bottom.

Place the cabbage rolls seam side down in a single layer in a shallow baking dish coated with no-stick spray. Pour the stock over the rolls and cover the dish with foil.

Bake at 325° for 1¼ hours or until the cabbage rolls are quite tender. Place on a serving plate, baste with pan juices, and serve.

173

Turkey Livers with Red Pepper and Raisins ★ ★ ★

Makes 6 servings

1   large onion, cut into rings
1   large sweet red pepper,
      cut into strips
2   tablespoons *Chicken Stock*
1½ pounds turkey livers
½   cup raisins
¼   cup apple cider
      kale leaves (garnish)
      cherry tomatoes (garnish)

Place the onions and peppers in a large skillet with the chicken stock. Cook over medium heat, stirring often, until the onions are translucent and the peppers begin to get tender.

Add the livers and raisins and cook, stirring occasionally, until the livers are browned. Add the cider and stir up any bits of vegetables or meat from the bottom of the pan. Cover and steam over low to medium heat until the livers are just done (still a bit pink inside), about 5 minutes. Serve hot, garnished with kale and cherry tomatoes, if desired.

★ ★ ★ *VARIATION: You can substitute chicken livers for the turkey livers.*

Grilled Rock Cornish Game Hens ★ ★

Makes 4 servings

2 Rock Cornish game hens, halved
2 tablespoons olive oil
½ cup orange juice or apple juice
½ cup lemon juice
¼ cup water
⅓ cup chopped onions
½ teaspoon rosemary, crumbled
½ teaspoon thyme
1 clove garlic
1 bunch parsley (garnish)

Place the game hens in a shallow roasting pan. Combine the oil, juices, water, onions, rosemary, and thyme in a small bowl and add the garlic by pushing it through a garlic press into the bowl. Pour over the hens. Cover and marinate in the refrigerator for 8 to 12 hours, turning once or twice.

Drain the hens and place on a grill or under a broiler, keeping the meat far enough away that it will cook slowly and not burn. When the meat is tender and cooked through, about 40 minutes, remove skin and place on a large serving plate garnished liberally with parsley, if desired.

174

Pecan-Stuffed Quail ★

Makes 6 servings

12 boneless quail, skin removed
2 tablespoons *Chicken Stock*
1 tablespoon minced shallots
½ cup shredded carrots
¼ cup minced celery
1½ cups minced mushrooms
dash of tarragon
dash of crumbled rosemary
1¾ cups cooked rice

Remove any loose, small bones from the inside of the quail. Sew the bottom of the birds closed with fine, white string or close with toothpicks. Cross the legs and tie them together. Set aside.

Place 2 tablespoons of the stock in a large skillet and set over medium heat. Stir in the shallots, carrots, and celery. Cook for about 4 minutes, stirring frequently. Add the mushrooms, tarragon, and rosemary and cook until the mushrooms have released their liquid and the liquid has evaporated.

Add the rice and pecans to the skillet and stir until combined. (Let the stuffing cool, then chill before filling the quail if they are not to be baked immediately.)

¼ cup chopped pecans
1 teaspon Dijon mustard
½ cup *Chicken Stock*
   Italian parsley sprigs
   (garnish)

Stuff the quail through the neck opening. Fold the neck skin underneath and hold in place with a small skewer or toothpick or sew closed. Any remaining stuffing can be baked separately in a small casserole. Preheat the oven to 450°.

Rub the quail with mustard, then place them in a shallow baking dish and place in the oven. Bake for 5 minutes then reduce the heat to 350°. Baste with rest of the chicken stock and bake about 15 to 20 minutes more or until the birds are golden brown. Remove the string, toothpicks, or skewers. Serve garnished with parsley, if desired.

Garlic Sausage Patties ★ ★ ★

Makes 8 servings

1½ pounds ground turkey
2 egg whites
1 tablespoon sherry wine
   vinegar
2 tablespoons minced fresh
   parsley
1 tablespoon tamari or soy
   sauce
2 teaspoons oregano
1 teaspoon cumin seeds
½ teaspoon fennel seeds
½ teaspoon black pepper
¼ teaspoon marjoram
¼ teaspoon ground sage
   dash of thyme
   dash of cayenne pepper
3 cloves garlic

Place the turkey in a large mixing bowl. Add the egg whites, vinegar, parsley, tamari, oregano, cumin seeds, fennel seeds, pepper, marjoram, sage, thyme, and cayenne. Add the garlic by pushing it through a garlic press into the bowl. Mix until thoroughly combined.

Form the mixture into 16 patties. Brown the patties in a no-stick skillet. Serve hot.

★ ★ *VARIATION: Serve in a whole wheat pita with garnish of your choice.*

Roast Pheasant with Apples ★

Makes 8 servings

1   4-pound pheasant
1   clove
1   small onion
2   tablespoons *Chicken Stock*
4   cups diced apples
¼   cup apple cider
    parsley sprigs (garnish)
    small bunches of grapes
        (garnish)

Rinse the pheasant and pat dry. Tie the legs together and fold the wings behind the back. Press the clove into the onion and place in the body cavity.

In a large skillet, brown the pheasant in the stock. Place on top of the apples in a deep casserole. Add the cider and cover.

Bake covered at 325° for about 1½ hours or until the pheasant is tender and cooked through. To serve, place the apples on a serving platter and top with the pheasant. Garnish with parsley and grapes, if desired.

176

Braised Rabbit with Vegetables ★

Makes 8 servings

4   pounds rabbit, cut into
        serving pieces and fat
        removed
1   leek, thinly sliced
½   sweet red pepper, diced
½   green pepper, diced
2   cups sliced mushrooms
3   large tomatoes, peeled,
        seeded, and chopped
½   teaspoon basil
¼   teaspoon rosemary,
        crumbled
1   cup *Chicken Stock*
2   cups hot cooked rice

Place the rabbit in a deep ovenproof casserole. Cover with the leeks, red peppers, green peppers, mushrooms, tomatoes, basil, and rosemary and pour the chicken stock over all.

Cover the casserole and bake at 300° for 2 hours. To serve, place the rice on a serving plate. Cover with vegetables and rabbit.

Rabbit
with Fruit Sauce ★ ★

Makes 8 servings

 4 pounds rabbit, cut into
    serving pieces and fat
    removed
2½ cups rice vinegar
1½ cups water
 2 medium-size onions,
    sliced
 ½ cup chopped celery
1½ tablespoons mixed
    pickling spices
 3 bay leaves
    whole wheat flour
 2 tablespoons *Chicken Stock*
 ½ cup raisins
1½ cups apple cider
 2 cups chopped, peeled
    apples
 2 teaspoons arrowroot
 2 tablespoons cold water
    watercress sprigs (garnish)

Place the rabbit in a large bowl. Add the vinegar, 1½ cups water, onions, celery, pickling spices, and bay leaves. Cover the bowl and refrigerate for at least 24 hours, turning the rabbit pieces occasionally. Remove the rabbit from the marinade and dry with paper towels. Strain the marinade and reserve.

Dredge the rabbit pieces in flour, then brown in the stock in a large flameproof casserole. Add the strained marinade, the raisins, and enough cider to cover the rabbit. Bring to a boil. Remove from heat, cover the casserole, and bake at 350° for 1 hour.

Remove the rabbit and keep warm. Strain the raisins from the braising liquid and reserve the liquid. Press the raisins with the back of a spoon to release juices, then discard the raisins.

Place 1 cup of the braising liquid in a blender with the apples and process on medium speed until smooth. Place with the remaining liquid in a medium-size saucepan and bring to a rolling boil, uncovered.

When the sauce has been reduced by nearly half, stir together the arrowroot and 2 tablespoons water and add to the saucepan. Stir until the sauce is thickened.

Place the rabbit on a large serving platter and top with the sauce. Garnish with watercress, if desired.

NOTE: It is important to use rice vinegar, which is milder than white or cider vinegar, in this recipe. It's available in health food stores and oriental food shops.

177

Ragout of Duck ★ ★

Makes 6 servings

4½–5   pounds duck, cut into serving pieces
1   cup *Chicken Stock*
½   cup chopped onions
½   cup diced green peppers
¼   cup celery
1   clove garlic, minced
½   teaspoon thyme
2   cups stewed tomatoes
  minced fresh parsley (garnish)

Remove all of the skin and underlying fat from the duck.

Heat 1 tablespoon of the stock in a large skillet over medium heat. Add the duck and brown. Remove the duck, drain it, and place in a deep 2-quart oven-proof casserole. Set aside and keep warm.

Add the onions, peppers, and celery to the skillet and cook until the onions are translucent. Add the garlic and thyme and stir together. Add the tomatoes and remaining stock and bring to a boil, stirring often.

Pour the tomato mixture over the duck and cover the casserole. Bake at 350° for 2 hours.

Serve with sauce on the side. Garnish with parsley, if desired.

NOTE: The duck meat can be removed from the bones before serving, if desired. Keep the rest of the casserole hot while boning the duck.

Roast Sliced Duck with Pecan Stuffing ★

A fancy buffet offering. The duck is low in fat, since it's roasted without the skin.

Makes 6 servings

1   4½–5-pound duck
2   cups *Chicken Stock*
1   clove garlic, halved
1   ¼-inch slice fresh ginger
2   cups hot *Pecan Stuffing*
  Italian parsley sprigs (garnish)

Remove all of the skin and underlying fat from the duck. Wrap the duck in three layers of cheesecloth that have been rinsed and squeezed dry. Place the duck breast side up in a roasting pan and pour the stock over it.

Place the garlic and ginger in the roasting pan, along with the duck neck. Bake at 350° for 2 hours, basting frequently with the pan juices to keep the cheesecloth moist.

When the duck is done, slice the meat thinly and keep it warm. Mound the stuffing on a round serving plate and arrange the sliced duck around the outside edge. Garnish the plate with parsley, if desired, and serve.

Fish and Seafood

What could be more satisfying than a food that is naturally low in fat and calories and lends itself to an immeasurable variety of recipes? Fish and shellfish are some of those rare seductive foods that also boast a healthy profile. Fish and shellfish have about one-third the calories of red meat, much less cholesterol, but the same good quality protein, and noteworthy amounts of vitamins and minerals. Fish even has some extra goodness for your heart and blood. The polyunsaturates in many types of fish have been shown to lower cholesterol and prevent blood from clotting in the arteries.

If you, or someone you know, can't get worked up over the idea of a meal based on fish, I'm willing to bet it's because freshness, variety, or proper cooking have been lacking in the fish meals you've known. And yet, you can easily remedy all three of these factors.

Freshness is imperative with any type of fish. Make sure the fish you purchase has firm flesh and a nice sheen.

For variety you need only find a reputable fish marketer in your area. Tuna, salmon, haddock, cod, trout, mackerel, snapper, and bluefish are just a few of the common finfish generally available now in most places. All lend themselves to an exciting array of low-calorie recipes.

Next to freshness, proper cooking is probably most crucial to enjoying fish. Fish is cooked only to develop its flavor, so you absolutely *must* avoid overcooking it. Generally fish is done just when its translucency becomes opaque and its flesh is easily flaked with a fork. Cooking beyond this point will dry fish out or diminish its delicate flavor.

Both freshwater and saltwater fish are classified according to their fat content (which may also dictate the best cooking method). Haddock, scallops, and cod have some of the lowest fat-to-calorie ratios. You'll find plenty of recipes here using these fish. Salmon, swordfish, and mackerel have some of the highest ratios of fat to calories but are still leaner than meat. Baking, broiling, steaming, or poaching are all suitable cooking methods for developing optimal flavor in low-calorie fish dishes.

Poaching fish is an especially flavorful, as well as easy, way to turn any fish into a wonderful low-fat repast. Two poaching liquids are offered here—*Court Bouillon for Freshwater Fish* and *Court Bouillon for Saltwater Fish*. They're your invitation to be innovative. Poach your favorite type of fish in one of these bouillons, then turn to "Dressings, Spreads, and Sauces" and choose a mouth-watering topping to suit your taste.

With so much variety and creativity, you'll find it easy and enjoyable to make fish a regular part of your weight loss menu.

180

Court Bouillon for Freshwater Fish ★ ★ ★

Makes enough to poach 2 pounds of fish (approximately 3 cups)

3	cups water
1	cup vinegar
½	cup thinly sliced carrots
½	cup thinly sliced onions
2	bay leaves
10	peppercorns

Combine all of the ingredients in a stockpot and simmer for 30 minutes. Strain.

Court Bouillon for Saltwater Fish ★ ★ ★

Makes enough to poach 2 pounds of fish (approximately 3 cups)

½ cup thinly sliced leeks
½ cup thinly sliced onions
3 cups water
1 cup cider vinegar
2 bay leaves
5 peppercorns
1 clove garlic
1 tablespoon tarragon,
       wrapped in cheesecloth
       and tied with string
¼ cup parsley sprigs

Combine all of the ingredients in a stockpot and simmer for 30 minutes. Strain.

181

Poached River Trout ★ ★ ★

Good with *Lemon Thyme Sauce.*

Makes 4 servings

1 recipe *Court Bouillon for Freshwater Fish*
4 river trout (½ pound each), scaled and gutted

Bring the bouillon to a rapid boil. Add the trout and continue to cook rapidly for 10 minutes. Remove the trout from the liquid and serve.

★ ★ ★ *VARIATION:* Cold River Trout—*Prepare as above but allow the trout to cool in the court bouillon. Serve with* Horseradish Sauce.

Rainbow Trout with
Walnut Herb Stuffing ★

Makes 4 servings

2   tablespoons minced shallots
2   scallions, sliced diagonally
1   tablespoon *Sausalito Fish Stock*
½   cup chopped celery with leaves
2   tablespoons water
¼   cup watercress leaves, chopped
1   tablespoon minced fresh dill or 1½ teaspoons dried dill
1   cup whole wheat bread crumbs
3   tablespoons minced walnuts
2   teaspoons tamari or soy sauce
4   rainbow trout (½ pound each), scaled and gutted
    orange slices
    watercress sprigs (garnish)

Place the shallots and scallions in a medium-size skillet with the stock. Cook over low to medium heat until the scallions are wilted. Stir in the celery and add the water. Cover and steam for 1 to 2 minutes, then stir in the watercress. Remove from the heat when the watercress is wilted.

In a medium-size bowl, combine the dill, bread crumbs, walnuts, and celery mixture. Sprinkle with the tamari and toss lightly.

If you prefer to serve the fish with heads and tails on, stuff each fish with one-fourth of the filling. Place each fish on a lightly oiled piece of aluminum foil or kitchen parchment and fold over the ends to protect the head and tail from scorching.

Arrange some orange slices over the exposed middle section of each fish to prevent drying out in the oven. Bake at 350° just until the fish is opaque and cooked through, about 15 to 20 minutes. Carefully remove the fish to a serving platter, remove the orange slices, and garnish with watercress, if desired.

To serve the fish without heads or tails, open up the fish and place skin side down on a lightly oiled baking sheet. Arrange the stuffing over the fish and top with some orange slices to prevent the stuffing from drying out. Bake at 350° until the fish is opaque and cooked through, about 10 to 15 minutes. Remove orange slices and serve garnished with watercress, if desired.

NOTE: If orange slices have not dried out and become unattractive while baking, they can be served in place on the fish. Or remove the baked orange slices and replace with fresh slices.

Crispy Baked Whole Fish, Szechuan Style ★

Makes 4 servings

FISH

4	whole bass (½ pound each), scaled and gutted
2	cloves garlic, one minced and one halved
1	teaspoon minced fresh ginger
2	scallions, chopped
1	tablespoon butter, melted
2	tablespoons chopped bamboo shoots
1	teaspoon ground coriander
1	tablespoon oriental sesame oil

SAUCE

1	tablespoon cornstarch
2	teaspoons tamari or soy sauce
1	cup water
1	teaspoon currant or apricot jelly
½	teaspoon cayenne pepper
¼	teaspoon red pepper
2-3	tablespoons minced flakes fresh ginger
	dash of hot pepper sauce
2	tablespoons toasted sesame seeds
2	scallions, thinly sliced
1	medium-size carrot, cut into ⅛-inch slices
1	green pepper, cut into ¼-inch strips
¼	cup sliced mushrooms

To make the fish: Rinse the bass and pat them dry. Rub the outside of each fish with the halved garlic clove. Place the fish on a lightly greased rack in a broiler pan.

In a small bowl, combine the minced garlic, the ginger, scallions, butter, bamboo shoots, and coriander. Stuff each fish with one-fourth of the mixture. Brush the top side of the fish with half of the oil. Broil the fish close to the heat until browned, about 10 minutes. Gently turn the fish and brush with the remaining oil. Broil until browned, about 10 minutes.

To make the sauce: While the fish cooks, combine the cornstarch and tamari in a medium-size saucepan. Slowly whisk in the water. Place over medium-high heat. Add the jelly, cayenne, red pepper flakes, ginger, hot pepper sauce, and sesame seeds, whisking constantly. After about 4 to 5 minutes, when the sauce becomes syrupy, stir in the scallions, carrots, peppers, and mushrooms. Reduce the heat and cook, stirring frequently, for 4 minutes. Pour the sauce over the fish and serve.

183

Snapper Poached with Fennel ★ ★ ★

Makes 4 servings

4 cups water
1 tablespoon fennel seeds
   juice of 1 lemon
1 bay leaf
2 whole red snappers (1
      pound each), scaled
      and gutted

In a fish poacher or oval roaster, boil the water, fennel, lemon juice, and bay leaf. Add the fish, cover, and poach for 15 minutes. Remove from liquid and serve.

Dill-Stuffed Red Snapper ★ ★

Have the fish scaled, but do not remove the head and tail—it makes an impressive presentation at the table.

Makes 4 servings

1 large leek, chopped
1 stalk celery, chopped
1 tablespoon *Sausalito Fish
      Stock*
1 cup whole wheat bread
      crumbs
¼ cup minced fresh dill or
      2 tablespoons dried dill
1 whole red snapper (4
      pounds), scaled and
      gutted
1 lemon, halved
   parsley sprigs (garnish)
   scallions (garnish)
1 cherry tomato, halved
      (garnish)
   lemon slices (garnish)

Sauté the leeks and celery in the stock in a medium-size skillet over medium heat, until they are slightly tender. Stir in the bread crumbs and dill and remove from heat.

Rub the fish inside and out with one half of the lemon. Stuff the bread crumb mixture into the fish and close with metal skewers or sew closed. Place on a shallow, rectangular baking dish coated with no-stick spray. Wrap the tail of the fish with foil to prevent burning. Squeeze the remaining lemon half over the fish.

Bake at 350° for about 40 to 45 minutes or until the fish flakes easily when tested with a fork. Place the fish carefully on a serving platter. Surround generously with parsley and scallions, if desired. Place one of the cherry tomato halves over the fish eye. Garnish with lemon slices and serve.

Grilled Tuna Steaks ★ ★

Makes 4 servings

½   cup lime juice
1   clove garlic, minced
1   teaspoon marjoram
4   6-ounce tuna steaks, about
     ¾ inch thick each,
     skinned

Combine the lime juice, garlic, and marjoram in an 8 × 8-inch glass baking dish and add the tuna. Marinate, covered, for 3 hours. Grill over medium heat for 8 to 10 minutes on each side, basting frequently with the marinade.

Stuffed Flounder Fillets ★ ★ ★
A beautiful dish to serve to guests.

Makes 4 servings

1½ teaspoons safflower oil
8   large mushrooms, sliced
½   pound spinach, coarsely
     chopped
1   tablespoon finely
     crumbled feta cheese
4   flounder fillets (4 ounces
     each)
     watercress (garnish)
4   cherry tomatoes (garnish)

Place the oil in a medium-size skillet. Turn the heat on low. Add the mushrooms. Cook over low heat until any moisture the mushrooms release has evaporated. Stir the spinach into the pan and continue to cook, stirring constantly, until the spinach is wilted. Remove from heat. Sprinkle feta over the spinach mixture and stir together.

Place one-fourth of the filling on one end of each flounder fillet and roll up. Secure with a toothpick. Place the fillets in a small shallow baking dish or pie plate. Add 2 or 3 spoonfuls of water and cover loosely with foil.

Bake at 350° just until the fish is flaky and opaque throughout, about 30 to 40 minutes. To serve, place watercress on a serving platter. Arrange the rolled fish fillets on the bed of watercress. Place a cherry tomato on each toothpick, if desired.

Flounder Florentine ★ ★

Makes 6 servings

1	pound spinach
2	tablespoons butter
2	tablespoons whole wheat flour
1½	cups skim milk
½	cup shredded Cheddar cheese
1½	pounds flounder fillets
	juice of one lemon
	watercress sprigs (garnish)
	lemon wedges (garnish)

Rinse the spinach well and remove the stems. Cook in a large saucepan just in the water that clings to the leaves. When the spinach is wilted, set aside to cool. Mince the spinach when it is cool enough to handle.

Melt the butter in a medium-size skillet over medium heat. Stir in the flour and cook, stirring, for about 3 minutes. Add the milk all at once and stir until smooth. Add the cheese and stir until melted. Stir in the spinach and remove from the heat.

Sprinkle the skin side of the fish fillets with lemon juice. Roll up the fish fillets and place seam-side down in a 9 × 13-inch baking dish lightly coated with no-stick spray. Spoon the spinach-cheese sauce over the fish fillets. (Reheat sauce slightly if it becomes too stiff.) Bake at 350° for about 25 minutes or until the fish is flaky throughout. Garnish with watercress and lemon wedges, if desired.

Oven-Poached Swordfish ★ ★ ★

Makes 6 servings

2	pounds 1-inch-thick swordfish steak, cut into 6 pieces
1½	cups water
	juice of 1 lemon
1	bay leaf
2	teaspoons thyme
½	cup *Lemon Thyme Sauce*

Place the swordfish in a glass baking dish. Combine the water, lemon juice, bay leaf, and thyme and pour over the swordfish. Bake uncovered for 20 minutes. Remove fish from liquid and serve with the sauce.

Baja Baked Haddock ★ ★ ★

Makes 2 servings

2 medium-size tomatoes, coarsely chopped
1 small hot red pepper, seeded
2 teaspoons tamari or soy sauce
½ teaspoon oregano
   dash of ground cumin
2 cloves garlic
¾ pound haddock fillets
2 *Corn Tortillas*, steamed
   parsley sprigs (garnish)
   cherry tomatoes (garnish)

Place the tomatoes, pepper, tamari, oregano, and cumin in a blender. Push the garlic through a garlic press into the blender. Process on medium speed until smooth.

Place the haddock in an 8 × 8-inch baking dish coated with no-stick spray and top with the sauce. Bake at 375° for 20 minutes or just until the fish flakes when tested with a fork.

To serve, divide the fish fillets into 2 portions, place on steamed corn tortillas and spoon the sauce on top. Garnish with parsley and cherry tomatoes, if desired.

Haddock with Mushrooms ★ ★

Makes 2 servings

2 cups sliced mushrooms
2 teaspoons sunflower oil
⅔ pound haddock fillets
1 tablespoon butter, melted
6 cherry tomatoes (garnish)
   parsley sprigs (garnish)

In a medium-size skillet, cook the mushrooms over medium heat in the oil. As soon as the mushrooms give up their liquid, place the fish fillets in one layer over the mushrooms and cover the pan. Turn the heat to low, just so the liquid simmers. After 5 minutes, spoon the butter onto the haddock, cover, and simmer for another 5 minutes or until the fish is opaque throughout. Using a spatula, carefully remove the fish and mushrooms to a serving plate or individual plates. Garnish with cherry tomatoes and parsley, if desired.

Haddock with Cauliflower White Sauce ★ ★

Makes 4 servings

½ cup brown rice
1 medium-size onion, minced
1 cup *Chicken Stock*
 dash of saffron
2 cups cauliflower
⅓ cup skim milk
½ cup shredded Monterey Jack cheese
1 pound haddock fillets
¼ teaspoon paprika
 minced fresh parsley (garnish)

Place the rice, onions, stock, and saffron in a medium-size saucepan and bring to a boil. Let boil for 2 to 3 minutes, then cover and reduce heat to lowest point. Cook for 45 minutes, then turn off heat and let stand 10 minutes more.

Steam the cauliflower until tender, about 15 to 18 minutes. Place in a blender with the milk and process on medium speed until smooth. Stir in the cheese with a spatula, then process again on medium speed until the cheese is incorporated into the sauce.

Place the hot rice in the bottom of a 10-inch quiche plate. Arrange the haddock on top, then spread the cauliflower mixture in a thin layer over the entire casserole. Sprinkle with the paprika and bake at 350° for 30 minutes. Sprinkle with the parsley, if desired, and serve.

Sweet and Sour Fish Fillets ★ ★ ★

Makes 4 servings

½ cup water
¼ cup cider vinegar
1 teaspoon cornstarch
2 tablespoons honey
¼ teaspoon grated fresh ginger
2 cloves garlic
2 tablespoons tomato paste
1½ pounds cod fillets
2 scallions, thinly sliced lengthwise (garnish)

Place the water, vinegar, and cornstarch in a small saucepan and stir until the cornstarch is dissolved. Place the pan over low heat. Add the honey and ginger. Push the garlic through a garlic press into the pan. Stir in the tomato paste. Bring to a boil, reduce heat, and simmer for 10 minutes, stirring occasionally. Set aside and keep warm until ready to use.

While the sauce simmers, place enough water in a large skillet to measure ½ inch deep. Bring to a boil. Reduce heat to a slow simmer and gently add the cod.

Cover and poach the fish for about 8 to 10 minutes or until opaque throughout. Remove the fish to a warm serving platter and spoon the sweet and sour sauce on top. Garnish with scallions, if desired.

Portuguese Cod Stew ★ ★

Makes 6 servings

2	medium-size onions, chopped
1	tablespoon *Sausalito Fish Stock*
2	cloves garlic, minced
4	medium-size potatoes, cubed
1	32-ounce can tomatoes with juice
1	bay leaf
½	teaspoon marjoram
1	teaspoon minced fresh parsley
½	teaspoon thyme
1½	pounds cod fillets, cut into 2-inch pieces
2	cups broccoli florets

Place the onions and stock in a large, heavy-bottom saucepan. Cook, stirring often, over medium heat until the onions are translucent and limp, then add the garlic and potatoes. Continue to cook, stirring often, just until the potatoes begin to stick to the bottom of the pan. Remove from heat and add the tomatoes and juice, bay leaf, marjoram, parsley, and thyme.

Place over medium heat until it just reaches a boil, reduce heat, cover, and simmer for 15 minutes. Add the fish and broccoli. Cover and simmer an additional 10 to 15 minutes or until the broccoli is tender.

189

Halibut with Dilled Tomatoes ★ ★ ★

Makes 2 servings

⅔	pound halibut fillets
2	medium-size tomatoes, sliced
2	red onion slices
2	tablespoons minced fresh dill or 1 tablespoon dried dill
1	tablespoon lemon juice

Place the halibut in one layer in the bottom of a shallow 8 × 8-inch ovenproof casserole coated with no-stick spray.

Arrange the tomatoes over the halibut. Separate the onion slices into rings and arrange over the tomatoes. Sprinkle with the dill. Drizzle the lemon juice over the ingredients.

Bake at 350° for 12 to 15 minutes or until the fish is cooked throughout and flakes easily with a fork.

Bluefish with Scallions and Cherry Tomatoes ★ ★

Makes 2 servings

1	teaspoon olive oil
8	scallions, chopped
¾	pound bluefish fillets
¼	cup *Chicken Stock* or *Sausalito Fish Stock*
	dash of thyme
12	cherry tomatoes watercress (garnish)

Place the oil in a medium-size skillet, set over low heat, add the scallions, and cook just until translucent.

Place the bluefish on top of the scallions, add the stock and thyme, and cover. Poach the bluefish over low heat until it is nearly cooked throughout, about 15 minutes. Add the cherry tomatoes during the final 1 to 2 minutes of poaching. Serve immediately, garnished with watercress, if desired.

Ginger-Marinated Bluefish ★ ★ ★

190

Makes 4 servings

3	tablespoons grated fresh ginger
¾	cup low-fat yogurt
¼	cup lemon juice
2	teaspoons tamari or soy sauce
1	teaspoon ground coriander
½	teaspoon ground cumin
4	cloves garlic
1	pound bluefish fillets lemon slices (garnish) Italian parsley sprigs (garnish)

Place the ginger in a piece of cheesecloth and squeeze all of the liquid out of the ginger into a small bowl. Add the yogurt, lemon juice, tamari, coriander, and cumin. Push the garlic through a garlic press into the bowl and stir to combine.

Place about one-third of this mixture in the bottom of a large, shallow glass baking dish. Place the bluefish in one layer in the dish and spoon the remaining marinade over the fish. Cover with foil or plastic wrap and refrigerate overnight.

Remove the fish from the marinade and place under a broiler. Broil for about 4 to 5 minutes or just until the fish begins to flake when tested with a fork. Carefully turn the fish fillets with a spatula. Broil the other side for about 4 to 5 minutes or just until the fish is cooked throughout.

Place the fish on a warm serving platter. Garnish with lemon slices and parsley, if desired.

Outdoor cooking lends a whole new taste treat to light summer fare. *Grilled Tuna Steaks,*
Summer Vegetable Kabobs, and *Steamed Mussels* star in this al fresco meal. These mussels were made
on the stove and brought to the grill for a brief warming.

Cioppino (California fish stew) is the star of this waist watchers summertime fest. Serve it with
Mini French Loaves, Salade aux Epinards, and nonalcoholic beer.

Marinated Mako Shark Steaks ★ ★ ★

The oil-based marinade gives the steaks just enough moisture to prevent them from drying out. Make sure you drain them well before broiling.

Makes 4 servings

4	mako shark steaks (about 4-6 ounces each)
¼	cup safflower oil
¼	cup lemon juice
1	tablespoon tamari or soy sauce
2	cloves garlic, sliced
1	⅛-inch slice fresh ginger
1	teaspoon grated orange rind
½	teaspoon Dijon mustard
¼	teaspoon ground coriander

Place the shark steaks in a large shallow ovenproof casserole. Combine all of the remaining ingredients in a small bowl and pour over the steaks.

Cover the dish and refrigerate for several hours or overnight, turning once. Drain the steaks and grill or broil, basting frequently, until the shark is opaque and cooked throughout (approximately 6 minutes on each side, depending on thickness).

193

Herbed Baked Abalone ★ ★

Abalone can be obtained frozen in most areas.

Makes 2 servings

¼	cup cracker crumbs
2	tablespoons wheat germ
1	tablespoon bran
1	teaspoon basil
½	teaspoon thyme
⅔	pound abalone steaks
2	tablespoons skim milk
	lemon wedges (garnish)
	parsley sprigs (garnish)

In a shallow bowl, mix together the cracker crumbs, wheat germ, bran, basil, and thyme. Dip the abalone into the skim milk. Then dip into the crumb mixture until coated.

Arrange the abalone in a shallow baking dish or a baking sheet lightly coated with no-stick spray. Bake at 375° for about 15 minutes or until the abalone is opaque and baked through. Serve on a platter garnished with lemon wedges and parsley, if desired.

Pompano Fillets with Orange Wheat Pilaf ★

Makes 2 servings

1   small onion, chopped
1   tablespoon *Sausalito Fish Stock*
1   tablespoon orange juice
½   cup cooked wheat kernels
    dash of grated orange rind
    dash of marjoram
½   pound skinned pompano fillets
6   orange slices, halved
    minced scallions (garnish)

Place the onions in a medium-size skillet with the stock. Cook the onions slowly over low heat until they are tender. Add a few drops of water, if necessary, to prevent scorching.

Add the orange juice, wheat kernels, orange rind, and marjoram. Stir until the wheat kernels are heated through. Cover and keep warm while preparing the fish.

Place the pompano in a large skillet with enough boiling water to nearly cover. Arrange the orange slices over the fish.

With the water barely simmering and the pan partially covered, poach the fish until opaque throughout, about 8 to 10 minutes.

Place the wheat pilaf on a serving plate. Arrange the fish fillets over the pilaf and garnish with the scallions, if desired.

Poached Monkfish with Lemon Thyme Sauce ★ ★ ★

Makes 2 servings

¾   pound monkfish fillets, cut into 2-inch pieces
1   clove garlic
5   lemon slices
¼   cup *Lemon Thyme Sauce*
    dill sprigs (garnish)

Place the monkfish in a medium-size skillet that is filled ½ inch full with boiling water. Add the garlic clove and lemon slices. Cover and gently poach the fish over low heat until cooked through, about 10 minutes.

Drain the water from the monkfish and place under a broiler until the top is lightly browned. Serve with sauce and garnish with dill, if desired.

Stir-Fried Monkfish with Black Bean Sauce ★ ★

A Cantonese classic.

Makes 4 servings

2 tablespoons fermented black beans
2 cloves garlic, minced
¼ teaspoon minced fresh ginger
¼ cup lean ground pork
1 pound monkfish, cut into 1-inch pieces
1 cup *Chicken Stock*
1 egg, beaten
1 teaspoon tamari or soy sauce
2 cups shredded spinach

Rinse the beans to remove excess salt. Pat dry and mash together with the garlic and ginger.

Spray a wok or medium-size skillet with no-stick spray and stir-fry the pork for 1 minute over medium-high heat. Add the monkfish and stir-fry 3 to 5 minutes more. Add the stock and black bean mixture and quickly bring to a boil. Reduce heat and add the beaten egg and tamari. Serve immediately over shredded spinach (instead of rice).

NOTE: Fermented black beans can be purchased at oriental groceries.

195

Salmon Steaks with Curried Avocado Sauce ★ ★ ★

Serve as a cold luncheon dish in warm weather.

Makes 4 servings

4 salmon steaks (4–6 ounces each)
2 lemons, sliced
½ avocado
2 teaspoons minced fresh tarragon or 1 teaspoon dried tarragon
¼ cup low-fat yogurt
¼ teaspoon curry powder
tarragon sprigs (garnish)

In a saucepan filled ½ inch full with water, poach the salmon with 2 lemon slices over each steak until cooked through, about 15 minutes. Remove the lemon slices and place the salmon on a plate. Cool, then chill.

When ready to serve, place the avocado in a blender with the tarragon, yogurt, and curry. Process on low speed until smooth.

Place a broad ribbon of avocado sauce across each salmon steak. Garnish with fresh lemon slices and tarragon, if desired. Serve immediately.

Baked Salmon with Tangerines ★ ★

Makes 4 servings

2 coho salmon (about 8–10 ounces each), boned and gutted
1 cup peeled tangerine sections
¼ cup thinly sliced scallions
2 teaspoons butter, melted
½ teaspoon minced fresh ginger
½ teaspoon tamari or soy sauce
minced fresh parsley (garnish)

Remove the heads and skins from the salmon and place in a 9 × 13-inch baking dish coated with no-stick spray. Arrange the tangerine sections over the salmon.

Combine the scallions, butter, ginger, and tamari in a small bowl. Spoon over the salmon.

Cover the dish loosely with foil. Bake at 350° for 20 minutes or until the salmon is opaque throughout. Serve hot, sprinkled with parsley, if desired.

196

Pike with Herbed Stuffing ★ ★

Makes 4 servings

1 teaspoon corn oil
2 shallots, minced
2 tablespoons minced fresh parsley
1¼ cup whole wheat bread crumbs
¼ teaspoon marjoram
¼ teaspoon basil
dash of thyme
1 egg, beaten
1 whole pike (3 pounds)
¼ cup mushrooms, minced
¼ cup tiny shrimp, minced
1 tablespoon lemon juice

Place the oil in a medium-size skillet. Add the shallots and cook until they are slightly tender. Stir in the parsley and remove from the heat. Stir in the bread crumbs, marjoram, basil, thyme, and egg.

Stuff the pike with the bread crumb mixture and sew closed. Wrap in foil and bake at 350° for 40 minutes.

Place the mushrooms, shrimp, and lemon juice in a medium-size no-stick skillet over medium-high heat and cook for about 3 minutes. Pour over the pike and serve immediately.

Steamed Mussels ★ ★ ★

Makes 4 servings

4   pounds mussels
8   cups water
2   large leeks, chopped
1   large onion, chopped
4   stalks celery with leaves,
      chopped
¼   teaspoon thyme
1   bay leaf

Scrub the mussels well, and using kitchen shears, cut off the "beards." Place the mussels in a large pot with all of the remaining ingredients. Bring to a boil over high heat, then reduce heat to medium and cook until all of the mussels are open, about 10 minutes. Discard the bay leaf and any of the mussels that do not open.

Serve the mussels from a large crock, letting each person take his or her own. Provide plates for the shells.

★ *VARIATION: Add cooked mussels to 1½ cups of* Tomato Sauce *and serve over ½ pound of cooked pasta.*

Cioppino ★ ★ ★
A fish stew from California.

Makes 8 servings

1   large onion, chopped
4   scallions, chopped
3   cloves garlic, sliced
1   tablespoon corn oil
4   chopped canned plum
      tomatoes with juice
3   cups *Chicken Stock*
½   cup minced fresh parsley
1   bay leaf
¼   teaspoon thyme
    dash of crumbled rosemary
    dash of black pepper
    dash of cayenne pepper
1   pound large shrimp,
      shelled and deveined
16 littleneck clams
1   pound haddock fillets,
      cut into large bite-size
      pieces
    minced fresh parsley
      (garnish)

Place the onions, scallions, and garlic in a large, heavy-bottom saucepan with the oil and cook over medium heat until the onions are translucent. Add the tomatoes and juice, stock, parsley, bay leaf, thyme, rosemary, black pepper, and cayenne. Cover, bring to a boil, then reduce heat and simmer for 1 hour.

Add the shrimp, clams, and haddock to the pot and cook for an additional 8 minutes or until the shrimp are pink, the clams are open, and the fish is opaque. Remove the bay leaf and serve hot. Garnish with parsley, if desired.

★ ★ *VARIATION: Serve over 1 pound of cooked spaghetti.*

Salmon Patties ★ ★ ★

Makes 3 servings

1 small carrot, shredded
1 small onion, grated
1 tablespoon sunflower seeds,
      ground
1 egg, beaten
1 7-ounce can red salmon,
      drained and flaked
   dash of thyme
   dash of tarragon
½ teaspoon parsley
   lemon wedges (garnish)
   parsley sprigs (garnish)

Combine the carrots, onions, sunflower seeds, and egg in a medium-size mixing bowl.

Remove any skin from the salmon, crush the bones, and add along with the salmon meat, thyme, tarragon, and parsley to the mixture in the bowl. Stir until combined.

Form into patties. Cook on a lightly oiled skillet, turning once, or broil until lightly browned and cooked throughout, 5 to 7 minutes on each side. Serve garnished with lemon wedges and parsley, if desired.

198

Clams with Red Pepper Mayonnaise ★ ★ ★

Makes 4 servings

2 shallots
1 teaspoon tarragon
1 bay leaf
½ cup water
2 tablespoons lemon juice
2 cloves garlic
32 cherrystone clams,
      scrubbed
1 sweet red pepper
3 tablespoons *Lighten-Up
      Mayonnaise*
2 tablespoons chopped
      fresh parsley (garnish)

Combine the shallots, tarragon, bay leaf, water, and lemon juice in a large, heavy-bottom saucepan. Add the garlic by pushing it through a garlic press into the pan. Bring to a boil and add clams. Reduce heat and simmer, covered, until the clams are open, about 8 to 10 minutes. Remove clams from their shells and keep warm. Reserve half of the shells.

Roast the pepper under a broiler for 8 to 10 minutes. Put the pepper in a paper bag and allow it to sit for 30 minutes, then peel off the skin.

In a food processor or a blender on medium speed, puree the pepper. Combine the pureed pepper with the mayonnaise, in a large bowl. Toss clams with the mayonnaise mixture until all are coated. Place one clam in each shell half. Garnish with parsley, if desired, and serve.

Florentine Oysters ★

Makes 4 servings

2	pounds spinach
½	small onion, minced
1	cup minced celery
2	tablespoons butter
¼	cup minced fresh parsley
1	tablespoon whole wheat pastry flour
½	cup skim milk
½	cup shredded Cheddar cheese
	dash of cayenne pepper
16	large oysters, well scrubbed
	parsley sprigs (garnish)

Rinse the spinach and place in a large saucepan with only the water that clings to the leaves. Steam just until wilted. Let cool, then chop.

Place the onions and celery in a medium-size skillet with 1 tablespoon of the butter. Cook over medium heat, stirring frequently, until the onions are translucent. Add the parsley and stir until wilted. Remove from heat.

In a small saucepan, melt the remaining butter and stir in the flour. Cook over low heat for 1 to 2 minutes, then stir in the milk. Remove from the heat when thickened, then add the cheese and cayenne. Stir until the cheese is melted.

Combine the spinach, onion mixture, and cheese sauce in a medium-size bowl. Open the oysters and arrange 16 of the shell halves on a baking sheet. Place one oyster in each shell.

Top each oyster with some of the cheese and spinach sauce. Bake at 350° for 15 minutes. Serve garnished with parsley, if desired.

199

Cataplana ★ ★

Crab legs steamed over vegetables.

Makes 4 servings

4	medium-size potatoes, cut into ¼-inch slices
1	cup chopped leeks
2	cloves garlic, minced
1	cup chopped tomatoes
2	tablespoons minced fresh parsley
1	bay leaf
2	pounds crab legs
½	cup dealcoholized white wine

Steam the potatoes for 5 minutes.

Line the bottom of a 1½-quart ovenproof casserole with the potatoes and sprinkle with half of the leeks, half of the garlic, half of the tomatoes, and half of the parsley. Add the bay leaf and all the crab legs. Sprinkle with rest of the leeks, garlic, tomatoes, and parsley. Add the wine, cover tightly, and bake, covered, at 400° for 20 minutes.

To serve, mound the vegetables on plates and arrange the crab legs over them. Serve immediately.

Scallops with Peppers and Pasta ★ ★

Makes 6 servings

1 pound sea scallops, halved
  whole wheat flour
¼ cup *Chicken Stock* or
  Sausalito Fish Stock
1 large onion, chopped
½ sweet red pepper, cut into
  thin strips
½ green pepper, cut into thin
  strips
½ pound sliced mushrooms
1 pound pasta spirals
½ cup *Tomato Sauce*
1 teaspoon fennel seeds
½ cup *Chicken Stock*

Dredge the scallops in flour, shaking off the excess. Bring a large pot of water to a boil.

Place the stock in a large skillet over medium-high heat. Add the onions, red peppers, and green peppers. Cook, stirring constantly, and when the onions are translucent, add the mushrooms. Continue cooking over low to medium heat, stirring occasionally, until the mushrooms have given up their liquid and it has evaporated.

Place the pasta in the boiling water and cook until al dente, about 8 to 9 minutes. Drain.

While the pasta cooks, add the scallops to the onion mixture in the large skillet and cook, stirring, until the scallops are opaque, about 5 minutes. Add the tomato sauce, fennel seeds, and ½ cup chicken stock to the pan, bring to a boil, then reduce heat and simmer for 1 to 2 minutes. Serve the scallops over the pasta.

Hawaiian Grilled Scallop Kabobs ★ ★

Makes 4 servings

1 pound sea scallops
¼ cup lemon juice
2 tablespoons tamari or soy
  sauce
2 tablespoons pineapple juice
½ tablespoon sunflower oil
¼ pound mushrooms
1 sweet red pepper, cut into
  1¼-inch squares
1 green pepper, cut into
  1¼-inch squares
1 cup cubed pineapple

Place the scallops in a shallow 8 × 8-inch baking dish. Combine the lemon juice, tamari, pineapple juice, and oil in a small bowl and pour over the scallops. Refrigerate for several hours or overnight.

Cut the stems off the mushrooms close to the caps. Steam the mushrooms and peppers for 2 minutes. Rinse under cold water until cooled.

To prepare the kabobs, place the mushrooms, peppers, pineapple, and scallops alternately on metal skewers. Set over a grill or under the broiler until the scallops are opaque and firm throughout, 3 to 5 minutes. Do not overcook.

★ *VARIATION: Serve with 2 cups cooked rice.*

Lobster Mornay with Crepes ★ ★

Makes 4 servings

1   pound lobster meat, cut into bite-size chunks
2   tablespoons butter
2   tablespoons whole wheat flour
¾   cup skim milk
2   tablespoons freshly grated Parmesan cheese
½   teaspoon lemon juice
½   teaspoon basil
8   *Golden Crepes*
¼   teaspoon paprika (garnish)

Steam the lobster until done, 5 to 10 minutes. (If using frozen lobster, just steam until heated through.) Keep the lobster warm.

In a small saucepan over medium heat, melt the butter. Add the flour and whisk until smooth. Remove from heat and add the milk, cheese, lemon juice, and basil, whisking to combine. Return to the heat and cook, stirring, until thick, 2 to 3 minutes.

In a medium-size bowl, toss the warm lobster with ½ cup of sauce, making sure to coat all the pieces. Lay out the crepes and place ¼ cup of the lobster mixture at the outer edge of each. Roll each crepe and arrange seam side down in pairs on serving plates. Drizzle with remaining sauce, sprinkle with paprika, if desired, and serve.

201

Grilled Garlic Shrimp ★ ★ ★

Makes 4 servings

1   tablespoon olive oil
3   tablespoons *Chicken Stock* or *Vegetable Stock*
2   tablespoons lemon juice
2   teaspoons tamari or soy sauce
6   cloves garlic, sliced
2   teaspoons minced fresh tarragon or ½ teaspoon dried tarragon
½   teaspoon fresh thyme leaves or dash of dried thyme
16   jumbo shrimp, shelled and deveined

Combine the oil, stock, lemon juice, tamari, garlic, tarragon, and thyme in an 8 × 8-inch baking dish.

Place the shrimp in the marinade, cover, and chill overnight. Drain well, then grill or broil 5 inches from the heat just until the shrimp are opaque throughout, about 5 to 7 minutes.

Shrimp and Broccoli Stir-Fry ★ ★ ★

Makes 6 servings

1   tablespoon safflower oil
2   small onions, halved and thinly sliced
2   cloves garlic, sliced
3   cups chopped broccoli
2   cups sliced mushrooms
1   pound shrimp, shelled and deveined
½   pound snow peas
1   tablespoon tamari or soy sauce
2   teaspoons minced fresh ginger
3   tablespoons water (optional)

Heat a very large skillet or wok over medium-high heat, then add the oil. Add the onions and garlic and stir quickly, until translucent. Add the broccoli and stir-fry until it is bright green. Add the mushrooms and stir-fry until they release their liquid.

Add the shrimp, snow peas, tamari, and ginger. If necessary, add water to prevent sticking. Stir-fry the ingredients until the shrimp are cooked through and the vegetables are crisp-tender.

★ ★ *VARIATION: Serve over 3 cups of hot cooked rice.*

Shrimp in Chili Sauce ★ ★ ★

Makes 4 servings

2   cloves garlic
⅓   cup minced onions
1   tablespoon minced fresh coriander or parsley
¼   cup *Chicken Stock*
1¼ pounds large shrimp, shelled and deveined
1   teaspoon chili powder
¼   teaspoon ground cumin
½   cup Mexican salsa or taco sauce

Push the garlic through a garlic press into a medium-size saucepan. Add the onions, coriander, and stock and sauté for 2 to 3 minutes. Add the shrimp and continue to sauté until shrimp just turn pink, about 4 to 8 minutes, depending on size. *Don't overcook.*

Combine chili powder, cumin, and salsa in a small bowl and add to the shrimp. Heat through and serve.

★ ★ *VARIATION: Serve over 2 cups hot cooked rice.*

Southampton Shrimp ★ ★ ★

Herb-poached shrimp.

Makes 4 servings

1	cup *Court Bouillon for Saltwater Fish*
1	cup dealcoholized white wine
2	cloves garlic, minced
1	tablespoon rosemary, crumbled
1¼	pounds shrimp, shelled and deveined
1	tablespoon lime juice
1	tablespoon apple juice
1	tablespoon minced fresh parsley
¼	teaspoon paprika

In a medium-size saucepan, combine the bouillon, wine, garlic, and rosemary. Cover the pan and bring to a boil. Add the shrimp and simmer, covered, for 3 to 5 minutes or until shrimp are pink. *Do not overcook.* Drain shrimp and run under cold water to stop the cooking process.

In a small saucepan, combine the lime juice, apple juice, parsley, and paprika and heat through. Toss shrimp with juices and serve.

203

Shrimp Foo Yong ★ ★ ★

Makes 4 servings

1	tablespoon sunflower oil
1	teaspoon minced fresh ginger
6	scallions, chopped
1	stalk celery, thinly sliced
2	cups bean sprouts
¼	pound shrimp, cooked and chopped
6	eggs, beaten
2	teaspoons tamari or soy sauce
2	teaspoons water

Place half of the oil in a small skillet over medium heat. Add the ginger, scallions, and celery. Cook until the vegetables are translucent but still quite crisp. Stir the cooked vegetables, the bean sprouts, cooked shrimp, and eggs together in a medium-size bowl.

Heat the remaining oil in a large skillet. Pour in the egg mixture, using ½ cup for each of the 4 "pancakes." Cook until golden brown, then turn and brown the other side.

Stir together the tamari and water. Serve the pancakes hot, sprinkled with a little of the tamari mixture.

Crabmeat and Salmon Casserole with Wild Rice ★ ★

Makes 8 servings

¾ cup brown rice
¼ cup wild rice
1 medium-size onion
2¼ cups *Chicken Stock*
½ teaspoon saffron
1 bay leaf
1 lemon slice
2 sprigs parsley
½ pound salmon fillets
1 pound cooked crabmeat
¾ cup shredded carrots
½ cup minced green peppers
¼ cup minced celery
¼ cup minced onions
1 tablespoon safflower oil
¼ teaspoon thyme
¼ teaspoon grated lemon
      rind
   dash of cayenne pepper
3 eggs, beaten
   lemon slices (garnish)
   parsley sprigs (garnish)

Combine the brown rice, wild rice, whole onion, stock, saffron, and bay leaf in a medium-size saucepan. Bring to a boil, simmer for 2 to 3 minutes, then cover, reduce heat as low as possible, and cook for 45 minutes. Turn off heat and let rice stand 10 minutes.

Fill a small skillet ½ inch full with water and add the lemon slice and parsley. Bring to a boil, then add the salmon. Return to a boil, then reduce heat and simmer just until the salmon is cooked throughout (about 5 minutes), turning once. Drain and flake the salmon.

Remove the onion and bay leaf from the rice mixture. Combine the rice, flaked salmon, and crabmeat in a large bowl.

Place the carrots, peppers, celery, and onions with the oil in a small skillet and cook just until the onions are translucent. Add to the rice mixture along with the thyme, lemon rind, cayenne, and eggs and stir until well combined. Place in a 9 × 13-inch baking dish. Bake at 350° for 20 minutes, then serve hot, garnished with lemon slices and parsley, if desired.

204

Vegetarian Main Dishes

One of my first encounters with vegetarian eating occurred in the 1970s. The occasion was a nationwide meat boycott. At the time, my diet was focused rather heavily on meat. I ate it *at least* once a day. When I thought of a full week without meat on the dinner table, my first concern was in getting adequate protein. With this in mind, I relied heavily on eggs, cheese, and nuts to provide the protein I thought I needed since I was giving up roasts, steaks, and chops. I still recall the "meatless loaf" I fashioned that week and served twice, the second time with a vegetarian gravy. The loaf was packed with ground walnuts, eggs, ground sunflower seeds, Cheddar cheese, and sautéed onions. I cringe to think of the calorie count in one serving of that loaf! I was overdoing everything, including eating, for fear of not getting enough protein. By the end of that week of experimentation, I had gained two pounds.

Slowly, over the years, I learned more about complementary proteins. I found out that by combining things like rice and beans or corn tortillas and lentils or wheat bulgur with a little bit of cheese I would be eating protein equal in value to that found in a steak. And that wasn't all I discovered. I found out that eating a variety of ethnic and creative vegetarian dishes was far more interesting and tasty than eating pan-fried steak or chops. Best of all, I found I was satisfied quickly on these foods. Calorie for calorie, when I compared these new dishes to the old meat standbys, I was eating less! I really started to notice the pounds dropping away and staying away!

That's why I consider this the most important chapter of *The Lose Weight Naturally Cookbook*. I'm going to introduce you to the type of vegetarian dishes my family and I have been hooked on for years. Dishes such as *Crepes*

Florentine, Vegetarian Ravioli, Chinese Stir-Fry, Greek Lasagna, Tamale Pie, and other foods of interesting taste and texture from far-off lands will prove to you that common-sense eating can be something you can truly enjoy and want to live with forever. You'll enjoy soy foods—tofu and tempeh—and come to consider the lowly potato as worthy main course fare.

With these and other dishes, you'll find that the food is satisfying, and because of the bulk, you won't be tempted to overeat. Your plate will look full and inviting, with no more calories than you would have found in a normal portion of meat, some stuffing perhaps, and a few vegetables.

One thing to keep in mind, if being a vegetarian—even part-time—is something you never considered but wish to try, don't expect to change all at once. Try one vegetarian meal a week, for starters. Keep going until you find a selection of dishes you love. Before you know it, you'll be eating vegetarian without even giving it any thought.

In addition to the weight loss, you'll notice other benefits. According to myriad surveys and studies, vegetarians aren't only leaner than their meat-eating counterparts, but they also have fewer health problems as well —less heart disease, lower blood pressure, fewer incidences of cancer. That fulfills the dual purpose of this book—to make you lose weight and become healthier!

Baked Stuffed Potatoes

One of the best things to come around in a long time is the stuffed baked potato—a whole meal of steaming goodness bulging with wonderfully tasty toppings like fresh, crunchy stir-fry vegetables and melted cheese. Who could ever complain about being on a diet eating such a meal!

But the baked potato *is* a diet dish. In fact, I've found it to be one of the best diet dishes around. It's brimming with protein and fiber, which keeps you pleasantly satisfied, and has plenty of flavor, to boot. At only 145 calories for one medium-size potato, it can hardly be considered fattening. (It's all that butter and sour cream we *used* to put on them that gave the baked potato it's nasty reputation.) And only 1.2 percent of those calories come from fat.

So, why not take advantage of the baked potato's new reputation as a *healthy* food and make it part of your diet. Following, you'll find a half-dozen recipes for turning a baked potato into a meal-in-one—all well below 250 calories. But by no means limit yourself to these. Experiment on your own, mixing and matching some of your favorite vegetables as toppings. But be honest with yourself. These recipes call for a *medium-size* potato. If you substitute a large potato, you will most likely be eating in the Maintenance (two-star) not Weight Loss (three-star) range.

There's no trick to making perfect baked potatoes. Just bake them as they are (no foil, please) at 400° for 1 hour. Just make sure the potato is hot when you pour the stuffing on top.

Oriental Stuffed Potato ★ ★ ★

A savory stir-fry.

Makes 4 servings

⅓   cup tamari or soy sauce
2   tablespoons rice vinegar
¼   cup honey
2   red chili peppers, broken in pieces
1½   teaspoons cornstarch
2   tablespoons *Vegetable Stock*
1¼   cups 2-inch pieces of broccoli
¾   cup fresh snow peas
½   cup julienned carrots
¼   cup diagonally sliced celery
¼   cup chopped water chestnuts
2   tablespoons sliced scallions
4   hot, medium-size baked potatoes

In a small bowl, mix together the tamari, vinegar, honey, and peppers and refrigerate overnight. Stir cornstarch into marinade and mix well.

In a wok or large frying pan, heat the stock. Stir-fry the broccoli, snow peas, carrots, celery, water chestnuts, and scallions in the stock for 3 minutes. Push vegetables to the side of the pan and heat the marinade until thick, stirring constantly. Remove from heat and stir in the vegetables, tossing until coated with marinade mixture. Split open the potatoes and spoon stir-fry mixture over them. Serve immediately.

Keystone Stuffed Potato ★ ★ ★

Makes 4 servings

1 cup low-fat cottage cheese
2 teaspoons lemon juice
2 teaspoons buttermilk
2 teaspoons low-fat yogurt
1½ teaspoons chives
2 cups crinkle-cut carrots
2 cups string beans, broken into 2-inch pieces
4 hot, medium-size baked potatoes
paprika
1 cup alfalfa sprouts

Combine cottage cheese, lemon juice, buttermilk, yogurt, and chives in a blender or food processor and process on medium speed until smooth. Let dressing stand for at least 30 minutes to blend flavors.

Steam carrots and string beans for 7 minutes. Split open the potatoes and spoon in vegetables. Top with cottage cheese mixture. Sprinkle with paprika and top with sprouts. Serve immediately.

208

Garden Puff Potatoes ★ ★ ★

Makes 4 servings

1½ cups broccoli florets
1 dill sprig (optional)
½ cup green peppers, coarsely chopped
¼ cup onions, chopped
4 hot, medium-size baked potatoes
2 tablespoons buttermilk
2 teaspoons dill
¼–⅓ cup skim milk
1 cup shredded carrots
1 tablespoon chopped chives (garnish)

Steam the broccoli for 3 minutes with the dill sprig (if available). Add the peppers and onions and steam 2 more minutes. Cut a slice from the top of each potato.

Scoop out potato pulp and put it in a blender with the buttermilk, dill, ¼ cup milk, and carrots. Whip on high speed for 5 minutes or until light and fluffy. (Add more milk, if needed.)

Put potato puree in a medium-size bowl. Gently fold in the steamed vegetables.

Spoon potato mixture back into potato shells. (More shells can be made with tin foil, to hold the extra potato mixture.) Place potatoes under a broiler for 7 minutes until the top has browned. Garnish with chives, if desired, and serve immediately.

Ratatouille
Stuffed Potato ★ ★ ★

Makes 4 servings

4   hot, medium-size baked
    potatoes
3   cups hot *Ratatouille*
¼   cup grated fresh Parmesan
    cheese

Split open the potatoes and spoon the ratatouille over them. Sprinkle with Parmesan and serve.

Armando's
Stuffed Potatoes ★ ★ ★

Makes 8 servings

4   cups *Chicken Stock*
⅔   cup tomato paste
2   medium-size carrots,
    sliced diagonally
2   cups chopped onions
1   cup sliced mushrooms
2   stalks celery, sliced
    diagonally
3   cloves garlic, sliced
½   teaspoon basil
½   teaspoon marjoram
¼   teaspoon cayenne pepper
2   small zucchini, cut into
    thin, 2-inch strips
¼   cup minced fresh parsley
4   hot, medium-size baked
    potatoes
    grated Parmesan cheese

Combine the stock, tomato paste, carrots, onions, mushrooms, celery, garlic, basil, marjoram, and cayenne in a large saucepan. Bring to a boil, then reduce heat, cover, and simmer for 30 minutes.

Stir in the zucchini and cook for another 15 minutes. Stir in the parsley and cook for another 1 to 2 minutes before serving.

Split open the baked potatoes, top with the vegetable stew, and sprinkle with Parmesan.

Big Sur
Stuffed Potatoes ★ ★ ★

Makes 4 servings

1 medium-size onion,
   chopped
2 teaspoons corn oil
½ cup low-fat cottage cheese
2 tablespoons crumbled feta
   cheese
   dash of nutmeg
4 hot, medium-size baked
   potatoes
2 tablespoons minced fresh
   chives

Sauté the onions in the oil until soft. Cool, then stir together with the cottage cheese, feta, and nutmeg.

Cut a slice from the top side of each potato, carefully scoop out most of the pulp, and reserve. Keep the skin intact.

Combine the potato pulp with the onion mixture. Stuff the mixture back into the potato skins. Bake at 375° for 15 minutes or until heated through. Sprinkle with the chives and serve.

Eggs

Hard-boiled eggs. They rank right up there with cottage cheese and lettuce leaves as one of the all-time boring "diet" foods. So, just forget about hard-boiled eggs on your diet! Instead, think of eggs as the main ingredient on which to build yourself a taste-worthy vegetarian meal.

After all, eggs *do* have their place in a reducing diet. A large egg contains only 79 calories (63 of these calories come from the yolk, by the way). They're rich in vitamins, too. Eggs contain a fair amount of vitamin A and a healthy dose of all other nutrients except vitamin C. However, they are not without their controversy. The yolk of the egg is also one of the richest sources of cholesterol, and high levels of cholesterol in the blood are believed to contribute to heart disease. So, should you or shouldn't you eat them? Medical experts say they see no harm in eating eggs once in a while, say once or twice a week, unless you have heart disease or a family history of it (after all, why take the risk?).

As far as I'm concerned, the best time to take advantage of an occasional egg is weekend brunch. There are many wonderful things you can do with eggs, and brunch-type food is high on the list. Vegetable souffles, quiches, frittatas, and elegant omelets are among the brunch fare you can enjoy on a diet. And the nice thing about brunch is that since you're combining two meals (breakfast and lunch), you don't have to be all that austere about the calories. That's where these recipes are a real treat to the weight conscious. The three-star egg dishes in this chapter all fall below 200 calories—a nice low sum when you consider it's for breakfast *and* lunch. So make a real occasion out of it. Start the day with a *Tomato-Buttermilk Cocktail* or other refreshing three-star drink from the beverage chapter. Select a nice green salad to go with your eggs. *Salade aux Epinards* or *Celebration Salad* are two particularly nice dishes. And cap it with a dessert (three-star, of course), if you'd like.

It's a nice way to enjoy a weekend repast—without doing harm to your diet.

211

Huevos Rancheros ★ ★ ★

These "ranch eggs," baked in a tangy hot sauce, are perfect for Sunday brunch.

Makes 6 servings

1	28-ounce can plum tomatoes, including the juice
1	small onion, chopped
½	green pepper, diced
½	sweet red pepper, diced
1	tablespoon corn oil
1	clove garlic, minced
1	tablespoon whole wheat flour
1	tablespoon chili powder
6	eggs
¼	cup shredded Cheddar cheese

Chop the tomatoes and set aside with the juice.

Cook the onions, green peppers, and red peppers in the oil in a large skillet over medium heat until slightly tender. Stir in the garlic and cook for 1 to 2 minutes more, then add the flour and stir until the vegetables are coated. Stir in the chopped tomatoes and juice and the chili powder. Cook for another 10 minutes, stirring occasionally.

Place the sauce in a 9 × 13-inch baking dish. Crack the eggs into the sauce carefully so that the yolks do not break. Spoon some of the sauce over each egg. Sprinkle with the cheese, and bake at 350° for 30 minutes or until the eggs are set.

NOTE: If making sauce ahead of time, reheat before assembling casserole.

Aztec Enchiladas ★ ★

Eggs with corn and a taste of chili, for brunch or lunch, are an easy and unusual offering.

Makes 4 servings

7 eggs
2 tablespoons skim milk
1 tablespoon *Chicken Stock*
1 cup corn
¼ teaspoon chili powder
4 *Corn Tortillas*
   sweet red pepper rings
      (garnish)
   parsley sprigs (garnish)

Beat the eggs in a medium-size bowl and whisk in the milk.

Heat the stock in a large skillet and add the corn. Cook 2 to 3 minutes. Stir in the eggs and sprinkle with the chili powder. Cook over low-medium heat, stirring occasionally, until the eggs are set. Place one-fourth of the mixture on each tortilla. Serve garnished with red pepper rings and parsley sprigs, if desired.

Herbed Eggs in Nests ★ ★ ★

Makes 6 servings

3 medium-size potatoes,
   cubed
1 stalk celery, minced
1 tablespoon whole wheat
   flour
½ cup skim milk
½ cup part-skim ricotta
   cheese
1 scallion, minced
1 tablespoon minced fresh
   parsley
6 eggs
¼ cup shredded Muenster
   cheese
½ teaspoon paprika
   parsley sprigs (garnish)

Place the potatoes and celery in a medium-size saucepan with enough water to cover and bring to a boil over high heat. Turn down heat and cook until the potatoes are very tender, about 15 to 20 minutes. Drain and mash.

Combine the flour and milk in a medium-size skillet and cook until thick, about 2 minutes. When the sauce is bubbly and thickened, place it in a blender with the ricotta cheese. Process on low speed until smooth.

Stir the blended cheese mixture, scallions, and parsley into the mashed potatoes and celery.

Coat 6 custard cups with no-stick spray. Spoon the potato mixture into the custard cups. Using a spoon, make a depression large enough to hold a raw egg in the top of each. Place an egg in the depression in each custard cup and sprinkle with some Muenster cheese and paprika.

Bake at 375° for about 15 minutes or until the eggs are set. Serve garnished with parsley sprigs, if desired.

Asparagus Omelet ★ ★ ★

Cottage cheese adds a surprising delicate taste to eggs.

Makes 2 servings

3   eggs, beaten
¼   cup low-fat cottage cheese
⅓   cup blanched asparagus
      tips

In a blender or food processor, at medium to high speed, whip eggs and cottage cheese. Heat a no-stick skillet and pour in the egg mixture. Stir until set. Turn onto a serving plate and arrange asparagus tips over the eggs.

★ ★ *VARIATION: Split 1 English muffin and toast. Place each half on a serving dish. Split the egg mixture in two. Place on the muffin halves and top with asparagus.*

Mushroom-Spinach Quiche ★ ★

Makes 6 servings

CRUST

1   cup whole wheat flour
¼   cup safflower oil
2   tablespoons water

FILLING

1   tablespoon *Vegetable Stock*
1   small onion, minced
1   cup sliced mushrooms
1   teaspoon tamari or soy
      sauce
10 ounces spinach, chopped
¼   teaspoon ground
      coriander
      dash of nutmeg
½   clove garlic
1¾ cups milk
3   eggs, beaten

To make the crust: Place the flour, oil, and water in a 9-inch pie plate. Toss with a fork until well combined, then press along the bottom and sides of the pie plate.

To make the filling: Heat the stock in a large, no-stick skillet, add the onions, and cook until translucent. Add the mushrooms and tamari and cook over medium heat, stirring, for about 5 minutes. Add the spinach, coriander, and nutmeg. Add the garlic by pushing it through a garlic press into the skillet. Cook, stirring, until the spinach is wilted.

Place the spinach and mushroom mixture in the pie crust. Combine the milk and eggs in a medium-size bowl and pour over the spinach. Bake at 375° for about 40 minutes or until the top is puffed and browned.

Herbed Zucchini Frittata ★ ★ ★

Cherry tomatoes make a colorful accompaniment to this dish.

Makes 4 servings

2   scallions, chopped
2   small zucchini, quartered
      and thinly sliced
1   tablespoon *Vegetable Stock*
1   teaspoon basil
½   teaspoon marjoram
6   eggs, beaten
2   tablespoons grated
      Parmesan cheese
      parsley sprigs (garnish)

In a medium-size ovenproof skillet, cook the scallions and zucchini in the stock over low heat just until crisp-tender. Sprinkle with the basil and marjoram and stir.

Add the eggs, pouring carefully over the zucchini and onions. Cook over low heat until the eggs are nearly set, but still runny on top.

Sprinkle with the Parmesan. Set under a broiler until the top of the frittata is browned lightly and the eggs are cooked through. Cut into 4 wedges and serve garnished with parsley, if desired.

214

New Orleans Frittata ★ ★ ★

Makes 4 servings

4   eggs
2   tablespoons skim milk
¼   teaspoon chili powder
2   teaspoons corn oil
1   medium-size onion,
      chopped
1   stalk celery, chopped
¾   cup cooked black-eyed peas
3   tablespoons grated
      Muenster cheese
      red pepper rings (garnish)
      parsley sprigs (garnish)

In a medium-size bowl, beat the eggs with the milk and chili powder.

Heat the oil in a medium-size ovenproof skillet, then add onions and celery. Cook until tender, stirring often. Add a few drops of water, if needed, to prevent scorching. Spread the cooked vegetables over the bottom of the skillet.

Pour the eggs gently over the vegetables and cook over medium heat, without stirring, for 1 to 2 minutes. Spoon the black-eyed peas over the surface of the eggs. Continue cooking the frittata, without stirring, over low to medium heat, until the eggs are firm on the bottom and begin to brown.

Sprinkle the top of the frittata with the cheese. Place the frittata under a broiler until the top is well puffed and golden and the eggs are cooked through. Garnish with red pepper rings and parsley sprigs, if desired. Cut in 4 wedges to serve.

Lemon Omelet
with Papaya ★ ★
Quick and pretty.

Makes 1 serving

2 eggs
1 teaspoon honey
½ teaspoon grated lemon
   rind
¼ teaspoon vanilla extract
¼ papaya, seeded and sliced
   watercress sprigs (garnish)

Beat the eggs with the honey, lemon rind, and vanilla until well combined.

Pour the egg mixture in an omelet pan or medium-size skillet coated with no-stick spray.

Cook over medium heat, pulling the edges of the omelet toward the center of the pan with a table knife and swirling the pan to allow uncooked egg to reach the edge.

When the eggs are cooked and just set on top, remove from heat. Lay two slices of papaya down the center of the omelet, fold the omelet over the papaya, and slide the omelet out of the pan onto a plate. Garnish with the remaining papaya slices and the watercress, if desired.

215

Broccoli Soufflé
Romano ★ ★ ★

Makes 4 servings

2½ cups broccoli florets,
    steamed
1   cup packed spinach leaves,
    coarsely chopped and
    steamed
2   egg yolks
⅓ cup grated Romano cheese
    dash of nutmeg
4   egg whites
    grated Parmesan cheese

Place the broccoli, spinach, and egg yolks in a blender and process on medium speed until smooth, scraping down the sides as necessary. Transfer to a large mixing bowl. Stir in the Romano and the nutmeg.

Beat the egg whites until they form stiff peaks. Stir one-fourth of the egg whites into the broccoli mixture, then gently fold in the rest of the egg whites.

Sprinkle the inside of a slightly oiled 2-quart soufflé dish with Parmesan. Gently pour the broccoli mixture into the soufflé dish. Bake at 325° for 30 minutes. Serve at once.

Broccoli and Cheese Soufflé ★ ★ ★

Makes 6 servings

4   eggs, separated
3   cups chopped broccoli, steamed
1   cup crumbled feta cheese
¼   teaspoon ground coriander
¼   teaspoon oregano
    dash of nutmeg
    dash of paprika

Place the egg yolks in a blender and add the broccoli. Process on low to medium speed until smooth.

Add the feta cheese, coriander, oregano, and nutmeg to the blender. Process on low to medium speed until combined, stopping to scrape down the sides of the blender if necessary. Transfer to a medium-size mixing bowl.

Beat the egg whites until they form stiff peaks.

Stir one-fourth of the egg whites into the broccoli mixture. Then gently fold in the remaining whites.

Place the mixture in a lightly oiled, 2-quart soufflé dish. Sprinkle with paprika and bake at 325° for 35 minutes. Serve immediately.

216

Frittata with Marinated Vegetables ★ ★ ★

Makes 6 servings

1   cup julienned zucchini
1   cup sliced mushrooms
1   green pepper, julienned
12 cherry tomatoes
2   tablespoons olive oil
1   tablespoon lemon juice
1   clove garlic, minced
2   tablespoons minced fresh parsley
1   tablespoon minced fresh rosemary or 1 teaspoon dried rosemary, crumbled

Combine the zucchini, mushrooms, peppers, and tomatoes in a medium-size mixing bowl.

Stir together the oil, lemon juice, garlic, parsley, rosemary, thyme, and mustard in a small bowl. Pour over the vegetables, stir, and let the vegetables marinate for 15 minutes.

Place the vegetables and marinade in a medium-size saucepan. Cook over medium heat until the liquid has evaporated and the vegetables are heated through. Let cool slightly.

Beat the eggs together with the Parmesan cheese. Stir the vegetables into the eggs.

Place an oiled, medium-size ovenproof skillet over medium heat for 1 to 2 minutes, then pour in the egg

1 tablespoon minced fresh
thyme or 1 teaspoon
dried thyme
½ teaspoon mustard
8 eggs
¼ cup grated Parmesan
cheese
parsley sprigs (garnish)
cherry tomatoes (garnish)

mixture. Lift the edge as the frittata cooks, so that uncooked egg runs underneath.

When the eggs are golden on the bottom, but the frittata is still runny on top (after about 5 to 7 minutes), remove from the flame and broil until the top is golden and puffed. Slide the frittata onto a serving plate. Cut into 6 wedges and garnish with parsley and cherry tomatoes, if desired.

Egg and Rice Pancakes with Vegetable Sauce ★ ★ ★

Makes 4 servings

PANCAKES
4 eggs, lightly beaten
⅔ cup cooked rice
½ cup bean sprouts
2 scallions, chopped
2 teaspoons tamari or soy
sauce
4 teaspoons sesame oil

SAUCE
1 tablespoon cornstarch
1 tablespoon tamari or soy
sauce
1 cup water
¼ cup diced celery
½ cup diced green peppers
2 water chestnuts, diced
¼ cup diced bamboo shoots
2 cloves garlic

To make the pancakes: In a medium-size mixing bowl, whisk together the eggs, rice, bean sprouts, scallions, and tamari.

Heat 1 teaspoon of the oil in a small omelet pan over high heat. Pour in one-fourth of the egg mixture. Turn heat to low and cook until the eggs are set, about 5 minutes. Gently turn over and brown the other side. Remove to an ovenproof platter, cover, and place in a warm oven. Repeat with the remaining batter.

To make the sauce: Combine the cornstarch and tamari in a medium-size skillet to form a thin paste. Whisk in the water and place over medium-high heat. Cook, whisking constantly, until the mixture becomes syrupy. Lower the heat and stir in the celery, peppers, water chestnuts, and bamboo shoots. Add the garlic by pushing it through a garlic press into the pan. Simmer for 3 minutes, stirring occasionally. Pour over the pancakes and serve.

Corn Soufflé ★ ★ ★

Its glorious golden color and rich taste mark this soufflé for special honors.

Makes 4 servings

¾ cup corn
¾ cup skim milk
2 tablespoons butter
2 tablespoons whole wheat
    flour
¼ cup finely crumbled feta
    cheese
4 eggs, separated
    grated Parmesan cheese

Place the corn and milk in a blender and process on medium speed until smooth.

Melt the butter in a large skillet and add the flour. Stir over low heat for 2 to 3 minutes. Add the corn mixture and cook, stirring, until slightly thickened. Add the cheese and continue to cook, stirring, for about 3 to 4 minutes over low heat. Remove from heat.

Beat the egg whites until they form stiff peaks.

Preheat the oven to 400°. When the corn mixture has cooled slightly, stir in the egg yolks. Then stir in about one-fourth of the egg whites. Gently fold in the remaining egg whites.

Dust the inside of a lightly buttered 2-quart soufflé dish with grated Parmesan. Gently pour in the corn mixture.

Place the soufflé in the preheated oven and immediately turn the heat down to 325°. Bake for 35 minutes. Serve at once, while the soufflé is still puffed and golden.

Other Vegetarian Dishes

Crepes Parmesan ★ ★ ★

Makes 4 servings

1 cup shredded zucchini
1 cup shredded yellow squash
½ cup minced scallions
1 cup chopped tomatoes
½ teaspoon basil
½ teaspoon thyme
2 tablespoons grated
    Parmesan cheese
8 *Whole Wheat Crepes* or
    Golden Crepes
1 teaspoon parsley (garnish)

In a medium-size skillet, coated with no-stick spray, sauté the zucchini, squash, scallions, tomatoes, basil, and thyme for about 2 minutes. Drain and add cheese. Place ¼ cup of filling on the outside edge of each crepe and roll. Sprinkle with parsley, if desired.

218

Spaghetti Squash with Alfredo Sauce ★ ★ ★

Makes 2 servings

1   medium-size spaghetti squash
½   cup buttermilk
½   cup low-fat cottage cheese
     dash of nutmeg
     dash of black pepper
2   tablespoons grated Parmesan cheese
     minced scallions (garnish)
     nutmeg (garnish)

Pierce the squash, then place in a saucepan with enough water to cover. Boil, covered, for 45 minutes. Cut the squash in half, remove the pulp strands with a fork, and reserve.

In a food processor or blender, combine the buttermilk, cottage cheese, nutmeg, and pepper and process on medium to high speed until smooth. Toss the squash with the Parmesan, then with the sauce. Garnish with scallions and nutmeg, if desired. Serve immediately.

★ ★ ★ *VARIATION: Serve the spaghetti squash with* Sauce Corsica.

Crepes with Watercress and Mushrooms ★

A nice, light dish for entertaining.

Makes 4 servings

2   cups sliced mushrooms
4   scallions, chopped
2   teaspoons sunflower oil
1   cup loosely packed watercress leaves, chopped
2   cups low-fat cottage cheese
¼   cup grated Parmesan cheese
2   eggs, beaten
1   teaspoon basil
     dash of nutmeg
2   cups *Tomato Sauce*
8   *Whole Wheat Crepes*
     watercress sprigs (garnish)

219

Place the mushrooms and scallions in a medium-size skillet with the oil. Cook over low to medium heat until the mushrooms have given up their liquid and the liquid has evaporated. The scallions should be translucent. Add the watercress and cook, stirring, just until the leaves are wilted.

In a large bowl, combine the cottage cheese, Parmesan, eggs, basil, nutmeg, and mushroom mixture. Stir together well.

Place a thin coating of tomato sauce on the bottom of a shallow 9 × 13-inch baking dish. Place about ⅓ cup of the filling on one end of each crepe and roll up. Place the filled crepes, seam side down, in the baking dish. Top with the remaining tomato sauce. Bake at 325° for 15 to 20 minutes or until heated through. Garnish with sprigs of watercress, if desired.

Vegetarian Ravioli ★ ★ ★

Makes 6 servings

1 pound *Basic Whole Wheat Pasta*
2 cups *Tomato Sauce*

Place 2 sheets of pasta of equal size (approximately 6 inches wide) on a lightly floured work surface. Using a pastry brush, paint one side of each sheet with water.

On one of the two sheets place mounds (1 heaping teaspoon each) of one of the accompanying stuffings in 2 rows with roughly 2 inches separating the center of each mound. Place the other sheet of dough over the one with the stuffing.

With your fingers press the dough together firmly between the mounds of stuffings and along the borders, removing as much air as possible. Cut into squares with a sharp knife or pastry wheel. Each ravioli should be about 2 inches square. Seal all edges. Repeat until all pasta is used.

To cook ravioli: Allow the stuffed ravioli to rest on a clean dry towel at least 30 minutes. Turn once to ensure that they dry evenly on both sides. Cook in 4 quarts of boiling water, 10 to 12 at a time, for 5 to 7 minutes. The cooking time will vary with the thickness of the pasta and length of drying time. They will rise to the surface as they cook. Remove with a large slotted spoon, drain well, and keep warm until ready to serve.

Serve ravioli with tomato sauce.

Mushroom-Spinach Ricotta Filling

¼ pound finely chopped mushrooms
dash of nutmeg
dash of black pepper
1 cup chopped cooked spinach
¾ cup part-skim ricotta cheese or low-fat cottage cheese

In a small skillet, coated with no-stick spray, sauté mushrooms until they are soft and their liquid has evaporated. Transfer the mushrooms to a medium-size bowl. Add the nutmeg, pepper, spinach, and ricotta and mix thoroughly.

220

Asparagus-Mushroom Filling

Follow the recipe for *Mushroom-Spinach Ricotta Filling*, substituting ¾ cup cooked chopped asparagus for the spinach and 3 ounces of Neufchâtel cheese (beaten until smooth) for the ricotta.

Broccoli Filling

¾	cup minced cooked broccoli
¼	cup minced scallions
¼	cup minced fresh parsley
½	cup part-skim ricotta cheese or low-fat cottage cheese

In a medium-size bowl, combine all ingredients.

Spinach-Carrot Cheese Filling

1	cup chopped cooked spinach
½	cup grated carrots
3	ounces Neufchâtel cheese, beaten until smooth
	dash of black pepper
	dash of nutmeg

In a medium-size bowl, combine all ingredients.

221

Spinach Risoto with Pasta ★ ★ ★

An eye-catching dish with everything going for it—nutritious whole grains and vegetables.

Makes 4 servings

2	tablespoons *Chicken Stock*
1	large leek, chopped
1	cup sliced mushrooms
½	cup shredded spinach
2	cups cooked rice
1½	cups cooked spaghetti, chopped
	tamari or soy sauce (to taste)

Place the stock in a large skillet over medium heat. Stir in the leeks. When the leeks are limp and beginning to get tender, add the mushrooms and cook until they have given up their liquid and the liquid has nearly evaporated. Stir in the spinach and cook over low heat until the spinach is tender.

Stir in the rice thoroughly. Carefully fold in the pasta. Heat through, then transfer the pilaf to a serving dish and sprinkle lightly with tamari. Serve hot.

Spinach Stuffed Artichokes ★ ★ ★

So low in calories! Eat two, if you care, and you're still within the three-star range.

Makes 4 servings

4	globe artichokes
4	cups minced mushrooms
2	tablespoons minced onions
1	tablespoon minced fresh parsley
½	cup chopped cooked spinach
1½	teaspoons lemon juice
½	cup low-fat cottage cheese
½	teaspoon basil
	dash of oregano
¼	teaspoon thyme
1	teaspoon chopped pine nuts
	paprika

Rinse the artichokes and trim off the loose leaves and leaf tips. Cut off 1 inch from the top of each artichoke. In a large, heavy-bottom pot, cook the artichokes in boiling water, covered, for 30 minutes. Drain and refresh under cold running water. Let them stand upside down until cold.

In a medium-size bowl, combine the mushrooms, onions, parsley, spinach, lemon juice, cottage cheese, basil, oregano, and thyme. Mix well. Add the pine nuts.

Pull out some center leaves from each artichoke and scrape well. Spoon about 3 tablespoons of the filling into each artichoke and sprinkle with paprika.

Stand the artichokes in a shallow 9 × 9-inch baking dish coated with no-stick spray. Bake artichokes at 350° for 30 minutes or until filling has heated through.

★ ★ ★ *VARIATION: For* Cold Stuffed Artichokes, *sauté the mushrooms and onions in a medium-size skillet coated with no-stick spray for 2 to 3 minutes or until moisture has evaporated. Transfer to a bowl and cool. Add remaining ingredients, except paprika, and mix well. Divide the mixture among the artichokes. Sprinkle with paprika and serve.*

222

Pizza Riso ★ ★ ★

This tasty recipe cuts the calories in pizza by replacing the traditional all-dough crust with one using rice as a base. The crust is quite thick and filling, making 1 slice per person an ample portion. Serve with a salad or a light soup for a complete meal.

Makes 8 servings

CRUST

1	cup coarsely grated carrots
2½	cups cooked brown rice
⅓	cup whole wheat flour
½	cup low-fat cottage cheese

To make the crust: Place the carrots in a strainer and weight them with an unopened can of fruit or vegetables. Let drain for 20 minutes. Pat dry.

Combine the carrots with the rice, flour, cottage cheese, onions, and ½ teaspoon basil.

Coat a 9 × 13-inch pan with no-stick spray, pour in the crust mixture, and spread it across the bottom of

2 tablespoons minced
    onions
½ teaspoon basil

TOPPING
½–¾ cup *Tomato Sauce*
1½ cups shredded, part-
    skim mozzarella
    cheese
½ teaspoon basil

the pan and about ¼ inch up the sides of the pan. Bake on the middle oven rack at 350° for 25 minutes. After crust bakes, put it under a broiler to seal the crust. Let the crust brown without burning the carrots. There's no need to cool the crust before topping it.

To assemble: Spread the tomato sauce over the crust and top with the cheese. Sprinkle the basil over the cheese and bake at 350° for 20 to 25 minutes or until cheese is brown and bubbly. Slice and serve.

★★★ *VARIATIONS: For* Vegetable Pizza, *dice and steam 1 cup of fresh vegetables and toss them with the tomato sauce. Cover with cheese and bake as directed.*

For Mexican Pizza, *substitute ½ cup of* Hot Taco Sauce *for the* Tomato Sauce. *Top with 1 cup of Monterey Jack cheese instead of mozzarella. Sprinkle with paprika and cumin instead of basil and bake as directed.*

★ *VARIATIONS: Cut* Pizza Riso *into 2-inch squares and serve as hors d'oeuvres.*

For Dessert Pizza, *dice 1 cup of fresh fruit (apples and pears are nice) and spread over the broiled crust. Top with Muenster cheese or other mild, white cheese and bake as directed.*

223

Crepes Florentine ★ ★
Perfect for a Sunday brunch.

Makes 4 servings

10 ounces spinach, chopped
    and steamed
1½ cups part-skim ricotta
    cheese
1 egg white
¼ cup grated Parmesan
    cheese
2 tablespoons minced fresh
    parsley
½ teaspoon basil
    dash of nutmeg
8 *Whole Wheat Crepes*
½ cup *Tomato Sauce*

Stir together the spinach, ricotta, egg white, Parmesan, parsley, basil, and nutmeg.

Divide the filling among the crepes. Roll the crepes around the filling and place seam side down in a shallow 9 × 13-inch baking dish.

Top each of the crepes with 2 tablespoons of sauce and bake at 325° for about 15 minutes or until heated through.

Greek Lasagna ★

I love Spanakopita, but that delicious buttery flavor comes from (you guessed it) lots and lots of butter. This dish retains the delightful flavor of that Grecian dish without going overboard on butter.

Makes 9 servings

12	ounces lasagna noodles
¼	cup *Vegetable Stock*
1	large leek, chopped
1	large onion, chopped
5	scallions, chopped
½	cup chopped fresh parsley
⅓	cup chopped fresh dill
1½	pounds spinach, chopped and steamed
1	cup low-fat cottage cheese
1	cup crumbled feta cheese
4	eggs, beaten
3	tablespoons butter
3	tablespoons whole wheat flour
2½	cups skim milk
¼	cup grated Parmesan cheese

224

Cook lasagna noodles in boiling water until al dente. Drain and rinse under cold water until cool. Spread out flat and cover so the noodles do not dry out.

Place the stock in a medium-size skillet. Add the leeks, onions, and scallions. Cook over low heat until soft. Do not brown. Add the parsley and dill. Stir until the parsley is wilted.

Drain the spinach and press out any excess moisture with the back of a wooden spoon. Stir the spinach into the onion mixture and set over the heat for a minute or two to evaporate any remaining moisture.

Turn the spinach mixture into a large mixing bowl and add the cottage cheese, feta, and eggs.

Melt the butter in the medium-size skillet. Stir in the flour and continue stirring over low heat for 2 to 3 minutes. Add the milk gradually, stirring well to avoid lumping. Stir the white sauce over low heat until it simmers and thickens. Stir in the Parmesan and remove from the heat.

To assemble the casserole, place ½ cup of the white sauce in the bottom of a 9 × 13-inch baking dish. Add a layer of lasagna noodles (use one-fourth of the noodles) and spread one-third of the spinach mixture over the noodles. Repeat the layering twice. Top with the remaining lasagna noodles. Pour the remaining white sauce over the top of the casserole. Bake for 25 minutes at 350°. Allow to stand about 15 minutes before cutting into serving pieces.

225

Pizza Riso takes the high calories out of this popular dish by using rice instead of dough for the crust. Tasty variations are *Vegetable Pizza*, top; *Mexican Pizza*, at right; and *Dessert Pizza*.

226

In the mood for vegetarian fare? Spaghetti squash with *Sauce Corsica* and *Italian Stuffed Squash*
are two of the main dishes from which you can choose. Accompany both with
Keystone Mixed-Grain Bread, Orange Ice Shells, and nonalcoholic wine.

Spanakorizo ★ ★ ★

Greek spinach and rice—a main dish and vegetable in one!

Makes 4 servings

¼	cup minced onions
1	tablespoon *Vegetable Stock*
1	pound spinach, chopped
2½	cups cooked rice
½	cup low-fat cottage cheese
¼	cup shredded sharp Cheddar cheese
1	egg, beaten
1	tablespoon minced fresh dill or 1½ teaspoons dried dill
1	tablespoon minced fresh parsley

Place the onions in a medium-size skillet with the stock and cook over low heat until the onions are translucent. Add the spinach and cook over low heat, stirring constantly, until the spinach has wilted. Continue cooking, stirring occasionally, until all liquid is evaporated from the pan.

In a large bowl, stir together the rice, cottage cheese, Cheddar, egg, dill, and parsley. Fold in the cooked spinach mixture. Place in a 1-quart ovenproof casserole and bake at 375° for 20 to 25 minutes or until the top is slightly golden.

Vegetable Paella ★ ★ ★

Makes 3 servings

3	tablespoons–¼ cup *Chicken Stock* or *Vegetable Stock*
½–1	teaspoon turmeric
2	cups cooked rice
1	sweet red pepper, sliced into ½-inch slices
2	Italian plum tomatoes, diced
1	medium-size zucchini, cut into thin rounds
1	tablespoon freshly grated Parmesan cheese
1	tablespoon minced fresh parsley (garnish)

In a paella pan or medium-size saucepan, heat 3 tablespoons of the stock. Add the turmeric and rice, stirring until rice is golden.

Add peppers, tomatoes, zucchini, and Parmesan and cook until vegetables are tender but crisp, about 5 minutes. Add more stock, if necessary. Garnish with parsley, if desired, and serve.

Rice Thread Noodles with Vegetable Julienne ★ ★ ★

Makes 4 servings

½ pound thin rice noodles
4 cloves garlic, minced
1 teaspoon minced fresh
    ginger
1 cup thinly sliced
    mushrooms
1 cup *Vegetable Stock*
1 teaspoon tamari or soy
    sauce
1 cup shredded Chinese
    cabbage
2 scallions, minced,
    including green part
½ cup thinly sliced sweet red
    peppers
1 tablespoon chopped
    fresh parsley or
    coriander (garnish)

Soak noodles for 20 minutes and drain.

In a medium-size saucepan, combine the garlic, ginger, mushrooms, stock, and tamari and heat through. Add the cabbage and scallions and bring to a boil. Reduce heat, add peppers and noodles, and cook until heated through.

Transfer to a serving bowl and garnish with fresh parsley, if desired.

NOTE: Rice noodles are available in oriental groceries and gourmet shops.

Chinese Stir-Fry ★ ★ ★

Makes 3 servings

1 package (3½ ounces)
    cellophane noodles
4 shiitake mushrooms (1½
    inches each), soaked for
    20 minutes and slivered

With scissors, cut the noodles in 2-inch pieces. Soak noodles in hot water for 30 minutes. Drain.

In a wok or medium-size no-stick skillet, stir-fry mushrooms, bamboo shoots, broccoli, carrots, and snow peas with the water for 2 minutes. Remove from wok.

½ cup shredded bamboo
  shoots
1 cup broccoli florets
½ cup julienned carrots
1 cup snow peas
2 tablespoons water
2 tablespoons tamari or soy
  sauce
2 tablespoons *Chicken Stock*
½ teaspoon cornstarch

In a small bowl, mix the tamari, stock, and cornstarch. Pour into wok and stir until thick, about 45 seconds. Add noodles and vegetables and toss. Serve immediately.

Vegetarian Stir-Fry ★ ★

Makes 4 servings

1 pound tofu, cubed
3 tablespoons apple juice
2 tablespoons tamari or soy
  sauce
1 teaspoon ground ginger
1 tablespoon safflower oil
1 medium-size onion, halved
  and thinly sliced
3 stalks broccoli, thinly sliced
  (peel the stems)
2 medium-size carrots, thinly
  sliced on the diagonal
2 celery stalks, thinly sliced
  on the diagonal
2 cloves garlic, sliced
2 cups cooked rice

Place the tofu in a medium-size bowl. Combine the juice, tamari, and ginger and pour over the tofu. Baste so that all of the tofu is marinated.

Heat a large skillet or wok, then add the oil. Quickly stir-fry the onions until translucent.

Add the broccoli and stir until bright green. Add the carrots, celery, garlic, and tofu, along with the marinade. Stir until the vegetables are crisp-tender. Serve over hot rice.

Sushi Bowl with Tamago ★ ★ ★

Sushi is a Japanese name for rice with vinegar. Tamago is a thin egg omelet.

Makes 4 servings

1	cup short grain brown rice
1¼	cups water
2	tablespoons rice vinegar
2	tablespoons mirin (sweet rice vinegar)
¼	cup shredded nori (Japanese sea vegetables)
½	cup shredded daikon radishes
½	cup cubed tofu
½	cup shredded cucumbers
1	egg, beaten

Soak rice in water for 30 minutes. Bring the rice to a boil, cover, and simmer over medium heat for 10 to 20 minutes or until all water is absorbed. Remove from heat and add vinegar and mirin. Mix well and set aside. When cool, gently add nori, radishes, tofu, and cucumbers.

Coat an 8-inch skillet with no-stick spray. Pour egg in and make a thin tamago by swirling the pan. Slice it in ½-inch strips and add to the rice. Serve in pretty bowls.

230

Bubbling Tofu ★ ★ ★

Cook this dish at tableside on an electric skillet.

Makes 4 servings

½	tablespoon tamari or soy sauce
2	tablespoons mirin (sweet rice vinegar)
2	cups shredded spinach
½	cup coarsely grated carrots
3	cups water
3	cups *Chicken Stock*
1	tablespoon grated fresh ginger
1	clove garlic
2	pounds tofu, cut into 1-inch cubes
¼	cup minced scallions
1	tablespoon sesame seeds

In a small bowl, combine tamari and mirin. Set aside to use as a dipping sauce.

Arrange spinach and carrots on a serving tray.

In a large, deep skillet combine water, stock, and ginger and add garlic by pushing it through a garlic press. Bring to a boil, then lower heat to a simmer. Add tofu and simmer gently for 2 to 3 minutes. (Cook slowly or tofu will harden.) Scoop tofu from liquid and arrange over spinach mixture. Sprinkle with scallions and sesame seeds and serve at once, with dipping sauce.

London Loaf ★ ★

Makes 8 servings

4	cups fresh whole wheat bread crumbs
2	cups shredded carrots
1	cup chopped onions
1	cup chopped celery
½	cup chopped mushrooms
¼	cup minced fresh parsley
¼	cup ground pecans or walnuts
3	eggs, beaten
⅓	cup skim milk
1½	teaspoons ground cumin
1	teaspoon ground coriander
½	teaspoon celery seeds
2	cups *Tomato Sauce*

In a large bowl, combine the bread crumbs with the carrots, onions, celery, mushrooms, parsley, and nuts. Combine the eggs and milk.

Stir the egg mixture, cumin, coriander, and celery seeds into the bread crumb mixture in the large bowl. Pack the loaf into 4½ × 8½-inch bread pan coated with no-stick spray. Bake at 375° for 1 hour.

Heat the tomato sauce. Cut the loaf into slices and top with some of the sauce.

NOTE: Pecans or walnuts can be ground in a blender with short bursts at high speed.

231

Westport Vegetable Bake ★ ★ ★

Makes 6 servings

10	cups sliced cabbage
2	cups chopped broccoli
1	small onion, chopped
3	tablespoons butter
3	tablespoons whole wheat flour
	dash of nutmeg
2	cups skim milk
1½	cups low-fat cottage cheese
2	cups whole wheat bread crumbs

Place the cabbage, broccoli, and onions in an 8-quart pot with a small amount of water and steam just until crisp-tender, about 5 minutes.

While the vegetables cook, melt the butter in a medium-size skillet and stir in the flour and nutmeg. Cook over medium heat, stirring constantly, for 1 to 2 minutes, then add the milk and cook, stirring, until thickened.

In a 3-quart ovenproof casserole coated with no-stick spray, layer one-half of the vegetables, cottage cheese, sauce, and bread crumbs. Repeat the layering. Bake uncovered at 350° for 30 to 40 minutes or until the vegetables are tender.

Summer Vegetable Stew ★ ★ ★

A mixture of vegetables provides a nutrient-rich stew that can be served over polenta squares, whole grain noodles, or brown rice for a main dish.

Makes 6 servings

4	cups *Chicken Stock*
⅔	cup tomato paste
2	medium-size carrots, sliced diagonally
2	cups chopped onions
1	cup sliced mushrooms
2	stalks celery, sliced diagonally
3	cloves garlic, sliced
½	teaspoon basil
½	teaspoon marjoram
¼	teaspoon cayenne pepper
2	small zucchini, cut in thin 2-inch strips
3	cups cooked rice
	freshly grated Parmesan cheese
¼	cup minced fresh parsley

Combine the stock, tomato paste, carrots, onions, mushrooms, celery, garlic, basil, marjoram, and cayenne in a large saucepan. Bring to a boil, then reduce heat and simmer, covered, for 45 minutes. Stir in the zucchini and cook 15 minutes longer. Serve over rice and sprinkle with Parmesan and parsley.

232

Summer Vegetable Kabobs ★ ★ ★

Makes 4 servings

1	medium-size yellow squash
1	medium-size zucchini
1	small eggplant

Blanch the squash in boiling water for 5 minutes, then drain and refresh under cold running water.

Blanch the zucchini, eggplant, and onions separately in boiling water for 7 minutes. Drain and refresh under cold running water.

8   small white onions
1   tablespoon vegetable oil
5   tablespoons cold water
2   tablespoons fresh lemon
    juice
1   tablespoon red wine
    vinegar
1½ teaspoons Dijon mustard
½   teaspoon basil
¼   teaspoon thyme
¼   teaspoon marjoram
1   small bay leaf, crumbled
1   clove garlic, minced
1   tablespoon minced fresh
    parsley
½   large sweet red pepper,
    cut into 6 equal pieces
½   large green pepper, cut
    into 6 equal pieces
8   mushrooms, rinsed and
    patted dry
8   cherry tomatoes

Cut the squash and zucchini crosswise into 16 slices each. Cut the eggplant into 1-inch cubes. Peel the onions.

In a large bowl combine the oil, water, lemon juice, vinegar, mustard, basil, thyme, marjoram, bay leaf, garlic, and parsley. Add the squash, zucchini, eggplant, onions, red peppers, green peppers, mushrooms, and tomatoes to the marinade, turning carefully to coat. Cover and marinate in the refrigerator for at least 2 hours or overnight.

Remove vegetables from marinade, reserving the marinade. Arrange the vegetables on skewers. Brush with reserved marinade. Broil or grill, turning and brushing often with reserved marinade until vegetables are tender, about 10 to 12 minutes.

233

Stuffed
Acorn Squash ★ ★

Makes 2 servings

2   acorn squashes, halved and
    seeded
1   medium-size tart red apple,
    chopped
1   tablespoon sunflower seeds
1   tablespoon honey
1   tablespoon apple cider
1   teaspoon lemon juice
    dash of cinnamon

Cut a thin piece from the bottoms of the squash halves so that they stand upright. Place cut side up on a baking sheet.

In a medium-size bowl, toss the apples with the sunflower seeds, honey, cider, and lemon juice. Divide the mixture among the squash halves. Sprinkle cinnamon over the stuffed squash halves and cover loosely with aluminum foil. Set in a shallow baking dish filled about ½ inch full with water. Bake at 350° for about 1½ hours or until the squash is quite soft.

Italian Stuffed Squash ★ ★

This is a big meal, but it is not heavy.

Makes 2 servings

3   medium-size tomatoes, quartered
1   sweet red pepper, coarsely chopped
1   small onion, halved
¼   cup *Tomato Sauce*
¼   teaspoon basil
    dash of oregano
    dash of marjoram
4   cloves garlic
1   medium-size zucchini
2   tablespoons *Vegetable Stock*
6   large mushrooms, chopped
1   medium-size onion, minced
1   cup packed spinach leaves, chopped
1   cup cooked rice
2   thin slices mozzarella cheese

Place the tomatoes, red peppers, onion halves, tomato sauce, basil, oregano, marjoram, and 3 of the garlic cloves in a blender. Process on low to medium speed until smooth, stopping the blender and scraping down the sides as necessary. Place in a medium-size saucepan and bring to a boil. Cover, reduce heat, and simmer for 30 minutes.

Cut the zucchini in half. Steam just until it begins to get tender yet is still firm, 8 to 10 minutes. Run under cold water until cool enough to handle.

While the zucchini is steaming, heat the stock in a large skillet. Stir in the mushrooms and minced onions. Cook over medium heat, stirring frequently, until the onions are tender.

When the zucchini is cool, use a sharp knife to remove the seeds and some of the pulp, leaving a shell about ¼- to ½-inch thick. Chop the removed pulp and seeds and add to the mushroom mixture along with the spinach. Mince the remaining garlic clove and add it to the mixture also.

Cook the mushroom mixture over medium heat, stirring frequently, until the spinach is wilted and any liquid in the pan has evaporated. Remove from heat. Fill the squash halves with the mushroom mixture.

Place the rice in two small, individual baking dishes or one shallow baking dish just slightly larger than the zucchini. Arrange the zucchini halves over the rice, cut sides up. Spoon the tomato sauce over the zucchini and rice.

Cut the cheese slices into strips and place over the zucchini. Cover loosely with foil and bake at 350° for 40 minutes.

Stuffed Summer Tomatoes ★ ★ ★

Makes 2 servings

4   large vine-ripened
    tomatoes
¾   cup *Chicken Stock*
1   small onion, chopped
2   tablespoons pine nuts
½   cup brown rice
2   tablespoons currants
2   tablespoons minced fresh
    parsley
1   teaspoon tamari or soy
    sauce
    dash of ground coriander
    dash of cinnamon
¼   cup low-fat yogurt (garnish)
    minced fresh parsley
    (garnish)

Cut off the tops of the tomatoes, remove the pulp, and set the pulp aside. Place the tomatoes, cut side up, in a shallow 8 × 8-inch baking dish.

Place ¼ cup of the stock and onions in a large skillet and cook, stirring, over low heat until the onions are tender. Stir in the pine nuts and rice and cook for 2 to 3 minutes.

Add the tomato pulp, the remaining stock, currants, parsley, tamari, coriander, and cinnamon. Bring to a boil, reduce heat, cover, and simmer on very low heat for 40 to 45 minutes.

Stuff the tomatoes with the rice mixture. Cover the baking dish with foil and bake at 350° for 20 minutes.

To serve, garnish each of the tomatoes with a tablespoon of yogurt and sprinkle with parsley, if desired. Serve hot or at room temperature.

235

Stuffed Tomatoes Myklos ★ ★ ★

Makes 2 servings

1   cup shredded spinach
4   large tomatoes
¾   cup cooked rice
¼   cup finely crumbled feta
    cheese
2   scallions, chopped
1   tablespoon *No-Oil Pesto*
1   tablespoon minced fresh
    dill
2   tablespoons low-fat yogurt
    (garnish)
    dill sprigs (garnish)
    lettuce leaves (garnish)

Blanch spinach for one minute.

Meanwhile, hollow out the tomatoes from the stem end. (Discard the pulp or save for another use.)

In a medium-size mixing bowl, combine the spinach, rice, feta cheese, scallions, pesto, and dill. Fill the tomatoes with the rice mixture. Garnish with a dollop of yogurt and dill sprigs, and serve on a bed of lettuce, if desired.

Broccoli and Cheese Bake ★ ★

Makes 4 servings

1	cup whole wheat macaroni
1½	pounds broccoli (1 large bunch)
2	eggs
1	cup low-fat cottage cheese
¼	cup skim milk
2	tablespoons grated Parmesan cheese
1	tablespoon whole wheat flour
	dash of nutmeg
	dash of cayenne pepper

Bring a 3-quart pot of water to a boil. Cook the macaroni in boiling water until al dente, about 9 to 11 minutes. Drain and rinse under cold water until cool. Set aside.

Cut the broccoli into stalks and remove the tough outer layer from the stems. Steam the broccoli until it just begins to get tender, about 10 minutes. The broccoli should still be bright green and quite firm. Rinse under cold water until cool and set aside.

Place the eggs, cottage cheese, milk, Parmesan, flour, nutmeg, and cayenne in a blender. Process on low speed until smooth.

To assemble the casserole, place the macaroni in the bottom of a 9- or 10-inch pie plate. Arrange the broccoli stalks in a circle around the outside edge of the pie plate so the top of each stalk covers the stem of the stalk in front of it. Save a couple of florets to place in the center of the dish.

Spoon the cheese mixture over the macaroni but not over the broccoli. Cover loosely with foil and bake at 350° for 40 minutes. Serve hot.

236

Tamale Pie ★

A vegetarian casserole, baked in cornmeal and chock-full of taste.

Makes 6 servings

1½	cups yellow cornmeal
1	cup cold water
3½	cups water
1	large onion, chopped
1	cup chopped sweet red peppers
10	cloves garlic, sliced
3	tablespoons *Chicken Stock* or *Vegetable Stock*

Stir together the cornmeal and the cold water until combined, pressing out any lumps. Set aside.

Bring the 3½ cups water to a boil in a large saucepan. Stir in the cornmeal mixture and immediately begin stirring rapidly with a wire whisk until the mixture begins to boil. Reduce heat and partially cover the saucepan. Simmer for 25 to 30 minutes, stirring frequently with the whisk. The cornmeal mixture should be rather stiff.

2 cups chopped tomatoes
  with juice
1 hot red or green chili
  pepper
⅔ cup tomato paste
3 cups cooked red kidney
  beans
3 tablespoons chili seasoning
½ cup shredded Monterey
  Jack cheese
1 teaspoon butter, melted

While the cornmeal mixture cooks, begin to make the filling. In a medium-size skillet, sauté the onions, red peppers, and garlic in the stock until the onions are limp.

Place the tomatoes in a blender with the chili pepper and tomato paste. Process on medium speed until smooth.

In a large bowl, combine the cooked onions, peppers, and garlic with the tomato mixture, beans and chili seasoning.

Remove the cornmeal from the heat when it is stiff. Spread about two-thirds of the cornmeal mixture across the bottom and up the sides of a 1½-quart ovenproof casserole.

Fill casserole with the bean mixture. Top with the cheese. Flatten the remaining cornmeal mixture and use it to cover the bean filling. Press to seal the cornmeal along the sides of the casserole. Using a fork, gently press a decorative design into the top of the cornmeal. Bake at 325° for 1 to 1¼ hours. Brush lightly with butter halfway through the baking time.

237

Chili Non Carne ★ ★

Makes 8 servings

4 cups cooked red kidney
  beans
4 cups water
2 large onions, minced
2 tablespoons olive oil
3 cloves garlic, minced
2½ cups chopped plum
  tomatoes with juice
1½ cups bulgur
1 tablespoon chili powder
1½ tablespoons tamari or soy
  sauce

Place the kidney beans and water in a large saucepan and bring to a boil over medium heat.

Meanwhile, cook the onions in the olive oil in a large skillet over medium heat until translucent. Add the garlic and cook, stirring, for an additional 1 to 2 minutes.

Add the onions and garlic, tomatoes, bulgur, and chili powder to the beans in the large saucepan. When it boils, reduce the heat, cover, and simmer for about 30 minutes, stirring frequently. Stir in the tamari and serve.

Lentil Chili ★ ★

Makes 6 servings

  2   small onions, chopped
 ¼   cup *Vegetable Stock*
  1   cup dried lentils
 1½   cups bulgur
 4½   cups water
  2   tablespoons chili
          powder
  1   clove garlic, minced
  1   tablespoon tamari or soy
          sauce
  3   scallions, minced (garnish)
  1   cup alfalfa sprouts
          (garnish)

Cook the onions in the stock in a large skillet over low heat until they are fairly tender. Stir in the lentils and bulgur and after 1 to 2 minutes, add the water. Stir well. Add the chili powder and the garlic.

Simmer for about 30 minutes or until the water is absorbed and the lentils are tender. Turn off the heat. Stir in the tamari. Place the chili in a serving bowl or on individual plates and garnish with the scallions and alfalfa sprouts, if desired.

238

Santa Fe Tostadas ★

Complete this satisfying lunch with a dessert of fresh fruit and herb tea.

Makes 4 servings

  1   small onion, chopped
 ½   stalk celery, chopped
  2   tablespoons *Vegetable
          Stock*
  5   cloves garlic
  1   cup dried lentils
 2½–3 cups water
 ⅓   cup *Tomato Sauce*
  1   tablespoon chili
          seasoning

Place the onions and celery in a large skillet with the stock. Cook until the onions are translucent, adding water, if necessary, to prevent sticking. Add the garlic by pushing the cloves through a garlic press into the skillet and stir for about 1 minute. Add the lentils, water, tomato sauce, chili seasoning, molasses, cumin, and oregano. Bring to a boil, then reduce heat and simmer, covered, for about 35 minutes or until the lentils are tender. Remove from the heat, stir in the tamari, and cover to keep warm.

2 teaspoons molasses
½ teaspoon ground cumin
½ teaspoon oregano
2 teaspoons tamari or soy
   sauce
4 *Corn Tortillas*
1 small zucchini,
   shredded
2 cups chopped lettuce
1 cup chopped tomatoes
½ cup chopped scallions
1 cup alfalfa sprouts
1 cup low-fat yogurt

To soften, dip the tortillas for 2 to 3 seconds in a small skillet filled 1 inch full with boiling water.

To assemble, place the tortillas on individual serving plates. Divide the lentil mixture among the tortillas and spread to the edges. Top each with some zucchini, lettuce, tomatoes, scallions, sprouts, and a dollop of yogurt. The yogurt can also be served on the side.

Mexican Bean Tacos ★

239

Makes 4 servings

8 taco shells
½ tablespoon butter
1 small onion, chopped
2 cups cooked red kidney
   beans
1 tablespoon chili powder
1 teaspoon ground cumin
½ teaspoon blackstrap
   molasses
½ cup shredded sharp
   Cheddar cheese
1 cup *Hot Taco Sauce*
1½ cups shredded lettuce
½ cup low-fat yogurt
   (optional)

Heat the taco shells in a 325° oven for 5 to 10 minutes.

Meanwhile, place the butter in a large skillet, then add the onions. Cook, stirring over medium heat until the onions are translucent and just begin to soften. Add a few drops of water, if necessary, to prevent sticking. Stir in the kidney beans, chili powder, cumin, and molasses. Mash the beans with the back of a wooden spoon while cooking. When the beans are mashed and heated through, remove from the heat.

Place the beans, cheese, sauce, lettuce, and yogurt in separate dishes on a buffet or on the table. Let each diner assemble his or her own tacos.

To assemble the tacos, place about 2 to 3 tablespoons of beans across the bottom of the taco shell. Sprinkle with some shredded cheese, then add sauce to taste. Top with shredded lettuce and a dollop of yogurt, if desired.

Red River Stew ★ ★ ★

A filling, protein-rich dish.

Makes 6 servings

1   tablespoon olive oil
1   medium-size onion,
         chopped
1   large carrot, thinly sliced
2   stalks celery, thinly sliced
4   cups *Chicken Stock*
4   cups chopped tomatoes
         with juice
½   cup packed watercress,
         chopped
1   cup dried red lentils
1   clove garlic

Place the oil in a large saucepan and cook the onions, carrots, and celery over low heat until the onions are translucent. Add the stock, tomatoes, watercress, and lentils. Add the garlic by pushing it through a garlic press into the pan. Bring to a boil, then reduce heat and simmer over low heat for 25 minutes or until the lentils are tender and the stew is the desired thickness.

240

Steamed Tempeh
with Two Sauces ★ ★ ★

Makes 4 servings

1   tablespoon minced fresh
         ginger
3   cloves garlic, minced
2   tablespoons minced
         shallots or onions
2   dried red chilies (about 2
         inches each), seeded
         and minced
1   pound tempeh
2   tablespoons minced fresh
         parsley
2   eggs, beaten
1   lemon, sliced

In a food processor or large mortar, puree the ginger, garlic, shallots, chilies, tempeh, parsley, and eggs. Roll into 2-inch balls.

Fill an 8-quart pot 2 to 3 inches full of water. Add the lemon slices to the water and bring to a boil. Place the balls on top of a steam rack coated with no-stick spray and steam for 15 to 20 minutes.

To make miso sauce: Combine miso and 2 teaspoons vinegar in a small bowl.

To make mustard sauce: Combine mustard, vinegar, parsley, and paprika in a small bowl.

Drizzle miso sauce over half the tempeh mixture and mustard sauce over the other half. Serve warm.

MISO SAUCE

1	teaspoon red miso (red soybean paste)
2	teaspoons rice vinegar

MUSTARD SAUCE

1	teaspoon Dijon mustard
1	teaspoon rice vinegar
½	teaspoon minced fresh parsley
¼	teaspoon paprika

Sweet and Sour Tempeh ★ ★ ★

Makes 8 servings

1½	cups water
½	cup cider vinegar
¼	cup tomato paste
¼	cup honey
1	teaspoon minced fresh ginger
2	cloves garlic
1	cup cubed pineapple
2	stalks celery, cut diagonally into thin slices
¾	cup diced sweet red peppers
2	teaspoons cornstarch
1	pound tempeh, cut into 1-inch cubes
1	cup snow peas
3	cups hot, cooked rice
4	scallions, sliced diagonally (garnish)

Place 1 cup of the water, the vinegar, tomato paste, honey, and ginger in a large saucepan. Push the garlic through a garlic press into the pan. Add the pineapple, celery, and peppers and bring to a boil. Reduce heat, cover, and simmer for 10 minutes or until the vegetables are crisp-tender.

Stir the cornstarch into the remaining half cup of water until it is dissolved, then add to the saucepan. Stir in the tempeh, cover, and simmer for 10 minutes. Add the snow peas and cook an additional 1 to 2 minutes or until the snow peas are bright green and still fairly crisp.

Arrange the cooked rice on a serving platter and top with the sweet and sour tempeh. Garnish with scallions, if desired, and serve at once.

Tempeh Stew ★ ★ ★

Makes 6 servings

1	pound tempeh, cut into 1-inch cubes
2½	cups *White Poultry Stock*
3	cups chopped Bermuda onions
2	cups chopped sweet red peppers
1	cup chopped leeks
1	large stalk celery, chopped
3	cloves garlic, minced
2½	cups chopped plum tomatoes with juice
1	teaspoon rosemary, crumbled
1	teaspoon parsley

In a medium-size saucepan, sauté the tempeh in 3 tablespoons of stock. Add onions, peppers, leeks, celery, and garlic and continue to sauté for 4 to 5 minutes. Add tomatoes, remaining stock, rosemary, and parsley. Simmer gently for 1 hour.

242

Double Pepper Tempeh ★ ★ ★

Use a finely textured brown rice tempeh rather than all soy, which could fall apart during braising.

Makes 4 servings

1	pound brown rice tempeh, cut into 2½ × ½-inch strips
1	tablespoon minced fresh ginger
2	cloves garlic, minced
1	cup *Chicken Stock*
½	teaspoon tamari or soy sauce
1	dried chili, seeded and cut into threads
1	green pepper, cut into ½-inch strips

In a medium-size saucepan, combine the tempeh, ginger, garlic, stock, tamari, and chilies. Bring to a boil, then quickly reduce heat and simmer, covered, for 2 to 3 minutes. Add green peppers and cook 1 to 2 minutes more. Serve hot.

Garbanzo Burgers ★ ★ ★

Makes 4 servings

1   egg
2   tablespoons chopped fresh
      parsley
1   teaspoon ground cumin
1   teaspoon ground coriander
¾   teaspoon chili powder
3   tablespoons tahini (sesame
      butter)
2   cloves garlic
¼   cup low-fat cottage cheese
1   cup cooked chick-peas
½   cup wheat germ

Place the egg, parsley, cumin, coriander, chili powder, and tahini in a blender. Add the garlic by pushing it through a garlic press into the blender. Process on low to medium speed until smooth.

Add the cottage cheese and process on low speed until smooth. Add the chick-peas and again process on low speed until smooth, scraping down the sides if necessary. Stir in the wheat germ by hand. Form the mixture into 4 patties. Sauté in a medium-size skillet coated with no-stick spray or a no-stick pan until golden brown on both sides and cooked throughout, about 6 minutes on each side.

★ ★ *VARIATION: To make into a sandwich, serve in* Whole Wheat Pitas, *garnished with chopped tomatoes, scallions, alfalfa sprouts, and a dollop of yogurt.*

243

Leek and Onion Pie ★ ★

Makes 6 servings

CRUST
1   cup whole wheat flour
¼   cup corn oil
2   tablespoons water

FILLING
3   medium-size leeks,
      chopped
1   small onion, chopped
1   tablespoon *Chicken Stock*
      dash of nutmeg
1   cup low-fat cottage cheese
½   cup skim milk
3   eggs
1   tablespoon chopped
      parsley (garnish)

To make the crust: Place the flour, oil, and water in a 9-inch pie plate. Toss the ingredients together with a fork, then press along the bottom and sides of the pie plate.

To make the filling: Place the leeks and onions in a medium-size skillet with the stock and dust with a little nutmeg. Cook over low to medium heat until the leeks are soft.

Place the cottage cheese, milk, and eggs in a blender. Process on low speed until smooth.

Scatter the cooked leeks and scallions over the bottom of the pie shell. Carefully pour in the cheese and egg mixture.

Bake at 375° for 35 to 40 minutes or until puffed and golden. Let cool slightly before cutting. Sprinkle with chopped parsley, if desired, and serve.

Corfu Cabbage with Bulgur ★ ★

Makes 6 servings

2¼   cups bulgur
4½   cups warm water
1½   teaspoons tamari or soy
       sauce
⅓   cup minced scallions
⅓   cup minced fresh parsley
1   tablespoon safflower oil
1   teaspoon caraway seeds
1   clove garlic
1   head cabbage or 24 small
       blanched cabbage leaves
1½   cups tomato juice
2   cups *Chicken Stock*
       lemon wedges (garnish)
       chopped fresh mint or
       parsley (garnish)

Soak the bulgur in the water for 45 minutes or until nearly soft. Stir in the tamari, scallions, parsley, oil, and caraway seeds. Add the garlic by pushing it through a garlic press.

Steam the cabbage for 10 minutes. Remove 24 leaves. (Large ones can be cut in half.) Place about ¼ cup of the bulgur mixture on the edge of each leaf and roll up.

Coat the bottom of a large skillet with no-stick spray. Place the stuffed leaves seam side down in a single layer in the skillet. Cover with tomato juice and stock.

Cover the pan and simmer over very low heat for 40 minutes, shaking pan occasionally. Add more water, if necessary, to keep rolls from sticking.

Serve each portion with a lemon wedge and a sprinkling of mint, if desired.

★ ★ ★ *VARIATION: Serve 3 cabbage rolls per serving.*

Whole Grains

Whole grains—wonderful foods such as oats, barley, whole wheat, millet, brown rice, buckwheat, and corn—are essential to weight control. So essential, they should be a part of your diet every day. Why? Because they're filled with fiber, and fiber acts as a *natural* appetite suppressant in two ways.

One, whole grains are chewy. You really have to take your time to eat them (unlike, say, a fluffy, low-fiber doughnut that you can practically inhale). That means you can't ram forkful after forkful of whole grain calories into your mouth—so even though they're a trifle high in calories, a little goes a long way. Two, the fiber in whole grains breaks down slowly in your digestive tract. And that means you're not hungry an hour later or three hours later. You feel pleasantly and energetically satisfied while you're eating and after you're done.

And there's a third weight loss benefit from fiber. It keeps the body's elimination system working normally—something that can be a problem for many dieters.

The benefits of rice and whole grains go beyond their ability to fill you up. They're chock-full of vitamins and minerals—B vitamins, zinc, and magnesium. And, combined with a sprinkling of nuts, low-fat dairy products, or beans and other legumes, rice and whole grains become an important source of protein. They can be turned into a hearty meal so tasty that you'll find them both physically and psychologically satisfying as you control your weight.

Breakfast Grains

Skipping breakfast? Think again. Studies have shown that those who eat breakfast are generally thinner than people who skip breakfast.

Whole grains have a long-standing reputation for "sticking to the ribs." This means that a protein-rich breakfast of filling oats, rice, barley, or wheat can provide an entire morning's worth of satisfaction.

I've found that the best way to control calories at breakfast is to make your own cereal from scratch. When you make your own, you know *exactly* what you're getting. And, in these recipes, you won't be getting any added salt, sugar, or unnecessary calories. Special care was taken in creating these recipes to bring them *well below* the calories you find in commercial varieties.

Also, by making your own, you have the luxury of sampling something different every day, if that's what you need to keep your diet from getting dull. There's no worry about having to empty one box before opening the next.

Following, you'll find two weeks worth of cereal recipes for your breakfast variety. Some are for two to six servings. Others you can make in large batches and store. I've also included a few pancake and waffle recipes that won't pile on the calories. Yes, you *can* have pancakes for breakfast!

The three-star rating in this chapter allows a half cup of cereal per serving, unless otherwise indicated. Milk, too, is included where suggested. Pancake and waffle ratings include the topping. Feel free to try other breakfast toppings from the "Dressings, Spreads, and Sauces" chapter. Just remember, don't overdo it. A tablespoon or two of topping is plenty.

Hot Apple Cider Breakfast Bowl ★ ★

Makes 4 servings

1½ cups cooked brown rice
1   cup apple cider
1   cup water
2   tablespoons ground
      almonds
      dash of cinnamon

Place all the ingredients in a medium-size sauce-pan and bring to a boil. Reduce heat, cover, and simmer for 1 hour. (All of this can be done the night before.)

Place the cooked mixture in a blender and process on medium speed until smooth. Reheat, if necessary, before serving.

Fruit and Rice Porridge ★

A sweet apricot taste without added honey.

Makes 2 servings

1   cup cooked brown rice
1   cup apple juice
¼   cup dried apricots,
      chopped
1   cup skim milk

Place the rice, juice, and apricots in a small sauce-pan and bring to a boil. Reduce heat and simmer about 10 minutes, until the juice is absorbed and the rice is soft. Serve hot with milk.

247

Raisin-Rice Porridge ★ ★

Makes 2 servings

1   cup cooked brown rice
½   cup water
1   tablespoon chopped raisins
1   tablespoon ground almonds
½   apple, chopped
1   teaspoon maple syrup
      skim milk or orange juice
      (optional)

Place the rice, water, raisins, almonds, apples, and maple syrup in a small saucepan. Bring to a boil, then reduce heat, cover, and simmer for about 15 minutes, until the rice is very soft and the water absorbed. Add a little milk or orange juice, if desired, and serve hot.

Date, Brown Rice, and Millet Cereal ★ ★

Makes 6 servings

1 cup brown rice
½ cup millet
4½ cups water
¼ cup chopped dates
2 teaspoons maple syrup
¼ teaspoon cinnamon
1 cup skim milk

Place the rice, millet, and water in a medium-size saucepan, bring to a boil, and allow to cook for a minute or two. Stir in the dates, syrup, and cinnamon. Cover the pan, turn the heat to its lowest setting, and steam the grains for 45 minutes. Remove from heat and let stand another 10 minutes. Serve with the milk.

NOTE: You can make the cereal ahead of time and reheat individual portions by adding a little water to the saucepan.

Apple Cinnamon Oatmeal ★ ★

248

Makes 2 servings

1 cup water
¼ cup apple juice
1 tart apple, diced
⅔ cup rolled oats
 dash of cinnamon
1 cup skim milk

Place the water, juice, and apples in a medium-size saucepan and bring to a boil. Stir in the rolled oats and cinnamon. Return to a boil, then reduce heat and simmer until the porridge is thick. Serve hot with milk.

Three Bears Porridge with Dates ★ ★

Makes 2 servings

1½ cups water
¼ cup bulgur
⅓ cup rolled oats
2 tablespoons chopped dates
1 cup skim milk

Place the water and bulgur in a small saucepan and bring to a boil. Reduce heat and simmer for about 8 minutes or until the bulgur is soft. Stir in the rolled oats and the chopped dates. Continue to simmer for another 1 to 2 minutes. Serve hot with milk.

Maple Wheat and Oats Cereal ★ ★ ★

Makes 2 servings

¼ cup wheat kernels
¼ cup oat groats
2 cups water
1 tablespoon maple syrup
⅓ cup skim milk

Place the wheat kernels and groats in a dry, large cast-iron skillet. Toast the kernels over low to medium heat, stirring constantly, until most of them have "popped" and are light golden brown.

Place the toasted grains in a blender or food processor and process with short bursts at high speed until most of the grains are cracked.

In a medium-size saucepan, combine the water and cracked grains. Bring to a boil, reduce heat, cover, and simmer for 10 to 15 minutes, until the cereal is thick.

Stir the maple syrup into the cereal and serve hot with the milk.

Polenta with Breakfast Fruit Sauce ★ ★

Prepare polenta the night before and let it chill.

Makes 6 servings

6½ cups water
2 cups cornmeal
2 teaspoons butter
2 cups *Brekafast Fruit Sauce*
6 orange slices (garnish)

Place 5 cups of the water in a large saucepan and bring to a boil. Meanwhile, stir the remaining water into the cornmeal.

When the water in the saucepan is boiling, stir in the cornmeal. Keep stirring until smooth.

Reduce the heat and cover the pan. Simmer for 25 minutes, stirring frequently, until the polenta is thick.

Rinse a 9 × 5-inch loaf pan with cold water. Pour the polenta into the pan and refrigerate overnight.

Next morning, cut the polenta into 12 slices. Cook the polenta, a few slices at a time, in a large skillet with the butter.

Serve polenta hot, with heated fruit sauce. Garnish with an orange slice, if desired.

Sunflower
Maple Porridge ★

Depart from the usual—try bulgur in place of rolled oats.

Makes 2 servings

1½ cups water
½ cup bulgur
¼ cup raisins
1 tablespoon ground sun-
    flower seeds
1 tablespoon maple syrup
½ cup skim milk

Place the water, bulgur, raisins, sunflower seeds, and maple syrup in a small saucepan. Bring to a boil, stirring frequently, then reduce heat and simmer, stirring occasionally, for 15 to 20 minutes or until creamy. Serve with milk.

NOTE: Coarse bulgur may require a slightly longer cooking time. Vary the amount of bulgur according to desired thickness of the porridge.

Crunchy
Wheat Treat ★ ★

Makes approximately 4 cups

1½ cups whole wheat flour
¼ cup wheat germ
½ teaspoon baking soda
¼ cup honey
1 cup buttermilk

In a medium-size mixing bowl, combine the flour, wheat germ, and baking soda. Stir in the honey and buttermilk until combined.

Spread the dough evenly on a cookie sheet coated with no-stick spray. Bake at 350° for 25 minutes.

Remove from the oven. Break off and discard any thin edges that may have become too browned in the oven.

When the dough has cooled, break into pieces and place in a blender, about 1 cup at a time. Process with short bursts at high speed until dough is broken up into small bits.

Place the cereal bits on the baking sheets and return to the oven. Bake at 250° for 25 to 50 minutes, or until crisp. Store cereal in an airtight container in a cool, dry place.

Use ½ cup of skim milk for each serving.

★ *VARIATION: Top each serving with ½ of a banana.*

Granola ★ ★ ★

Everyone loves granola, but the added sweeteners usually put it off limits to the weight watcher. This version cuts out a lot of these unneeded calories, while still preserving the granola flavor. Figure on a ⅓-cup serving for this recipe.

Makes approximately 7½ cups

3	cups rolled oats
1½	cups wheat germ
1	cup bran
½	cup soy flakes
¼	cup shredded coconut
¼	cup chopped walnuts
1	teaspoon cinnamon
3	tablespoons honey
3	tablespoons water
½	cup raisins

Combine oats, wheat germ, bran, soy flakes, coconut, walnuts, and cinnamon in a large bowl.

In a small bowl combine honey and water. Pour over the oat mixture and stir well.

Spread the mixture on two ungreased baking sheets. Bake at 225° for about 1 hour or until the granola is golden brown, stirring every 15 minutes. Allow to cool on the baking sheets, then stir in the raisins.

Place in a covered jar and store in a cool, dry place or refrigerate. Use ½ cup of skim milk for each serving.

Buckwheat Breakfast Cereal ★ ★ ★

Makes 4 servings

2½	cups water
¾	cup buckwheat groats
1	tablespoon honey
⅓	cup raisins
¼	teaspoon cinnamon
¾	cup skim milk

Bring the water to a boil in a medium-size saucepan. Stir in the groats, reduce heat, cover, and simmer for 20 to 25 minutes, until they are quite soft.

Stir in the honey, raisins, and cinnamon. Cook an additional 5 minutes. Serve with milk.

★ ★ ★ *VARIATION: Substitute chopped dried apricots for the raisins. You'll save even more calories.*

Barley Breakfast Bowl ★ ★

Makes 6 servings

1	cup barley
4	cups water
2	tablespoons honey
1	teaspoon cinnamon
1	cup skim milk

Place the barley and water in a medium-size saucepan. Bring to a boil, then cover, reduce heat, and simmer for 1½ hours.

Add the honey and cinnamon. Stir and cover. Simmer an additional 10 minutes. Stir in milk and serve.

251

Muesli ★ ★

Makes about 7 cups

3	cups rolled oats
1½	cups wheat germ
1	cup bran
½	cup soy flakes
¼	cup chopped walnuts
1	teaspoon cinnamon
½	cup raisins

Combine oats, wheat germ, bran, soy flakes, walnuts, and cinnamon in a large bowl.

Spread the mixture on two baking sheets coated with no-stick spray. Bake at 225° for about 45 minutes or until the mixture is golden brown. Stir occasionally.

Allow to cool on the baking sheets, then stir in the raisins.

Place in a covered jar and store in a cool, dry place.

Use ½ cup of skim milk for each serving.

★ ★ *VARIATION: Serve with ¼ cup of yogurt and half a sliced banana.*

252

Raisin Pancakes ★ ★

Makes 4 servings, 3 pancakes each

1	cup skim milk
1	cup quick-cooking rolled oats
⅓	cup whole wheat flour
1	teaspoon baking powder dash of cinnamon
2	eggs
2	tablespoons water
¼	cup raisins
¾	cup *Strawberry Sauce*

Place the milk and oats in a small saucepan, set over low to medium heat, and bring to a boil, stirring occasionally. Stir well, then remove from heat.

Place the cooked oats in a medium-size mixing bowl and add the flour, baking powder, and cinnamon.

Beat the eggs in a small bowl and then stir in the water. Add this to the oat mixture and stir together until combined.

Using ¼ cup of batter per pancake, pour the batter onto a hot, no-stick skillet or griddle or a skillet coated with no-stick spray. Sprinkle the top of each pancake with a few raisins before turning. Turn when the pancakes are golden brown on the bottom and bubbles appear on the surface.

Serve with sauce on the side.

Cottage Cheese Pancakes ★ ★ ★

Makes 2 servings, 3 pancakes each

½ cup low-fat cottage cheese
1 egg, separated
1 teaspoon maple syrup
¼ cup whole wheat flour
¼ teaspoon baking powder
    dash of nutmeg
½ cup *Strawberry-Rhubarb Sauce*

Place the cottage cheese, egg yolk, and maple syrup in a blender or food processor and process on low speed until smooth, scraping down the sides as necessary.

Place the egg white in a medium-size bowl and beat until stiff peaks form.

Add the cottage cheese mixture, flour, baking powder, and nutmeg to the egg white. Fold together gently with a spatula until combined.

Using ¼ cup of batter per pancake, spoon out and slightly spread the batter on a hot, no-stick skillet or griddle or a skillet coated with no-stick spray. Turn when the pancakes are golden brown on the bottom and bubbles appear on the surface.

Serve with sauce on the side.

253

Buttermilk Waffles ★ ★

Makes 4 servings, 1 waffle each

1 cup whole wheat flour
¼ cup wheat germ
1 teaspoon baking soda
1½ cups buttermilk
1 egg, beaten
2 tablespoons water
½ cup hot *Pineapple Sauce*

Place the flour, wheat germ, and baking soda in a medium-size mixing bowl and stir together.

Begin heating the waffle iron.

Place the buttermilk, beaten egg, and water in a blender and process on low speed until smooth. Pour into the dry ingredients and stir just until combined.

When the waffle iron is at the proper temperature, pour some of the batter onto it and bake until done. Remove and keep warm. Repeat until all 4 waffles are cooked. Top each with 2 tablespoons of sauce and serve.

★ ★ ★ *VARIATION: For a light vegetarian lunch or dinner, top the waffles with an assortment of steamed vegetables of your choice.*

Rice and Other Grains

When making a meal featuring poultry or fish, I like to serve rice on the side. But I never make it the same way twice in a row. Rice is extremely versatile and can take on any number of wonderful tastes, depending on what you boil it in or add to it during the cooking process. I, of course, prefer brown rice over white. For one thing, brown rice has more fiber—and staying power—than white. Calorie for calorie, it also contains more niacin and potassium and less salt than white. And I always like to get the most nutrition for my calories. You should, too.

You needn't stop at rice when you're looking for a side dish with staying power. I'll show you how to include barley, buckwheat, rye, millet, bulgur, and even cornmeal in your meals.

With the exception of *Indonesian Fried Rice,* all the following recipes are for side dishes, serving about ½ cup of grain per person.

When increasing recipes, keep this guideline in mind: 1 cup of raw brown rice makes 3 cups cooked; 2 cups of raw brown rice makes 8 cups cooked.

254

Basic Brown Rice ★ ★ ★

Cooking in stock rather than water gives plain rice much more flavor. This recipe makes a firm rice, perfect for reheating. If you like softer rice, add 2 to 3 tablespoons of additional stock. Never disturb the rice while it cooks.

Makes 6 servings

1   cup brown rice
2   cups *Chicken Stock* or
      Vegetable Stock

Place the rice and stock in a medium-size saucepan over medium-high heat and bring to a boil. Lower heat and simmer 5 minutes, uncovered. Place a lid on the pan and turn the heat as low as possible. Steam the rice for 40 to 45 minutes, until rice is tender and stock has been absorbed. Turn off the heat and allow the rice to stand for 10 minutes before serving.

NOTE: You can double the recipe and freeze leftover rice in pint containers for future use. A pint of rice makes 4 servings.

Saffron Rice ★ ★ ★

The saffron gives the rice beautiful colors; the coriander, wonderful taste.

Makes 6 servings

1	small onion, minced
2	teaspoons *Chicken Stock*
¼	teaspoon saffron
¼	teaspoon ground coriander
1	cup brown rice
2	cups *Chicken Stock*

In a large saucepan, slowly cook the onions in the stock until translucent. Stir in the saffron and cook for about 3 minutes. Add the coriander and the rice. Stir the rice until any liquid in the pan has been absorbed. Add the stock and bring to a boil. Cover and turn the heat down as low as possible. Cook for 45 minutes, until all of the liquid has been absorbed. Keep covered until ready to serve.

Rice Paprikash ★ ★

A rosy rice from Budapest.

Makes 6 servings

1	cup brown rice
2	cups *Chicken Stock*
1	small onion, chopped
½	sweet red pepper, chopped
1½	teaspoons tamari or soy sauce
1½	teaspoons paprika

255

Place all the ingredients in a large saucepan. Bring to a boil, then reduce heat and simmer for 4 to 5 minutes. Cover and turn heat to lowest setting. Cook for 40 minutes or until the rice is tender and the liquid has been absorbed.

Curried
Brown Rice ★ ★ ★

I like this with stews or broiled fish.

Makes 6 servings

1	cup brown rice
1	small onion, chopped
2	teaspoons curry powder
¼	teaspoon freshly grated ginger
2½	cups water

Place all of the ingredients in a large saucepan. Bring to a boil, stir, cover, and reduce heat to lowest setting. Steam for about 45 minutes, until rice is tender and liquid has been absorbed.

Lemon Rice with Vegetables ★ ★

Makes 6 servings

1	cup brown rice
1	egg, beaten
1½	cups *Chicken Stock*
½	cup lemon juice
½	sweet red pepper, chopped
1	small carrot, thinly sliced
3	scallions, chopped

Place the rice and egg in a large, heavy-bottom saucepan and stir together. Turn the heat to medium and continue to stir the rice until the grains are separated and dry.

Add the stock, lemon juice, peppers, carrots, and scallions and bring to a boil. Reduce heat and simmer for about 4 to 5 minutes, then cover. Turn the heat to the lowest setting and cook for 45 minutes, until rice is tender and liquid has been absorbed. Remove from heat and let stand 5 to 10 minutes before fluffing the rice with a fork and serving.

Scotch Kale and Rice ★ ★

256

Makes 4 servings

2	cups cooked brown rice
½	cup finely chopped kale
½	cup shredded carrots
2	tablespoons grated Parmesan cheese

Toss the rice, kale, and carrots together in a medium-size bowl, then turn mixture into a steaming basket.

Steam about 4 to 5 minutes over boiling water, just until the rice is heated through and the vegetables are slightly tender.

Place in a serving bowl and dust with cheese.

Garden Rice ★ ★ ★

You can substitute chopped scallions for the celery.

Makes 6 servings

1	cup brown rice
½	cup chopped celery
1	large carrot, shredded
2¼	cups *Vegetable Stock*

Place the rice, celery, and carrots in a medium-size saucepan. Add the stock and bring to a boil. Boil the rice and vegetables for 5 minutes, then cover the pan and turn the heat to low. Simmer for about 40 minutes, until rice is tender and liquid has been absorbed. Remove pan from the heat and let stand, still covered, for about 10 minutes before serving.

Vegetable Rice Pilaf ★ ★

The sesame oil gives a tasty, distinctive flavor to this dish.

Makes 6 servings

1 tablespoon sesame oil
2 cups grated carrots
6 scallions, chopped
1 tablespoon minced carrot
    tops or fresh parsley
1 cup brown rice
2 cups water
1 teaspoon tamari or soy
    sauce

Place the oil in a large saucepan or skillet. Turn the heat on low, then add the carrots and scallions. Cook over low heat for about 5 minutes, stirring occasionally. Add the carrot tops or parsley and the brown rice. Cook, stirring, for another 1 to 2 minutes.

Add the water and tamari. Bring to a boil, then cover, reduce heat to its lowest setting, and cook for about 40 minutes, until rice is tender and liquid has been absorbed. Remove from heat and let stand, uncovered, until serving.

★ ★ ★ *VARIATION: Substitute 1 tablespoon of* Chicken Stock *for the oil and replace the 2 cups of water with 2 cups of* Chicken Stock.

257

Calico Rice ★ ★

Nice with fish or chicken.

Makes 6 servings

1 tablespoon *Chicken Stock*
1 small onion, minced
½ cup shredded carrots
¼ cup minced celery
1 cup brown rice
1¼ cups *Chicken Stock*
1 cup tomato juice
    dash of ground cloves

Place the stock in a medium-size saucepan and add the onions. Cook over low heat until the onions are translucent. Add the carrots and celery and cook, stirring, over low heat for about 5 minutes or until tender.

Add the rice, stock, tomato juice, and cloves. Stir. Bring to boil, then cover and turn the heat down very low. Cook for about 40 minutes or until rice is tender and liquid has been absorbed, then remove the pan from the heat. Let stand, covered, for about 5 to 10 minutes before serving.

Arroz Rosa ★ ★ ★

Tomatoes and rich chicken stock give a hearty flavor and fine color to brown rice.

Makes 6 servings

1	large tomato, peeled and coarsely chopped
1¾	cups *Chicken Stock*
1	cup brown rice
¼	teaspoon paprika
	dash of cayenne pepper
	minced fresh parsley (garnish)

Place the tomatoes, partially seeded, in a blender with 1 cup of the stock. Process on medium speed until smooth.

Place the tomato mixture, the remaining stock, the rice, paprika, and cayenne in a large saucepan. Bring to a boil, tightly cover, and reduce heat to its lowest setting. Cook for about 45 minutes, until rice is tender and liquid has been absorbed. Toss the rice before serving. Garnish with parsley, if desired.

Rice with Mushrooms ★ ★ ★

Makes 6 servings

1	small leek, chopped
2	tablespoons *Chicken Stock*
1	cup sliced mushrooms
¼	teaspoon thyme
	dash of nutmeg
3	cups cooked brown rice
2	scallions (garnish)

In a large skillet or large heavy-bottom saucepan, slowly cook the leeks in the stock until tender, adding water, if necessary, to prevent scorching. Add the mushrooms, thyme, and nutmeg and cook, stirring often, until the mushrooms have released their liquid.

Add the rice and stir gently to combine. Turn the heat down to low and cook just until heated through. Place in a serving bowl and garnish with scallions, if desired.

Chestnut Brown Rice ★ ★

Makes 8 servings

1½	cups brown rice
1	cup peeled chestnuts, halved
2	cups water
1	cup apple cider
	dash of nutmeg

Place all the ingredients in a medium-size saucepan. Bring to a boil, reduce heat, and simmer for 1 to 2 minutes, then cover and turn heat to lowest setting. Cook for 45 minutes or until rice is tender and liquid has been absorbed. Turn off the heat and let stand for about 10 minutes. Toss and serve.

Mixed fruit, *Cottage Cheese Pancakes,* and a frosty glass of *Orange Glorious* is a great way to start the day.

Three stars go to this Sunday brunch—*Broccoli and Cheese Soufflé, Corn Muffins,* and
Tomato-Buttermilk Cocktail.

Indonesian Fried Rice ★ ★

A complete meal, making good use of leftover chicken.

Makes 4 servings

2	small onions, chopped
1	sweet red pepper, chopped
1	green pepper, chopped
2	tablespoons *Chicken Stock*
2	cloves garlic, minced
1	teaspoon minced hot peppers
2	teaspoons tamari or soy sauce
1	cup chopped, cooked chicken
3	cups cooked long grain brown rice
½	cup bean sprouts
1	egg
1	tablespoon water
1	teaspoon butter

In a large skillet, cook the onions, red peppers, and green peppers in the stock until just crisp-tender. Add a little water, if necessary, to prevent scorching. Add the garlic and hot peppers. Cook over low heat, stirring constantly, for 1 minute, then add the tamari and chicken. Heat through, then add the rice and sprouts. Cook until heated through, stirring occasionally.

While the rice is cooking, beat the egg with the water. Place the butter in a small no-stick skillet and when it is melted and has stopped foaming, add the egg. Cook without stirring, making a thin omelet.

When the rice is heated through, mound on a serving plate. Cut the omelet into thin strips and arrange these in the center of the fried rice.

NOTE: Since this is a full meal, follow the star rating for vegetarian main dishes.

261

Herbed Wheat Pilaf ★ ★ ★

Look for the dark bulgur, with a layer of bran, for a heartier, nuttier flavor.

Makes 4 servings

½	cup bulgur
1¼	cups *Chicken Stock* or *Vegetable Stock*
1	tablespoon minced onions
2	teaspoons tamari or soy sauce
1	tablespoon minced fresh parsley (garnish)

Place the bulgur, stock, onions, and tamari in a small saucepan and bring to a boil. Reduce heat to low and partially cover the pan. Simmer for about 20 minutes or until the bulgur is tender and the liquid is absorbed. Place the cooked bulgur in a serving bowl with a pinch of parsley in the center, if desired. Toss before serving.

Millet Croquettes ★ ★

Makes 4 servings

CROQUETTES
1   cup cooked millet
¼   cup minced red onions
¼   cup shredded carrots
1   clove garlic, minced
1   egg
½   teaspoon marjoram
½   teaspoon thyme
1   teaspoon chopped fresh
      parsley
3   tablespoons *Chicken Stock*

SAUCE
2   tablespoons rice vinegar
1   tablespoon Dijon mustard
½   teaspoon minced fresh
      parsley

To make the croquettes: Combine the millet, onions, carrots, garlic, egg, marjoram, thyme, and parsley in a medium-size bowl. Heat a no-stick skillet to medium and add the stock. Divide the mixture into fourths, shape each fourth in a patty and fry for 5 minutes on each side.

To make the sauce: Combine the vinegar, mustard, and parsley in a small bowl. Serve with the croquettes.

Piedmont Polenta Squares ★ ★ ★

Serve as a garnish with poultry dishes.

Makes 6 servings

3   cups water
1   cup cornmeal
1   tablespoon freshly grated
      Parmesan cheese
      dash of paprika

In a medium-size saucepan, combine water and cornmeal and bring to a boil. Reduce to a low simmer and cook for 20 minutes, stirring constantly. Add Parmesan.

Coat an 8 × 8-inch pan with no-stick spray and pour in the hot mixture, smoothing the top. Sprinkle with paprika. Cover loosely with waxed paper and allow to set, at least 3 hours. Gently cut into 2-inch squares and serve.

Kasha with Seashells ★
A Russian winter favorite.

Makes 6 servings

1   cup coarse buckwheat
      groats
1   egg, beaten
4   cups *Vegetable Stock*
1   cup cooked pasta seashells
1   teaspoon marjoram

Coat a large heavy skillet with no-stick spray and brown the buckwheat, stirring constantly. Stir in the egg, coating all grains. Slowly add the stock and cook, stirring, until all liquid is absorbed, about 25 to 30 minutes. Add pasta and marjoram and toss. Serve immediately.

Scandinavian Barley Pudding ★ ★ ★
Originally from western Finland, this is a hearty winter side dish.

Makes 6 servings

½   cup barley
1½ cups *Vegetable Stock*
2   cups skim milk
1   apple, cored and sliced
2   tablespoons apple juice
      dash of cinnamon

In a large saucepan, cook barley and stock for 30 minutes. Add milk and bring to a boil. Stir and pour into a 1½-quart ovenproof casserole. Bake uncovered for 3 hours at 250°, stirring occasionally.

Remove from oven and arrange apple slices on barley. Brush with apple juice, sprinkle with cinnamon, and bake for 20 to 30 minutes more.

263

German Rye Timbale ★ ★

Makes 4 servings

1   cup cooked rye flakes
1   teaspoon ground caraway
      seeds
1   cup chopped celery
1   cup chopped tomatoes
½   cup chopped onions
1   egg
1   teaspoon minced fresh
      parsley

In a medium-size bowl, combine rye, caraway, celery, tomatoes, onions, and egg. Coat a 1-quart ovenproof casserole with no-stick spray and add rye mixture. Cover and bake at 350° for 30 minutes. Remove from oven and sprinkle with parsley. Serve hot.

NOTE: Cook rye flakes by adding 1 cup of flakes to 3 cups boiling water. Simmer for 20 minutes or until liquid is absorbed, stirring frequently.

Pearl Barley
with Porcini ★

Makes 4 servings

1   cup barley
4   cups *Vegetable Stock*
¼   cup slivered Italian porcini
        mushrooms, rinsed and
        soaked for 20 minutes, or
        any dried mushrooms
¼   cup chopped scallions
¼   cup shredded carrots
1   clove garlic, minced
¼   cup white wine vinegar
1   teaspoon Dijon mustard
½   teaspoon basil

Combine barley and stock in a medium-size sauce-pan and bring to a boil. Cover and simmer for 50 to 60 minutes or until stock is absorbed. Add mushrooms, scallions, carrots, and garlic and toss. Chill for 1 hour.

In a small jar, combine vinegar, mustard, and basil. Shake to combine and toss with barley mixture. Serve chilled.

Side Dishes

Show me a person who doesn't like vegetables and I'll show you a person who doesn't know how to cook them.

To me, opening a box of frozen vegetables and boiling them in water until they just about resemble soup is about the worst way to eat them. Unfortunately, it's the way many people—particularly those who say they hate vegetables—were brought up to eat them.

Not me. I *love* vegetables. But I also know how to get the most out of them—both in nutrition and taste. I always buy fresh vegetables and I *never* overcook them or smother them in butter, oil, or heavy sauces. Why ruin a good thing with needless calories?

Simply quick steaming them for a few minutes is by far the best way to get the most natural taste out of cooked vegetables. It's also the method that best preserves nutrients and color and keeps calories at a minimum.

The flavor of vegetables can be enhanced even more through the knowledgeable use of herbs and spices. And by carefully combining two or more vegetables or pairing vegetables with fruit, you can bring out the best taste in all of them.

The fact that this is a big chapter is not the result of overzealous cooks. The variety is here for good reason—to encourage you to eat more vegetables and genuinely enjoy them. I cannot stress enough that in order to lose weight naturally you must learn to eat less fat and more complex carbohydrates. That means eating more vegetables. Vegetables are naturally low in calories, low in fat, and high in fiber, which makes them a natural weight loss food.

These are the dishes you should be turning to when you get a hankering for seconds during a meal. Most of the three-star side dish recipes, particularly those featuring greens, are well below 50 calories a serving. But if you really must have seconds, you can even reach for extras of the one-star dishes. In the long run, you'll be a lot better off adding the high-carbohydrate, high-fiber foods to your diet—even if they are higher in calories—than anything else you might want.

But vegetables are a lot more than just something to fill up on. They can also add to the eye appeal of the entire meal. They can make an empty-looking plate look full. (Imagine your fine china with nothing but a half of a chicken breast on it.) They can add a range of color to the meal. And when the meal looks appetizing, it provides satisfaction beyond the mere eating of it.

Make good use of this chapter. Eat a side dish—even two—at both lunch and dinner. Try making an entire meal out of some of these dishes—they certainly are appealing enough. *Winter Solstice Stew, Rainbow Fruit and Vegetable Casserole, Zucchini-Stuffed Zucchini, Welsh Vegetable Pot,* and *Fruit and Sweet Potato Bake* are but a few side dishes that can make satisfying main dish meals. So experiment. Count on a variety of side dishes to add nutrients, fiber, and good taste to your menus.

266

Side dishes should take first place in a healthy weight loss program, never last.

Asparagus Ariana ★ ★ ★

Makes 4 servings

12 large asparagus spears
1 tablespoon sesame seeds
1 teaspoon butter
1 teaspoon lemon juice
   lemon slices (garnish)
   parsley sprigs (garnish)

Remove a thin layer of the skin from the asparagus spears to a point about 2 inches from the top. Steam the asparagus just until crisp-tender, about 10 to 15 minutes, depending on the size.

Place the sesame seeds in a small, heavy-bottom skillet and toast over low to medium heat just until golden. Remove from heat, add the butter to the pan and stir into the seeds. Stir in the lemon juice. Place the asparagus on a warmed serving dish. Toss with the sesame seeds. Garnish with lemon slices and parsley, if desired, and serve.

Green Beans Amandine ★ ★ ★

Makes 6 servings

1   pound green beans
1   tablespoon *Chicken Stock*
2   tablespoons slivered
      almonds
2   tablespoons minced fresh
      dill or 1½ teaspoons
      dried dill
1   tablespoon lemon juice

Steam the beans just until they are crisp-tender, about 8 to 10 minutes.

While the beans steam, place the stock in a small saucepan. Heat the almonds in the stock for about 5 minutes. Remove from heat. Stir in the dill and lemon juice.

Arrange the beans on a serving plate and spoon the almond mixture over the top. Serve hot.

Green Beans with Rosemary ★ ★ ★

Makes 6 servings

1   pound green beans
1   tablespoon *Chicken Stock*
¼   teaspoon rosemary,
      crumbled
      dash of nutmeg
      orange slice (garnish)
      parsley sprigs (garnish)

Steam the beans until crisp-tender, about 8 to 10 minutes.

While the beans are steaming, place the stock in a small pan and heat. Stir in the rosemary, then turn off heat.

Arrange the green beans all in the same direction on a serving plate. Sprinkle with the rosemary sauce and nutmeg.

Cut the orange slice halfway through to the center. Twist and set atop the beans and place parsley sprigs on either side of the beans, if desired.

Bravo Green Beans ★ ★

Makes 6 servings

1   pound green beans, halved
½   teaspoon grated fresh
      ginger
2   medium-size tart red
      apples, diced
      dash of nutmeg

Place the green beans in a steaming basket over boiling water. Sprinkle the ginger over the beans. Steam the beans for about 5 minutes. Add the apples and nutmeg and steam for another 3 to 4 minutes or until the green beans are crisp-tender. Toss the beans and apples together in a medium-size serving bowl. Serve hot.

Peas and Carrots
with Ginger ★ ★

Makes 4 servings

4   small carrots, cut diagonally
      into thin slices
2   tablespoons *Chicken Stock*
1   cup peas
½   teaspoon grated fresh
      ginger
1   clove garlic, minced
      dash of ground coriander
¼   cup water

In a medium-size saucepan, sauté the carrots in the stock for 5 minutes. Add the peas, ginger, garlic, coriander, and water. Partially cover the pan and when the water boils, turn down heat and steam for 5 to 7 minutes or until the carrots are crisp-tender. Serve hot.

Herbed Peas
with Orange ★ ★

268

The combination of parsley and orange gives peas a special flavor, without adding calories.

Makes 4 servings

2   cups peas
3   tablespoons water
½   teaspoon grated orange rind
1   teaspoon minced fresh
      parsley

Place the peas, water, and orange rind in a medium-size saucepan over low heat. Cover and steam until the peas are crisp-tender, about 5 minutes. Remove the cover, add the parsley, and cook over medium heat, stirring constantly, for about 1 minute, allowing the water to evaporate. Serve hot.

Gingered
Snow Peas ★ ★ ★

Wonderfully low in calories!

Makes 6 servings

2   tablespoons *Chicken Stock*
1   clove garlic, halved
1   small piece fresh ginger
1   pound snow peas
      watercress (garnish)

Place the stock in a medium-size skillet over medium heat. Add the garlic and ginger and cook for about 2 minutes. Remove the garlic and ginger. Add the snow peas all at once and cook quickly over medium to high heat until the peas are crisp-tender and bright green, about 1 minute.

Serve the snow peas garnished with sprigs of watercress, if desired.

Peas with Tarragon ★ ★

Tarragon is a perfect companion for delicate peas.

Makes 4 servings

6–7   scallions, thinly sliced
½   tablespoon *Chicken Stock* or *Vegetable Stock*
2   cups peas
¼   cup *Chicken Stock* or *Vegetable Stock*
1   tablespoon minced fresh tarragon or ½ teaspoon dried tarragon
  dash of ground coriander
  tarragon sprigs (garnish)

Cook the scallions briefly in ½ tablespoon of stock in a medium-size saucepan or skillet until they begin to soften. Add the peas, ¼ cup stock, tarragon, and coriander. Cover and cook over low heat just until the peas are crisp-tender but still bright green, about 5 minutes. Place in a serving bowl and garnish with fresh tarragon, if desired.

269

No-Crust Spinach Pie ★

Makes 6 servings

1   cup low-fat cottage cheese
¼   cup skim milk
3   eggs
¼   teaspoon Dijon mustard
1   teaspoon sunflower oil
4   scallions, chopped
4   cups packed spinach leaves, chopped
1   tablespoon minced fresh dill or 1½ teaspoons dried dill
  dash of nutmeg

Place the cottage cheese, milk, eggs, and mustard in a blender. Process on medium speed until smooth.

Place the oil in a large skillet. Add the scallions and cook over low to medium heat until translucent. Add the spinach leaves. Cook, stirring, until the spinach is wilted, then stir in the dill.

Spread the spinach mixture evenly in an 8-inch pie plate coated with no-stick spray. Gently pour the cottage cheese and egg mixture over the spinach. Sprinkle with nutmeg and bake at 350° for 40 minutes. Serve hot or at room temperature.

Coach House Spinach ★ ★ ★

Makes 4 servings

1 pound spinach
1 tablespoon thyme
¼ cup chopped scallions
¼ cup shredded carrots
1 clove garlic

Place the spinach in a steaming basket over boiling water. Add the thyme, scallions, and carrots. Push the garlic through a garlic press over the spinach. Cover and steam just until the spinach is wilted and bright green.

Newport Room Cauliflower ★ ★ ★

Makes 6 servings

1 large head cauliflower, separated into florets
1 sweet red pepper, cut into thin strips
2 tablespoons minced fresh basil or 1 tablespoon dried basil

270

Place the cauliflower in a large steaming basket. Arrange the pepper strips over the cauliflower. Set the steaming basket over boiling water and steam, covered, until the cauliflower is tender, about 15 minutes. Remove to a serving bowl. Sprinkle with the basil and serve hot.

Broccoli a la Grecque ★

Makes 4 servings

4 cups broccoli florets
2 tablespoons olive oil
1 tablespoon white wine vinegar
½ teaspoon Dijon mustard
½ teaspoon grated Parmesan cheese

Steam the broccoli just until crisp-tender, about 7 minutes. Place in a medium-size serving bowl.

Combine the oil, vinegar, mustard, and Parmesan in a small jar or bowl. Shake or stir until blended and pour over the broccoli while the broccoli is still hot. Toss. Allow to cool to room temperature before serving. If refrigerated, allow to return to room temperature before serving.

Sorrel Squares ★
Adapted from the French Chiffonnade D'Oseille.

Makes 6 servings

1½   cups cooked rice
¼   cup shredded carrots
¼   cup diced leeks
¼   cup chopped mushrooms
⅓   cup toasted wheat germ
1   teaspoon Dijon mustard
1½   cups low-fat cottage cheese
1   teaspoon parsley
1   teaspoon dill
1   cup shredded sorrel
     (choose the tender
     "underleaves")
1   teaspoon paprika

In a large bowl, combine the rice, carrots, leeks, mushrooms, and wheat germ.

Whip mustard and cottage cheese on medium to high speed in a blender or food processor. Add to the vegetables. Add the parsley and dill and mix well.

Coat an 8 × 8-inch baking pan with no-stick spray and add half of the vegetable-cheese mixture. Sprinkle sorrel in an even layer over the mixture. Add second half of mixture and sprinkle with paprika. Bake at 350° for 30 minutes. Cool and cut into 12 squares.

NOTE: Extra portions may be refrigerated and eaten cold or reheated.

271

Vegetable Puree ★ ★ ★

Makes 6 servings

3   cups peeled and cubed
     kohlrabi
2   cups sliced broccoli stems
     and florets
1   cup packed watercress
¼   teaspoon marjoram
2   tablespoons *Chicken Stock*
1   teaspoon whole wheat flour
¼   cup skim milk
     watercress sprigs (garnish)

Steam the kohlrabi for 10 minutes, then add the broccoli stems. Steam for another 10 minutes, then add the broccoli florets. Steam an additional 10 minutes.

While the broccoli steams, place the watercress and marjoram in a small skillet with the stock. Cook, stirring, over low heat just until the watercress is wilted. Add the whole wheat flour and continue stirring over low heat for another 2 minutes.

Place the watercress in a blender with the milk and most of the steamed vegetables. Process on low to medium speed until smooth. Remove most of the pureed mixture from the blender and place in a serving dish. Add any remaining vegetables and process until smooth. Add to the serving dish, stir, and garnish with sprigs of watercress, if desired.

Brussels Sprouts Italienne ★ ★

Makes 8 servings

4   cups halved brussels
    sprouts
1   tablespoon *Chicken Stock*
1   small onion, minced
1   large tomato, peeled and
    chopped
¾   cup peas
1   tablespoon tomato paste

Bring a large saucepan half filled with water to a boil. Add the brussels sprouts and return to a boil. Cook the sprouts just until crisp-tender, about 8 to 10 minutes. Drain.

While the brussels sprouts cook, place the stock and onions in a large skillet. Cook over low heat, stirring until the onions are just about tender. Add the tomatoes and the peas. Cook, stirring occasionally, until the peas are crisp-tender, about 5 minutes. Stir in the tomato paste, then stir in the brussels sprouts and heat through. Serve at once.

NOTE: Do not overcook, or both peas and brussels sprouts will lose their attractive color and taste. If onion-tomato mixture is not ready when sprouts are cooked, drain and run sprouts under cold water until cooled. Heat through with the onion-tomato mixture as above.

272

Brussels Sprouts in Mustard Sauce ★ ★

Makes 6 servings

4   cups brussels sprouts
1   tablespoon sunflower oil
1   tablespoon butter
2   teaspoons Dijon mustard
1   tablespoon lemon juice
    lemon slices (garnish)

Trim the bottoms of the brussels sprouts and cut an "x" in the bottoms about one-third of the way through the sprouts. Steam for about 6 minutes or until just slightly tender.

Place the oil and butter in a small skillet over low heat. Stir in the mustard and lemon juice.

Place the steamed brussels sprouts in a shallow 9 × 13-inch baking dish in one layer, cut side down. Spoon the mustard sauce over the top of the sprouts. Fit a piece of lightly buttered waxed paper over the baking dish. Bake at 350° for 15 to 20 minutes or until the brussels sprouts are tender. Serve from the baking dish, garnished with lemon slices, if desired.

NOTE: If you will not be braising the brussels sprouts immediately, run them under cold water until cool. Bake for 20 to 25 minutes or until tender, basting with the sauce, if desired.

Brussels Sprouts with Chestnuts and Oranges ★

The brussels sprouts can be steamed ahead of time, then braised in the oven just before serving.

Makes 8 servings

4   cups brussels sprouts
½   cup boiled chestnuts
2   tablespoons *Chicken Stock*
¼   teaspoon grated orange
      rind
2   oranges

Trim the bottoms of the brussels sprouts and cut an "x" in the ends, about one-third of the way through the sprouts. Steam the sprouts for about 6 minutes or just until they begin to get tender.

If the sprouts will not be used immediately, run them under cold water briefly, then spread them out on a kitchen towel to cool.

If the chestnuts are large, halve them. Place the stock in a small saucepan over low heat and stir in the chestnuts and orange rind.

Place the brussels sprouts in a shallow 1-quart baking dish coated with no-stick spray. Add the chestnuts in a single layer, then cover the ingredients with a lightly buttered piece of waxed paper, cut to fit the dish. Bake at 350° for 15 minutes.

While the brussels sprouts braise, section the oranges and peel the membrane off each section.

Add the orange sections in a single layer over the sprouts and chestnuts. Cover again with the waxed paper and return to the oven for another 5 minutes. Toss together before serving. Serve hot.

273

Sweet Lime Carrots ★ ★ ★

Makes 4 servings

3   large carrots
½   tablespoon corn oil
1   tablespoon lime juice
2   tablespoons water
1   clove garlic
½   teaspoon honey

Cut the carrots into long, thin sticks. Place in a medium-size saucepan with the oil and cook, stirring, over medium heat for 2 to 3 minutes. Add the lime juice and water. Push the garlic through a garlic press into the pan. Stir in the honey. Cover and steam over low heat until the carrots are crisp-tender, about 10 to 15 minutes.

Puree of Dilled Carrot ★ ★

Makes 4 servings

1   teaspoon *Chicken Stock* or *Vegetable Stock*
1   small onion, chopped
5   small carrots, sliced
⅓   cup skim milk
⅓   cup water
½   teaspoon dill
    dash of nutmeg
    dill sprigs (garnish)

Place the stock in a small saucepan over low heat. Add the onions and cook, stirring occasionally, until translucent. Add the carrots, milk, water, dill, and nutmeg. Bring to a boil, then reduce heat, cover, and simmer until the carrots are tender.

Place the ingredients in a blender and process on low, then medium speed, until smooth. Place in a serving bowl and garnish with dill, if desired.

Rainbow Fruit and Vegetable Casserole ★

Makes 4 servings

4   small carrots, cut into sticks
2   medium-size tart red apples, sliced
2   thick slices red onion
½   cup apple juice
    dash of nutmeg
    minced fresh mint (garnish)

Place the carrots in an 8 × 8-inch baking dish. Place the apples on top of the carrots. Separate the onion slices into rings and arrange over the apples and carrots. Pour the apple juice into the baking dish. Sprinkle with the nutmeg and cover tightly with foil. Bake at 350° for 1 hour. Serve garnished with mint, if desired.

★ *VARIATION: Substitute pears for the apples.*

Chelsea Squash ★ ★

A unique side dish, which can be served chilled or at room temperature.

Makes 4 servings

3   cups cubed butternut or hubbard squash
¼   cup chopped scallions
½   cup low-fat yogurt
¼   teaspoon ground coriander

Place the squash in a large saucepan and cover with water. Bring to a boil, then reduce heat and simmer just until the squash is tender.

Drain the squash and set aside to cool. Place the squash in a serving bowl and toss with the scallions, yogurt, and coriander. Serve immediately or chill.

274

Scalloped Summer Squash ★

Makes 8 servings

4 cups sliced yellow squash
1 medium-size Spanish onion, sliced
2 tablespoons butter
2 tablespoons whole wheat flour
1 cup skim milk
1 cup low-fat cottage cheese
1 tablespoon wheat germ

Place the squash and onions in a large pan with a small amount of boiling water. Return to a boil, then reduce heat and simmer until the squash is tender, about 10 minutes.

Meanwhile, melt the butter in a medium-size skillet. Add the flour and cook, stirring, over medium heat for 1 to 2 minutes. Stir in milk and continue cooking, stirring constantly, until the sauce begins to thicken. Place the cottage cheese in a blender. Add the sauce and process on low speed until smooth.

Layer a small amount of the cheese sauce in the bottom of a 9-inch ovenproof casserole or pie plate. Drain the cooked squash and onions and arrange a layer across the bottom of the baking dish. Pour the remaining sauce evenly over the squash. Sprinkle with the wheat germ and bake at 350° for 20 minutes.

275

Steampot Vegetables ★ ★ ★

Simplicity itself, yet a colorful and nutritious addition to any meal.

Makes 4 servings

1 stalk broccoli
2 cups sliced cauliflower florets
1 sweet red pepper, diced
1 bay leaf
2 medium-size carrots, julienned
1 cup cherry tomatoes
½ lemon
1 tablespoon minced fresh parsley

Separate the broccoli stem from the florets. Peel the thick layer of skin from the stem and cut the stem diagonally into thin slices.

Place the stem, florets, cauliflower, peppers, bay leaf, and carrots in a steaming basket over boiling water. Steam for about 6 to 8 minutes, until the vegetables are crisp-tender. Add the cherry tomatoes and continue to steam, just until tomatoes are heated through, about 1 minute.

Place the vegetables in a serving dish. Squeeze the juice from the lemon half over the vegetables. Sprinkle with parsley and serve.

Winter Solstice Stew ★ ★ ★

Plain, good fare.

Makes 8 servings

12 small, white onions
1 large rutabaga, diced
4 medium-size carrots, diced
4 cups water
4 teaspoons tamari or soy sauce
1 tablespoon thyme
1 teaspoon marjoram
1 teaspoon parsley
2 cloves garlic

Peel the onions but leave them whole. Place them in a large ovenproof casserole with the rutabagas, carrots, water, tamari, thyme, marjoram, and parsley. Push the garlic through a garlic press into the casserole and stir. Cover and bake at 350° for about 45 minutes or until all of the vegetables are tender.

276

Eggplant Grill ★ ★ ★

Eggplant is best in its simplest form.

Makes 8 servings

1 large eggplant, cut into ½-inch slices
2 cloves garlic
2 teaspoons grated onions
1 tablespoon olive oil

Steam the eggplant for about 8 minutes or just until it begins to soften.

While the eggplant steams, push the garlic through a garlic press into a small bowl. Stir in the onions and oil until well mixed.

Arrange the eggplant slices in one layer on a baking sheet coated with no-stick spray. Brush with half of the garlic mixture. Broil about 5 inches from the heat for about 5 minutes or until the slices begin to turn golden. Turn, brush with the remaining oil mixture, and broil until golden brown. Serve hot.

NOTE: The eggplant can also be grilled out doors.

★ ★ ★ *VARIATION: Add leftovers to* Tomato Sauce *and serve over whole wheat spaghetti as a vegetarian main meal.*

Zucchini-Stuffed
Zucchini ★ ★ ★

Makes 4 servings

4	small zucchini, shredded
2	medium-size zucchini
1	medium-size onion, minced
1	clove garlic, minced
1	tablespoon *Chicken Stock* dash of nutmeg
¼	cup low-fat yogurt
4–8	squash blossoms (garnish)

Place the shredded zucchini in a steaming basket. Steam for about 6 minutes, or until tender.

While the shredded zucchini steams, cut the medium-size zucchini in half lengthwise. Hollow out the centers and discard the pulp.

Cook the onions and garlic in the stock in a medium-size skillet over low heat until the onions are tender.

When the shredded zucchini is tender, set aside. Place the zucchini halves in the steaming basket and steam for 10 to 12 minutes or until crisp-tender.

When the onions are tender, stir the shredded zucchini and the nutmeg into the skillet. Heat through. Remove from heat. Let cool slightly, then stir in the yogurt.

Fill the zucchini halves with the shredded zucchini mixture. Arrange on a serving plate and garnish with squash blossoms, if desired.

277

Red Rooster
Zucchini ★ ★ ★

A traditional combination.

Makes 4 servings

4–5	scallions, thinly sliced
2	teaspoons *Chicken Stock* or *Vegetable Stock*
3	small zucchini, cut into thin sticks
2	large tomatoes, peeled, seeded, and chopped
¼	teaspoon oregano

In a large skillet over medium heat, sauté the scallions in the stock until they begin to soften.

Add the zucchini and sauté over medium heat for about 3 to 4 minutes, then add the tomatoes and oregano. Cover, lower heat, and cook, stirring occasionally, until the vegetables are soft, about 15 minutes.

Chantilly Acorn Rings ★ ★

Attractive enough for a party dish.

Makes 4 servings

1	medium-size acorn squash
¾	cup orange juice
	dash of cinnamon
	watercress sprigs (garnish)

Cut the squash crosswise into ½-inch slices. Remove the seeds from the inside of the rings. Peel. Place the rings in a 9 × 13-inch baking dish. Pour on the orange juice and sprinkle with the cinnamon. Loosely cover with aluminum foil and bake at 350° for 1 hour, basting once about halfway through the baking time. Serve garnished with watercress, if desired.

278 Eggplant Sto Fourno ★ ★

Greek eggplant in casserole.

Makes 6 servings

1	tablespoon grated Parmesan cheese
1	tablespoon minced onions
1	tablespoon wheat germ
1	tablespoon Greek oregano
1	tablespoon parsley
1	medium-size eggplant, thinly sliced (about 2 cups)
2	cups thinly sliced white potatoes
½	cup *Chicken Stock*
1	teaspoon paprika

Combine the Parmesan, onions, wheat germ, oregano, and parsley in a small bowl.

Coat a 1½-quart ovenproof casserole with no-stick spray. Line the bottom with half of the eggplant. Sprinkle about one-third of the cheese mixture over the eggplant. Layer with half of the potatoes. Continue with another layer of eggplant, cheese mixture, and potatoes.

Pour stock over the casserole and sprinkle with paprika. Bake, covered, at 350° for 45 minutes. Uncover, top with remaining cheese, and bake 15 minutes more. Serve immediately.

Kyoto Eggplant ★ ★ ★

Japanese steamed eggplant steaks.

Makes 4 servings

2 small eggplants
1 tablespoon red miso (red soybean paste)
2 tablespoons hot water
2 tablespoons chopped scallions

Cut the eggplants into ½-inch slices, then cut in half to form half moons. Steam the eggplant for 30 minutes.

In a small saucepan, heat miso, water, and scallions. Arrange eggplant on a platter and pour miso sauce over it. Serve immediately.

Ratatouille ★ ★

Makes 8 servings

1 tablespoon olive oil
4 cups cubed eggplant
5 tablespoons water
1½ cups coarsely chopped onions
2 sweet red peppers, diced
3 cloves garlic, minced
2 cups cubed zucchini
6 medium-size tomatoes, seeded and chopped
2 tablespoons minced fresh parsley

Place the oil in a large skillet, heat, add the eggplant, then add 3 tablespoons of the water. Cook quickly over medium heat until the eggplant begins to soften.

Add the remaining water to the pan along with the onions, peppers, and garlic and steam-sauté until slightly tender. Add the zucchini and steam-sauté until crisp-tender, adding a few spoonfuls of water, if necessary, to prevent sticking. Stir in the tomatoes. Cover and cook for 5 minutes, until the tomatoes release their juices.

Remove the cover from the pan and cook, stirring, over medium-high heat until most of the liquid has evaporated. Spoon into a 2-quart ovenproof casserole, cover, and bake at 350° for 20 to 25 minutes. Sprinkle with parsley and serve.

Tomatoes Oregano ★ ★ ★

This dish is best using vine-ripened tomatoes.

Makes 4 servings

2   teaspoons butter
2   cups cherry tomatoes
1   teaspoon oregano

Melt the butter in a medium-size skillet or saucepan, cook the cherry tomatoes and oregano over medium heat, stirring frequently, just until heated through, about 3 to 4 minutes. Remove the cherry tomatoes from the heat before they begin to burst.

Cucumber Raita ★ ★

This specialty from India, which has a cooling effect on the palate, is a must when serving curry dishes.

Makes 4 servings

1   cup peeled, seeded, and shredded cucumber
2   cups low-fat yogurt
¼   teaspoon mint

Chill cucumber. Meanwhile, strain yogurt through cheesecloth for 2 hours. Combine with cucumber and mint and serve immediately. Do not store.

Palm Court Leeks ★ ★

Attractive, with delicate flavor.

Makes 4 servings

4   large leeks
1   cup *Chicken Stock*
2   cloves garlic, minced
    dash of nutmeg

Remove any tough outer layers and trim the top ends from the leeks. Slice the leeks through the center, leaving about 3 inches of the root end intact. Spread open the green tops and rinse well under running water to remove the sand.

Cut the leeks completely in half and place cut side down in a 9 × 13-inch baking dish. Pour on the stock, then sprinkle with the garlic and nutmeg and cover with foil. Bake at 350° for about 45 minutes or until the leeks are tender. Serve hot.

Ragout of Summer Vegetables ★ ★

Makes 6 servings

1	medium-size eggplant
6	medium-size tomatoes
2	cups *Vegetable Stock*
1	sweet red pepper, cut into 2-inch strips
2	small red onions, thinly sliced
3	celery stalks, sliced
1	clove garlic, minced
2	teaspoons tamari or soy sauce
¼	teaspoon thyme
¼	teaspoon marjoram

Cut the eggplant into $2 \times \frac{1}{2} \times \frac{1}{2}$-inch sticks. Steam the eggplant for 8 to 10 minutes.

Place the tomatoes in a blender with 1 cup of the stock. Process on low speed until smooth.

Place the steamed eggplant in a large saucepan with the pureed tomatoes, remaining stock, peppers, onions, celery, garlic, tamari, thyme, and marjoram. Bring to a boil, reduce heat, and simmer for 30 minutes. Serve hot or at room temperature.

Braised Fennel with Marjoram ★ ★

The slight taste of anise departs from the usual vegetable routine.

Makes 4 servings

2	small fennel bulbs
1	small onion, minced
1	cup *Chicken Stock*
1	teaspoon minced fresh marjoram or ½ teaspoon dried marjoram
1	tablespoon grated Parmesan cheese

Trim any feathery sprigs from the fennel bulb tops and reserve for garnish.

Cut the bulbs in half lengthwise, removing any tough or discolored outer layers from the bulb.

In a small saucepan, cook the onions in 1 tablespoon of stock until they are translucent. Remove from the heat. Stir in the marjoram.

Spread the onions in the bottom of a shallow 8×8-inch ovenproof casserole. Arrange the fennel, cut side down, on top of the onions. Add the remaining stock, sprinkle with cheese, and cover the dish tightly with foil.

Bake at 325° for about 1 hour or until the fennel is quite tender. Garnish with the fennel sprigs, if desired, and serve.

Garden-In-A-Skillet ★ ★ ★

Makes 6 servings

1	medium-size onion, chopped
1	tablespoon *Chicken Stock* or *Vegetable Stock*
1	sweet red pepper, chopped
1	cup cooked corn
½	teaspoon thyme
	dash of nutmeg
4	cups sliced zucchini, steamed
	parsley sprigs (garnish)

In a large saucepan, cook the onions in the stock until they are translucent. Add the peppers and cook until the onions and peppers are crisp-tender. Add the corn, thyme, and nutmeg. Heat through, then add the zucchini. Simmer uncovered until any excess moisture has evaporated. Serve garnished with parsley, if desired.

282

Shanghai Manor Cabbage ★ ★

Makes 4 servings

8	cups coarsely shredded cabbage
½	cup *Chicken Stock*
2	teaspoons tahini (sesame butter)
2	teaspoons grated fresh ginger
4	cloves garlic, minced
1	teaspoon ground coriander
½	teaspoon ground cumin
½	teaspoon chili powder
2	teaspoons tamari or soy sauce

Place the cabbage in 2 tablespoons of stock in a large skillet over medium-high heat. Stir quickly until the cabbage begins to wilt. Remove from heat.

Add tahini, ginger, garlic, coriander, cumin, chili powder, ¼ cup of stock, and tamari and turn the heat to low. Cover the pan and steam the cabbage for about 10 to 15 minutes or until tender. Stir occasionally and add more stock, if necessary, to prevent the cabbage from sticking to the pan. Serve hot.

Kapalua Cabbage ★ ★ ★

Makes 6 servings

3   cups shredded red cabbage
1   cup chopped pineapple
     with juice
1   cup shredded carrots
½   cup apple juice
     dash of nutmeg

Place all of the ingredients in a medium-size saucepan. Bring to a boil, then reduce and simmer over low heat until tender, about 30 minutes.

Creamed Corn ★

You can serve a delicious, creamy vegetable without relying on butter and cream.

Makes 8 servings

8   ears of fresh corn
¼   cup skim milk
     dash of nutmeg

Cut the corn from the cobs, then scrape the cobs to remove the nutritious corn germ. Place ½ cup of the corn in a blender with the milk. Processs on low speed until smooth. Place the remaining corn and the blended mixture in a medium-size saucepan. Bring to a boil, then reduce heat and simmer 4 to 5 minutes. Place in a serving bowl, dust with nutmeg, and serve hot.

283

Chili Corn Cornie ★ ★

Try this as an unusual accompaniment to fish or with main dishes that have a Mexican flair.

Makes 6 servings

1   small onion, chopped
1   sweet red pepper,
     chopped
1   stalk celery, chopped
¼   cup water
¼   teaspoon chili powder
     dash of ground cumin
2   cups corn
1   cup sliced green beans
     minced fresh parsley
      (garnish)

Place the onions, peppers, celery, and water in a medium-size saucepan and bring to a boil. Add the chili powder and cumin, cover, reduce heat, and simmer for 5 minutes. Stir in the corn and beans. Return to a boil, cover, and simmer over low heat until the beans are tender, about 10 minutes. (The water should be nearly evaporated by the end of cooking time. Add a few extra spoonfuls of water, if needed, to prevent scorching.) Serve hot, garnished with parsley, if desired.

Corn Pudding ★

Makes 6 servings

2 cups fresh or cooked corn
2 eggs
1 teaspoon honey
1¾ cups milk
   dash of nutmeg
   dash of cayenne pepper
1 tablespoon wheat germ

Place 1 cup of the corn with the eggs in a blender. Process on medium to high speed until smooth. In a large mixing bowl, combine the remaining corn with the blended corn mixture and honey.

Place the milk in a small saucepan over low heat. When the milk is hot, stir rapidly into the egg and corn mixture. Stir in the nutmeg and cayenne.

Pour into a medium-size baking dish, coated with no-stick spray. Sprinkle the wheat germ on top. Place the baking dish in a pan of hot water and bake at 325° for 45 minutes to 1 hour or until the pudding is firm.

Welsh Vegetable Pot ★ ★

284

There's a satisfying flavor that comes from this combination of traditional winter vegetables. See if you don't agree.

Makes 6 servings

3 cups shredded cabbage
2 cups cubed potatoes
1 cup sliced carrots
1 stalk celery, sliced
¼ teaspoon thyme
1 cup water

Place all of the ingredients in a large saucepan. Bring to a boil, then reduce heat to simmer. Partially cover and simmer for about 30 minutes or until quite tender. Serve with the cooking liquid.

Sharon's Succotash ★

A touch of herbs brings a whole new taste to this traditional side dish.

Makes 4 servings

1½ cups lima beans
¾ cup corn
2 tablespoons low-fat yogurt
1 teaspoon minced fresh dill
   or ¼ teaspoon dried dill

In a medium-size saucepan, bring a small amount of water to a boil and add the lima beans. Simmer for about 15 to 20 minutes, until nearly tender. Add the corn and simmer together for about 2 to 3 minutes.

Combine the yogurt and dill in a serving bowl. Drain the vegetables and place in the serving bowl. Toss with the yogurt and dill mixture. Serve hot.

Poached Mushroom Caps ★ ★ ★

Low-calorie mushrooms usually become high-calorie dishes when they are sautéed in butter. This is a tasty low-calorie option.

Makes 3 servings

12 large mushroom caps
¼ cup *Chicken Stock*

Cut the mushroom stems even with the caps. If you desire, cut a fluted design in the top of the mushroom caps with the tip of a very sharp knife.

Bring the stock to a boil in a large skillet. Add the mushroom caps, return to a boil, then simmer for about 10 minutes, turning the caps once. Turn up the heat and cook until the liquid in the pan is nearly evaporated. Serve hot or cold.

Oven-Baked Potatoes ★

A nice touch to routine potatoes—with no added calories.

Makes 4 servings

1 tablespoon basil
1 teaspoon paprika
4 small baking potatoes

Coat a cookie sheet with no-stick spray and sprinkle basil and paprika on it. Cut potatoes in half lengthwise and place them, cut side down, on the herbed sheet. Bake at 350° for 45 minutes or until done.

Mixed Vegetable Mash ★ ★ ★

Makes 6 servings

4 cups cubed new potatoes
4 small carrots, thickly sliced
1 small onion, chopped
¼–⅓ cup skim milk
minced fresh parsley (garnish)
2 thin carrot slices (garnish)

Place the potatoes, carrots, and onions in a large saucepan and cover with water. Bring to a boil, reduce heat, cover, and simmer until the vegetables are tender, about 20 minutes.

Drain the cooked vegetables, then mash them thoroughly in the saucepan with a vegetable masher. Mix in milk to make desired consistency.

Place the mashed vegetables in a serving dish, add a large pinch of parsley in the center, and arrange the 2 carrot slices over the parsley, if desired.

Toll Gate
Sweet Potatoes ★ ★

Makes 4 servings

2 large sweet potatoes,
      peeled and cubed
3 tablespoons low-fat yogurt
      dash of cinnamon
      dash of ground cloves
      grated lemon or orange rind
        (garnish)

Place the sweet potatoes in a medium-size saucepan, partially cover with water, and bring to a boil. Reduce heat, cover, and simmer for about 15 minutes or until the sweet potatoes are soft when pierced with a fork.

Mash the potatoes in the pan with a potato masher. Add the yogurt, cinnamon, and cloves and mash until combined. Transfer the potatoes to a warmed serving dish. Top with a touch of grated lemon or orange rind, if desired, and serve.

★ *VARIATION: Fold in ½ cup of* Homemade Applesauce *and heat through before serving.*

286

Spiced Sweet
Potato Terrine ★
Nice for the holidays.

Makes 4 servings

2 medium-size sweet
      potatoes
2 medium-size tart apples,
      sliced
½ cup apple cider or *Chicken
      Stock*
¼ teaspoon grated fresh
      ginger
      dash of cinnamon

Cut the sweet potatoes in half lengthwise, then cut crosswise into thin slices.

Place the sweet potatoes and apples in layers in an 8 × 8-inch baking dish. Pour the cider over the apples and potatoes and sprinkle with the ginger and cinnamon. Bake at 350° for about 45 minutes or until the sweet potatoes are tender.

Fruit and
Sweet Potato Bake ★

Makes 8 servings

4 cups cubed sweet potatoes
2 medium-size pears, diced
1 medium-size apple, diced
2 tablespoons apple juice
   dash of nutmeg
   minced fresh parsley
      (garnish)

Place the sweet potatoes, pears, apples, and juice in a medium-size ovenproof casserole. Dust with nutmeg and toss lightly.

Cover tightly. Bake at 350° for 1 hour. Garnish with a pinch of parsley, if desired, before serving.

Puree of
Sweet Potatoes ★

Makes 6 servings

4 large sweet potatoes
1 tablespoon butter
¼ cup low-fat vanilla yogurt
   dash of nutmeg

Cut the sweet potatoes in half, place in a large saucepan, and cover with cold water. Bring to a boil, then reduce heat and simmer, covered, until tender. Drain.

Hold the sweet potato halves with a fork and peel them while they are hot. Mash the potatoes with the butter, then add the yogurt and nutmeg and mash until smooth.

★ ★ *VARIATION: Eliminate the butter.*

Orange Mashed
Sweet Potatoes ★

Makes 4 servings

3 medium-size sweet
      potatoes, cubed
2 medium-size carrots, sliced
¼ cup low-fat yogurt
¼ teaspoon grated orange
      rind
¼ teaspoon cinnamon
   dash of nutmeg
   orange slices (garnish)
   watercress sprigs (garnish)

Place the sweet potatoes in a medium-size saucepan with the carrots. Cover with cold water. Bring to a boil, reduce heat, cover, and simmer until tender, about 25 minutes. Drain.

Mash the potatoes and carrots with the yogurt, orange rind, cinnamon, and nutmeg. Garnish with orange slices and watercress, if desired.

Oranged Beets ★ ★ ★

Makes 8 servings

5   large beets
2   oranges
½   cup orange juice
1   teaspoon cornstarch
2   tablespoons water
    dash of nutmeg

Place the unpeeled beets in a large saucepan with enough water to cover. Bring to a boil, then reduce heat, cover, and cook until tender when pierced with a fork, about 30 minutes.

While the beets cook, section the oranges and peel the membrane off each section.

Bring the orange juice to a boil in a small saucepan. Dissolve the cornstarch in the water and stir into the boiling orange juice. Reduce heat and simmer, stirring constantly, until the sauce is slightly thickened. Add the orange sections and nutmeg. Heat through and keep warm until ready to use.

Drain the beets. Peel each beet by holding it with a fork and removing the skin with a knife. Slice the beets and arrange in a shallow serving dish. Pour the orange sauce over them and arrange the orange sections on top.

288

Princeton Beets ★ ★ ★

Makes 8 servings

8   medium-size beets, with
        tops
1   cup rice vinegar
1   tablespoon honey
2   cloves garlic
5   whole cloves
1   small bay leaf
¼   teaspoon celery seeds

Cut the tops from the beets, leaving about 1 inch of stem attached. Place beets in a large saucepan and cover with water. Bring to a boil, cover, reduce heat, and simmer just until tender, about 20 minutes. Remove from heat and drain, reserving 1 cup of the cooking water. Set the beets aside to cool.

In a medium-size saucepan, combine the reserved cooking water, the vinegar, honey, garlic, cloves, bay leaf, and celery seeds. Bring to a boil over low heat.

While the marinade heats, peel and slice the cooked beets and place in a serving bowl.

Pour the hot marinade over the beets. Cool slightly, then cover and chill overnight. Drain before serving.

Homemade Applesauce ★

Makes 8 servings

8 medium-size tart red
   apples, quartered
2 cups water
1 tablespoon lemon juice
1 tablespoon honey
½ teaspoon cinnamon

Place one-fourth of the apples in a blender, along with ½ cup of the water. Process on low speed, then medium, until the apples are smooth, scraping down the sides of the blender as necessary. Place in a large saucepan. Repeat with the remaining apples and water.

Add the lemon juice, honey, and cinnamon to the pan. Bring to a boil, then reduce heat and simmer, stirring occasionally, about 15 to 20 minutes, until the applesauce has the desired consistency.

Real-Apple-Sauce ★ ★

The season's best fresh apples and delicious cider make an unbeatable applesauce. Try it! Make several batches and freeze.

Makes 6 servings

4 cups diced apples
1 cup apple cider
   dash of cinnamon

Place the apples in a blender with the cider. Process on low, then medium speed until smooth.

Place the blended mixture in a medium-size saucepan. Bring to a boil over medium heat, then reduce heat, cover, and simmer 15 minutes. Serve warm or chilled with a dash of cinnamon.

Barley Stuffing ★

Makes 4 servings

1 cup minced onions
1 cup chopped celery
3 tablespoons *Chicken Stock*
1 cup cooked barley
1 egg, beaten
1 teaspoon thyme
1 teaspoon marjoram
1 clove garlic, minced
¼ cup grated Parmesan
   cheese

Sauté the onions and celery in the stock until translucent. In a large bowl, combine the onions and celery with the barley, egg, thyme, marjoram, garlic, and cheese.

Reserve to stuff a bird or bake in a 1-quart oven-proof casserole at 350° for 30 to 45 minutes.

NOTE: This recipe makes 2 cups.

Pecan Stuffing ★

Makes 8 servings

2 tablespoons *Chicken Stock*
2 tablespoons minced
    shallots
¾ cup shredded carrots
¼ cup minced celery
2 cups minced mushrooms
¼ teaspoon tarragon
    dash of crumbled
    rosemary
2½ cups cooked brown rice
½ cup chopped pecans
¼ cup *Chicken Stock*

Place the 2 tablespoons of stock in a large skillet and set over medium heat. When the stock is heated, stir in the shallots, carrots, and celery. Cook for about 4 to 5 minutes, stirring frequently. Add the mushrooms, tarragon, and rosemary and cook until the mushrooms release their liquid and the liquid has evaporated. Add the rice and pecans to the skillet and stir until combined.

Place the stuffing in a 1½-quart baking dish and spoon ¼ cup of stock over the top.

Reserve to stuff a bird or bake at 350° for 40 minutes, covering loosely with foil toward the end of baking if the stuffing browns too much.

NOTE: This recipe makes 4 cups.

290

Bennie's Baked Beans ★

Makes 8 servings

4 cups cooked baby lima
    beans
1 cup water or cooking
    liquid from beans
½ cup *Tomato Sauce*
2 tablespoons chopped
    onions
1 tablespoon tamari or soy
    sauce
2 cloves garlic
1 orange, thinly sliced

Place the lima beans in a deep, 1½-quart oven-proof casserole. Place the water in a blender with the tomato sauce, onions, and tamari. Push the garlic through a garlic press into the blender. Process on medium to high speed until smooth. Pour the tomato sauce over the beans and stir lightly so that the liquid is distributed throughout. Top the beans with the orange slices. Cover and bake at 350° for 1 hour. Uncover and bake an additional 1½ hours.

Sandwiches

Remember all the times you wrapped your fist around a wonderfully thick sandwich piled high with lots of meat, mayonnaise, tomatoes, lettuce, and other sandwich fixings? Remember how guilty you felt? The diet. Gulped away again.

Sandwiches can be a tough one to resist. Yet, somehow giving in leaves dieters with a feeling they've done something wrong. Bread, we think. It's fattening.

Now's the time to straighten out a few errors in thinking where sandwiches are concerned. It's not the bread that makes the sandwich so wrong for the diet. It's what you put *between* the slices.

Take tuna fish salad, for example. A tuna fish salad sandwich is a pretty popular item with a lot of dieters. Tuna fish in itself isn't all that slimming (at least when you compare it to the sandwich fillers I'll be introducing you to). Mix it with a tablespoon or two of mayonnaise (at 99 calories a tablespoon), pile it between a couple of pieces of mayonnaise-smeared toast, top with a couple of pieces of lettuce and, well, you might as well be eating a dish of ice cream.

We know (or at least we should) that luncheon meats have no place in a diet—they're much too high in calories. But chicken, tuna, or eggs turned into "salad" with high-calorie spreads don't belong in a diet either.

So what's there to make a sandwich with then? Plenty. The sandwiches in this chapter are made with many of the low-calorie, high-fiber, nutritious, and crunchy fillers you find in other sandwiches. Only what you'll find here is a lot more filler and a lot less (and in some cases not any at all) other sandwich fare. Sure, you'll find eggs, chicken, and turkey in these sandwiches but not mixed with mayonnaise. There's also cheese—but used sparingly to give you the taste, not the calories.

Some of the sandwiches are featured open faced, so you don't have the calories of an extra piece of bread. (Add an extra slice of chicken and cheese; take off a slice of bread. That should be easy enough to remember.)

Pita is a great bread for stuffing, especially the pita in this book. A sandwich made with pita has fewer calories than one made with bread. Pita and fresh raw vegetables were made for each other. Take any of the vegetables you have on hand. Shred them, mix them. Spread the pita with *Chick-Pea Puree* and stuff it as full as you like. Even top it with a little cheese if you care. You'll have a great three-star sandwich you can devour without the calories.

The sandwiches you'll find in this chapter are not served dry, either. We make generous use of mayonnaise, Russian dressing, and other spreads and toppings, but we only use the low-calorie versions developed for this book (you'll find a wide selection in the "Dressings, Spreads, and Sauces" chapter). Stick with these recipes if you want to stick with low calories.

On the following pages, I've given you a baker's dozen of sandwich ideas to show you how easy it is to create a tasty, attractive, and low-calorie treat. You'll find out how cabbage, sprouts, scallions, radishes, cucumbers, mushrooms, carrots, tomatoes, spinach (you'll find no Iceburg here), poultry, and even hamburger combined in different ways can create different tastes. Try some of these, then experiment on your own. If you're a real sandwich lover, you should be able to design even more and better sandwich ideas. Pile them high; wrap your fist around them; and enjoy—without the guilt.

292

293

Your good intentions never need to be left behind with these sandwiches to go.
From top clockwise are *Egyptian Pita, Vegetarian Rye Sandwich, Falafel in Romaine, Toasted Cheese and Mushroom Sandwich,* and *Moo Shiu Mushrooms.*

Italian Wedding Soup and *Seeded Rye Bread* make a great fill-me-up meal for lunch or dinner.

Toasted Cheese and Mushroom Sandwiches ★ ★ ★

A hot sandwich served open faced and piled high. One of my favorites.

Makes 2 servings

1	teaspoon tamari or soy sauce
2	tablespoons water
2	scallions, chopped
1	cup sliced mushrooms
	dash of nutmeg
2	slices *Whole Wheat Bread* or other whole grain bread
¼	cup shredded Swiss cheese
1	small carrot, shredded
½	cup alfalfa sprouts
2	orange slices (garnish)

Place the tamari and water in a small skillet. Add the scallions and stir over medium heat until the scallions are limp. Add the mushrooms and reduce heat to low. When the mushrooms have released their liquid and the liquid has evaporated, remove from heat. Dust with the nutmeg and stir.

Toast the bread. Arrange the mushrooms and scallions on the bread slices. Top with the cheese. Place under a broiler until the cheese is melted. Top with the carrots and sprouts. Garnish with orange slices, if desired.

295

Hungarian Cucumber Sandwiches ★ ★

In this traditional campfire sandwich we replaced salt pork with watercress.

Makes 4 servings

1	cup thinly sliced cucumbers
1	tablespoon white wine vinegar
1	cup trimmed watercress
¼	cup low-fat cottage cheese
½	teaspoon dill
8	slices whole grain bread

Combine cucumbers and vinegar in a colander. Toss and let drain for 1 hour.

In a medium-size saucepan, blanch watercress for 45 seconds. Drain well and combine with cucumbers.

In a blender or food processor, whip cottage cheese and dill. Spread evenly on 4 bread slices, add cucumber mixture, and top with remaining bread slices. Serve immediately.

Sunnyside Sandwiches ★ ★

Makes 2 servings

¼ cup thinly sliced radishes
2 slices *Keystone Mixed-Grain Bread*, toasted if desired
4 large mushrooms, sliced
1 small carrot, shredded
2 ounces Muenster cheese, thinly sliced
½ cup alfalfa sprouts
2 orange slices (garnish)
   parsley sprigs (garnish)

Divide the radishes and place in the center of the bread slices. Top with mushrooms and carrots and cover with cheese slices. Set under a broiler until the cheese is melted. Place sprouts on top of cheese. Serve each sandwich with an orange slice and parsley sprigs, if desired.

296 Open-Faced Club Sandwiches ★ ★

These attractively garnished sandwiches make a nice luncheon for guests.

Makes 2 servings

2 slices *Keystone Mixed-Grain Bread*
2 tablespoons *Russian Dressing*
2 thin slices Swiss cheese
2 thin slices cooked turkey or chicken breast
2 leaves Boston lettuce
2 thin tomato slices
2 tablespoons shredded zucchini
1 tablespoon shredded carrots
2 tablespoons alfalfa sprouts
4 leaves spinach (garnish)
2 orange slices (garnish)

Spread each of the bread slices with about a teaspoon of the dressing. Place on individual serving plates. Layer each slice of bread with a slice of cheese, then turkey, lettuce, and tomato. Then add a layer of zucchini, carrots, and sprouts. Place a dollop of the remaining dressing on top of each sandwich.

If desired, arrange the spinach next to the sandwich. Cut the orange slices halfway across, twist, and place on the spinach.

Vegetarian Rye Sandwiches ★

Wonderful for picnics or outdoor lunches.

Makes 2 servings

4   slices *Onion Rye Bread* or
      Seeded Rye Bread
¼   cup *Russian Dressing*
¼   cup shredded cabbage
2   tablespoons shredded
      carrots
¼   cup alfalfa sprouts
      spinach leaves
2   thin slices Swiss cheese
4   orange slices (garnish)
      parsley sprigs (garnish)

Spread each of the bread slices with about ½ teaspoon of the dressing. Combine the cabbage, carrots, and half the sprouts in a small bowl and toss with the remaining dressing.

Place two bread slices on each plate. Layer with the cabbage mixture, remaining sprouts, spinach, and cheese. Top with remaining slices of bread. Garnish with orange slices and parsley, if desired. Cut in half and serve.

297

Country Chicken Sandwiches ★ ★

Makes 2 servings

1   whole chicken breast,
      halved, boned, and
      skinned
1   tablespoon *Chicken Stock*
1   whole wheat English
      muffin, halved
1   tablespoon whipped,
      low-fat cottage cheese
2   thin tomato slices
½   teaspoon marjoram
2   thin slices part-skim
      mozzarella cheese

Flatten each chicken piece by placing it between two sheets of waxed paper and pounding it with a mallet or the flat side of a meat cleaver until about ½-inch thick.

Heat the stock in a large skillet. Quickly sauté the chicken pieces on both sides, just until cooked through, about 10 minutes on each side.

Meanwhile, toast the muffin halves. Spread the cottage cheese on the muffins and place them on a baking sheet and broil for about 20 seconds.

Arrange each piece of chicken on the muffin halves, add tomatoes and marjoram, and top with cheese. Broil until cheese melts and begins to turn golden.

Serve hot and open faced.

Popeye's
Egg Sandwiches ★ ★

Great for brown baggers. Just wrap bread and filling separately, then assemble when ready to eat.

Makes 2 servings

4	slices *Keystone Mixed-Grain Bread* or other whole grain bread
1	chopped hard-cooked egg
½	cup shredded spinach
2	tablespoons shredded carrots
1	tablespoon minced scallions
2	tablespoons *Russian Dressing*

Place bread on 2 serving plates.

In a medium-size bowl, toss the egg, spinach, carrots, and scallions with the dressing.

Divide the mixture in half, spread on two slices of bread, and top with remaining bread. Cut in half and serve.

★ ★ ★ *VARIATION: Serve open faced on one slice of bread per person.*

298

Skinny
Beef Burgers ★ ★

Ultra-thin hamburgers with quite a special flavor. Choose your own toppings.

Makes 4 servings

4	whole wheat English muffins
1	teaspoon Dijon mustard
¼	pound lean ground beef
4	thin tomato slices
¼	cup minced onions
¼	cup alfalfa sprouts
¼	cup shredded carrots
	parsley sprigs (garnish)

Cut the muffins in half. Spread 4 of the muffin halves with mustard. Press a thin layer of ground beef into each muffin half, about a tablespoon per muffin.

Place the muffins, beef side down, in a heated, lightly oiled skillet. Lightly press the muffin on the cooking surface. Sauté over low to medium heat just until the beef is cooked through. Remove from the pan carefully with a spatula.

While the beef is cooking, toast the remaining muffin halves. Place the muffins on a serving plate with the toppings arranged around them.

★ ★ *VARIATION: If you can afford a few extra calories, top the cooked beef with half a tablespoon of shredded cheddar cheese and place under a broiler until the cheese is melted. Serve as above.*

Yogi Hoagie ★ ★ ★

Stuff low-calorie vegetables and sprouts in whole grain pitas and enjoy a thick (but sensible) sandwich.

Makes 4 servings

4	*Whole Wheat Pitas*
2	tablespoons *Lighten-Up Mayonnaise*
¼	cup shredded spinach
¼	cup shredded lettuce
¼	cup shredded carrots
¼	cup chopped red cabbage
¼	cup chopped mushrooms
½	cup alfalfa sprouts

Slice open the top of each pita and spread with mayonnaise. Combine spinach, lettuce, carrots, cabbage, and mushrooms in a medium-size bowl and toss. Stuff in pitas and top with sprouts.

299

Moo Shiu Mushrooms ★ ★ ★

A tasty, southeast Asian sandwich so low in calories we've allowed for seconds.

Makes 2 servings

1	cup sliced mushrooms
½	cup shiitake mushrooms, slivered and soaked for 20 minutes
1	tablespoon *Chicken Stock*
½	cup shredded Chinese cabbage
¼	cup minced scallions
½	teaspoon red miso (red soybean paste)
4	thin, 6-inch spring roll skins
1	tablespoon soy sauce

In a medium-size skillet or wok, stir-fry the mushrooms and shiitake mushrooms over medium-high heat in stock for 3 minutes. Add the cabbage and stir-fry another minute. Add the scallions and miso. Combine and remove from heat. Drain and cool. Steam spring roll skins for 3 minutes. Lay them flat and place one-fourth of the mushroom mixture at the edge of each. Roll like a jelly roll, tucking corners in along the way.

Serve immediately with soy sauce for dipping.

NOTE: Egg roll wrappers will not work well in assembling these sandwiches. Spring rolls can be found in many supermarkets or at a Korean grocery store.

Falafel
in Romaine ★ ★ ★

Crispy lettuce replaces bread in these sandwiches.

Makes 4 servings

2	cups shredded carrots
1	medium-size onion, minced
2	eggs, beaten
1	clove garlic
¾	cup mashed cooked chick-peas
1	tablespoon chopped fresh parsley
¼	teaspoon ground cumin
¼	teaspoon ground coriander
	dash of ground allspice
4	large leaves romaine lettuce

In a large bowl, combine the carrots, onions, and eggs. Push the garlic through a garlic press into the bowl and mix.

Grind the chick-peas in a blender or food processor on medium to high speed.

Add the chick-peas, parsley, cumin, coriander, and allspice to the egg mixture and stir together until well combined. Chill until the mixture is firm.

Form into patties and cook in a large hot no-stick skillet over medium heat until lightly browned on both sides. Wrap each in a lettuce leaf and serve immediately.

300

Vegetarian
Pitas ★ ★ ★

A real low-calorie treat.

Makes 2 servings

2	*Whole Wheat Pitas*
⅓	cup *Chick-Pea Puree*
2	leaves romaine lettuce, shredded
½	cup shredded spinach
1	tomato, coarsely chopped
¼	cup minced scallions
½	cup alfalfa sprouts
6	cherry tomatoes (garnish)
	parsley sprigs (garnish)

Slit open the pitas. Spread the inside of each pocket with *Chick-Pea Puree*. Add the lettuce, spinach, tomatoes, scallions, and sprouts. Arrange the sandwiches on serving plates and garnish with cherry tomatoes and parsley, if desired.

Egyptian Pitas ★ ★ ★

This filling keeps well in the refrigerator, ready to go when you are.

Makes 6 servings

2   cups shredded cabbage
2   cups shredded spinach
½   cup chopped tomatoes
1   cup low-fat cottage cheese
¼   cup minced yellow onions
2   tablespoons minced fresh
      parsley
2   tablespoons red wine
      vinegar
¼   teaspoon oregano
6   *Whole Wheat Pitas*

Combine the cabbage, spinach, tomatoes, cottage cheese, onions, and parsley in a large mixing bowl.

Combine the vinegar and oregano in a small bowl or jar and stir or shake well. Pour over the cabbage mixture and chill, tightly covered.

Slice open the top of each pita and stuff each with about ⅔ cup of filling.

Breads, Muffins, and Crepes

Why would dieters want to subject themselves to an afternoon in the kitchen, surrounded by the enticing aroma of homemade bread baking in the oven? Because super nutritious, whole grain breads that are deliciously satisfying and low in calories cannot be gotten any other way. (Unless, of course, you have somebody else do the baking *for* you.)

We don't like to call the breads and other baked goods in this chapter "diet" food. They taste much too good for that. But they *are* good food for dieters. That's because they contain an essential ingredient so important to natural weight loss—whole grains. And they don't contain any of the ingredients that make other breads and baked goods so high in calories—things like lots of oils and butter, whole milk, nuts, and lots of honey and eggs.

We arrived at the bread and muffin recipes in this chapter in sort of a backward fashion. Instead of looking at a table full of raw ingredients and deciding how we could develop tasty low-calorie recipes, we decided to take a look at some already proven, great-tasting, high-calorie recipes and see how we could cut back on the calories without losing the taste. From the response of our taste testers, we succeeded quite well.

What we found was that plain ordinary water, fruit juices, buttermilk, and skim milk work quite well as substitutes for whole milk, oil, and other liquid ingredients in baking. The nuts we removed from some of the breads were never even missed by our taste testers. Sweeteners—honey and molasses—were cut to the minimum. So, too, was oil. The result was that we turned breads—some as high as 200 calories a slice—into tasty loaves well within the 80-calorie-a-slice range.

The muffins were a little trickier. The high-calorie nuts you often find in muffin recipes were replaced by rolled oats or more flour. Dried fruit was cut to a minimum—just enough to lend the muffins some taste. And skim milk, fruit juice, or water took the place of oils, sweeteners, and eggs. Two eggs became one egg and one egg white.

Similar things were done with the rolls, bagels, and crepes. Where whole milk or buttermilk was called for, we simply substituted skim. Oil and butter were reduced to the minimum necessary. Here again two eggs became one egg and one egg white (that saves about 50 calories).

For some recipes we simply reduced size. The corn tortillas, for example, were reduced from seven inches in diameter to six inches—enough to lower the tortillas from a two-star to a three-star range. Who would ever notice the difference? The pitas were slightly reduced to a size still ample enough to make a great sandwich.

With the exception of the French bread, all the breads in this chapter are baked in 9 × 5-inch loaf pans. Each recipe makes two loaves of either 18 or 20 generous slices (bigger than the slices you get from store-bought bread). The slices are ample enough that you can, if you wish, make a sandwich with one slice cut in half—a nice way to save on calories.

We suggest cutting the bread into slices after it cools and storing it in the freezer. This helps in two ways: it keeps the breads fresher, and it prevents you from digging your hand into the bread drawer and eating more than you should.

You should find that baking your own is a great way to control your diet.

Whole Wheat Bread ★ ★

A delicious basic bread.

Makes 20 slices per loaf

2 tablespoons active dry yeast
4 cups lukewarm water
1 tablespoon honey
1 teaspoon salt
7–8 cups whole wheat flour

In a large bowl, dissolve the yeast in ½ cup of lukewarm water. Stir in the honey. When yeast mixture is bubbly, add remaining water and salt.

Stir in 4 cups of whole wheat flour. With a hand mixer, beat the batter at high speed for at least 5 minutes, until the batter is "stretchy." The dough will become too heavy to continue using the mixer.

Add the remaining flour, one cup at a time, stirring well after each addition. The dough will be too soft to knead, so let dough remain in bowl, cover with a damp towel, and let rise in a warm place for 1 hour.

Punch the dough down after it has risen and allow to rise a second time in the bowl with a damp towel over it for about 1 hour.

Coat two 9 × 5-inch bread pans with no-stick spray. When the dough has risen a second time, punch it down, divide in half, and place it into each pan.

Let the bread rise uncovered for 10 minutes. Place in a cold oven and turn heat to 400°. Bake for 15 minutes, then turn heat to 350° and bake 30 minutes more.

When the bread is done, it will pull away from the sides of the pan and sound hollow when tapped. Cool on racks before slicing.

Keystone Mixed-Grain Bread ★ ★ ★

For those who like to eat light at breakfast, a slice of this bread, toasted and served with *Keystone Breakfast Cheese*, is a nutritious—and low-calorie—way to start the day.

Makes 20 slices per loaf

2½ cups lukewarm water
2 tablespoons corn or barley malt
2 tablespoons active dry yeast

Mix the water and malt in a large bowl. Add the yeast and stir to dissolve. Add the rye flakes, wheat flakes, oat bran, and cornmeal and stir until well blended. Gradually add the unbleached and whole wheat flours ½ cup at a time, until the mixture can be kneaded (it'll be sticky).

1 cup rye flakes
1 cup wheat flakes
¾ cup oat bran
¼ cup cornmeal
2–2½ cups unbleached flour
2 cups whole wheat flour

On a well-floured surface, knead for 8 minutes or until the dough is elastic. Coat a large bowl with no-stick spray and place the dough in it, turning once to bring the coated side up. Cover with plastic wrap and let rise in a warm place for 45 to 60 minutes or until doubled in volume.

Punch down the dough, cut in half, and fit into two 9 × 5-inch loaf pans coated with no-stick spray. Let rise again until doubled in volume, about 30 minutes. Spray each loaf with water from a plant mister. Place in a 375° oven and bake for about 45 minutes or until the loaves sound hollow when tapped, spraying again midway through baking. Remove from pans and cool on wire racks.

Seeded Rye Bread ★ ★ ★

Makes 18 slices per loaf

2 tablespoons active dry yeast
2¾ cups lukewarm water
1 tablespoon blackstrap molasses
¼ cup lemon juice
½ teaspoon finely grated lemon rind
1 teaspoon salt
1 cup gluten flour
1 cup rye flour
¼ cup carob powder
2 tablespoons caraway seeds
4½–5 cups whole wheat flour

In a large bowl, dissolve the yeast in ½ cup of the water and stir in the molasses. When the yeast is bubbly, add the remaining water, lemon juice, lemon rind, and salt.

Stir in the gluten flour, rye flour, carob powder, caraway seeds, and enough of the whole wheat flour (about 4 cups) to make the dough hold together.

Place the dough on a lightly floured surface and knead for 5 to 10 minutes, until it is smooth.

Place the dough in a large bowl coated with no-stick spray, turning the dough once. Cover with a damp kitchen towel and set in a warm place for 45 to 60 minutes or until doubled in bulk. Punch down, knead, and divide the dough in half. Roll up the dough and place seam side down in two 9 × 5-inch bread pans coated with no-stick spray.

Let the dough rise again, covered with a damp towel, until nearly doubled in bulk (about 30 minutes). Place in a preheated 350° oven and bake for 30 to 35 minutes or until the bread is browned and sounds hollow when tapped. Cool on racks before slicing.

Herbed Carrot Bread ★ ★ ★

Makes 18 slices per loaf

3	medium-size carrots, sliced
2	tablespoons active dry yeast
2¼	cups lukewarm water
1	tablespoon honey
1	tablespoon oil
6	scallions, chopped
3	tablespoons minced fresh parsley
2	tablespoons minced fresh dill or 1 tablespoon dried dill
1	teaspoon salt
6½–7	cups whole wheat flour

Steam the carrots for about 20 minutes or until tender. Drain and mash. There should be ¾ cup. Set aside.

Dissolve the yeast in ½ cup of the water in a large bowl and stir in the honey. When yeast is bubbly, stir in remaining water.

Meanwhile, cook the oil and scallions in a small skillet over medium heat. When scallions are translucent, stir in the parsley and dill. Remove from heat, stir in salt, and cool slightly.

Stir the mashed carrots, scallions, and 2 cups of the flour into the yeast mixture. Add enough of the remaining flour (about 3 cups) to make a dough firm enough to handle.

Place dough on a lightly floured surface and knead in enough additional flour until the dough is smooth. Knead 6 to 8 minutes to develop gluten.

Place dough in a large bowl coated with no-stick spray, turning the dough once. Cover with a damp towel and set in a warm place until doubled in bulk, about 45 minutes. Punch down, knead lightly, and divide into two pieces. Roll up the dough and place seam side down in two 9 × 5-inch loaf pans coated with no-stick spray.

Cover and let rise again until nearly doubled in bulk, about 30 minutes. Bake in a preheated 350° oven for 35 minutes or until the bread sounds hollow when tapped. Cool before slicing.

Orange Wheat Germ Bread ★ ★

A sweet-tasting bread that's great for breakfast—or even dessert!

Makes 18 slices per loaf

2	large navel oranges, washed
1	egg
	buttermilk (optional)
2	tablespoons active dry yeast
1¼	cups lukewarm water
3	tablespoons honey
1	cup wheat germ
½	cup gluten flour
¼	teaspoon ground mace
5–5½	cups whole wheat flour

Place the oranges in a large saucepan of boiling water. Boil for 30 minutes. Cut the oranges in half across, remove any seeds, and place in a blender.

Add the egg. Process the egg and cooked oranges on medium speed until smooth. Add buttermilk, if needed, to make 3 cups of liquid.

Meanwhile, in a large bowl, dissolve the yeast in ½ cup of the water. Stir in the remaining water, honey, wheat germ, gluten flour, mace, orange mixture, and enough of the whole wheat flour to make the dough hold together.

Place the dough on a lightly floured surface and knead until the dough is smooth, about 5 minutes. Set the dough in a large bowl coated with no-stick spray, turning the dough once. Cover with a damp kitchen towel and set in a warm place for 45 to 60 minutes or until the dough doubles in bulk.

Punch down the dough. Divide in half and knead. Flatten out the dough and roll up to fit two 9 × 5-inch bread pans. Coat the pans with no-stick spray. Place the dough in the pans, cover with a damp kitchen towel, and let rise until almost doubled in bulk, about 30 minutes.

Place the bread in a preheated 350° oven. Bake for 35 to 40 minutes, until the bread is golden brown and sounds hollow when tapped. Let cool on a rack before slicing.

307

Onion Rye
Bread ★ ★

Makes 20 slices per loaf

3	medium-size onions, chopped
2	tablespoons sunflower oil
1	teaspoon salt
2	tablespoons active dry yeast
2¼	cups lukewarm water
2	tablespoons light unsulphured molasses
1½	cups rye flour
½	cup gluten flour
¼	teaspoon ground cardamom
5–5½	cups whole wheat flour

Place the onions and the oil in a medium-size skillet over low heat. Cook the onions until soft but do not brown them. Reserve one-third of the onions and set aside. Place the remaining onions in a blender with the salt and process on medium speed until smooth.

Meanwhile, dissolve the yeast in ½ cup of the water in a large bowl and stir in the molasses. When the yeast is bubbly, add the remaining water, reserved onions, rye flour, gluten flour, cardamom, and enough whole wheat flour to make the dough hold together.

On a lightly floured surface, knead the dough until it is smooth, about 5 to 10 minutes. Place in a large bowl lightly coated with no-stick spray, turning the dough once. Cover with a damp kitchen towel, and set in a warm place to rise until doubled in bulk, 45 to 60 minutes.

Punch down the dough and divide in two. Knead briefly, then roll up to fit two 9 × 5-inch bread pans. Coat the pans with no-stick spray. Place the dough, seam side down, in the pans, and cover with a damp kitchen towel. Set aside again until doubled in bulk, about 30 minutes.

Place the bread in a preheated 350° oven and bake for 35 minutes or until the bread is browned and sounds hollow when tapped. Cool on racks before slicing.

Pumpernickel
Bread ★ ★

Makes 18 slices per loaf

2	tablespoons active dry yeast
2⅓	cups lukewarm water
2	tablespoons light unsulphured molasses

Dissolve the yeast in ½ cup of the water in a large bowl and stir in the molasses and buttermilk. When the yeast is bubbly, stir in the remaining water, oil, salt, rye flour, buckwheat flour, carob powder, mace, and 4 cups of the whole wheat flour. Stir to combine.

2 cups buttermilk
2 tablespoons safflower oil
1 teaspoon salt
1½ cups rye flour
1 cup buckwheat flour
½ cup carob powder
¼ teaspoon ground mace
4½–5 cups whole wheat flour

Place the dough on a lightly floured surface and knead in enough of the remaining whole wheat flour to make a smooth and elastic dough, kneading about 5 to 10 minutes. Place the dough in a very large bowl lightly coated with no-stick spray, turning the dough once. Cover with a damp kitchen towel and let rise in a warm place for 45 to 60 minutes or until doubled in bulk.

Punch down the dough in the bowl, knead briefly, and divide in half. Knead and flatten the bread, then roll up to fit two 9 × 5-inch bread pans. Coat the pans with no-stick spray. Place the dough in the pans, cover with the damp towel, and allow to rise until nearly doubled in bulk, about 30 minutes.

Place the bread in a preheated 350° oven and bake for 30 to 35 minutes, until the bread is browned and sounds hollow when tapped. Let cool on racks before slicing.

309

Popovers ★ ★ ★

Makes 12 popovers

2 eggs
2 egg whites
1 cup skim milk
1 tablespoon butter, melted
1 cup whole wheat pastry
    flour

In a medium-size bowl, beat the eggs and egg whites with an electric mixer at high speed until foamy. Continue beating as you add the milk, butter, and flour.

When the mixture is smooth and all the ingredients well combined, divide the batter among muffin cups or custard cups lightly coated with no-stick spray. Do not fill the cups more than two-thirds full.

Bake at 400° for 15 minutes. Reduce heat to 350° and bake an additional 10 to 15 minutes or until golden brown. Do not open the oven door until baking time has elapsed, or the popovers may fail to rise properly.

NOTE: Do not use a blender to prepare the popover batter. Some air must be beaten into the eggs, and a blender is unsuitable for this task.

Whole Wheat
Pitas ★ ★ ★

These are slightly smaller than the store-bought variety, but their firm texture makes them superb for their primary purpose—to hold lots of good sandwich fixings.

Makes 18 pitas

2 teaspoons active dry yeast
1¼ cups lukewarm water
1 tablespoon olive oil
2½–3 cups whole wheat flour

In a large bowl, dissolve the yeast in the lukewarm water. Add the oil and 1½ cups of flour. Using an electric mixer, beat the dough on medium to high speed for 2 minutes.

Add the remaining flour by hand, beating it in with a wooden spoon at first, then kneading the dough by hand.

Coat a large mixing bowl with no-stick spray and set the dough in the bowl. Turn the dough once to coat. Cover with a damp towel and set in a warm place until the dough has doubled in bulk, about 30 minutes.

Punch down the dough and place it on a floured surface. Divide the dough into 18 pieces and roll each into a ball, about the size of a golf ball. Cover with a damp towel or waxed paper and let the dough rest at least 10 minutes.

Roll out each ball of dough to a diameter of 5 inches and a ⅛-inch thickness. Dust the countertop and rolling pin with additional flour, if needed, to prevent sticking.

Preheat the oven to 500°. Use a baking sheet lightly coated with no-stick spray and place it in the hot oven for about 5 minutes.

Carefully place 2 pita dough circles on the hot baking sheet and close the oven door immediately. Keep the oven door closed for 2 minutes, giving the pita breads enough time to puff.

After the pitas have puffed, flip them over and continue to bake for 2 minutes. Remove the pitas from the baking sheet. Bake remaining pitas.

After the pitas are baked, wrap the loaves in a slightly damp tea towel until they are cool. Then wrap in plastic and place in the refrigerator or freezer until ready to use.

   NOTE: Use a small serrated knife to open the "pockets" of any pita breads that have not puffed open fully.

   Pitas can be reheated by sprinkling lightly with water and placing the bread, wrapped in foil, in a 400° oven for a couple of minutes.

★ VARIATION: For larger pitas, divide the dough into 12 pieces instead of 18 and proceed as above.

Whole Wheat Rolls ★ ★

Freeze these so you can reach for them one at a time when you get a craving for a dinner roll.

Makes 2 dozen rolls

1	tablespoon active dry yeast
1¾	cups lukewarm water
1	tablespoon honey
2	tablespoons olive oil
½	tablespoon salt
½	cup wheat germ
3½–4	cups whole wheat flour

In a large bowl, dissolve the yeast in ¼ cup water. Add the honey without stirring. When yeast is bubbly, add remaining water, oil, and salt and stir to combine.

   Stir in the wheat germ and 2 cups of flour. Beat the dough with a wooden spoon or electric mixer until it becomes "stretchy." This develops the gluten, which helps the bread rise.

   Add enough of the remaining flour to make dough solid enough to knead. Knead the dough on a floured surface until smooth.

   Clean out the large bowl and coat with no-stick spray. Place the dough in the bowl, cover with a damp towel, and allow to rise in a warm, draft-free spot for about 30 minutes.

   Punch down the dough and form into 24 balls of equal size.

   Place the balls of dough in muffin tins coated lightly with no-stick spray. Allow to rise until almost doubled in bulk, about 30 minutes.

   Place the rolls in a 400° oven and after 15 minutes, turn the heat to 350°. Bake an additional 10 minutes or until the rolls are golden and baked throughout.

311

Mini French Loaves ★ ★ ★

Makes 12 slices per loaf

1	tablespoon active dry yeast
2	cups lukewarm water
4–4½	cups unbleached white flour
1–1½	cups whole wheat bread flour
4	teaspoons yellow cornmeal
	cold water

312

In a large bowl, dissolve the yeast in ¼ cup of the water. When yeast mixture is bubbly, add remaining water.

Combine white and whole wheat flours. Add to the yeast mixture, one cup at a time, kneading until dough is very stiff. Turn dough onto a floured surface.

Knead for about 10 minutes, until the dough is smooth and elastic. Place the dough in a large bowl coated with no-stick spray. Turn the dough to coat the top. Cover with plastic wrap, then a damp towel. Place the bowl in a warm area and let it rise about 30 to 45 minutes or until doubled in bulk.

Punch down and divide the dough into 4 equal pieces. Place on a floured surface and let it rest for 15 minutes. With a floured rolling pin, roll one piece of dough into a 12 × 8-inch rectangle. Roll up the dough from the long side as for a jelly roll. Pinch the ends and seams to close. Place on a baking sheet coated with no-stick spray and sprinkled with 1 teaspoon of cornmeal.

Repeat with the rest of the dough. Let the loaves rise, uncovered, in a warm spot, about 25 to 30 minutes or until doubled. With a serrated or very sharp knife, cut diagonal slashes 2 inches apart and ½ inch deep on the top of each loaf. Brush or spray loaves with cold water. Place in a cold oven, set oven to 400°, and bake about 30 minutes or until loaves are browned and sound hollow when tapped. About halfway through the baking time, brush or spray again with cold water.

NOTE: Because these loaves are small, the calories are lower than all the other breads. A two-slice serving would put you in the one-star range.

★ ★ ★ *VARIATION: You can spread 2 tablespoons of finely chopped parsley onto each loaf before rolling up and rising the second time.*

Maple Bran Muffins ★ ★ ★

Makes 18 muffins

2 cups whole wheat pastry flour
2 cups bran
2 teaspoons baking powder
1 teaspoon baking soda
1 egg
1½ cups skim milk
⅓ cup maple syrup

In a large bowl, combine the flour, bran, baking powder, and baking soda.

In a medium-size bowl, beat the egg, then add the skim milk and maple syrup.

Stir the wet ingredients into the flour mixture just until combined. Divide the batter among 18 muffin cups lightly coated with no-stick spray.

Place in a preheated 375° oven and bake for 15 to 20 minutes. Remove muffins to a wire rack to cool.

Corn Muffins ★ ★ ★

Makes 1 dozen muffins

¾ cup skim milk
¼ cup low-fat yogurt
3 tablespoons maple syrup
2 eggs
1 cup whole wheat pastry flour
¾ cup cornmeal
½ teaspoon baking soda

In a medium-size mixing bowl, combine the milk, yogurt, maple syrup, and eggs. Blend well.

In another bowl, mix together the flour, cornmeal, and baking soda and add to liquid ingredients. Spoon batter into a muffin tin lightly coated with no-stick spray. Bake at 375° for 15 to 20 minutes. Cool on a wire rack.

313

Oatmeal Date Muffins ★ ★

Makes 1 dozen muffins

1 cup whole wheat flour
1¼ cups rolled oats
2 teaspoons baking powder
½ teaspoon baking soda
¼ teaspoon cinnamon
¼ cup chopped dates
1 egg
¾ cup skim milk
2 tablespoons corn oil
3 tablespoons honey

Place the flour, oats, baking powder, baking soda, and cinnamon in a medium-size bowl and combine. Add the dates and mix until the dates are coated with flour.

Beat the egg in a small bowl. Add the milk, oil, and honey. Stir into the dry ingredients.

Pour the batter into a muffin tin coated with no-stick spray. Bake at 375° for 15 to 20 minutes.

Apple and Date Muffins ★ ★ ★

Makes 1 dozen muffins

1½	cups whole wheat pastry flour
¾	cup bran
2	teaspoons baking powder
½	teaspoon cinnamon
¾	cup chopped firm, tart apples
¼	cup chopped dates
¾	cup skim milk
¼	cup honey
2	eggs, beaten

Place the flour, bran, baking powder, and cinnamon in a large bowl and stir together until combined.

Add the apples and dates and toss to coat with the dry ingredients.

Combine the milk, honey, and eggs in a small bowl. Stir into the dry ingredients until combined.

Divide the batter among 12 muffin cups coated with no-stick spray. Bake in a preheated 375° oven for 15 to 20 minutes, until browned.

314

Banana-Orange Muffins ★ ★

The sweetness comes from banana and orange juice—not honey or molasses.

Makes 1 dozen muffins

1	ripe banana
1	egg
3	tablespoons safflower oil
1	cup whole wheat flour
1½	cups rolled oats
2	teaspoons baking powder
½	teaspoon finely grated orange rind
¾	cup orange juice

Place the banana, egg, and oil in a blender. Process on low speed until smooth.

In a medium-size bowl, combine the flour, oats, baking powder, and orange rind. Stir in the banana mixture and the orange juice.

Pour the batter into a muffin tin lightly coated with no-stick spray. Bake at 425° for 15 minutes.

Orange-Currant Muffins ★

Makes 1 dozen muffins

2 cups whole wheat pastry flour
1½ teaspoons baking powder
1 egg, beaten
¾ cup orange juice
¼ cup safflower oil
⅓ cup honey
2 drops almond extract
¼ cup dried currants
1 teaspoon grated orange rind

In a large bowl, combine the flour and baking powder.

In a small bowl, combine the egg, orange juice, oil, honey, and almond extract. Add to the dry ingredients with the currants and orange rind and stir just until combined.

Pour the batter into a muffin tin coated with no-stick spray. Bake at 350° for 20 minutes, until the muffins are golden brown.

Corn Tortillas ★ ★ ★

The calories you'll save (these are a tad smaller than the commercial variety) are well worth the effort of making your own tortillas. Besides, it's fun. You'll have to find masa harina, a specially processed corn flour, to make them. (Regular cornmeal will not do.) It usually can be found in Spanish groceries or gourmet shops.

Makes 12 tortillas

1⅔ cups masa harina
⅓ cup whole wheat flour
approximately 1 cup warm water

Blend the 2 flours, then mix in just enough water to make a stiff dough. It should just hold together in a ball.

Knead by hand or in a food processor until smooth. Wrap well in a plastic bag or plastic wrap and set aside for 20 minutes.

Divide dough into 12 equal pieces and roll each piece into a ball. Flatten slightly. Take two pieces of waxed paper, about 12 inches square, and dust with whole wheat flour.

Place the flattened dough ball on one piece of the waxed paper and cover with the other piece. Use a rolling pin and starting in the center, roll out toward the edges until the tortilla is round and thin, about 6 inches in diameter. Repeat with remaining dough balls.

On a skillet or griddle lightly coated with no-stick spray, cook tortillas on medium to medium-high heat for 3 minutes on each side or until lightly browned.

315

Whole Wheat Bagels ★

Makes 2 dozen bagels

1	medium-size potato, quartered
1½	cups water
2	tablespoons active dry yeast
2	teaspoons honey
1	egg, beaten
1	cup gluten flour
4–4½	cups whole wheat flour
1	egg white, beaten sesame or poppy seeds (optional)

Place the potatoes and water in a small saucepan and bring to a boil. Reduce heat, cover, and simmer until tender, about 15 minutes.

Place the potatoes and water in a blender, processing on medium speed until smooth. Measure the amount of blended mixture and add additional water to make 2 cups.

Place the potato mixture in a large bowl. When it has cooled to lukewarm, add the yeast and honey. When the yeast is bubbly, stir in the egg and the gluten flour.

Add ½ cup of the whole wheat flour and, using an electric mixer, beat the mixture on medium speed for about 5 minutes to develop the gluten. Add enough of the remaining flour to make a dough firm enough to knead, working the dough by hand as it becomes stiff.

Place the dough on a lightly floured sturdy work surface and knead for about 5 to 8 minutes. Place the dough in a large bowl lightly coated with no-stick spray, cover with a damp towel, and let the dough rise in a warm place for 45 to 60 minutes.

When the dough has doubled in bulk, punch it down and knead it briefly. Divide the dough into 24 pieces. Roll each into a "rope" about 7 inches, with tapered ends.

Form circles with the dough, overlapping the ends and moistening with a few drops of water to make them stick together.

Allow the bagels to rise on the lightly floured work surface and bring a large 4-quart pan of water to a boil. When the bagels have risen for 15 minutes or so, drop them, 4 at a time, into the boiling water.

316

When the bagels have floated to the surface, let them boil for about 2 minutes, then turn them over and boil for an additional 2 to 3 minutes. Remove bagels with a slotted spoon and let them drain on cake racks.

Place the bagels on baking sheets lightly coated with no-stick spray. Brush bagels with egg white, and sprinkle with sesame seeds, if desired. Bake at 400° for 12 to 15 minutes. Flip bagels and bake an additional 12 to 15 minutes. Remove from baking sheet and let cool on a rack.

Whole Wheat Crepes ★ ★ ★

A basic crepe to use in main dishes or desserts. Make them in batches and freeze, separating them with sheets of waxed paper.

317

Makes 10 crepes

1	cup skim milk
1	egg
1	egg white
¾	cup whole wheat flour

Place the milk, egg, and egg white in a blender. Process on medium speed until combined. Add the whole wheat flour and process again on medium speed until smooth, about 1 minute, stopping and scraping down the sides of the container as necessary.

Lightly oil a crepe pan and heat. Pour about 2 to 3 tablespoons of batter into the heated pan and swirl the pan gently to distribute the batter in a thin layer across the bottom of the pan. Over medium to medium-high heat, cook the crepe until the surface appears dry, about 1 minute.

Invert the pan over a kitchen towel draped over a cooling rack so the crepe falls onto the towel. Let cool. Repeat for the remaining crepes, blending the batter briefly before making each crepe.

Cinnamon Whole Wheat Crepes ★ ★ ★

You don't need sugar or other sweeteners for a dessert crepe. Cinnamon gives these crepes a special flavor that tastes good in a dessert.

Makes 1 dozen crepes

1   cup whole wheat pastry
      flour
1½ cups skim milk
2   eggs
½   teaspoon cinnamon

Place all of the ingredients in a blender. Process on medium speed until smooth, stopping and scraping down the sides with a spatula as necessary. Place the blender container with the batter in the refrigerator for 30 minutes.

Process again briefly on medium speed. Pour about 2 to 3 tablespoons of batter in a heated, lightly oiled crepe pan. Swirl the pan gently to spread a thin layer of batter across the bottom. Cook the crepe for about 1 minute over medium heat or until the surface of the crepe appears dry and the bottom is golden brown.

Invert the pan over a cooling rack covered with a kitchen towel. Repeat with the remaining batter, blending the batter briefly before making each crepe.

Golden Crepes ★ ★ ★

Although whole wheat crepes have more fiber and nutrients, you might want to consider these white flour crepes on those occasions when eye appeal is important to the meal. These crepes go well with fish and seafood.

Makes 10 crepes

1   egg, slightly beaten
1   cup skim milk
1   teaspoon butter, melted
¾   cup white flour

In a small bowl, place the egg, milk, and butter and mix well. Add the mixture to the flour and blend until smooth. Cover and set aside for 30 minutes to 1 hour.

Lightly oil a crepe pan and set over medium heat. Pour about 2 tablespoons of batter into the pan and swirl to spread evenly. Cook for 1 to 2 minutes or until golden. Turn over and cook for 1 to 2 minutes more.

Invert the pan over a cooling rack covered with a kitchen towel. Repeat with the remaining batter, blending the batter briefly before making each crepe.

Beverages

A tall, cool quencher on a hot summer day. . . . A warm, soothing sip on a wintry night. . . . There are times when it just doesn't feel right *not* to have a tasty beverage in hand. Unfortunately, that tasty beverage usually contains a heap of calories. But not if you mix your own.

Oh, sure, making your own is more difficult than picking up a six-pack of diet cola at the market. But for my money, such drinks just can't match the flavor satisfaction of combining fresh fruit and juices, herbal teas, or sparkling mineral water in a beverage.

Besides, when you make your own you won't be getting the added sugar (and the calories) you find in many colas, fruit drinks, or traditional home recipes. Sugar can leave you listless or, worse yet, knock your sugar level out of kilter, a condition that can set many people up for an eating binge. You won't be getting any added salt either, a common ingredient in many commercial soft drinks. Salt is something you *don't* want. It helps you retain liquid, which, in turn, prevents the scale from going *down*.

By blending your own, you won't be getting unwanted caffeine, another ingredient in many shelf beverages. Caffeine only stimulates your system— not what you're really after if your aim is to sit back and enjoy. And there's another plus. The drinks we offer here are all packed with nutrition— something you can't get out of the no-cal or low-cal bottled drink.

All you need to make your own healthy drinks is a blender, a selection of the season's freshest fruits, some yogurt, skim milk, sparkling mineral water, and maybe some herbal teas. And I'll let you in on a little secret. Many of the drinks in this chapter are well *below* the 50-calorie limit for the three-star category. So feel free to enjoy. Fifty calories is barely a dent in your daily calorie intake, and it's about a third of the calories you'll find in a soft drink or a bottle of beer!

As for alcohol, you won't feel deprived if you turn to our *Tomato-Buttermilk Cocktail, Ruby Cooler,* or *Strawberry Sipper*—all tasty nonalcoholic choices for cocktail time or brunch. At about 80 to 100 calories a shot, you don't need the alcohol. Besides, alcohol only stimulates the appetite.

Experiment to find your favorite beverage. Mix and match. Keep a pitcher on hand. Blend in some berries, a half of a banana, or some mint and have a liquid breakfast or lunch. Then just sit back and enjoy—without the burden of counting calories.

Strawberry Sipper ★ ★

Cool, refreshing, and summertime delicious!

Makes 2 servings

1	cup sliced strawberries
½	cup apple juice
½	cup sparkling mineral water
1	tablespoon lemon juice
3	ice cubes
2	sprigs mint (garnish)

Place the strawberries, apple juice, mineral water, lemon juice, and ice in a blender. Process on medium speed until smooth and frothy.

Pour into glasses, over additional ice, if desired. Garnish with mint sprigs, if desired.

Peach Fizz ★ ★ ★

A sophisticated summer drink without sweeteners.

Makes 2 servings

1	ripe peach, pitted
½	ripe banana
1	cup sparkling mineral water
2	ice cubes
	drop of vanilla extract (optional)
2	sprigs mint (garnish)

Place the unpeeled peach with the banana, mineral water, ice, and vanilla, if desired, in a blender. Process on high speed until frothy.

Serve in tall, chilled glasses, garnished with mint sprigs, if desired.

Peach Frosty ★ ★

Added buttermilk and cinnamon turns the fizz into a frosty.

Makes 2 servings

½   cup buttermilk
1   ripe peach, pitted
½   large ripe banana
3   ice cubes
¼   teaspoon vanilla extract
     dash of cinnamon

Place all the ingredients in a blender. Process on medium, then high speed, until smooth. Serve immediately.

Orange Glorious ★

This makes a nice breakfast drink.

Makes 2 servings

¾   cup orange juice
½   cup skim milk
1   egg white
½   teaspoon honey
     drop of vanilla extract
3   ice cubes

Place all the ingredients in a blender. Process on high speed until smooth and foamy. Serve immediately.

321

Minted Pineapple-Orange Juice ★ ★

A hot weather pick-me-up, with vitamin C and potassium to help you weather those sweltering days.

Makes 2 servings

1   cup cubed fresh pineapple
2   tablespoons fresh mint
     leaves (about 12)
1   cup freshly squeezed orange
     juice
2   orange slices (garnish)
2   sprigs mint (garnish)

Place the pineapple and mint in a blender. Process on medium speed until smooth. Place the blended pineapple in 3 or 4 thicknesses of cheesecloth or a strainer and squeeze the liquid into a bowl. Discard the pulp.

Add the orange juice to the bowl. Stir together and serve in chilled glasses over ice.

Garnish the glasses with orange slices and mint sprigs, if desired.

Golden Shake ★ ★

This drink shows that you don't always need ice cream to make a thick and sweet-tasting shake.

Makes 4 servings

1½	cups skim milk
1	cup cubed cantaloupe
½	peach, pitted and diced
½	medium-size sweet apple, cored
4	ice cubes
4	drops vanilla extract

Place all the ingredients in a blender. Blend on low, then medium speed, until the ice is thoroughly crushed and the mixture is smooth. Serve in tall, chilled glasses.

Frozen Fruit Shake ★ ★ ★

Makes 2 servings

½	ripe banana, frozen
4	large strawberries, frozen
1½	cups sparkling mineral water
2	fresh strawberries (garnish)

Place the banana, strawberries, and mineral water in a blender. Process on medium speed until smooth. Pour the fruit shake into two frosted glasses, decorating the rims with the fresh strawberries, if desired.

Banana Shake ★ ★

Makes 2 servings

½	large ripe banana
⅔	cup skim milk
¼	teaspoon vanilla extract
2	ice cubes
	dash of nutmeg (optional)

Coarsely chop the banana and add to the blender with milk, vanilla, and ice. Process on medium to high speed until smooth. Serve in tall glasses, and sprinkle with nutmeg.

Creamy Cantaloupe Cooler ★

Makes 2 servings

1   cup cubed cantaloupe
1   cup orange juice
½   cup sparkling mineral
     water
2   tablespoons low-fat yogurt
2   drops vanilla extract

Place all the ingredients in a blender. Process on medium speed until very smooth. Serve at once, over ice.

★★★ *VARIATION: This is satisfying enough to serve as a liquid breakfast or lunch. You can even double the recipe!*

Cran-Grape Cooler ★

Makes 2 servings

⅔   cup cranberry juice
⅓   cup white grape juice
3   strawberries
2   ice cubes
2   strawberries (garnish)

Place the cranberry juice, white grape juice, strawberries, and ice in a blender. Process on medium speed until the ice cubes are crushed. Serve in chilled, stemmed glasses over ice and garnish with a strawberry, if desired.

323

Lemon Cooler ★ ★ ★
Tart and refreshing. A nice alternative to the traditional version.

Makes 6 servings

4–5   lemons
  7   cups water
 10   spearmint leaves
  2   tablespons honey
  6   lemon slices (garnish)
  6   sprigs mint (garnish)

Finely grate the rind of 1 lemon. Squeeze enough of the lemons to make 1 cup of juice.

Place 1 cup of water and the spearmint leaves in a blender. Blend on medium speed for about 30 seconds. Strain through a sieve into a 2-quart container.

Add the 1 cup of lemon juice, the grated rind, the remaining water and the honey. Stir or shake well until the honey is dissolved.

Chill. Serve over ice in glasses garnished with a lemon slice and mint sprig, if desired.

Grape-Lemon Cooler ★ ★

Makes 1 serving

¼ cup grape juice
¾ cup *Lemon Cooler*
5 ice cubes

Combine the juices over ice in a tall, frosted glass. Stir and enjoy!

Ruby Cooler ★ ★ ★

A lovely punch for entertaining.

Makes 6 servings

1½ cups white grape juice
2 cups red hibiscus tea, cooled
1 cup cold sparkling mineral water
6 sprigs mint (garnish)

Combine the white grape juice and tea in a pitcher. When ready to serve, stir in the mineral water. Pour over ice in six tall glasses garnished with mint, if desired.

324

Steaming Golden Punch ★ ★ ★

A hot fruit punch, nice for cold-weather entertaining.

Makes 8 servings

¼ cup honey
½ cup water
1 cinnamon stick
1 teaspoon grated lemon rind
1½ teaspoons grated orange rind
¼ cup orange juice
¼ cup pineapple juice
2 tablespoons lemon juice
3½ cups boiling water
3 tablespoons decaffeinated tea leaves

Combine honey, ½ cup water, cinnamon, lemon rind, and orange rind in a saucepan. Bring to a boil and boil for 5 minutes. Remove cinnamon stick. Add orange juice, pineapple juice, and lemon juice. Keep hot.

Pour boiling water over tea leaves and steep 5 minutes.

Combine tea and fruit mixture. Serve hot in tea or punch cups.

Pineapple-Melon Punch ★ ★ ★

Makes 2 servings

½   cup chopped pineapple
½   cup cubed cantaloupe
¼   cup buttermilk
3   ice cubes
¼   teaspoon vanilla extract
    dash of grated nutmeg
2   lemon slices (garnish)
2   sprigs mint (garnish)

Place the pineapple, cantaloupe, buttermilk, ice, and vanilla in a blender. Process on high speed until smooth.

Pour the punch into two glasses. Dust with a little nutmeg. Slit the lemon slices to the center and set one on the rim of each glass. Add a mint sprig to each glass, if desired, and serve.

Grapefruit Refresher ★ ★ ★

Makes 2 servings

½   cup grapefruit juice
¼   cup orange juice
1¼ cups sparkling mineral
    water
2   orange slices or lime
    wedges (garnish)

Combine grapefruit juice, orange juice, and mineral water. Immediately pour over ice in tall glasses.

Garnish with orange slices or wedges of lime, if desired.

325

Tomato-Buttermilk Cocktail ★ ★ ★

Makes 2 servings

½   cup tomato juice
½   cup buttermilk
½   teaspoon tamari or soy
    sauce
    dash of cayenne pepper
3   ice cubes
2   6-inch stalks of celery, with
    leaves (garnish)

Place the tomato juice, buttermilk, tamari, cayenne, and ice in a blender. Process on medium speed until smooth.

Serve in chilled glasses, garnished with celery stalks, if desired.

Raspberry-Lime Spritzer ★ ★ ★

Makes 6 servings

1	cup black raspberries
½	cup apple juice
1	teaspoon honey
1	tablespoon lime juice
4	cups sparkling mineral water
6	lime slices (garnish)

Place the raspberries, apple juice, and honey in a small saucepan. Bring to a boil, reduce heat, and simmer, partially covered, for 5 minutes.

Put the mixture through a strainer, pressing the berries with the back of a spoon to squeeze out all the juice. There should be about ⅔ cup.

In a pitcher, stir together the strained berry mixture, lime juice, and mineral water. Serve over ice. Garnish glasses with lime slices slit to the center and placed over the rim, if desired.

Apple-Spice Iced Tea ★ ★ ★

Iced tea lovers will enjoy this version.

Makes 1 serving

⅓	cup apple juice
½	cup orange spice herbal tea, chilled
1	apple slice (garnish)
1	sprig mint (garnish)

Pour the apple juice and tea over ice in a tall glass. To garnish, slip an apple slice, skin side up, over the rim and place a mint sprig in the drink, if desired.

Cranberry Iced Tea ★ ★ ★

Makes 2 servings

½	cup cranberry juice
1	cup orange spice herbal tea, chilled
2	orange slices (garnish)

Combine the cranberry juice and tea in a pint container. Pour over ice in two tall glasses.

Garnish each glass with an orange slice cut to the center and slipped over the rim, if desired.

High-calorie pork can be turned into a low-calorie entrée when tender meat pieces are mixed with fruit in *Diamond Head Pork with Pineapple*. Serve with *Gingered Snow Peas*.

Variety is the spice of light when it comes to desserts. From top clockwise are
Raspberry Whip, Apple Tart, Orange Angel Cake with *Orange Crème, Cheesecake Mousse,*
and *Poached Ginger Peaches.*

Desserts

We've got something in common if this is the first chapter you've turned to. I still remember when I went on my first diet—and the dessert that sent me reeling off of it. I don't remember its exact name, but I *do* remember that it was gooey, creamy, and delicious! Many subsequent diets had similar unhappy (but tasty) endings. Some sinful food I'd succumb to (usually a rich dessert, of course) left me with the feeling that I'd ruined weeks of work, sending me back to square one and the all-consuming feeling that I never was meant to get thin and stay thin.

But that was before I discovered how to lose weight naturally. I no longer believe the theory that diets and desserts aren't to be mentioned in the same breath. If you follow the philosophy that no food has to be off limits as long as you know *your* limits, then, please, help yourself to some dessert. But help yourself to the desserts in this book.

These desserts were developed using only whole grains and fresh ingredients and a minimum of fats and sweeteners. Some contain no sweeteners at all, depending solely on the natural sweetness of fresh fruit as the basis for a truly delicious dessert. And you won't find any "imitation" ingredients in these recipes. So you won't be left with that less-than-satisfied feeling of eating "imitation" dessert that you get from so many "diet" recipes. These are real desserts—cakes, pies, souffles, and even stuffed crepes—all carefully designed with low calories and high nutrition in mind.

Of course you will have to limit the number of desserts you eat if your intention is to lose weight. During the week, you might choose to skip dessert altogether, opting for a piece of fruit instead. Or, you might turn to an occasional three-star dessert. On weekends, you could select something a little higher in calories. And for very special occasions, you can treat yourself thin and still keep moving toward your weight loss goal.

Adult
Fruit Pops ★ ★ ★

The lack of sugar is what makes these treats adult. It's nice to have them ready in the freezer when the urge for a snack hits. They're sweet but not sinful.

Makes 5 2-ounce pops

¾ cup black or red raspberries
½ cup frozen apple juice
    concentrate
½ cup water

In a food processor or blender, puree raspberries, juice, and water at a low speed. Strain through a fine sieve to remove the seeds. Let foam die down. Ladle into fruit pop molds. (If you don't have molds, use small waxed-paper baking cups placed in a muffin tin. Fill and cover with freezer-grade plastic wrap. When fruit pops are partially frozen, insert fruit pop sticks.) Freeze for at least 6 hours.

Banana Glace ★ ★

Makes 4 servings

2 frozen bananas (about 1
    cup sliced)
1½ cups skim milk
2 tablespoons honey
½ teaspoon cinnamon
½ teaspoon vanilla extract
    freshly grated nutmeg

Slice the bananas and place them in a blender or food processor with ½ cup of milk and the honey. Blend until smooth. Add the remaining milk, cinnamon, and vanilla. Freeze until slushy, then blend again until smooth. Refreeze. Sprinkle with nutmeg and serve.

Frozen Fruit
Yogurt ★ ★ ★

Makes 4 servings

1 cup low-fat yogurt
1 cup fresh fruit, such as
    raspberries, blueberries,
    peaches, apricots, sweet
    cherries or kiwi fruit
1 tablespoon honey
1 teaspoon vanilla

Freeze yogurt for 3 to 4 hours. Meanwhile, in a food processor or blender on medium to high speed, puree the fruit, honey, and vanilla. Add frozen yogurt and combine. Refreeze for another 3 to 4 hours. To smooth, process again before serving. Serve immediately.

★ ★ *VARIATION: Make a yogurt pie by scooping* Frozen Fruit Yogurt *into a pre-baked 9-inch pie shell. Freeze. When ready to serve, cut into pieces with a knife that's been dipped in hot water.*

Raspberry Whip ★ ★ ★

Believe it—skim milk whips.

Makes 4 servings

⅔ cup skim milk
¾ cup fresh raspberries
1 tablespoon honey
1 egg white

Place the milk in the freezer for 2 hours or until it just begins to freeze.

Reserve 4 raspberries for garnish. In a blender on high speed or in a food processor, puree the remaining raspberries with the honey and set aside.

Whip the skim milk for about 7 minutes or until thick. Beat egg white until stiff but not dry. Fold egg white into the whipped skim milk. Stir in raspberry puree and serve immediately, topping each serving with one of the reserved raspberries.

Tangerine and Papaya Float ★ ★

A light, airy, delicate-tasting dessert.

331

Makes 2 servings

1 papaya, cubed
1 tangerine
1 egg white
½ teaspoon honey
   dash of vanilla extract
   dash of ground cardamom
      (optional)
   mint sprigs (garnish)

Place the papaya in a freezer container and freeze until firm.

When you are ready to serve the dessert, section the tangerine and peel the sections, removing all membranes.

Remove the papaya from the freezer and place in a food processor. Process with several short bursts until the papaya is smooth.

In a medium-size mixing bowl, beat the egg white with an electric mixer, first on medium, then high speed. When the egg white is foamy, add the honey, vanilla, and cardamom and continue beating until it forms stiff peaks.

Fold the papaya into the beaten egg white until thoroughly combined. Fold in the tangerine sections.

To serve, spoon the papaya mixture into glass serving dishes or stemware. Garnish with mint, if desired, and serve immediately.

Poached Ginger
Peaches ★ ★ ★

Makes 4 servings

4 peaches, halved
½ cup water
2 tablespoons lemon juice
1 slice fresh ginger, 1 inch by
    ¼ inch
1 cinnamon stick (2 inches
    long)
   dash of cinnamon

Place the peaches skin side up in a baking dish. Combine the water, lemon juice, ginger, and cinnamon stick and pour over the peaches. Cover and bake at 350° for 30 minutes. Sprinkle with cinnamon and serve hot.

332 ## Baby Meringues
with Currants ★ ★ ★

Oh, so low in calories! Serve 3 or 4 as a dessert or keep on hand for snacking.

Makes 2½ dozen

2 egg whites, at room
    temperature
1 teaspoon lemon juice
2 teaspoons honey
¼ cup dried currants,
    softened in warm water
    and well drained

Beat the egg whites until frothy. Add the lemon juice and continue beating until soft peaks form. Add the honey, 1 teaspoon at a time, and continue beating until stiff peaks form. Fold in the currants.

Cover a baking sheet with heavy brown paper and coat with no-stick spray. Drop the meringue by level tablespoons onto the paper, about 1 inch apart. Bake at 275° for about 20 minutes or until the meringues begin to turn golden. Turn off the oven and let the meringues stand in the oven for 1 hour.

Remove from oven and let cool. As soon as the meringues are cool, store them in a tightly covered glass or plastic container so they won't become soggy.

Orange
Ice Shells ★ ★

Makes 4 servings

2   pretty oranges
1   6-ounce can frozen orange
    juice concentrate
2   cups skim milk
4   mint sprigs (garnish)

Cut the oranges in half and loosen pulp with a sharp paring knife. Remove the pulp with a spoon and discard or reserve for another use. Freeze the orange shells.

In food processor or blender on medium to high speed, whirl the frozen juice concentrate and milk for 30 seconds or until combined. Freeze for at least 5 hours. To serve, whirl in a blender or food processor for 20 seconds, stuff into the orange shells, garnish with mint, if desired, and serve immediately.

NOTE: This can be made ahead and stored, lightly covered, in the freezer.

Chilled
Strawberry Soup ★ ★ ★

Makes 4 servings

4   cups strawberries
2   tablespoons apple juice
2   tablespoons low-fat yogurt

Reserve 4 berries for garnish. Puree the remaining berries with the apple juice in a food processor or blender on medium to high speed and chill, covered, for at least 3 hours. When ready to serve, pour the soup into bowls and float a dollop of yogurt in each. Slice the reserved berries 3 times, from the pointed end, *not* quite through to the stem end. Fan out and gently place on the yogurt.

Iced Honeydew
Dessert Soup ★ ★ ★

Delightful and refreshing.

Makes 4 servings

4   cups cubed honeydew
5   tablespoons lime juice
2   tablespoons low-fat yogurt
1   teaspoon grated lime rind

Puree the melon with the lime juice in a food processor or in a blender on medium to high speed and chill, covered, for at least 3 hours. To serve, pour the soup into bowls and top each bowl with a swirl of yogurt. Sprinkle lime rind on top of the yogurt.

Caribbean
Cassava Pudding ★ ★ ★

Cassava, not to be confused with casaba melon, is the inner stalk of the yucca plant. It is similar to potato but slightly sweeter and thicker. It can be found frozen in 3-inch pieces in the Hispanic section of most large supermarkets. There's no need to defrost it.

Cassava is popular in the Caribbean, where it is boiled, pureed, then combined with sweetener and coconut milk. Following is a northern adaptation.

Makes 8 servings

1	pound cassava
½	cup skim milk
1–2	tablespoons honey
1	teaspoon vanilla extract
1	teaspoon cinnamon
2	tablespoons coconut, toasted and shredded

Put the cassava in a medium-size saucepan with enough water to cover. Bring to a boil, then simmer, uncovered, for 30 minutes or until a fork will easily pierce the flesh. Drain.

In a food processor, puree the cassava with the milk, honey, vanilla, and cinnamon until smooth.

Scoop into one large serving dish or individual dishes and sprinkle with coconut. Serve immediately.

NOTE: A blender should not be used to puree the cassava.

★ ★ *VARIATION: Layer with fresh blueberries or other fresh fruit in large parfait glasses.*

334

Whipped
Apricot Mousse ★ ★

Makes 2 servings

¼	cup dried apricots
1	cup water
1	small banana
½	cup low-fat yogurt
1	egg
¼	teaspoon vanilla extract
2	ice cubes
	mint sprigs (garnish)

Place the apricots and water in a small saucepan and bring quickly to a boil over high heat. Turn down heat and simmer for 10 minutes. Remove from the stove and cool for 5 minutes.

While the apricots cook, place the banana, yogurt, egg, and vanilla in a blender.

Stir the ice cubes into the apricots. When the apricots are thoroughly cooled, pour them into the blender. Process on medium speed until velvety smooth. Garnish with mint, if desired, and serve immediately or chill.

Cheesecake Mousse ★ ★

A light mixture that offers the same taste but not the calories of traditional cheesecake.

Makes 10 servings

½ cup skim milk
1 envelope unflavored gelatin
1 tablespoon lemon juice
1 teaspoon grated lemon rind
¼ cup honey
1 cup crushed ice
2 eggs
1 cup low-fat cottage cheese
1 cup low-fat yogurt
½ teaspoon vanilla extract
½ cup wheat germ
   thin lemon slices (garnish)

Place the milk in a small saucepan over low heat and bring to a boil. Place the gelatin in a blender and add the boiling milk. Process on medium to high speed for 30 seconds or until the gelatin is completely dissolved, scraping down the sides of the container, if necessary. Add the lemon juice, lemon rind, and honey. Process until the honey is dissolved. Add the ice and blend until the ice is melted. Add the eggs, cottage cheese, yogurt, and vanilla. Process until smooth.

Lightly oil a 9-inch springform pan or coat it with no-stick spray. Sprinkle the bottom and sides of the pan with the wheat germ.

Gently pour the blended cheese mixture into the pan. Cover with plastic wrap. Chill in a refrigerator for 6 to 8 hours or overnight.

To serve, carefully remove the band from the springform pan. Garnish with a border of thin lemon slices, if desired.

335

Mango Mousse ★ ★

An easy, colorful, and creamy dessert. Just whip it up and serve it.

Makes 4 servings

2 ripe mangoes, peeled and coarsely chopped (about 2½ cups)
½ cup low-fat yogurt
1 small banana
3 drops vanilla extract
3 ice cubes
4 sprigs mint (garnish)
4 slices kiwi fruit (garnish)

Place the mangoes in a blender with the yogurt, banana, vanilla, and ice. Process on low, then medium speed, until smooth. Remove any large pieces of ice that might remain.

Place the mixture in shallow sherbet dishes and garnish with the mint sprigs and a slice of kiwi fruit, if desired. Serve at once.

Orange Blossom Soufflé ★ ★

Makes 8 servings

¼ cup low-fat cottage cheese
2 tablespoons sweet rice flour or cornstarch
2 tablespoons skim milk
½ cup frozen orange juice concentrate, thawed
1½ teaspoons grated orange rind
4 eggs, separated

In a food processor or in a blender on medium to high speed, combine the cottage cheese and flour until almost smooth. Add the milk, orange juice concentrate, orange rind, and egg yolks and process again.

In a separate bowl, beat the egg whites until stiff but not dry. Add about one-fifth of the beaten egg whites to the egg yolk mixture and blend well and quickly. Fold the remaining egg whites into the egg yolk mixture gently until well mixed. Pour the batter into a 1½-quart soufflé dish coated with no-stick spray. Bake at 350° for about 30 minutes. Remove from the oven and serve immediately.

NOTE: Sweet rice flour is available in oriental groceries.

336

Cinnamon Date Soufflé ★ ★

An elegant dessert that must be served as soon as it is taken from the oven.

Makes 4 servings

½ cup pitted dates
½ cup skim milk
¼ teaspoon vanilla extract
  dash of ground cardamom
4 egg whites
  dash of cinnamon
½ cup *Maple Yogurt Sauce*

Place the dates and milk in a small saucepan and bring to a boil. Reduce heat and simmer for 7 to 8 minutes, stirring occasionally, until the dates are soft and the mixture is creamy.

Place the date mixture in a blender with the vanilla and cardamom. Process on low speed until smooth, stopping and scraping down the sides of the container as necessary.

Beat the egg whites and cinnamon with a hand beater or electric mixer on low, then medium speed, until stiff peaks are formed.

Place the blended date mixture in a large mixing bowl. Gently stir in one-fourth of the beaten whites to lighten the mixture, then gently fold in the remaining whites.

Pour the mixture into a medium-size soufflé dish coated with no-stick spray. Bake at 350° for about 30 minutes or until puffed and golden brown. Do not open the oven door until near the end of the required baking time, or the soufflé may fall.

Bring the soufflé to the table immediately. Spoon into individual serving dishes and top each with a dollop of sauce.

Georgia Peach Soufflé ★ ★ ★

A hot soufflé that's easy to prepare.

Makes 8 servings

3	peaches, chopped (about 1½ cups)
3-4	tablespoons honey
½	teaspoon nutmeg
1	tablespoon lemon juice
5	egg whites
	dash of cinnamon

Puree the peaches in a food processor or a blender on medium speed.

In a small saucepan over moderately low heat, combine the puree with the honey, stirring often, for about 20 minutes or until thickened. Remove from heat and add nutmeg and lemon juice. Cool the mixture to lukewarm.

Beat the egg whites until stiff peaks form. Whisk one-third of the egg whites into the peach mixture. Gently fold peach mixture into the remaining egg whites. Spoon into a 1½-quart, ungreased soufflé dish. Sprinkle top with cinnamon.

Place the dish in a pan of hot water and bake on the bottom oven rack at 300° for 1 hour or until firm to the touch and browned. Do not open the oven door until near the end of the required baking time or the soufflé may fall.

NOTE: If ripe peaches are not available, frozen and thawed or canned and drained peaches will work nicely.

337

Cherry-Almond Soufflé ★ ★

Makes 6 servings

1   envelope unflavored gelatin
2   tablespoons lemon juice
2   tablespoons cold water
1   cup low-fat yogurt
1   cup pureed cherries
2   tablespoons honey
½   teaspoon vanilla extract
½   teaspoon almond extract
2   egg whites
1   tablespoon lime rind curls
    (garnish)

In a small saucepan, combine the gelatin, lemon juice, and water. Place over low heat and stir until the gelatin is completely dissolved, about 3 minutes.

In a medium-size mixing bowl, beat the yogurt with a wire whisk until smooth. Stir in the cherries, honey, vanilla, and almond extract, then fold in the gelatin mixture. Whisk lightly until well blended.

In a medium-size mixing bowl, beat the egg whites until stiff but not dry. Fold the whites into the yogurt mixture gently but completely. Pour into a 1-quart soufflé dish. Chill for 6 hours or until set. Garnish with lime rind, if desired.

338

Cheshire Stuffed Apples ★ ★

Nice picnic fare. For informal picnic parties, double or triple the recipe, then chill the apples and serve in a large bowl.

Makes 2 servings

2   medium-size tart red apples
1   tablespoon lemon juice
2   tablespoons low-fat cottage
    cheese
2   tablespoons shredded sharp
    Cheddar cheese
1   tablespoon minced dates
2   sprigs mint (garnish)

Cut the apples in half crosswise and core. Dip the cut edges of the apples in the lemon juice.

In a small bowl, combine the cottage cheese, Cheddar, and dates. Pack the cheese mixture into the hollowed apple halves and spread some over the cut surface of the apples.

Put the apple halves back together. A small amount of filling should be visible, but the apples should appear whole. Place a mint sprig at the end of each apple, if desired.

Wrap tightly in foil or plastic wrap if packing.

Apple Tart ★ ★

Pears, peaches, or nectarines are delicious substitutes for apples in this recipe.

Makes 10 servings

3–4	medium-size apples, peeled and cut into ¼ inch slices
2	eggs
½	cup low-fat yogurt
¼	cup honey
¼	cup flour
¼	teaspoon vanilla extract
1	tablespoon apple jelly
2	tablespoons apple juice

With no-stick spray, coat a 9-inch tart pan, with a removable bottom. Arrange apple slices in 2 concentric circles, slightly overlapping each other in the pan.

In a medium-size bowl, combine the eggs, yogurt, honey, flour, and vanilla. Spoon over the apple slices until all are covered but their shapes are still visible. Bake at 375° for 30 minutes.

In a small saucepan, combine the jelly and juice over low heat. Brush evenly over tart and bake 10 minutes more or until toasty brown.

NOTE: Other light, clear jellies and juices can be used instead of apple.

Orange Angel Cake ★ ★ ★

Light and aromatic.

Makes 10 servings

5	egg whites, room temperature
¼	teaspoon cream of tartar
½	teaspoon orange extract
3	tablespoons honey
½	cup whole wheat pastry flour, sifted
½	cup *Orange Creme*

Beat the egg whites at high speed until frothy. Add the cream of tartar and beat until the egg whites are stiff but not dry. Add the orange extract and mix. Gradually add the honey and mix thoroughly. Sprinkle 1 tablespoon of the flour over the mixture, folding in the flour carefully with a spatula until blended. Repeat until all of the flour is used.

Spoon the batter carefully into a 9 × 5-inch loaf pan coated with no-stick spray. Bake at 325° for 35 to 40 minutes or until lightly browned on top. Invert onto a cake rack and let cool completely.

Loosen the cake sides carefully with a knife. Remove the cake from the pan. Slice the cake lengthwise into 2 layers and spread ¼ cup *Orange Creme* on the bottom layer. Replace the top layer and drizzle the remaining ¼ cup of *Orange Creme* on the top.

Pineapple Sponge Cake ★ ★

Makes 16 servings

1   8-ounce can unsweetened
    crushed pineapple
6   eggs, separated
½   teaspoon cream of tartar
¾   cup honey
1   teaspoon vanilla extract
1½ cups whole wheat pastry
    flour, sifted

Drain the pineapple, reserving the juice. Add enough water to the juice to make ½ cup.

In a medium-size bowl, beat the egg whites at high speed until foamy. Add the cream of tartar and continue to beat until whites form soft peaks. Gradually add ¼ cup of the honey and continue to beat until whites form stiff peaks.

In a large bowl, beat the egg yolks at high speed until thick and lemon-colored, about 5 minutes. Add reserved pineapple juice and vanilla and beat 5 minutes longer. Gradually add the remaining honey.

Beat 12 to 15 minutes longer (the lightness of the cake depends on this final beating). Fold in the flour then the drained pineapple until blended. Fold in one-fourth of the egg whites until blended, then fold in the rest.

Pour into a 9- or 10-inch tube pan coated with no-stick spray. Bake at 350° for 60 to 65 minutes or until the cake springs back when lightly touched. Cool, inverted on a bottle. Loosen with a knife or spatula. Garnish with fresh fruit to serve, if desired.

Pumpkin Pie ★

Fresh pumpkin makes all the difference in this pie, offering a sweet dessert with only a touch of maple syrup.

Makes 8 servings

2   cups pumpkin puree
½   cup skim milk
2   eggs, beaten
2   tablespoons maple syrup
1   teaspoon cinnamon
¼   teaspoon ground allspice
    dash of nutmeg
    dash of ground cloves
1   9-inch pie shell, baked

In a medium-size mixing bowl, combine the pumpkin puree, milk, eggs, maple syrup, cinnamon, allspice, nutmeg, and cloves.

Pour the pumpkin filling into the pie shell. Bake at 375° for about 1 hour or until a knife inserted in the center of the filling comes out clean. Let cool before serving.

Orange-Carob Cake ★

Carob is similar in taste and color to chocolate, but it is far lower in fat than chocolate, and it is high in fiber. This gets one star with or without the frosting.

Makes 12 servings

2   navel oranges
¾   cup ground almonds
¾   cup whole wheat pastry
        flour
⅓   cup carob powder
1   teaspoon baking soda
¼   teaspoon cinnamon
1   teaspoon vanilla extract
¼   teaspoon almond extract
½   cup honey
3   eggs
2   egg whites
½   cup *Orange Creme* (optional)

Place the oranges in a large saucepan filled with water. Bring to a boil, cover, reduce heat, and simmer for 30 minutes. Drain and cool.

Sift the almonds, setting aside the coarser granules for another dish. In a large bowl, combine sifted almonds with the pastry flour, carob powder, baking soda, and cinnamon.

Coarsely chop the oranges but do not peel. Place half the orange pieces in a blender with the vanilla extract, almond extract, and the honey. Process on low to medium speed until smooth. Add to the dry ingredients.

In a blender, process the remaining orange pieces with the eggs and egg whites on medium to high speed and add to the dry ingredients. Stir until well combined. Place the batter in a lightly oiled and floured 8-inch springform pan.

Bake at 375° for 1 hour. Remove the rim from the springform pan and cool. Frost with *Orange Creme*, if desired.

341

Cinnamon Apple Crepes ★

Makes 4 servings

2   cups minced tart apples
2   tablespoons ground
        walnuts
½   teaspoon cinnamon
8   *Whole Wheat Crepes*
½   cup *Maple Yogurt Sauce*
        pomegranate seeds
        (garnish)

Place the apples, walnuts, and cinnamon in a small saucepan over low heat. Cook, stirring occasionally, until the apples are tender, about 10 minutes. Add a few drops of water, if needed, to prevent scorching.

Place 2 to 3 tablespoons of the mixture on the edge of each crepe and roll. Place seam side down on a serving platter or individual plates.

Spoon a ribbon of sauce over the crepes. Sprinkle some pomegranate seeds on top of the sauce, if desired, and serve.

Ricotta Pie ★

Makes 12 servings

CRUST

1½	cups whole wheat pastry flour
1	teaspoon grated lemon rind
¼	teaspoon cinnamon
½	cup butter
2–4	tablespoons ice water

FILLING

2	cups low-fat cottage cheese
1	cup part-skim ricotta cheese
2	egg yolks
⅓	cup honey
1	teaspoon vanilla extract
2	tablespoons whole wheat flour
1½	teaspoons grated lemon rind
5	tablespoons minced toasted almonds, pecans, or walnuts
¼	teaspoon cinnamon
¼	teaspoon ginger

To make the crust: In a medium-size mixing bowl, combine the flour, lemon rind, and cinnamon. Place the flour on a table or countertop. Cut the butter into 8 chunks and add to the flour. Toss the butter in the flour, then break the butter into smaller chunks with your fingers, until the butter is in ½-inch bits and is well covered with flour. With the heel of your hand, smear the butter into the flour by rubbing against the countertop.

Gather the mixture together and make a well in the center. Add water, 1 tablespoon at a time, tossing after each addition to blend. (You can also use a food processor to do this.) When the flour forms a ball, stop adding water. Form into a flattened circle and wrap in foil or plastic wrap. Refrigerate for at least 1 hour. (The dough may be made 1 to 2 days in advance, wrapped, and chilled.)

Put the ball of dough on a lightly floured surface. Roll out to fit a 9-inch pie pan. Put the dough in the pan and chill for 15 minutes.

Line the inside of the pie crust with aluminum foil and fill with dried beans or rice to keep crust from rising. Bake for 8 to 10 minutes at 425°. (The crust may be prebaked and frozen if well wrapped.)

To make the filling: Beat the cottage cheese and ricotta in a blender on medium to high speed until creamy.

In a medium-size mixing bowl, beat the egg yolks until thick and creamy. Gradually add the honey and vanilla and mix well.

In a small bowl, toss the flour, lemon rind, nuts, cinnamon, and ginger together.

Add the cheese mixture to the egg yolk mixture, then stir in the flour mixture until it is well incorporated. Pour the filling into the pie crust. Bake at 350° for about 40 minutes.

Golden Dream Pie ★ ★

Makes 10 servings

1   envelope unflavored gelatin
¼   cup cold water
4   egg yolks
1   teaspoon cornstarch
1   20-ounce can unsweetened
     crushed pineapple,
     drained and juice
     reserved
3   egg whites
1   9-inch pie shell, baked
2   tablespoons toasted,
     unsweetened coconut
     (garnish)

Soften the gelatin in the water. In a medium-size saucepan, beat the egg yolks until light and fluffy and add the cornstarch, 1 cup of the reserved pineapple juice, and softened gelatin. Cook over low heat, stirring constantly, until thickened. Set aside until cool.

Fold the pineapple into the custard mixture.

Beat the egg whites until they form soft peaks. Fold the whites into the fruit mixture. Pour into the pie shell. Refrigerate until set. Garnish with coconut, if desired.

★ *VARIATIONS: Top with ½ cup of sliced strawberries or other seasonal fresh fruit or ½ cup of* Strawberry Sauce.

343

Cheese-Stuffed Crepes with Fruit Topping ★ ★

Makes 12 servings

1   cup part-skim ricotta
       cheese
1½   cups low-fat cottage
       cheese
2   tablespoons maple syrup
½   teaspoon finely grated
       lemon rind
¼   teaspoon vanilla extract
12   *Cinnamon Whole Wheat
       Crepes*
2   cups sliced strawberries
½   cup halved and seeded
       grapes
1   cup blueberries
       mint sprigs (garnish)

With a spoon, beat together the ricotta cheese, cottage cheese, maple syrup, lemon rind, and vanilla in a medium-size bowl. Place about 3 tablespoons of filling on the edge of each crepe and roll up.

Combine the strawberries, grapes, and blueberries in a medium-size bowl. Arrange the crepes seam side down on a large serving platter. Spoon the fruit over the crepes. Garnish with mint, if desired.

★ *VARIATIONS: Use 2 cups chopped, fresh pineapple in place of the strawberries or 4 cups of pineapple in place of all the fruit.
Add 1 thinly sliced kiwi fruit.*

Apple Crisp ★

A simil.. recipe I've seen calls for 1 cup of sugar and 6 tablespoons of butter. Be good to yourself... this dish tastes terrific!

Makes 8 servings

6 medium-size tart apples, cut in thin slices
1 teaspoon lemon juice
½ teaspoon cinnamon
¼ teaspoon finely grated lemon rind
   dash of ground cloves
1 cup rolled oats
½ cup whole wheat flour
   dash of nutmeg
2 tablespoons sunflower oil
2 tablespoons maple syrup
1 cup *Maple Yogurt Sauce*

Place apples in an 8 × 8-inch baking dish coated with no-stick spray. Sprinkle with the lemon juice, cinnamon, lemon rind, and cloves. Toss until the slices are coated.

In a medium-size bowl, combine the oats, flour, and nutmeg. Pour the oil and maple syrup over the oats and stir with a spoon until the mixture is well combined and crumbly.

Sprinkle the topping over the apples. Bake at 350° for 45 minutes. Serve warm with chilled *Maple Yogurt Sauce*.

NOTE: Don't use a watery apple, such as MacIntosh. Macoun and Granny Smith apples are good choices.

344

Apple-Raisin-Walnut Bake ★

Makes 6 servings

3 medium-size apples, chopped
¼ cup chopped walnuts
3 tablespoons raisins, chopped
3 tablespoons whole wheat flour
½ teaspoon baking powder
½ teaspoon cinnamon
1 egg, beaten
¼ cup honey
½ cup *Creamy Whipped Dessert Topping*

Place the apples, walnuts, and raisins in a medium-size mixing bowl.

In a small bowl, combine the flour, baking powder, and cinnamon. Toss with the apples until the fruit is coated.

In the small bowl, combine the egg and honey. Pour over the apple mixture and toss until the ingredients are well combined.

Coat a medium-size soufflé dish with no-stick spray. Place the apple mixture in the soufflé dish. Bake at 350° for 50 minutes. Serve with topping.

Fruits Fantasia ★ ★

Makes 4 servings

1   cup low-fat yogurt
1   small banana
1   teaspoon lemon juice
1   teaspoon honey
    dash of grated whole
        nutmeg
1   cantaloupe
    mint sprigs (garnish)

Place the yogurt, banana, lemon juice, honey, and nutmeg in a blender and process on low speed until smooth.

Split the cantaloupe and cut into small balls, using a melon baller. Divide among four individual serving dishes. Pour the yogurt mixture over top and garnish with mint sprigs, if desired. Serve chilled.

Fresno Fruit Nuggets ★ ★ ★

California-style Granola treats. Eat like you should eat candy—one at a time and once in a while.

Makes 5 servings

10   dried, pitted apricots
10   pitted prunes
½   cup chopped walnuts or
        rolled oats
 1   teaspoon cinnamon
 2   tablespoons apple juice

In a blender or food processor, finely chop the apricots, prunes, and walnuts. Stir the cinnamon and apple juice into the apricot mixture. Shape with hands into 10 balls. Store covered in a cool, dry place.

Calories at a Glance

Food	Portion	Calories	Major Nutrient
Acerola (Barbados cherry)	10	20	C
Acerola juice	½ cup	26	C
Alfalfa sprouts	1 tablespoon	1	C
All-Bran cereal	½ cup	107	magnesium
Allspice, ground	1 teaspoon	5	calcium
Almond extract	1 teaspoon	—	—
Almonds, dry, whole	¼ cup	212	E
Almonds, roasted, salted	¼ cup	246	B_2
Anise seed	1 teaspoon	7	iron
Apple	1	81	C
Apple, cooked	½ cup	46	potassium
Apple, dried	½ cup	105	potassium
Apple butter	1 tablespoon	33	potassium
Apple cider	½ cup	59	potassium
Apple cider, sparkling	½ cup	124	potassium
Apple juice	½ cup	58	potassium
Apple-raspberry juice	½ cup	59	potassium
Applesauce, unsweetened	½ cup	53	potassium
Apricot nectar	½ cup	71	A
Apricot juice	½ cup	61	A
Apricots	3	51	A
Apricots, dehydrated	½ cup	192	A
Apricots, dried	½ cup	155	A
Arrowroot	1 tablespoon	37	—
Artichoke	1 globe	32	C
Asparagus	4	12	C
Avocado	1	324	potassium
Bacon	3 strips	109	B_{12}
Bacon, Canadian-style	2 slices	86	B_1

Food	Portion	Calories	Major Nutrient
Baking powder	1 teaspoon	2	—
Bamboo shoots	¼ cup	10	potassium
Banana	1	105	B₆
Banana, dehydrated	½ cup	173	potassium
Barbecue sauce	1 teaspoon	4	A
Barley, cooked	½ cup	120	magnesium
Barley, pearled, raw	½ cup	348	B₁, iron
Basil, ground	1 teaspoon	4	calcium
Basil, leaves	¼ cup	4	calcium
Bass, black sea, stuffed	3 ounces	249	B₁₂
Bass, smallmouth and largemouth	3 ounces	165	B₁₂
Bass, striped	3 ounces	168	B₁₂
Bay leaf (1 whole leaf, crumbled)	1 teaspoon	2	iron
Beans:			
adzuki	½ cup	131	potassium
black	½ cup	136	potassium
Great Northern	½ cup	106	potassium
green, French-style	½ cup	17	C
green, snap	½ cup	16	C
kidney	½ cup	109	potassium
lima	½ cup	131	C
mung, sprouted	½ cup	18	folate
navy	½ cup	112	magnesium
pinto	½ cup	108	B₁
soybeans	½ cup	117	magnesium
yellow	½ cup	14	C
¹Beef:			
brisket, choice grade	3 ounces	189	B₁₂
brisket, good grade	3 ounces	169	B₁₂
chipped, dried	3 ounces	174	B₁₂
chuck rib roast, choice grade	3 ounces	212	B₁₂
chuck rib roast, good grade	3 ounces	186	B₁₂
chuck steak, choice grade	3 ounces	164	B₁₂
chuck steak, good grade	3 ounces	152	B₁₂
club steak, choice grade	3 ounces	207	B₁₂
club steak, good grade	3 ounces	184	B₁₂

NOTE: Where calories or a major nutrient were not given for a food, their amount was negligible.
¹trimmed of fat, meat only
²skin and bone removed

Calories at a Glance—*continued*

Food	Portion	Calories	Major Nutrient
[1]Beef *(continued)*:			
flank steak, choice grade	3 ounces	167	B_{12}
flank steak, good grade	3 ounces	162	B_{12}
foreshank, choice grade	3 ounces	156	B_{12}
foreshank, good grade	3 ounces	150	B_{12}
heart	3 ounces	160	B_{12}
heel of round, choice grade	3 ounces	153	B_{12}
heel of round, good grade	3 ounces	148	B_{12}
hindshank, choice grade	3 ounces	156	B_{12}
hindshank, good grade	3 ounces	150	B_{12}
ground, lean	3 ounces	186	B_{12}
ground, regular	3 ounces	243	B_{12}
liver	3 ounces	195	B_{12}
porterhouse steak, choice grade	3 ounces	190	B_{12}
porterhouse steak, good grade	3 ounces	167	B_{12}
round steak, choice grade	3 ounces	162	B_{12}
round steak, good grade	3 ounces	149	B_{12}
rump roast, choice grade	3 ounces	177	B_{12}
rump roast, good grade	3 ounces	162	B_{12}
sirloin steak, choice grade	3 ounces	204	B_{12}
sirloin steak, good grade	3 ounces	178	B_{12}
stewing beef	3 ounces	183	B_{12}
T-bone steak, choice grade	3 ounces	190	B_{12}
T-bone steak, good grade	3 ounces	169	B_{12}
tongue	3 ounces	208	B_{12}
Beef broth	1 cup	19	niacin
Beef gravy	1 tablespoon	8	zinc
Beef and vegetable stew, homemade	1 cup	109	potassium
Beet greens, cooked	½ cup	13	A
Beet greens, raw	1 cup	13	A
Beets	½ cup	27	C
Biscuit, baking powder	1	103	B_1
Bitter lemon	6 ounces	96	—
Blackberries	½ cup	37	C
Blackberry juice	½ cup	46	C
Blueberries	½ cup	41	C
Blueberry juice	½ cup	68	C

Food	Portion	Calories	Major Nutrient
Blue cheese dressing	1 tablespoon	77	calcium
Bluefish	3 ounces	99	B_{12}
Bologna:			
beef	1 ounce	89	B_{12}
lebanon	1 ounce	64	B_{12}
pork	1 ounce	70	B_1
turkey	1 ounce	54	niacin
Bran, oat	1 tablespoon	4	B_1
Bran, wheat	1 tablespoon	4	magnesium
Bran Buds cereal	½ cup	109	niacin
Bran Chex cereal	½ cup	78	niacin
Bratwurst	1 ounce	85	B_1
Braunschweiger	1 ounce	102	B_{12}
Brazil nuts	¼ cup	229	B_1
Bread:			
cracked wheat	1 slice	66	B_1
French	1 slice	102	B_1
Italian	1 slice	83	B_1
pumpernickel	1 slice	79	magnesium
raisin	1 slice	66	iron
rye	1 slice	61	B_1
white, firm crumb	1 slice	74	magnesium
white, soft crumb	1 slice	76	magnesium
whole wheat, firm crumb	1 slice	61	magnesium
whole wheat, soft crumb	1 slice	67	magnesium
Bread crumbs, white, dry	1 cup	392	magnesium
Bread crumbs, whole wheat, dry	1 cup	244	magnesium
Bread sticks, 7¾ inches long	2 sticks	38	magnesium
Brewer's yeast	1 tablespoon	23	B_1
Broccoli, cooked	½ cup	20	C
Broccoli, raw	½ cup	20	C
Broccoli, raw	1 medium-size stalk	48	C
Brussels sprouts, cooked	4	30	C

NOTE: Where calories or a major nutrient were not given for a food, their amount was negligible.
[1] trimmed of fat, meat only
[2] skin and bone removed

Calories at a Glance—*continued*

Food	Portion	Calories	Major Nutrient
Bulgur, dry	¼ cup	138	iron
Butter	1 tablespoon	102	A
Butter, whipped	1 tablespoon	68	A
Cabbage, raw	½ cup	11	K
Cabbage, Chinese, raw	½ cup	6	K
Cabbage, cooked	½ cup	16	K
Cabbage, red, raw	½ cup	14	K
Cantaloupe	¼	47	C
Caraway seeds	1 tablespoon	22	iron
Cardamom	1 teaspoon	6	iron
Carob powder	¼ cup	63	potassium
Carrot, raw	1 medium-size	30	A
Carrot juice	½ cup	48	A
Carrots, cooked	½ cup	23	A
Carrots, raw, grated	½ cup	23	A
Casaba	⅛	54	C
Cashew nuts, roasted in oil	¼ cup	196	magnesium
Cassava, raw	1 ounce	39	A
Catsup	1 teaspoon	5	A
Cauliflower, cooked	½ cup	14	C
Cauliflower, raw	½ cup	43	C
Cayenne pepper	1 teaspoon	6	C
Celery, chopped, cooked	½ cup	11	potassium
Celery, chopped, raw	½ cup	10	potassium
Celery seeds	1 teaspoon	8	iron
Celery stalk	1 large	7	potassium

Food	Portion	Calories	Major Nutrient
Chard, Swiss, cooked	½ cup	16	A
Chard, Swiss, raw	1 cup	15	A
Cheese:			
blue	1 ounce	100	calcium
brick	1 ounce	105	calcium
Brie	1 ounce	95	B_{12}
Camembert	1 ounce	85	calcium
caraway	1 ounce	107	B_{12}
Cheddar	1 ounce	114	calcium
Cheshire	1 ounce	110	calcium
Colby	1 ounce	112	calcium
cottage, creamed	½ cup	109	B_{12}
cottage, dry curd	½ cup	62	B_{12}
cottage, low fat, 1 percent	½ cup	82	B_{12}
cream	1 ounce	99	B_{12}
Edam	1 ounce	101	calcium
feta	1 ounce	75	calcium
fontina	1 ounce	110	calcium
Gjetost	1 ounce	132	calcium
Gorgonzola	1 ounce	111	calcium
Gouda	1 ounce	101	calcium
Gruyère	1 ounce	117	calcium
Limburger	1 ounce	93	calcium
Monterey Jack	1 ounce	106	calcium
mozzarella	1 ounce	80	calcium
mozzarella, low moisture	1 ounce	90	calcium
mozzarella, part skim	1 ounce	72	calcium
Muenster	1 ounce	104	calcium
Neufchâtel	1 ounce	74	calcium
Parmesan	1 tablespoon	23	calcium
Port du Salut	1 ounce	100	calcium
provolone	1 ounce	100	calcium
ricotta, part skim	½ cup	171	calcium
ricotta, whole milk	½ cup	216	calcium
Romano	1 ounce	110	calcium
Roquefort	1 ounce	105	calcium
Swiss	1 ounce	107	calcium
Tilsit	1 ounce	96	calcium

351

NOTE: Where calories or a major nutrient were not given for a food, their amount was negligible.
[1] trimmed of fat, meat only
[2] skin and bone removed

Calories at a Glance—*continued*

Food	Portion	Calories	Major Nutrient
Cheese sauce	1 tablespoon	19	calcium
Chervil, dried	1 teaspoon	1	potassium
Chestnuts	½ cup	155	potassium
[2]Chicken:			
back	3 ounces	204	niacin
breast	3 ounces	140	niacin
drumstick	3 ounces	147	niacin
giblets	3 ounces	134	B_{12}
leg	3 ounces	163	niacin
liver	3 ounces	133	B_{12}
neck	3 ounces	252	niacin
thigh	3 ounces	178	niacin
wing	3 ounces	174	niacin
Chicken broth or stock	1 cup	39	niacin
Chicken gravy	1 tablespoon	12	potassium
Chicken liver pâté	3 ounces	171	niacin
Chick-peas, cooked	½ cup	180	folate
Chick-peas, dried	¼ cup	180	folate
Chicken roll	1 ounce	45	niacin
Chicken spread	1 ounce	55	niacin
Chicory	1 cup	14	calcium
Chili powder	1 teaspoon	8	A
Chili sauce	1 teaspoon	5	A
Chives	1 tablespoon	1	A
Cinnamon	1 teaspoon	6	iron
Clams:			
cherrystones	6	84	B_{12}
chowders	6	156	B_{12}
little necks	6	67	B_{12}
Cloves	1 teaspoon	7	C
Club soda	6 ounces	0	—
Cocktail sauce, seafood	1 tablespoon	22	C
Cocoa powder	4 heaping teaspoons	106	—

352

Food	Portion	Calories	Major Nutrient
Coconut meat	¼ cup	69	potassium
Cod	3 ounces	144	B_{12}
Coffee, brewed	1 cup	4	—
Cola	12 ounces	159	—
Cola, sugar-free	12 ounces	2	—
Collards, cooked	½ cup	32	A
Collards, raw	1 cup	25	A
Coriander leaf, dried	1 teaspoon	5	magnesium
Coriander seeds	1 teaspoon	5	magnesium
Corn	1 ear	70	B_6
Corn	½ cup	69	B_6
Corn Bran cereal	½ cup	62	iron
Cornbread, whole ground	1 slice	161	B_6
Corn Chex cereal	½ cup	56	B_1
Corn Flakes cereal	½ cup	52	B_1
Corn grits	½ cup	73	B_1
Cornmeal, whole ground	¼ cup	108	B_1
Cornstarch	1 tablespoon	29	—
Crab, deviled	3 ounces	160	A
Crab, imperial	3 ounces	125	A
Crab, king	3 ounces	79	A
Crab apple, sliced	½ cup	42	C
Cracker crumbs, whole wheat	1 cup	368	magnesium
Crackers:			
cheese	10	52	B_1
graham, plain	1 large	55	potassium
graham, sugar honey	1 large	58	potassium
oyster	10	33	iron
saltine	10	123	iron
sandwich type, cheese and peanut butter	6	209	niacin
soda	10	125	iron
whole wheat	10	124	niacin

NOTE: Where calories or a major nutrient were not given for a food, their amount was negligible.
[1]trimmed of fat, meat only
[2]skin and bone removed

353

Calories at a Glance—*continued*

Food	Portion	Calories	Major Nutrient
Cracklin' Bran cereal	½ cup	115	B_1
Cranberries	½ cup	23	C
Cranberry juice cocktail	1 cup	147	C
Cream:			
half and half	1 tablespoon	20	B_{12}
heavy whipping	1 tablespoon	52	calcium
light	1 tablespoon	29	calcium
light whipping	1 tablespoon	44	calcium
Cream of Wheat cereal	½ cup	67	iron
Crispy Rice cereal	½ cup	56	niacin
Crispy Wheats 'n Raisins cereal	½ cup	75	B_{12}
Croissant	1	117	B_2
Croutons	½ cup	28	magnesium
Cucumbers, sliced	½ cup	8	potassium
Cumin seeds	1 teaspoon	8	iron
Currant juice, black	½ cup	69	C
Currants, black	¼ cup	18	C
Currants, dried	¼ cup	102	potassium
Currants, red	¼ cup	16	C
Curry powder	1 teaspoon	6	iron
Curry sauce	1 tablespoon	17	calcium
Dandelion greens, cooked	½ cup	18	A
Dandelion greens, raw	1 cup	27	A
Dates, chopped	¼ cup	122	potassium
Dill, dried	1 teaspoon	6	calcium
Dill, fresh	1 tablespoon	2	iron
Duck, domesticated	3 ounces	171	riboflavin
Egg, fried	1	83	B_{12}
Egg, raw or hard-cooked	1	79	B_{12}
Egg, scrambled	1	95	B_{12}

354

Food	Portion	Calories	Major Nutrient
Eggnog	1 cup	342	calcium
Eggplant	½ cup	19	potassium
Egg white	1	16	B_2
Egg yolk	1	63	B_{12}
Elderberries	½ cup	53	C
Endive	1 cup	10	A
Escarole	1 cup	10	A
Farina	½ cup	58	B_1
Fennel	¼ cup	12	calcium
Fennel bulb	½	92	calcium
Fennel seeds	1 teaspoon	7	calcium
Fenugreek seeds	1 teaspoon	12	iron
Figs	2 medium-size	74	magnesium
Figs, dried	¼ cup	127	potassium
Filberts	¼ cup	214	E
Fish cakes	5 bite-size	103	B_{12}
Flounder	3 ounces	171	potassium
Flour:			
brown rice	¼ cup	113	B_6
buckwheat, dark	¼ cup	82	magnesium
buckwheat, light	¼ cup	85	magnesium
corn	¼ cup	108	B_1
gluten	¼ cup	128	B_1
pastry, whole wheat	¼ cup	100	B_1
peanut, defatted	¼ cup	56	niacin
rye, dark	¼ cup	105	B_1
rye, light	¼ cup	79	B_1
rye, medium	¼ cup	77	B_1
soybean, defatted	¼ cup	82	magnesium
sweet rice	¼ cup	113	B_6
wheat, white	¼ cup	114	B_1
wheat, whole	¼ cup	100	B_1
Fortified oat flakes	½ cup	89	B_{12}

355

NOTE: Where calories or a major nutrient were not given for a food, their amount was negligible.
[1]trimmed of fat, meat only
[2]skin and bone removed

Calories at a Glance—*continued*

Food	Portion	Calories	Major Nutrient
40% bran flakes	½ cup	64	B_{12}
Frankfurters:			
beef	1	184	B_{12}
chicken	1	116	niacin
turkey	1	102	niacin
French dressing	1 tablespoon	67	potassium
Fruit punch drink	1 cup	132	—
Garlic	1 clove	4	potassium
Garlic powder	1 teaspoon	9	potassium
Gelatin	½ cup	71	—
Ginger, fresh	1 tablespoon	6	potassium
Ginger, ground	1 teaspoon	6	potassium
Ginger ale	12 ounces	113	—
Ginger juice	1 tablespoon	2	potassium
Goose, domesticated	3 ounces	202	B_2
Gooseberries	½ cup	34	C
Granola, homemade	½ cup	298	B_1
Grapefruit, pink	½	37	C
Grapefruit, white	½	39	C
Grapefruit juice	½ cup	48	C
Grapefruit–orange juice	½ cup	55	C
Grape juice	½ cup	78	C
Grape-Nuts cereal	½ cup	202	B_{12}
Grape-Nuts flakes cereal	½ cup	58	B_{12}
Grapes	10	15	C
Ground-cherries	½ cup	37	C
Guava	½ cup	42	C
Guava juice	½ cup	86	C
Haddock	3 ounces	141	B_{12}

Food	Portion	Calories	Major Nutrient
Halibut	3 ounces	144	niacin
Ham, chopped	1 ounce	65	B_1
Ham and cheese loaf	1 ounce	73	B_1
Ham salad spread	1 ounce	61	B_1
Heartland Natural cereal, plain	½ cup	250	magnesium
Herring, pickled	3 ounces	189	B_{12}
Herring, plain	3 ounces	177	B_{12}
Herring, smoked	3 ounces	179	B_{12}
Hollandaise sauce	1 tablespoon	84	calcium
Honey	1 tablespoon	64	potassium
Honeydew	⅛	58	C
Honey loaf luncheon meat	1 ounce	36	B_{12}
Horseradish	1 teaspoon	2	potassium
Italian dressing	1 tablespoon	69	E
Kale	½ cup	22	A
Kielbasa	1 ounce	88	B_{12}
Kiwi fruit	1 medium-size	46	C
Kix cereal (corn, puffed)	½ cup	37	B_{12}
Knockwurst	3 ounces	261	B_{12}
Kohlrabi	½ cup	20	C
Kumquats	3	36	C
[1]Lamb:			
leg	3 ounces	158	B_{12}
loin chops	3 ounces	160	B_{12}
rib chops	3 ounces	180	B_{12}
shoulder	3 ounces	170	B_{12}
Leek	1	61	C
Lemon	⅙ (wedge)	3	C
Lemonade	1 cup	107	C

357

NOTE: Where calories or a major nutrient were not given for a food, their amount was negligible.
[1]trimmed of fat, meat only
[2]skin and bone removed

Calories at a Glance—*continued*

Food	Portion	Calories	Major Nutrient
Lemon juice	1 tablespoon	4	C
Lemon rind, grated	1 teaspoon	—	C
Lentils	½ cup	106	B_6
Lettuce:			
Boston	1 cup	8	A
iceberg	1 cup	7	C
looseleaf	1 cup	10	A
Romaine	1 cup	10	A
Life cereal, plain	½ cup	81	B_1
Lime	⅙ (wedge)	3	C
Lime juice	1 tablespoon	4	C
Liverwurst	3 ounces	279	B_{12}
Lobster	3 ounces	81	B_{12}
Lobster Newburg	½ cup	243	B_{12}
Loganberries	½ cup	40	C
Macadamia nuts	6	109	B_1
Mace	1 teaspoon	8	iron
Mackerel	3 ounces	201	B_{12}
Maltex cereal	½ cup	90	B_1
Malt-O-Meal cereal	½ cup	61	iron
Mango	½	68	A
Maple syrup	1 tablespoon	50	—
Margarine, stick	1 tablespoon	51	E
Margarine, tub	1 teaspoon	34	E
Marjoram, dried	1 teaspoon	2	iron
Mayonnaise, regular	1 tablespoon	99	E
Maypo cereal	½ cup	85	B_{12}
Meatballs, homemade	3 ounces	234	B_{12}
Meatloaf, homemade	3 ounces	137	B_{12}

Food	Portion	Calories	Major Nutrient
Milk:			
buttermilk	1 cup	99	calcium
chocolate	1 cup	208	calcium
coconut	1 cup	605	iron
condensed, sweetened	¼ cup	246	calcium
dry, buttermilk, powder	¼ cup	100	calcium
dry, nonfat, powder	¼ cup	109	calcium
dry, whole, powder	¼ cup	159	calcium
evaporated, skim	¼ cup	50	calcium
evaporated, whole	¼ cup	85	calcium
goat	1 cup	168	calcium
malted, natural	1 cup	236	calcium
1 percent low fat	1 cup	102	calcium
skim	1 cup	86	calcium
soybean	1 cup	87	magnesium
2 percent low fat	1 cup	121	calcium
whole, 3.3 percent fat	1 cup	150	calcium
Millet, cooked	½ cup	71	B_1
Millet, raw	¼ cup	142	B_1
Mineral water	8 ounces	0	—
Mint	8 ounces	0	C
Miso	1 tablespoon	10	magnesium
Molasses:			
blackstrap	1 tablespoon	43	potassium
medium	1 tablespoon	46	potassium
unsulphured	1 tablespoon	54	potassium
Most cereal	½ cup	88	B_{12}
Muffin:			
blueberry	1	112	B_2
bran	1	104	iron
cornmeal, whole ground	1	115	B_1
plain	1	118	B_2
Mulberries	¼ cup	15	C
Mushrooms, porcini, dried	4	65	niacin
Mushrooms, raw	4	16	niacin
Mushrooms, sauteed	4	78	niacin

NOTE: Where calories or a major nutrient were not given for a food, their amount was negligible.
[1]trimmed of fat, meat only
[2]skin and bone removed

359

Calories at a Glance—*continued*

Food	Portion	Calories	Major Nutrient
Mushrooms, shiitake	4	65	niacin
Mushroom sauce	1 tablespoon	14	niacin
Mussels	6	29	B_{12}
Mustard, brown	1 teaspoon	5	magnesium
Mustard, yellow	1 teaspoon	4	magnesium
Mustard greens, cooked	½ cup	16	A
Mustard greens, raw	1 cup	19	A
Mustard seeds	1 teaspoon	2	magnesium
Mustard spinach, cooked	½ cup	15	A
Nature Valley Granola cereal	½ cup	252	magnesium
Nectarine	1	67	A
Nutmeg, ground	1 teaspoon	12	magnesium
Nutri-Grain cereal, barley	½ cup	77	B_2
Nutri-Grain cereal, corn	½ cup	80	B_2
Nutri-Grain cereal, rye	½ cup	72	B_2
Nutri-Grain cereal, wheat	½ cup	79	B_2
Oatmeal	½ cup	73	B_1
Oats, dry	¼ cup	78	B_1
Ocean perch	3 ounces	195	B_{12}
Oil:			
almond	1 tablespoon	120	E
apricot kernel	1 tablespoon	120	E
coconut	1 tablespoon	120	E
corn	1 tablespoon	120	E
cottonseed	1 tablespoon	120	E
grape-seed	1 tablespoon	120	E
hazelnut	1 tablespoon	120	E
linseed	1 tablespoon	120	E
olive	1 tablespoon	119	E
palm, kernel	1 tablespoon	120	E
peanut	1 tablespoon	119	E
poppy-seed	1 tablespoon	120	E
safflower	1 tablespoon	120	E
sesame	1 tablespoon	120	E

Food	Portion	Calories	Major Nutrient
soybean	1 tablespoon	120	E
sunflower	1 tablespoon	120	E
walnut	1 tablespoon	120	E
wheat germ	1 tablespoon	120	E
Okra	½ cup	23	calcium
100% Bran cereal	½ cup	89	B_1
100% Natural cereal, plain	½ cup	245	magnesium
Onion powder	1 teaspoon	7	potassium
Onions, cooked	¼ cup	15	potassium
Onions, raw	¼ cup	16	potassium
Orange, navel	1	65	C
Orange, valencia	1	59	C
Orange juice	½ cup	56	C
Orange rind, grated	1 teaspoon	—	C
Oregano, ground	1 teaspoon	5	iron
Oxtail	3 ounces	207	B_{12}
Oysters, cooked	6	163	B_{12}
Oysters, raw	6	60	B_{12}
Pancake, buckwheat	1	146	B_6
Pancake, plain or buttermilk	1	164	B_2
Papaya	½	59	C
Papaya juice	½ cup	60	C
Paprika	1 teaspoon	6	iron
Parsley, dried	1 teaspoon	1	A
Parsley, sprigs	10	4	C
Parsnips	½ cup	51	potassium
Passion fruit	1	18	C
Pasta:			
buckwheat	1 ounce	38	magnesium
egg noodles	1 ounce	36	B_1
rice noodles	1 ounce	25	iron

361

NOTE: Where calories or a major nutrient were not given for a food, their amount was negligible.
[1]trimmed of fat, meat only
[2]skin and bone removed

Calories at a Glance—*continued*

Food	Portion	Calories	Major Nutrient
Pasta *(continued)*:			
sesame	1 ounce	35	magnesium
soy	1 ounce	35	magnesium
white	1 ounce	42	B_1
whole wheat	1 ounce	38	magnesium
Peach	1	37	C
Peach nectar	½ cup	67	C
Peanut butter	1 tablespoon	95	E
Peanuts, dry raw	¼ cup	205	niacin
Peanuts, roasted, salted	¼ cup	211	niacin
Pear	1	98	potassium
Pear nectar	½ cup	75	C
Peas:			
blackeye	½ cup	89	magnesium
early green	½ cup	57	C
snow	½ cup	34	C
split	½ cup	115	B_1
sweet green	½ cup	59	C
Pecans	¼ cup	186	E
Pepper, black	1 teaspoon	5	iron
Pepper, white	1 teaspoon	7	iron
Peppercorn	1	0	—
Peppered loaf luncheon meat	1 ounce	42	B_{12}
Pepperoni	1 ounce	139	B_{12}
Peppers:			
green, cooked	½ cup	12	C
green, raw	1	36	C
hot chili, raw	1	18	C
sweet red, raw	1	51	C
Pheasant	3 ounces	181	B_{12}
Pickle, dill	1 medium-size	7	—
Pickle, sweet gherkin	1 large	51	—
Pickle and pimiento loaf luncheon meat	1 ounce	74	B_{12}
Pickle relish	1 teaspoon	7	—

Food	Portion	Calories	Major Nutrient
Pickling spice	1 teaspoon	—	—
Pie shell, 9 inch, white	1	900	B₁
Pie shell, 9 inch, whole wheat	1	1,106	B₁
Pineapple (3½ inches wide, ¾ inch thick)	1 slice	42	C
Pineapple juice	½ cup	70	C
Pine nuts	1 tablespoon	59	B₁
Pistachio nuts	10	29	potassium
Pita bread, whole wheat	1	128	magnesium
Pizza (⅛ of 13¾-inch diameter pizza):			
with cheese topping	1 slice	153	calcium
with sausage topping	1 slice	157	calcium
Pizza sauce	½ cup	57	C
Plums	3	108	C
Pomegranate	1	104	potassium
Popcorn, oil and salt added	1 cup	41	zinc
Popcorn, plain	1 cup	23	zinc
Poppy seeds	1 tablespoon	47	calcium
¹Pork:			
blade roll, cured	3 ounces	244	B₁
Boston blade, fresh	3 ounces	218	B₁
ham, cured	3 ounces	140	B₁
ham, fresh	3 ounces	187	B₁
loin chops	3 ounces	232	B₁
picnic, cured	3 ounces	251	B₁
picnic, fresh	3 ounces	194	B₁
spareribs	3 ounces	545	B₁
Potato chips	10	114	—
Potatoes:			
baked	1 medium-size	145	C
boiled with skin	1 medium-size	173	C
french fried	10 strips	137	potassium
hash brown	½ cup	178	potassium
mashed, with milk added	½ cup	69	C
scalloped, au gratin, with cheese	½ cup	178	C

NOTE: Where calories or a major nutrient were not given for a food, their amount was negligible.
¹trimmed of fat, meat only
²skin and bone removed

363

Calories at a Glance—*continued*

Food	Portion	Calories	Major Nutrient
Potato salad	½ cup	182	C
Poultry seasoning	1 teaspoon	5	iron
Prawns	6	19	calcium
Pretzel, rod	1	55	iron
Pretzel, twisted	1	62	iron
Prickly pear	1	42	magnesium
Product 19 cereal	½ cup	63	niacin
Prune juice	½ cup	91	potassium
Prunes, dried	½ cup	193	potassium
Pumpkin	½ cup	41	A
Pumpkin pie spice	1 teaspoon	6	iron
Pumpkin seeds	¼ cup	194	iron
Quince	1	53	C
Rabbit	3 ounces	185	niacin
Radishes	3 large	4	C
Raisin bran cereal	½ cup	84	B_{12}
Raisins, golden seedless	¼ cup	125	potassium
Raisins, seedless	¼ cup	124	potassium
Ralston cereal	½ cup	67	B_1
Raspberries	¼ cup	15	C
Raspberry juice	½ cup	49	C
Rhubarb	½ cup	13	potassium
Rice:			
brown, long grain, cooked	½ cup	116	B_6
brown, short grain, cooked	½ cup	125	B_6
white, long grain, cooked	½ cup	112	B_1
wild, uncooked	¼ cup	167	B_2
Rice, puffed, cereal	½ cup	28	niacin
Rice Chex cereal	½ cup	50	B_1
Rice Krispies cereal	½ cup	56	B_1

Food	Portion	Calories	Major Nutrient
Rockfish	3 ounces	90	B$_{12}$
Rolls:			
brown-and-serve	1	84	B$_1$
frankfurter	1	119	B$_1$
hard, kaiser	1	156	B$_1$
hoagie	1	392	B$_1$
Roman Meal, plain, cereal	½ cup	74	B$_1$
Root beer	12 ounces	163	—
Rosemary, dried	1 teaspoon	4	iron
Russian dressing	1 tablespoon	76	C
Rye, whole grain	¼ cup	107	magnesium
Rye wafer	1	22	magnesium
Saffron	1 teaspoon	2	potassium
Sage, ground	1 teaspoon	2	calcium
Salami:			
beef, cooked	1 ounce	72	B$_{12}$
beef and pork	1 ounce	71	B$_{12}$
hard, pork	1 ounce	115	B$_{12}$
Salmon:			
chinook	3 ounces	179	B$_{12}$
pink	3 ounces	120	B$_{12}$
smoked	3 ounces	150	B$_{12}$
sockeye (red)	3 ounces	145	B$_{12}$
steak	3 ounces	156	B$_{12}$
Sardines	3 ounces	175	B$_{12}$
Sauerkraut	½ cup	25	K
Sausage:			
Italian	3 ounces	274	B$_{12}$
Polish	3 ounces	276	B$_{12}$
pork, smoked, link	3 ounces	331	B$_{12}$
Vienna	3 ounces	239	B$_{12}$
Savory, ground	1 teaspoon	4	calcium
Scallion	1	4	C
Scallops:			
bay	6	67	B$_{12}$
sea	6	113	B$_{12}$

NOTE: Where calories or a major nutrient were not given for a food, their amount was negligible.
[1]trimmed of fat, meat only
[2]skin and bone removed

Calories at a Glance—*continued*

Food	Portion	Calories	Major Nutrient
Scotch broth	1 cup	80	—
Sesame seed dressing	1 tablespoon	68	E
Sesame seeds	1 tablespoon	47	niacin
Sesame tahini	1 tablespoon	85	niacin
Shad	3 ounces	170	niacin
Shallots	¼ cup	28	potassium
Shark steak, Mako	3 ounces	117	B_{12}
Shortening, vegetable	1 tablespoon	113	—
Shrimp	6	22	B_{12}
Shrimp, french fried	6	44	B_{12}
Snapper, raw	4 ounces	105	B_{12}
Soda, fruit-flavored	12 ounces	166	—
Soda, fruit-flavored, sugar-free	12 ounces	3	—
Soda, lemon-lime	12 ounces	146	—
Soda, lemon-lime, sugar-free	12 ounces	0	—
Sole	3 ounces	67	B_{12}
Sour cream sauce	1 tablespoon	32	calcium
Spaghetti sauce	1 tablespoon	42	C
Spaghetti sauce with mushrooms	1 tablespoon	45	C
Special K cereal	½ cup	42	B_1
Spinach, cooked	½ cup	21	A
Spinach, raw	1 cup	14	A
Squash:			
acorn	½ cup	57	A
butternut	½ cup	70	A
hubbard	½ cup	36	A
summer	½ cup	13	A
yellow	½ cup	14	A
zucchini	½ cup	11	potassium
Strawberries	¼ cup	11	C
Stroganoff sauce	1 tablespoon	17	calcium

Food	Portion	Calories	Major Nutrient
Sunflower seeds	¼ cup	203	E
Sweet potato, baked	1	161	A
Sweet potato, candied	1	245	A
Sweet and sour sauce	1 tablespoon	18	—
Swordfish	3 ounces	138	niacin
Taco shell	1	80	B_1
Tamari	1 tablespoon	12	potassium
Tangerine	1	37	C
Tangerine juice	½ cup	54	C
Tarragon, fresh	1 sprig	1	iron
Tarragon, ground	1 teaspoon	5	iron
Tea, brewed	1 cup	0	—
Team cereal	½ cup	82	B_{12}
Tempeh	4 ounces	182	magnesium
Teriyaki sauce	1 teaspoon	3	—
Thousand island dressing	1 tablespoon	59	A
Thyme, ground	1 teaspoon	4	iron
Tilefish	3 ounces	117	B_{12}
Tofu	¼ cup	58	magnesium
Tomatoes:			
cherry, raw	1	3	C
cooked	½ cup	32	C
green, raw	½ cup	25	C
plum, raw	½ cup	26	C
raw	1 medium-size	27	C
Tomato juice	½ cup	23	C
Tomato juice cocktail	1 cup	51	C
Tomato paste	¼ cup	54	C
Tonic water	12 ounces	132	—
Total cereal	½ cup	58	B_{12}
Trout	3 ounces	115	B_{12}

NOTE: Where calories or a major nutrient were not given for a food, their amount was negligible.
[1]trimmed of fat, meat only
[2]skin and bone removed

Calories at a Glance—*continued*

Food	Portion	Calories	Major Nutrient
Tuna, in oil	3 ounces	245	niacin
Tuna, in water	3 ounces	108	niacin
Tuna steak, raw	4 ounces	150	niacin
Turkey:			
breast	3 ounces	115	niacin
giblets	3 ounces	142	B_{12}
leg	3 ounces	135	B_6
liver	3 ounces	144	A
wing	3 ounces	139	B_6
Turkey gravy	1 tablespoon	8	—
Turkey roll, light meat	1 ounce	42	niacin
Turmeric, ground	1 teaspoon	8	iron
Turnip greens, cooked	½ cup	15	K
Turnips	½ cup	18	C
Vanilla extract	1 teaspoon	5	—
¹Veal:			
boneless veal for stew	3 ounces	200	B_{12}
cutlet	3 ounces	185	B_{12}
liver	3 ounces	222	B_{12}
loin cut	3 ounces	199	B_{12}
plate	3 ounces	256	B_{12}
rib roast	3 ounces	230	B_{12}
round roast	3 ounces	184	B_{12}
Venison	3 ounces	168	B_{12}
Vinegar	1 tablespoon	2	—
Waffle	1	138	B_2
Walnuts, black	¼ cup	196	iron
Walnuts, English	¼ cup	195	iron
Watercress	¼ cup	2	C
Watermelon	1 slice (10 × 1 inch)	152	C
Wheat, puffed, cereal	½ cup	22	niacin
Wheat, shredded, large biscuit	2 biscuits	166	magnesium

Food	Portion	Calories	Major Nutrient
Wheatberries	½ cup	301	B_1
Wheat Chex cereal	½ cup	85	niacin
Wheatena cereal	½ cup	68	magnesium
Wheat germ, raw	½ cup	174	E
Wheat germ, toasted, plain	½ cup	216	E
Wheaties cereal	½ cup	51	calcium
Wheat 'n' Raisin Chex cereal	½ cup	93	B_{12}
White sauce	1 tablespoon	15	magnesium
Whole Wheat Hot Natural cereal	½ cup	76	B_1
Worcestershire sauce	1 tablespoon	13	—
Yeast, active dry	1 tablespoon	20	—
Yogurt:			
low fat, coffee and vanilla varieties	8 ounces	194	calcium
low fat, fruit varieties	8 ounces	225	calcium
low fat, plain	8 ounces	144	calcium
skim milk, plain	8 ounces	127	calcium
whole milk, plain	8 ounces	139	calcium

NOTE: Where calories or a major nutrient were not given for a food, their amount was negligible.
[1] trimmed of fat, meat only
[2] skin and bone removed

Index

Boldface page numbers indicate entries in charts; *italic* page numbers refer to photographs.

375

376

377

379

381

385

389